Storytelling and Ecology

Bloomsbury Advances in Ecolinguistics

Series Editors:
Arran Stibbe and Mariana Roccia

Advisory Board:
Nadine Andrews (Lancaster University, UK)
Maria Bortoluzzi (University of Udine, Italy)
Martin Döring (University of Hamburg, Germany)
Sue Edney (University of Bristol, UK)
Alwin Fill (University of Graz, Austria)
Diego Forte (University of Buenos Aires, Argentina)
Amir Ghorbanpour (Tarbiat Modares University, Iran)
Nataliia Goshylyk (Vasyl Stefanyk Precarpathian National University, Ukraine)
Huang Guowen (South China Agricultural University, China)
George Jacobs (Independent Scholar)
Kyoohoon Kim (Daegu University, South Korea)
Katerina Kosta (Oxford Brookes University, UK)
Mira Lieberman-Boyd (University of Sheffield, UK)
Keith Moser (Mississippi State University, USA)
Douglas Ponton (University of Catania, Italy)
Robert Poole (University of Alabama, USA)
Alison Sealey (University of Lancaster, UK)
Nina Venkataraman (National University of Singapore, Singapore)
Daniela Francesca Virdis (University of Cagliari, Italy)
Sune Vork Steffensen (University of Southern Denmark, Denmark)

Bloomsbury Advances in Ecolinguistics emerges at a time when businesses, universities, national governments and many other organizations are declaring an ecological emergency. With climate change and biodiversity loss diminishing the ability of the earth to support life, business leaders, politicians and academics are asking how their work can contribute to efforts to preserve the ecosystems that life depends on.

This book series explores the role that linguistics can play in addressing the great challenges faced by humanity and countless other species. Although significant advances have been made in addressing social issues such as racism, sexism and social justice, linguistics has typically focused on oppression in human communities and overlooked other species and the wider ecosystems that support life. This is despite the disproportionate impact of ecological destruction on oppressed groups. In contrast, this book series treats language as an intrinsic part of both human societies and wider ecosystems. It explores the role that different areas of linguistic enquiry, such as discourse analysis, corpus linguistics, language diversity and cognitive linguistics, can play at a time of ecological emergency.

The titles explore themes such as the stories that underpin unequal and unsustainable industrial societies; language contact and how linguistic imperialism threatens the ecological wisdom embedded in endangered languages; the use of linguistic analysis in ecocriticism, ecopsychology and other ecological humanities and social sciences; and emerging theoretical frameworks such as Harmonious Discourse Analysis. The titles also look to cultures around the world for inspirational forms of language that can lead to new stories to live by. In this way, the series contributes to linguistic theory by placing language fully in its social and ecological context, and to practical action by describing the role that linguistics can play in addressing ecological issues.

Storytelling and Ecology

*Empathy, Enchantment and Emergence
in the Use of Oral Narratives*

Anthony Nanson

BLOOMSBURY ACADEMIC
LONDON • NEW YORK • OXFORD • NEW DELHI • SYDNEY

BLOOMSBURY ACADEMIC
Bloomsbury Publishing Plc
50 Bedford Square, London, WC1B 3DP, UK
1385 Broadway, New York, NY 10018, USA
29 Earlsfort Terrace, Dublin 2, Ireland

BLOOMSBURY, BLOOMSBURY ACADEMIC and the Diana logo are trademarks of
Bloomsbury Publishing Plc

First published in Great Britain 2021
Paperback edition published in 2023

Copyright © Anthony Nanson, 2021

Anthony Nanson has asserted his right under the Copyright, Designs and Patents Act,
1988, to be identified as Author of this work.

For legal purposes the Acknowledgements on pp. x–xi constitute an extension
of this copyright page.

Cover design: Ben Anslow

All rights reserved. No part of this publication may be reproduced or transmitted
in any form or by any means, electronic or mechanical, including photocopying,
recording, or any information storage or retrieval system, without prior
permission in writing from the publishers.

Bloomsbury Publishing Plc does not have any control over, or responsibility for,
any third-party websites referred to or in this book. All internet addresses given
in this book were correct at the time of going to press. The author and publisher
regret any inconvenience caused if addresses have changed or sites have ceased
to exist, but can accept no responsibility for any such changes.

A catalogue record for this book is available from the British Library.

Library of Congress Cataloging-in-Publication Data
Names: Nanson, Anthony, author.
Title: Storytelling and ecology: empathy, enchantment and emergence in the
use of oral narratives / Anthony Nanson.
Description: London; New York, NY: Bloomsbury Academic, 2021. |
Series: Bloomsbury advances in ecolinguistics |
Includes bibliographical references and index. |
Identifiers: LCCN 2021000351 (print) | LCCN 2021000352 (ebook) |
ISBN 9781350114920 (hardback) | ISBN 9781350114937 (ebook) |
ISBN 9781350114944 (epub)
Subjects: LCSH: Ecolinguistics. | Storytelling. | Human ecology. |
Social ecology.
Classification: LCC P39.5.N36 2021 (print) | LCC P39.5 (ebook) |
DDC 808.5/43–dc23
LC record available at https://lccn.loc.gov/2021000351
LC ebook record available at https://lccn.loc.gov/2021000352

ISBN: HB: 978-1-3501-1492-0
PB: 978-1-3502-4622-5
ePDF: 978-1-3501-1493-7
eBook: 978-1-3501-1494-4

Series: Bloomsbury Advances in Ecolinguistics

Typeset by Integra Software Services Pvt. Ltd.

To find out more about our authors and books visit www.bloomsbury.com
and sign up for our newsletters.

To Maya

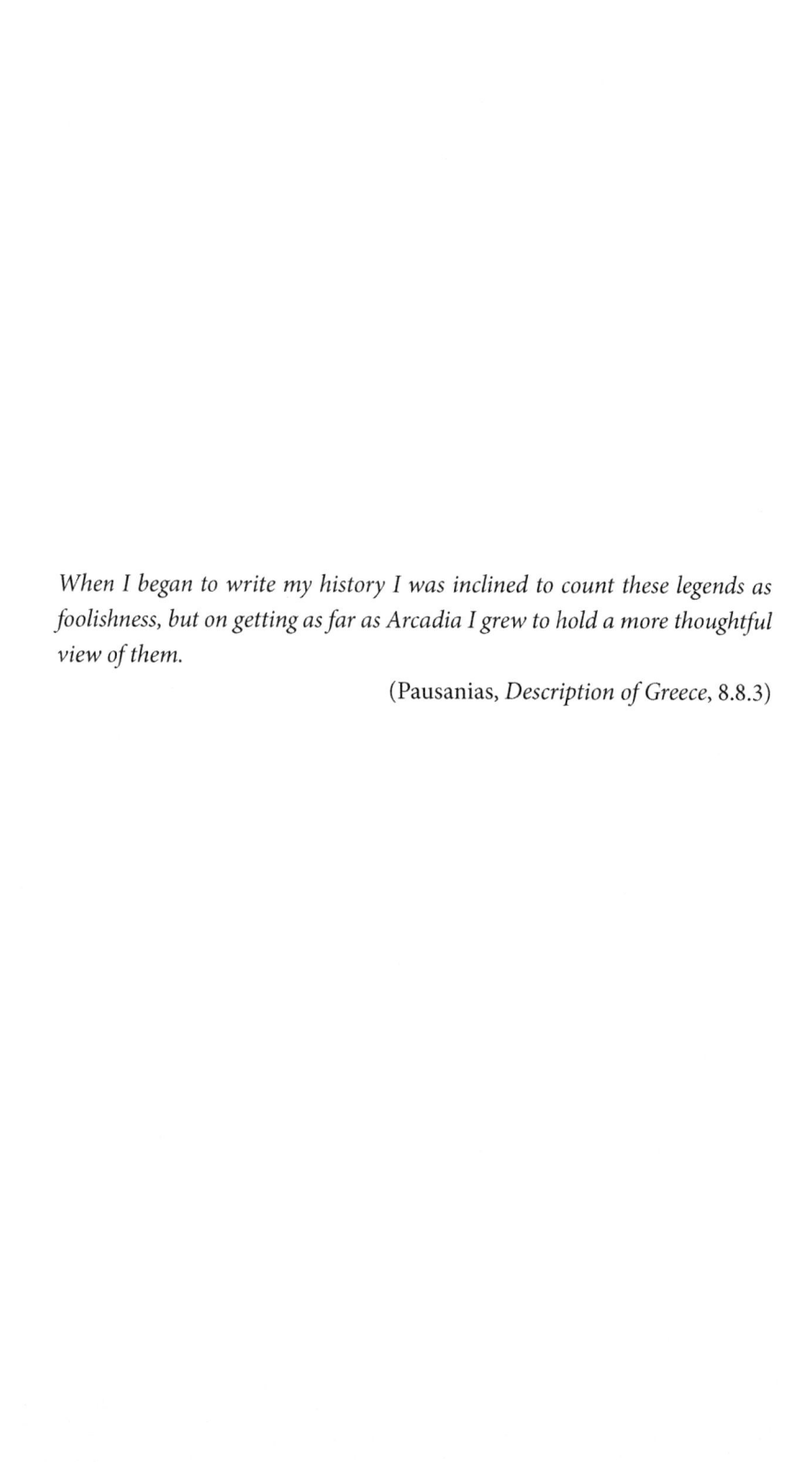

When I began to write my history I was inclined to count these legends as foolishness, but on getting as far as Arcadia I grew to hold a more thoughtful view of them.

(Pausanias, *Description of Greece*, 8.8.3)

Contents

Acknowledgements		x
Introduction		1
1	Storytelling and ecology: Reconnecting people and nature through oral narrative	9
2	Storytelling as a means of conversation about ecology and sustainability	49
3	Time, desire and consequence in ecological stories	93
4	Composting snakes and dragons: Ecological enchantment of local landscapes	119
5	The listening place: The space of transformative stillness	153
6	Supernatural ecology and the transcendence of normative expectation	177
Notes		213
Bibliography		239
Index		266

Acknowledgements

The writing of this book would not have been possible without the generous cooperation of the storytellers who allowed me to interview or observe them and the many other people who helped me in many different ways. My heartfelt thanks therefore to Peter Adams, Ana Adnan, Dave Aftandilian (and NILAS), Minna Åkerman (and Otava), Chris Allen (and UWE Land and Biology Society), David Arnold, Misty L. Bastian, Tina Bilbé, Sam Bloomfield, Hazel Bradley, Pat Brayshaw, Beatrice Camallonga, Jo Chapman (and the Lanan Foundation), Jon Cree, Charlene Collison, Peter Cripps, Simon Croft, Michael Dacre, Wendy Dacre, Amélence Darbois, Ian Darwin Edwards, Allan Davies, Gwilym Davies, Val Dean, Leisa de Burca, Lynne Denman, Ron Donaldson, Diana Durham, Fiona Eadie, Laurent Heetoua Epetahui, Elanora Ferry, Patrice Fesselier-Soerip, Francis Firebrace, Jane Flood, Heather Forest, Hamish Fyfe (and the George Ewart Evans Centre for Storytelling), Simon Garrett, Patrick Génin, Waej Génin-Juni, Alida Gersie, Michael Glen, Patrice Godin, Chloë Goodchild, Philip Goodchild, Mark Graham, Malcolm Green, Ben Haggarty, Kelvin Hall, Tristan Hankins, Julie Harris, Sophie Hastie, Cedric Haverkamp, Julie Hayman, Simon Heywood, Jane Hislam, Léopold Hnacipan, Becky Holland, Chris Holland, Michael Houseman, Becky Holland, Ronald Hutton, Greg Huth, Jean-Paul Jeanrenaud (and WWF-International), Mike Jones, Nan Kammann-Judd, Austin Keenan, Richard Kerridge, Laura Kinnear, Sonia Kondolo, Martin Large, Isabelle Leblic, Andy Letcher, Hugh Lupton, Gordon MacLellan, Eric Maddern, Kevan Manwaring, Pippa Marland, Martin Maudsley, Maya, Ivor McGillivray, Alistair McNaught, Theo Meder, Mary Medlicott, David Metcalfe, Michael Moran, Dawn Morgan, Jack Morrison (and the Eden Project), Cathy Mosley, Warren Palajota, Martin Palmer, Roy Palmer, John Parham, Tonia Payne, David Phelps, Dorothy Plater, Peter Please, Rebecca Poani, Shanmathi Priya Sampath, Rachel Rehin, Karola Renard, Emma Restall-Orr, Sam Richards, Bliss Russell, Marjut Sadeharju, Chris Salisbury, Edward Schieffelin, Richard Selby, Tim Sheppard, Riita Silk, Tom Simenauer, Scott Slovic, Chantelle Smith, Glenn Smith, Mags Smith, Fran Stallings, John Stevinson, Arran Stibbe, Tracey Strange, Helene Su, Chris Sunderland, Eleni Svoronou, Gilbert Tein, Wali Tetuanui, Peter Thayer, Mimi Thebo, Chris Thomas, Josine Tiavouane, Adrian Tissier, François Tran-

Hong, Nick Twilley, Leslie Van Gelder, Léonard Var, Rebecca Vincent, Ghislaine Walker, Andrew Wardell, Simon West, Mike Wilson, Linda Yemoto, Jack Zipes – and Kirsty Hartsiotis, who shares the stories with me.

Chapter 1 is a revision of *Storytelling and Ecology: Reconnecting Nature and People through Oral Narrative*, originally published by the Society for Storytelling (2005). Chapter 4 incorporates material from 'Composting Dragons: Recovery and Eco-radicalisation of Local Folk Tales in a Gloucestershire Landscape', originally published in *Green Letters* 18, no. 1 (2014). I thank Gwilym Davies for permission to reproduce a stanza from 'The Deerhurst Dragon Song'; Ron Donaldson for permission to present a summary of 'Bat Milk'; Jane Flood for permission to present a summary of 'Gracie's Story'; Ben Haggarty for permission to present a summary of 'Bull Hunt' from *Mezolith*, vol. 1 (David Hickling, 1996); and Kirsty Hartsiotis for the epigraph from Pausanias.

Introduction

Words have power. You can think of them as a kind of magic. Linguistic analysis demonstrates how verbal messages contained in speech and writing condition what people believe and thus what they do.[1] Such messages thus affect people's response to the global ecological crisis, which is not merely a physical crisis, but a crisis of culture and mind,[2] and threatens both the continuation of joyful human existence and the survival of much of the biosphere. Yet words by themselves may not be enough to produce change.

The word 'story' gets used to refer to many different aspects of language, such as a description, opinion, interpretation or meaning. This book uses 'story' specifically to refer to a narrative, a sequence of events through time which usually are linked by some pattern of causality. Stories carry messages, like other texts, but in a story these messages tend to be less explicit. Language shaped into story can be productive of action in life, Don Cupitt argues, because it conveys 'actforms' – 'a temporally extended pattern or form of action'.[3] However, in a good story, well told, something can happen quite the opposite of targeting a message: the audience has space to discover their own response, in meaning and feeling and any consequent action.

'Storytelling' is another beguiling word, now commonly applied to any narrative medium. Novelists and film-makers are lauded as good 'storytellers'. However, this book is about 'storytelling' exclusively in the sense of the oral narration of stories to listeners who are physically present before the storyteller. Such storytelling is usually extempore, not scripted, and is entirely distinct from reading a text aloud. English has no other word to name this activity. Within the mimesis of a story, in any medium, actforms are imagined as embodied through our identification with protagonists who are embodied within the story's world.[4] In storytelling the empathetic impact of such imagined embodiment is amplified through the bodily presence of the storyteller.

In much writing about 'story' and 'storytelling' there's slippage between the general and specific senses of these two words. It's important to distinguish the particular meanings I've specified if we want to understand the particular qualities of a *story*, as distinct from other kinds of discourse, and the particular dynamics of *storytelling*, as distinct from other narrative media.

An exploration of storytelling, in this sense, in relation to ecology may seem a very specialized pursuit. Especially so when we note the relatively small numbers of people in modern Western societies who experience storytelling as a distinct art form, whether as storytellers or listeners, compared with the numbers producing or receiving stories in other forms. The perspective changes if we look back to periods before the coming of mass literacy, or to the diminishing number of cultures that remain predominantly oral, wherein storytelling, with music, dance and ritual drama, is a primary form of cultural expression. In everyday contexts elsewhere it still is, in the informal sharing of experiences and hearsay.[5]

The science of ecology is a synthesizing discipline that brings together the various natural sciences to seek understanding of the complex web of connections among the biosphere's multiplicity of living and non-living components. Peace studies is a similarly synthesizing discipline among the humanities and social sciences. The human causes and consequences of ecological crisis bring together these manifold areas of study. When, in 2005, I wrote what is now Chapter 1 of this book, as a pamphlet for the Society for Storytelling, my initial inspiration was ecocriticism, or ecological literary criticism.[6] However, my research was wide-ranging, bringing together field studies of storytellers in Britain with insights from diverse disciplines across the sciences and humanities – an approach sympathetic to the multidisciplinary awareness of today's environmental humanities.[7]

This broad-spectrum approach, continuing in this book, comes in part from my having an educational and professional background in the sciences but a vocation to storytelling and creative writing. It perhaps also reflects the emphasis on synthesis in creative work: seeking fertile connections amidst disparate and conflicting material. In much of the book, I write as a reflective practitioner, bringing critical awareness and theoretical ideas to bear on my own storytelling work as well as others'. Experimentation in devising new kinds of ecological stories has been part of my ongoing research practice (examples are discussed in Chapters 2 and 3), as has the reworking of local folktales (Chapter 4). The theoretical argumentation of this book is interwoven with narrative in the form of summarized stories and also of snapshots of personal experience, including situations in which storytelling took place.

In the academic context, creative work places a greater demand, than critical studies, on thinking constructively. You're not only critiquing things; you're making something new. This is apposite to the challenge of ecological crisis. The natural sciences can seek to identify exactly what damage humankind has done to the biosphere. The humanities and social sciences can provide insight into the cultural dynamics that underpin that damage. What, though, is to be done? The shaping of cultural activity in constructive ways that may be conducive to positive change thus follows from the intention of the environmental humanities to attempt 'simultaneous critique and action'.[8]

Artists can be wary of agendas of commitment because of the danger these will suck the life out of art and reduce it to propaganda. But the claim to have no such agenda may make you complicit with a default ideology, such as one endorsing an unsustainable or unjust status quo. In 2008 I co-authored, with my colleagues in the performance group Fire Springs, *An Ecobardic Manifesto*, promoting the notion of an emergent artistic movement that is responsive to the strained relationship between humankind and the ecosystem by means of qualities in keeping with art as something valuable for its own sake. This manifesto accords with Suzi Gablik's demand that art in our time should be socially responsible, but not with her rejection of aesthetic tradition.[9] It is ecocritical in taking the reality of ecological crisis as reason to reject postmodern capitalism's conviction that commercial success is the only measure of art's worth, but is receptive to supra-rational spaces of mystery and paradox from which creative inspiration may arise. Taking inspiration from aspects of medieval and modern bardic tradition in the British Isles,[10] the manifesto suggests five motive principles for 'ecobardic' art:

- to connect with one's roots in time and place and at the same time celebrate cultural diversity;
- to discern and critique in order to offer cultural leadership;
- to respect and engage with one's audience as creative partners;
- to cultivate the appreciation of beauty by means of well-wrought craft;
- to enchant the world and existence as filled with significance.[11]

The influence of these aims on my storytelling work became coupled with that of three core principles distilled from an exercise in thematizing the insights of participants in the 2009 gathering of Tales to Sustain, a network of storytellers engaged with ecological sustainability:

- to seek clarity of intention;
- to cooperate or collaborate with others;
- to hold a space of stillness.

Tales to Sustain met for a weekend each year between 2005 and 2010 to share thinking and best practice about storytelling and sustainability. Another outcome of these meetings was the publication of *Storytelling for a Greener World*, in which twenty-one ecological storytellers share aspects of their practice for use by anyone involved in environmental and sustainability education. The emphasis there is on applied storywork – educational or developmental groupwork using story-based activities. The premise of this kind of work is that simply hearing a story won't necessarily lead to change; there need to be further 'conversations [that] are conducted in a change-promoting manner'.[12]

Although the present book does consider broader contexts of conversation (Chapter 2) and storywork (Chapter 5), the focus is upon storytelling itself, as a particular mode of spoken language and an art form in its own right. Storytelling has continually been marginalized as the written word has been privileged over the spoken; as oral cultures have been suppressed by colonizing invaders; as television, cinema and internet have colonized people's attention. In academia, interest in storytelling is inhibited by the demand for written assessment outcomes; by sceptical attitudes towards counterculture; by the conflation of storytelling with other things, like performance poetry or public readings, or with 'digital storytelling' or 'interactive storytelling', which have coopted the word but have little in common with storytelling except that they mediate narrative. My aim here is to explore, in ecological perspective, what qualities and experiences are peculiar to storytelling and to the kinds of stories suited to this medium.

Contemporary storytelling cannot escape the cultural context in which it exists. Jack Zipes has spelt out how, by competing in the globalized entertainment industry, professional storytellers become complicit in the ways that commercial entertainment blinds people to the power relations of society and so prevents them challenging what needs to change. When storytellers are hired to provide a service to an organization, they're subject to the expectations of whoever's paying them, which may disallow them from telling the very stories that most need to be heard. Zipes thus characterizes storytellers as 'chameleons', ever trying to shapeshift their habitus to serve whatever opportunities arise; he reads 'success' in storytelling as a marker of ethical failure, as indicating you've likely sold out your integrity and the authenticity of who you really are.[13] His analysis places the storyteller in a bind: he wants the storyteller to serve community, yet the conditions of society make that purpose impossible unless you're already socially or financially privileged. The implication is that society first needs to be restructured. But how is that to come about? There's an elided question here about sustainability: efforts to build a more equitable and ecologically sustainable society require the economic sustainability of those who are active in that cause.

The unhappy implication is that storytellers can better save their integrity if their storytelling rides upon some other source of income. The bleakness of Zipes's critique risks rendering immutable the very structures of society he condemns, and thus becoming unintentionally complicit with the neoliberal rhetoric proclaiming there's no plausible alternative to the economic doctrines driving the world towards ecological disaster. Meanwhile neoliberalism's failure to deliver on its promises of endless growth, under the constraints of finite natural resources, has produced a predictable turn towards far-right nationalism.

All of these political positions tend to close down possibility. What's needed is more room for hope. The aim of this book is to encourage critical awareness but also to explore what authentic, radical storytelling might look like; the ideas, tools and stories it can employ to serve the needs that people feel and at the same time to be part of the change that's needed. When stories are told, writes Rupert Sheldrake, our 'minds can embrace possibilities that go far beyond our own experience. Conscious minds choose among possibilities, and their choices collapse possibilities into actions.'[14]

There's a tension to be acknowledged between the well-being of the individual and the well-being of the collective. Exponents of particular ideological positions may sometimes locate the entirety of 'the good' in a particular quarter – a cooperative equitable society, for instance – and then perceive everything that does not directly serve that centre of good as, by default, opposed to it and therefore suspect. The thing is, there are different centres of good, within different ideological frameworks – individual fulfilment, say, or beautiful biodiverse landscape – and these may not be mutually exclusive, even when they seem to pull in different directions. If the tension of such dialectics can be held, creative ways forward may emerge from the space opening within them.

Ecocriticism agonizes about the pathways of effect by which literature may impact upon the actuality of the physical world. How to jump the gap between words and action?[15] A story may be a 'symbolic act', strategically speaking to a real situation, but that's not the same as a practical act.[16] Studies of biosemiotics infer how the semiotics of the written word are embedded in the larger web of communication permeating the biosphere.[17] Cultural ecology tries to integrate literature with ecology via notions of textuality and empathy that transcend the duality of mind and body.[18] Studies of ecopoetics trace the connection between reading a poem and the experience of being outdoors in nature.[19] So much of this work privileges written texts, takes for granted that narrative will be written.

Sometimes the reasoning feels contrived, the chain of consequence tenuous. The strength of storytelling is that it skips several links in the chain. The storyteller stands in the immediate presence of their listeners in a shared physical space, meeting their gaze directly, breathing the same air. 'Spoken words', writes Walter J. Ong, 'are always modifications of a total, existential situation, which always engages the body.'[20] This situation is already more ecological, in its embodied connectedness, than are reading and screen-viewing.

Since 2005 the intensification of electronic communication has made storytelling look even more archaic than it already did. It has driven the norms of communication towards greater degrees of remoteness and of unfamiliarity with the etiquette and reciprocity of speaking and listening face to face. At the same time, it has produced an expanded sense of connectedness that collapses the barrier of geographical distance. There's money and prestige to be had from being at the cutting edge of new technology. It's cutting-edge to affirm that cyberspace is truly a 'place' where people now 'are'. Ecologically, this is simply not true. The place where they are is the room where they're viewing the screen, a place subject to environmental impacts, such as floods and storms, and their economic repercussions, which could mean the loss of one's home. Moreover, they're viewing the screen in a body subject to ecological impacts such as malnutrition or disease.

I'm writing this during 2020's Covid-19 pandemic, when online solutions have become the panacea for all needs for communication, education, therapy, entertainment and togetherness – including storytelling. There's a sad irony that in a world already in crisis and needing greater connectedness the immediate remedy for this particular effect of ecological crisis is physical separation. What long-term change will ensue from the pandemic remains to be seen. If online communication should become yet more normative, that might help reduce travel to meetings that could just as well fulfil their purposes online, but I'm sceptical it would benefit activities like teaching, training, coaching and counselling. Storytelling has helped me appreciate that teaching and learning have a tacit dimension in which something beyond knowledge and know-how is shared, something that can only be shared through the interpersonal dynamics of physical presence known to countless generations of our forebears. Moreover, computer use has an oft-ignored ecological cost: the production and use of information and communications technology (ICT) have an enormous carbon footprint and profligately waste material resources in the endless cycle of upgrading equipment.[21] Storytelling consumes no resources except transport and lighting when needed, albeit the *marketing* of storytelling today routinely depends on ICT, and the web provides a wealth of story sources.

One premise of this book is that the ever more pervasive penetrations of people's lives by ICT, and the consequences for human relations with the natural world, make it all the more precious and necessary to cultivate the particular qualities of embodied, oral conversation (see Chapter 5). Only in the event of the collapse of industrial civilization, especially if this halted the mass production of books as well as bringing down the internet, might we expect storytelling to regain the pre-eminence it enjoyed in traditional cultures.

The pandemic, likely caused by the exploitation of wildlife and facilitated by the density of human population and frequency of air travel, is a reminder that global warming is not the sole component of ecological crisis.[22] In recent years the prominence of 'climate change' in public conversation has made it a metonym for the ecological crisis as a whole and thereby displaced from awareness the bigger, more complex picture of humankind's multipronged degrading and destruction of the earth's ecosystems.

Given that the ecological crisis is underpinned by industrial civilization's failure to recognize that human beings and all our works are inseparably part of the biosphere, the word 'nature' has become problematized as implying there's something, called 'nature', that's separate from human culture. Hence a plethora of synonyms – 'natural world', 'more-than-human world', 'ecosystem' – to which the same critique could be applied. But if we avoid using any such term, to avoid distinguishing between 'nature' and 'culture', then we verbally erase that which human activities are physically destroying, and we also erase our alienation from it. With due acknowledgement that culture is imbricated within ecology and that in countries like Britain almost no habitats are untouched by human agency, I will use the word 'nature' – usually in the lay sense it's used in 'nature writing', to refer to wild organisms and the elements they inhabit.[23]

Having established, at the beginning of Chapter 1, the challenge of contemporary society's alienation from nature, the book explores a wide range of ways in which storytelling can help people to connect with nature as they simultaneously connect with each other and with themselves. Although the subject may seem specialized, the scope of relevant topics – and stories – is enormous. The book therefore makes no pretence of comprehensive coverage. Chapters 2–5 have roots in the intersections between my personal explorations and various opportunities presented by other people and organizations. They expand in detail a number of topics from Chapter 1's widescreen survey and in doing so develop a paradigm of how storytelling can help to facilitate change. The concluding Chapter 6 broadens the frame to consider how different models of reality conveyed in mythic stories disclose how our response to the world's woes may be transformed by aspects of experience that transcend the individual human will.

Much may be learnt about different ways of thinking by looking at different cultures. The global character of the ecological crisis demands international as well as national and local awareness and cooperation. Though much engaged in local community-building activities, the storytelling movement in Britain has been keenly celebratory of international cultural diversity. Many insights in this book draw from further afield, including from so-called 'indigenous' peoples – meaning native communities that have retained into recent times an oral culture coupled with a hunting-gathering or subsistence-cultivating economy requiring a conscious relationship with the environment and its wildlife.

Any application of ideas or stories from non-Western cultures raises ethical questions. The ecological crisis places the crucial concerns of identity politics within a larger perspective (see Chapters 2 and 4). The enormity of the crisis requires the transformation of nearly every aspect of human existence, from social, political and economic systems to education, ethics and fundamental attitudes and motivations. This needs to happen on every scale, from the institutions of global governance to the individual human heart. Just as the biosphere's diversity should be loved and protected, so we may affirm a diversity of stories, storytellers and approaches to storytelling – and a diversity of ways of understanding the world.[24]

One useful springboard for thinking about positive change in this challenging context is Patrick D. Murphy's 'triad' of dialogue, ecology and feminism.[25] If it's to help to facilitate change, storytelling needs to be understood as dialogic, not self-expressive. The crisis *is* ecological. The prospect of reconciling the 'masculine' with the 'feminine', in the multiple connotations of those terms, is what, more than anything else, inspires my hope.

1

Storytelling and ecology: Reconnecting people and nature through oral narrative

We experience ourselves, our thoughts and feelings as something separate from the rest – a kind of optical delusion of consciousness. Our task must be to free ourselves from this prison by widening our circle of compassion to embrace all living creatures, and the whole of nature in its beauty.[1]

The storytelling movement in Britain is permeated by ecological sympathies and overlaps in part with the 'green' or 'alternative' subculture descended from the counter-culture of the 1960s. Many storytellers express in their work a sensitivity to living landscapes and have been influenced by the practice of storytelling among peoples who live in more conscious relationship with nature than do most people in industrialized countries; storytelling has found a growing professional niche in environmental education; and storytelling also has an important place among communities of people seeking to nurture a spirituality that's rooted in the landscape and honours nature as sacred. Critics warn against naive desires to *return* to a romanticized pre-industrial past.[2] Better, in contemporary circumstances of ecological crisis and intercultural exchange, is to invite into the future new ways of being that reincorporate from the past that which is useful and discard that which is not.

How exactly do storytelling and ecology interface with each other? What kind of synergy exists between them? This chapter brings together insights from scholarship and from observation of and interviews with a number of storytellers in Britain to reflect upon ecological applications of storytelling. I begin by outlining the deep-rooted disconnection between nature and modern industrial society which I believe underlies the escalating ecological crisis and is linked to a gap of understanding between a dominant discourse of science and economics and a marginalized discourse of experience and imagination. I then examine – in both theory and practice – the ways that storytelling can help to bridge this ravine of modern society's alienation from nature and to counterbalance the logic of economic self-interest with values rooted in ecology, community and compassion. I explore, in turn, the challenge of bringing science and story together in environmental education, the power of storytelling to facilitate a sense of connection with that which is physically present around you, the openness of the storytelling moment to nature's active agency, and the capacity of stories to facilitate compassion for non-human entities and reverence for natural landscapes. Finally, I venture beyond the domain of education and awareness to consider how storytelling might contribute to processes that could make an actual, transforming difference to people's treatment of nature – at both personal and collective levels.

Modern society's disconnection from nature

Humans evolved as hunter-gatherers, one species among an ecology of wild species in a wild landscape. In many parts of the world, people continued to live this kind of life until quite recently. In some places, though, people chose to control and modify their environment in such a way that their daily life became progressively more distanced from awareness of participating in ecology. In Europe this process escalated rapidly after the rise of modern capitalism and the scientific and industrial revolutions. European colonization of the rest of the world imposed similar change on other peoples, most devastatingly on the hunter-gatherers of Oceania, the Americas and Southern Africa. The exploitation of nature continues to this day, consuming and polluting the earth's resources to meet the needs of a rapidly increasing human population and a growth-driven globalized economy. Hand in hand with the destruction of nature goes the destruction of oral traditions of knowledge that once mediated relations with the ecosystem but are not valued by the colonizing ideologies of capitalism and science, except when commercially exploited in the entertainment industry.

Humans have not changed genetically since the onset of modernity; an ancestral hunter-gatherer sensibility remains within us all. Hence the alienation that is inherent in a modern way of life distanced from nature and may find expression in mental illness.[3] Ecopsychologists interpret psychological problems as deriving as much from the environmental stresses of modern life as from the social domain in which psychotherapy conventionally pursues them.[4]

A procession of technologies – motor cars, aircraft, telephones, television and the burgeoning plethora of ICT – that are designed to facilitate communication and access have also had the consequence of disconnecting us more and more from what's physically present around us. This has a social facet – a tendency to disregard people around you as if they are not real people with whom you have any relationship – and an environmental one: a veiling of the senses to the destruction of nature and to the ugliness that often replaces it.

Those who've experienced in their own lives a displacement from nature may be more conscious of the process of alienation. I experienced this in a modest way at the age of ten when I moved from a village where I had the run of the meadows and woods to a town where my freedom was circumscribed by fast roads, housing estates and industrial sites. Far greater is the alienation of indigenous people who've seen their land taken from them and transformed by industrialized development, and their culture obliterated by the colonizing forces of modernity. Indigenous storytelling traditions convey knowledge about the land and its creatures and how to sustain a living from them.[5] The storytelling of the Hebrides and the Scottish Travellers, writes Donald Smith, is a remnant in Britain of comparable traditions that 'animat[e] the social, psychological and natural worlds as a single living whole'.[6] When the land is completely converted to human use, such traditional knowledge counts for nothing and is replaced by the colonizers' written and audiovisual culture – geographically transferable knowledge that's not rooted in the physical reality of the land.

The silencing of indigenous languages and stories has meant the loss of local ecological knowledge that took millennia to build – knowledge not only about the creatures native to the lands in question, but about the relationships of predation, pollination, competition and cooperation among them. The indigenous language of an area includes specialized vocabulary for its natural phenomena, including terms that refer specifically to such connections between different species. Much of this knowledge is unknown to science. If both the indigenous language and the ecology are destroyed, then these phenomena will be wiped out of mind and existence as if they've never been.[7] And nature is silenced too, both physically, as in the disappearance of birdsong, and spiritually, in the loss of any idea of what nature may have to teach us.[8]

The arrival of television has been potent in the demise of local storytelling traditions.[9] Gary Paul Nabhan has investigated among desert children of the American southwest 'the phenomenon that Robert Michael Pyle has termed "the extinction of experience," or the termination of direct, hands-on contact between children and wildlife'.[10] Children's learning from direct experience outdoors and from the storytelling of elders is displaced by learning from television and classroom schooling, so that what they gain in knowledge of national or globalized culture they lose in knowledge of local ecology:

> Tell me, why do you think the younger generation is not keeping up these traditions?
>
> Laura [an O'odham elder and educator] listened, stopped dead in her tracks ... and pointed straight at the camera, frowning. *'it's that TV!* They're all watching *that TV!* They just sit around in front of it, they hardly go outside anymore ... That's the problem, *right there!*'[11]

In urban and suburban Britain, where children have little access to natural spaces, this 'extinction of experience' has become progressively more complete. My own early knowledge of wild flowers, trees and birds, for example, was much poorer than that which my parents acquired during their childhood. For teenagers from inner-city London, even a large city park can be terrifyingly alien.[12] These kinds of circumstances have led to the provision of compensatory activities by specialist facilitators of outdoor play and learning.[13]

Technological media facilitate a dislocation between image and reality. A television wildlife documentary may present an image of East Africa as endless savannah teeming with wild animals, but the reality I experienced living in Kenya was of land mostly given over to livestock and crops; only in game reserves were you likely to see wildlife. In advertising, popular photo-art and many products aimed at children, wild animals are commodified as charming images that reveal little of the animals' true being.[14]

In prioritizing output that will optimize their return on investment – material that nourishes consumers' 'self-gratification and self-justification'[15] – the mass media can be perceived as 'engaged in the mass production of social ignorance'.[16] Their purveyance of 'spectacle' sustains people's alienation and passivity through an overwhelming impact on the senses and valorizes violence as the means to resolve conflict.[17] Lacking much direct experience of the natural environment, the public may believe by default in a romanticized and generalized picture of the world and thereby fail to comprehend the scale of ecological damage it has sustained.[18] This disconnect between image and reality can widen the gap between thinking and action. You may espouse green views – believe that something should be done about particular issues – and yet fail to modify your own actions accordingly. The displacement of the real by the virtual allows you to behave as if nature doesn't really exist.[19]

Despite its rising profile in the public eye, the ecological crisis remains to many a theoretical idea. In wealthy countries the media's relentless promotion of products to consume seems to belie the notion the living earth's resources are endangered. The consequences of consumption are often invisible to consumers.[20] The impression you may gain is that ecological crisis lies too distant in the future to require much response right now. But the reality of the crisis is already demonstrated through the roll-call of lost species and habitats and, in parts of Africa for example, the consequences of starvation, disease and war that follow when the need for resources exceeds their supply. Humans have caused ecological crises before, only not on such a global scale. The lessons of history are there to be told, such as the deforestation of Easter Island which led to its society's decline and/or collapse;[21] the extermination of the world's most populous bird, the passenger pigeon (*Ectopistes migratorius*);[22] or the destruction of the Aral Sea and its entire ecosystem through the diversion of water to irrigation projects.[23]

Evolution has bestowed upon humans an intelligence that gives us unusual power over nature and at the same time a sense of morality and our own mortality. In mythic terms, this intelligence can be seen as the fruit of the Tree of Knowledge which brought human beings out of the Eden of animal innocence.[24] Human power has become so great that, unless tempered by a higher ethics, the biological imperative towards self-interest and procreation may be expected to continue to wreak destruction upon nature and other people.

Indigenous peoples are motivated by self-interest like everyone else, but their dependence on resources from their immediate environment clarifies for them how their self-interest depends on the well-being of the ecology they inhabit.[25] This is why indigenous peoples need, as a tool of enlightened self-restraint, their stories that transmit knowledge and ethics about how to live sustainably in their environment.

More severe ecological destruction seems to happen when human populations move into new territories; biodiversity being most stable in areas where the population is least transient.[26] Arrival in a new land is a defamiliarizing experience. Migrants tend to be younger people, with an impoverished knowledge of the oral tradition known to the elders left behind.[27] Ecological knowledge in the stories they do remember may not be applicable in the new land. It takes time to become attuned to the new land, to cultivate knowledge and stories about it.[28] The arrival of humans in Oceania and the Americas was evidently the decisive cause of mass extinctions of megafauna in these regions. By the time Europeans arrived, thousands of years later, ecological constraints had compelled the descendants of those first settlers to adapt to their environment and develop cultural traditions mediating a sustainable relationship with the local ecology.

The European colonists in turn brought a devastating new wave of ecological damage which has yet to run its course.[29]

In this light, I'm aware, as an Englishman, that my people have a problematic history. The Anglo-Saxon settlers in Britain were alienated from the traditions of the ancestral lands they'd come from and then converted to a Christian spirituality based more upon scripture than relationship with the land. The Norman conquest brought a new ruling elite who had themselves previously migrated from Scandinavia to France and who subsequently led English invasion of the other countries of the British Isles. The 'British' thenceforth colonized enormous territories around the world, including ones that became the United States. Lacking local traditions in these lands to guide their activities, they caused immense destruction of ecology and indigenous culture as they exploited these colonies' resources according to uncompromising capitalist imperatives that were consolidated in seventeenth-century England and have since produced a globalized economic system that, championed by US and British governments, has driven the world ever deeper into ecological crisis.[30]

One need this history suggests is for elements in modern culture that are sufficiently resistant to capitalist assimilation to mediate, like indigenous people's storytelling, a respectful relationship between society and nature. Britain has produced fine works of art, literature and television that celebrate nature; an impetus arising partly in reaction to the industrial transformation of the land. It's perhaps no accident that this, one of the most developed countries, where nature is so dominated by human activity and where biodiversity continues to decline, should also be such a centre of environmentalist campaigning. The influence of such creativity and campaigning upon economic activity remains modest, yet their existence inspires hope. Today's unprecedented knowledge of science and history offers humankind the possibility to devise means by which we can choose to constrain our impact on nature rather than blindly pursue economic and demographic growth up to the breaking points when population and happiness are forcefully curtailed through the painful processes of famine, disease and war. Covid-19 brought such a moment, globally, but will the lesson yet be learnt? Before we can hope that truly effective action will be undertaken to meet the ecological crisis, truthful ecological history must be spoken in place of the rhetoric by which the rich and powerful defend their interests, and the public must be moved to care what kind of world our collective actions will shape for posterity.

All aspects of culture, not science only, need to contribute to this task. What distinctive contribution can storytelling make? Let's begin to answer that question by looking at storytelling's potential to resist the discourse of powerful vested interests.

Contradicting the consensus of the powerful

We might expect scientists to be best placed to take on the mantle of ecological prophet. Many have done so. Their role, in diagnosing the problems and proposing solutions, is essential and there is wide scientific consensus about, for example, the reality of global warming, habitat destruction and declining biodiversity.[31] But scientific hypotheses are abstract and rely on quantitative data. If insufficient data are available to demonstrate a hypothesis to a high degree of statistical certainty, then it's likely to be contested by those with an immediate economic interest in doing so. Application of the scientific paradigm to decision-making in public life thus means that decisions will be based on factors that can more easily be measured and indeed valued in monetary terms.

Science can more precisely describe phenomena that can readily be broken down into the simplest components, as in classical physics and chemistry, than it can the more complex phenomena of ecology. So the difficulty of presenting conclusive quantitative data about many ecological problems becomes a reason for denying their significance and failing to address them adequately until the damage has been done, as in the cases of carcinogenic pesticides, carbon emissions and the overharvesting of seal and whales.[32] Even when the lethality of Covid-19 was evident in other countries, as were the measures needed to contain the virus, conservative US and British governments wouldn't take pre-emptive action so long as the immediate local risk of infection remained small.[33]

The application of an industrial model of management to agriculture, environment and society fails to comprehend the intricacy and subtlety of what it's dealing with: in attempting to control organisms, ecosystems and people as if they're simple mechanisms it abuses them.[34] Understanding in these areas requires us to make sense of complex patterns of causation, purpose and relationships. The best way to understand *purposes* is through stories, since stories are usually propelled by their characters' motivations.[35]

The mass media purvey a consensus narrative of what's going on which tends to override people's personal experience and forge conformity of thought. This discourse privileges the voices of the powerful and wealthy and filters out content that might threaten audience figures. It expresses and is controlled by the ideology of free-market capitalism, which is framed as serving everyone's best interests but in fact serves mainly the financial returns of those with capital to invest.[36]

There are other stories – from history and contemporary life – that present alternative pictures of what's actually happened. Stories from environmental history tell us how land was deforested, topsoil denuded, seas polluted, animals hunted; how these actions were justified in terms of economic imperative and the abundance of the resources in question; and about the consequences: mass starvation, vanished cultures, ruined habitats, species extinctions.[37] From our own time we can find stories about the efforts of ecowarriors and conservation agencies and the experiences of ordinary people in the places they inhabit.[38] The publications of conservation organizations, for example, provide many stories about conservationists' and local people's interaction with wildlife. Such true-life stories may expose the political realities that resist environmental progress, such as events in Guatemala in 1992 when conservation officials investigating deforestation in the Mayan Biosphere Reserve were beaten up by loggers and soldiers,[39] or the fossil fuel lobby's very personal attacks upon the climatologist Benjamin Santer over his work on the Second Assessment Report of the Intergovernmental Panel on Climate Change.[40]

Attending to the personal stories of people normally without a public voice has been an important ingredient of human rights movements, beginning with the campaigns to end slavery. Such stories have challenged the supposed objectivity of the dominant account of events. Today the stories of ordinary people's lived experience challenge science's uncertainties about the significance of environmental change: the farmer whose livelihood is ruined by repeated drought or flooding; the woman who must walk ever further to find firewood or water; the birdwatcher who notices species wintering in Britain which used always to fly south.

Real life consists of a morass of experience and circumstance. The shaping of experience into a coherent story enables the storyteller to make sense of their experience and so share it meaningfully with their listeners. A story connects cause and effect and interrogates purposes: it shows us that because X was done, then Y followed; it may thereby suggest solutions to problems by questioning why X was done and raising the possibility that if Z were done instead of X, then something other than Y might have come about. Exactly what, we can't be sure (see Chapter 3).

Capitalist domination of expensive media such as film and television constrains opportunities for communicating counter-hegemonic stories through these media. The more expensive a medium is to produce and distribute, the more likely is its freedom of expression to be compromised. There's no denying television's role in evoking interest in nature and raising ecological awareness, yet the programmes of even 'celebrity conservationists' like David Attenborough are required to meet consumer expectations.[41] Salman Rushdie is no doubt right that literature, being cheaper to produce than film and television, retains greater freedom of expression,[42] but production costs and the barriers to distribution do subject publishing, too, to commercial imperatives. Social media provide users with great freedom of expression; the question is: who's listening to you? Opportunities for storytellers, too, to speak truth that needs to be heard are commercially constrained, yet storytelling remains the cheapest of all narrative media, therefore the most independent of corporate gatekeepers and shareholders and so potentially the most subversive – if storytellers have the will and skill to make it so.[43] In its minimal consumption of material resources it's also the greenest. It resists commodification inasmuch as its greatest strength – of face-to-face communication in the here and now – cannot be 'mechanically reproduced'.[44] The modest scope of remuneration means that its practitioners have to be motivated by something other than money.

Needing no equipment, storytelling can seize impromptu opportunities, as Eric Maddern did to contribute an unscheduled story and song at the opening ceremony of the Soweto Mountain of Hope during the Earth Summit in 2002.[45] Once a storyteller is in front of a live audience, they cannot easily be censored except by themselves.

Although the discourse of the powerful may discount narratives of personal experience as mere anecdote, when someone tells in person the story of something they've actually experienced, their account has authority among those listening to contradict the consensus of the powerful.[46] Speaking the truth of one's experience aloud is important to healing, 'not just for ourselves but for society at large', says Inger Lise Oelrich.[47]

The extent to which a story may be deemed 'true' has important ramifications for its impact and thus for how the storyteller presents it. In ecological applications of storytelling, two distinct concerns about truth arise: one pertains to the emotional and political impact of a story that's presented as true, which implies a moral responsibility to convey the facts of the matter accurately and honestly; the second concerns the distinction between scientific and mythopoeic truth and leads to the question of how stories work differently from exposition.

Truth, message and trust in storytelling and interpretation

Storytelling in environmental education utilizes both true-life and traditional stories. These two categories of stories make different impacts on a modern audience. Stories presented as truth that actually happened demand sympathy and judgement, whereas traditional stories depend on metaphors and morals whose implications may be deep but are easier to ignore. When a storyteller segues from traditional material to a strong true-life story, the audience may shift into a grave stillness of emotional receptivity and be moved to form a strong opinion about the subject the story addresses. Therefore respect for the audience, and the possible consequences of the story being passed on, demands integrity in shaping such stories. Real life has a tangled complexity that doesn't always provide stories with an ideal structure for telling. If the effect of the story depends upon it being accepted as truth that actually happened, says Chris Sunderland, the storyteller has a responsibility to research the facts and preserve the essential pattern of events even if the story's emotional structure will need to be crafted to make the story sing.[48]

The second concern about truth is more particular to the use of storytelling in nature interpretation. Interpreters often have a background in the natural sciences, which may instil a commitment to scientific knowledge as objective truth that must be communicated accurately to the public.[49] Storytelling is seen as one tool among an array of interpretive techniques. Some interpreters love it; others are sceptical about its utility. Simon West, a Forestry Commission ranger I observed using storytelling in the New Forest, was sceptical himself when first introduced to the practice. He noticed a swing towards more widespread acceptance of its use in interpretation.[50]

Storytelling makes knowledge more accessible, enjoyable and memorable.[51] On forest walks with school groups West mixed storytelling with exposition and experiential exercises, believing, 'If they don't remember anything else, they'll remember the stories.'[52] I noticed how the quality of teenage pupils' listening deepened when he shifted – smoothly, without announcement – from exposition into storytelling. The storyteller-naturalist Malcolm Green tested the mnemonic power of storytelling with a group of students by describing the Manx shearwater's life cycle separately in a lecture and as a story: all agreed they could remember the information better from the story.[53]

The anxiety among interpreters is about communicating facts correctly: they may worry that traditional stories often play loose with science's picture of the world.[54] When a story presents animals behaving like humans or gods, Western listeners usually understand this behaviour to be fantasy and that the truth of the story is to be sought in its subtext and symbolism; but the Enlightenment paradigm of verifiable scientific truth has difficulty comprehending mythopoeic or psychological truth. It may dismiss the veracity of indigenous stories out of hand,[55] curtail fantasy and wonder as suitable only for children,[56] and cause an anxious interpreter to nullify the effect of a story by deconstructing it into true and false elements.[57]

On the other hand, traditional stories have propagated nefarious false ideas about wildlife, notably in Europe, where the disconnection between society and wild nature is so ingrained that folktales often represent animals as stereotypes upon which society has projected aspects of its collective psyche. Tales like 'Little Red Riding Hood', 'The Three Little Pigs' and 'The Wolf and the Seven Little Kids' propagate such a negative stereotype of wolves, as evil killer and thief, sanctioning their extermination in Britain and the United States, that we might question the telling of these stories just as we'd question the telling of stories that propagate racial stereotypes.[58] Here the observations of biologists stand as corrective to a problematic tradition. The storyteller can choose to subvert 'Little Red Riding Hood' to give more credit to both wolf and girl, as in Angela Carter's 'The Company of Wolves', or to provoke critical thought by presenting the tale alongside alternative perspectives of the same animal in, say, a non-Western story and a story based on natural history.[59] Indigenous stories tend to represent creatures more accurately and respectfully, as in Native American understanding of the wolf as an intelligent hunter, respected as a teacher.[60] But sometimes even indigenous stories represent creatures unfairly. In such instances the storyteller may seek to honour the creature better by incorporating the findings of natural history.[61]

The use of storytelling in environmental education also raises concerns about whether the story conveys a useful message. Pressure for storytelling to do this may especially arise in large organizations managed according to an outcomes-based business paradigm in which little is left to chance. I've noticed the keenness of executives in a large conservation charity to know how telling a story will elicit from listeners a desired response of modifying their actions or making a donation.

There is cultural variation on the question of highlighting a message: in some more conservative traditions the story's moral may be spelt out at the end.[62] Francis Firebrace, an (Australian) Yorta-Yorta elder and performer who works extensively in Britain, moves freely between storytelling and frank moral instruction, not unlike the way that interpreters like West move between storytelling and exposition. With the authorization of his people, Firebrace seeks to share with Western audiences the Aboriginal wisdom that he believes it's in the earth's best interests they should learn. Because he manifestly comes from a different culture, British audiences perhaps accept from him a frankness of teaching that they wouldn't welcome from a native British storyteller. Yet Firebrace believes that storytelling is 'the most powerful and spiritual way of teaching' because it 'opens people's hearts and plants seeds'.[63] As we shall see, storytelling is most potent when it trusts people to draw lessons for themselves, when it moves people enough to make them think.

Among the practitioners I interviewed, employees of environmental organizations were more inclined to tell stories to convey specific ecological messages than were freelance storytellers. While employed at Kew Gardens in London, Ghislaine Walker told stories to convey messages about biodiversity, sustainable development and walking gently on the earth, and to instil a general association of plants with having a nice time.[64] The storytellers employed at the Eden Project in Cornwall also aimed to convey a message, though sometimes the message was hidden in the subtext so people had to think harder to get the point.[65] Gordon MacLellan, a freelance storyteller, argues that stories that don't have a specific message can provoke more thought than those which do. He's more interested in provoking a sense of wonder about the world.[66] Green too wants his storytelling to evoke a sense of wonder about nature, such as he experienced as a child, then lost during his education in zoology and recovered through encountering storytelling in Cameroon. As manager of a country park, he initially told stories to convey ecological messages, but gradually learned to trust storytelling to work in a more open-ended way.[67] Susan Strauss believes that an experience of wonder and authenticity can elicit from listeners an attitude of respect – the essential basis of ecological ethics.[68]

The storytellers I interviewed enjoyed great freedom to work on their own initiative. At the Eden Project, which when I visited had eleven full-time storyteller-actors serving a clientele of up to 14,000 visitors a day, this trust was built into the official relationship between management and performers in a way that mirrors the trust a storyteller places in the story and the audience's capacity to respond. The 'storytellers' there had much more freedom of action than the 'guides', who had a structured brief to present the 'five messages of Eden'.[69] Michael Moran notes that his aim in telling ecological stories – to 'stir people in their depths' – is not something that can be measured. The only thing he evaluates is whether listeners are enjoying themselves; he's gratified that the management at Slimbridge Wildfowl and Wetland Centre evaluated his efforts simply by turning up to listen to the stories and see how listeners were reacting.[70]

Scientific exploration of wilderness regions usually discounted the knowledge of their indigenous inhabitants as unreliable anecdote or superstition. Without writing or mathematics, indigenous peoples gathered from direct experience over a long timescale vast amounts of tacit knowledge about the environment in which they lived. Stories provide pathways through this body of 'analogue knowledge' and, like dreams and visions, facilitate the leaps of intuition required to make important decisions.[71] The scientific knowledge needed to address today's ecological crisis is available. The barrier is political and public will. Maddern sees hope in the power of stories 'to leapfrog the morass of statistics' and touch people's hearts.[72] Jon Cree, long-time education and training officer at the Bishops Wood Centre in Worcestershire, values the capacity of mythological stories to provoke the imagination in ways that challenge the assumption that science will have all the answers.[73]

In the United States, Linda Yemoto has observed a gradual growth of understanding between the interpretation and storytelling communities. Although there's little overlap in the membership of the National Association for Interpretation and the National Storytelling Network (NSN), these organizations have exchanged keynote speakers at their annual conferences, storytelling-based workshops are offered to interpreters, and NSN hosts an Environmental Storytelling Discussion Group and has offered an entire track of environmental storytelling at its annual conference. Yemoto would like to see greater weaving together of the two paradigms: as an interpreter, she wants more respect for natural history in the stories told; as a storyteller, she wants to see interpretive stories that have a better story arc and create more emotional connection with nature.[74]

The modest scale of the storytelling and interpretation communities in Britain has facilitated networking between them and some fusion of methodology.[75] Storytellers are hired to run storytelling courses for interpreters and teachers, such as at the Bishops Wood Centre (one of the National Grid's environmental education centres), National Park Study Centre in Derbyshire, Royal Botanic Gardens Edinburgh and various National Trust properties, or through the Environmental Trainers Network.[76] In some organizations, such as Kew Gardens and the Eden Project, in-house storytellers have trained their interpreter colleagues in storytelling skills. Chris Salisbury and Chris Holland incorporate storytelling in their bushcraft programmes.[77] Forestry Commission rangers have hosted storytelling festivals in which professional storytellers have performed.[78] West's experience of storytelling came to inform his interpretation in general; when expounding natural history, I observed, he had a storyteller's sensitivity to the dynamics between self and audience. In practice there's a fluid continuum between the extremes of pure storytelling and interpreting modes. When introducing storytelling to the Scottish ranger services, Allan Davies consciously sought to 'build bridges between the two languages of science and story'.[79]

Strauss encourages nature interpreters to look in the science they're communicating for mythopoeic elements that could be shaped into story. In indigenous cultures, mythic and ecological knowledge are united rather than antagonistic.[80] Sometimes myth and Western science uneasily converge, as in Bruce Chatwin's observation of the similarity of Darwinian and Australian Aboriginal accounts of the origin of individual species in isolated localities from which they then spread.[81] Other times the commitments on both sides are too strong to allow any fusion, as in the failure of a Royal Commission workshop of archaeologists and indigenous elders to formulate a common story about Canada's prehistory because the elders rejected the archaeological story that their ancestors reached North America across a land bridge from Siberia rather than emerging autochthonously from the land their peoples today inhabit.[82] The conflict between the story of evolution and the Genesis creation story is a familiar test case for comprehending that religious mythology has to be understood symbolically.

Evolution and processes of geological or climatic change are but two categories of an enormous range of natural processes that lend themselves to presentation as story because they consist of a sequence of events in time. Others include: ecological succession from pioneering species to climax community; species' experience of changing circumstances; species life cycles; and intergenerational sagas of social animals. Maddern sees in the story of evolution a progress in grace, sophistication and the capacity to love.[83] Such a perception raises questions about the Darwinian doctrine that evolutionary processes, being driven by random forces, are devoid of purpose (see Chapter 3). However, purpose is certainly evident in animal behaviour: Green's story of the Manx shearwater's life cycle is driven by the intense purpose this bird exhibits in migrating between the ends of the earth.[84]

Ecological storytelling makes extensive use of traditional stories; collections have been compiled of folktales from the British Isles which feature particular plants, animals or other aspects of nature.[85] When there are no native stories about particular species or ecological topics, storytellers use stories from elsewhere that convey a desired message or involve a similar creature, sometimes translocating them into local settings. There are published collections of ecological tales from around the world.[86] The Eden Project storytellers have a 'bible' of information about all the plants on show and routinely take a strong story from the world repertoire and 'strip in' details about the species they wish to draw attention to.[87] Such practices raise questions about the sacrosanctity versus mutability of traditional material. Stories are always evolving – the hyena of African folktale, transported to America, became Br'er Fox – but if stories and creatures are treated as simply interchangeable there's a risk of corrupting the authentic knowledge that stories can contain about real organisms and places. This illustrates once again that building bridges between science and story, the actual and the imagined, means seeking creative synthesis between antithetical positions. In North America and Australia the telling of traditional tales about local ecology is complicated by political sensitivities because the relevant tales largely come from the indigenous peoples (see Chapter 2).

But the challenges are not only intellectual or political. In many ways, observes Scott Russell Sanders, the 'gospel of ecology has become an *intellectual* commonplace. But it is not yet an *emotional* one.'[88] The healing of the ecological, social and psychological ills arising from modern society's disconnection from nature requires, says Sarah Conn, the reconnection of people to nature at an emotional and sensual level.[89] Jhan Hochman raises the moral question, should we not care about things, far away, with which we have *no* connection?[90] However, the Hindu myth of 'Indra's Net', echoed by network theory, teaches that *everything* is connected: a motion in any part of the net that Indra spread above his palace causes a sparkling of *all* of the jewels fastened to every crossing of the net's threads.[91] The motivation to actually care has to begin somewhere. There's good evidence that a sense of connectedness with nature supports positive attitudes and behaviour towards the environment.[92] How can storytelling help to facilitate this sense of connection?

Making connections between self and other

Environmental educators use diverse creative activities to help people acquire knowledge about a locality and its ecology and at the same time conceive a feeling connection with them.[93] Lucy Goodison writes,

There is a difference between a story told to a child about woods, and a real child in a real forest ... 'the child entering the real woods becomes involved in its life cycle, treads upon leaves that fell yesterday, rests beneath trees far older than his or her memory, and looks up at night to see a moon that will soon disappear'.[94]

Stories can be used to provide a framework for educational programmes that involve inquisitive and creative interaction with the natural environment. Participants can be invited to respond to stories in structured ways or to make up stories about things they've observed and their own experiences in the locality. Or stories can simply be told to an audience outdoors in the midst of nature.[95]

When a story is told in an outdoor setting, says Green, the story should add something to whatever is there to be seen and the environment should add something to the story. The way this works may not be obvious. Green will open his awareness to the surrounding landscape and ask himself, 'What speaks to me here as I stand in this place?' He recalls a powerful experience of telling an African story in the seemingly incongruous setting of a Derbyshire wood, in which he was conscious of allowing the presence of the trees and river into his imagination 'to help the story grow'.[96]

Before anything else, says Moran, the storytelling must be entertaining, so the listeners go away with an association of nature with an enjoyable time.[97] The memory of listening to the stories becomes part of each listener's life experience and will inflect their memory of that locality ever after. That memory can be recalled or shared as a narrative in itself, and thus a flow of positive feeling may be perpetuated.[98] Alida Gersie points out that the ecological crisis threatens the joyful existence of humankind and other creatures; and storytelling has the capacity both, as entertainment, to evoke our experience of joy in the here and now and, as teaching, to clarify our long-term self-interest in preserving the conditions in which joy remains a possibility.[99] Good storytelling in the midst of nature's beauty can unite these means and ends as one and the same experience.

Thus many ecological storytellers' primary objective is to elicit a sense of connection: an emotional investment in the locality where the storytelling takes place, so that people will care what happens to it.[100] The goal is not so much a generalized feeling for nature as a more tangible connection with specific places where nature flourishes, especially those in the area where one lives. Local audiences enjoy the significance of a story hinging upon a precise locality known to them.[101]

Some of those I interviewed spoke of creative work such as storytelling as a 'giving back' in return for what one receives from nature. Moran volunteered to tell stories at Slimbridge as a way of giving something back for the 'lifeline of connection to the earth' which that place had given him.[102] The immediate recipient of this giving is not nature, but the human audience. The hope is that further down the line this giving to the audience will feed through to a giving back to nature. It may do so, but let's remain aware that, although listeners may be touched by the stories they hear, it doesn't necessarily follow that this will lead to any action that will replenish nature.

The emphasis in Peter Please's outdoor storytelling is on cultivating an attitude of open awareness, of 'noticing' without judging or even straining to observe; on accepting that which you can remember as that which is significant for you, and trusting the listeners to respond in their own way. The stories he tells are inspired by what he remembers from his own noticing.[103] He avoids any deliberate agenda for change. Again there's a trusting, that this stimulation of awareness through giving attention may sow seeds that will give rise to some transformative consequence.

Neurological research suggests that habitual giving of attention to what is around you rearranges the synaptic networks in the brain and thereby gradually transforms your perception of reality, so that you become more sensually connected to your surroundings.[104] David Abram describes a story that 'makes sense' as one that enlivens the senses into an awareness of what's actually around you.[105] That being so, the physical situation in which a story is told will influence the impact it makes. When our awareness is extended, we see the beauty and intricacy of our surroundings, but also the ugliness and pollution. When we focus our attention on the here and now – Walter Benjamin's 'jetztzeit' in which a story is told[106] – the present expands to fill our perception of space and time; and if we are outdoors we encounter the earth that defines the ground and the horizon of the place where we are. Abram believes that such direct sensory awareness is necessary for us to truly comprehend the needs of the world and respond to them.[107]

The way that storytelling centres upon the present moment echoes the way that, in the experience of Barry Lopez, hunter-gatherers are attuned to the moment when they are out on the land.[108] Both storyteller and hunter enter a state of 'flow', as Mihaly Csikszentmihalyi calls it, in which 'there is little distinction between self and environment, between stimulus and response, or between past, present, and future'.[109]

The continuous exchange of attention between storyteller and listener encompasses not only the story but also the surroundings. Sensuous connection is desirable with beautiful scenery, living creatures, fine architecture, but we feel repelled from such connection with a polluted beach, motorway traffic, barbed wire, a concrete wall. Images on a screen give the appearance of a connection, but what's represented on the screen is not actually present to your embodied being.

Ecology comprises a web of connections between multifarious living and non-living entities: the cyclic exchanges between them of energy, air, water and nutrients. For human beings, it's air that mediates the most obviously pervasive and intimate physical connection with the rest of the ecosystem. We share the same air with the creatures around us, inhaling it deep inside our bodies, absorbing into our blood the oxygen expired by plants. In many cultures, air or wind is identified with some notion of spirit that links all creatures together. When the air is polluted with anthropogenic chemicals, the pollutants enter the bodies of humans and other creatures alike. When the air is polluted with technological noise, the noise disturbs everyone within hearing, drowns out the sounds of nature and makes storytelling impossible.

Speech is carried into the air on our breath. When you speak to me, some of your breath is entering my lungs, as mine enters yours, and the sound of your words vibrates through my body, making storytelling an intimate and sensual experience (see Chapter 5). A microphone and loudspeaker's intermediation of the transmission of sound between lips and ears is one reason a mike reduces the quality of connection between teller and listeners. Storytelling elicits a relationship demanding that, right now in this moment, both teller and listeners acknowledge the presence and respect the needs of others. For some new to the experience, this means learning to restrain the impulse to use one's mobile phone.

From the connection between storyteller and listeners, further connections may branch out: between one listener and another; between the people and the immediate space in which the storytelling is happening and also the larger locality in which that space is situated; between the people and the kinds of animals and plants that feature in the story and perhaps inhabit the locality too. Maddern and Hugh Lupton ran a workshop, inspired by the Welsh poem *Cad Goddeu*, in which each student worked up a story about a different species of native tree. As examples of all these species occur at Cae Mabon, Maddern's retreat centre in Snowdonia, the workshop culminated in a walk in which each student told their story in the physical presence of the respective tree. This proved a powerful way to attend to each kind of tree and to experience a sense of the trees as distinct beings.[110]

In such ways storytelling may catalyse an extension of the boundaries of the self from the 'skin-encapsulated ego'[111] to encompass a group of other people, the place where you are in this moment, and perhaps your larger neighbourhood and the people and other creatures who inhabit it.[112] Such an extension of the self begins to make porous the boundaries between self and other, and between human and non-human.

The dynamic between storyteller and listeners can easily acquire an erotic charge, an intimate exchange of gaze. I use 'erotic' in a broad sense, implying a wish for intimacy with others and a care for their well-being. Attentive listening – including the storyteller's listening to their audience's non-verbal presence – may be considered a kind of loving attention. In the best storytelling situations, with a congenial group around a campfire in a wood on a summer night, you can feel a profound sense of connection to and love for everyone present and the environment around you.

Film and television, by contrast, mediate no real relationship between performer and viewer, though television presenters convey the illusion of such a relationship.[113] 'Reality has been lifted beyond our participation,' writes Ted Hughes, arguing that the camera and screen epitomize the objectifying perception of the modern age which denies the validity of inner life.[114] The 'ubiquity of television [and] canned and capitalized media imagery', argues Laura Sewall, can blunt people's capacity for active imagination and hence responsible action.[115] Film narratives can take you on an emotional journey that stirs deep feelings, but the imaginative work is done for you, externalized on the screen, and is thus more easily left behind. Online media differ in bringing to the screen diverse possibilities of interaction, including audiovisually. These allow even an online experience of storytelling – witness the widespread efforts to deliver storytelling through videotelephony during the Covid-19 pandemic. To what extent does the objectifying effect of camera and screen compromise that experience? How much does embodied presence really matter? That's something we'll return to in Chapters 5 and 6.

Storytelling demands acknowledgement of each other as a conscious being. It engages the listener as an active agent in imagining the story and thereby, I suggest, invites the awakening of their sense of responsibility. Whereas the film-maker is distant, untouchable, wielding powerful technologies to manipulate the viewer's emotions, the storyteller is a vulnerable figure, whose activity depends on two-way communication and trust. It works through provocation, the sowing of seeds. The listeners find their own response within themselves, and in finding it themselves, using their own imagination, they may be more likely to then express it in responsible action.

The agency and voices of nature

Storytelling outdoors is exposed not only to the active agency of the audience but also to nature's own initiative and power. Unexpected sounds and movements may distract from the storyteller and dissipate the energy of the performance, yet can also contribute a fitting intervention with stunning timing – such as a crack of thunder at a critical pause in a ghost story.[116] The elements do pose challenges to storytelling outdoors. It's wise to choose a space where the energy will be contained, there'll be shelter if needed, the sun will not shine into the audience's eyes, there are no distractions behind the storyteller, and the audience will be downwind. On a story walk, each stop needs to have these properties, so the stops have to be scouted out beforehand. In such ephemeral venues where often no seating is available the stories need to be kept short lest discomfort undermine the listeners' attention. Small groups are best to minimize the danger of some people being excluded from earshot and to maximize the intimacy of connection between teller, listeners and location. And everyone needs to be suitably dressed for the weather and to have gone to the toilet beforehand. Around the campfire after dark, everything comes together: a containment of space by the darkness around the pool of firelight, the alchemical focus of the fire, the background sounds of nature, and the power of the night to open your imagination to other worlds of possibility.[117]

This power of nature, challenging though it may be, is something that people need to engage with if they're going to learn to respect and cherish the ecosystem. Storytelling is more flexible than scripted performance genres to respond to the dynamics of the moment, to accommodate nature's agency. Outdoors there's an exaggerated need for flexibility. The storyteller has to go with the flow and accept the listeners' shifting interest in the surroundings as well as the story. Such attention to the environment may well be forging in them the desired sense of connection.

Moran's experience telling stories to psychiatric patients with erratic powers of attention pre-adapted him for the unpredictability of outdoor storytelling, so he was able to accommodate without strain unexpected interactions between nature and audience. At Slimbridge, where visitors drifted through with no expectation of listening to stories, performances at set times weren't feasible; so Moran, installed in a shady spot, would gently waylay visitors as they passed by and invite them to stop for a story. From a repertoire of bird stories he chose whichever one felt right for the particular group of listeners.[118] When a moorhen invaded the space in search of scraps of food, Moran remarked, 'She likes to come and listen to the story,' and gave the children time to enjoy the bird's exciting proximity before she moved on and he resumed telling.

Nature's agency is expressed partly through weather and seasons. Adrian Tissier, a National Trust consultant on interpretative techniques, emphasizes that the optimum style of storytelling outdoors is defined by the physical conditions: on a Peak District moorland, for example, the need to keep warm demands an interactive approach in which the audience get to move about.[119]

Outdoor storytelling and interpretation can be mixed with experiential exercises that get people using their senses to become more aware of what's around them and to notice their own responses to what they observe.[120] For the sense of hearing, for example, a simple exercise is to close your eyes and listen to the soundscape around you without speaking. This can be coupled to a response activity of either blindly 'drawing the sound' with pencil on card while listening, *or*, after the period of listening, writing quick descriptive notes of what you remember hearing.[121]

When stories are told in a natural setting, the background sounds of elements and creatures make a potent contribution to the experience. The storyteller who listens closely to nature can learn to imitate its sounds. Green includes bird calls at relevant points in his stories: the curlew's call evoking the moorland, the shearwater's the loneliness of the sea.[122] This skill may even elicit a response from nature, as when Yemoto once ended an owl story with an owl call and then heard, far off, the hoot of a real owl returning her call.[123]

For a story to 'make sense' and have transformative potency, Abram says, it needs to be told in language that sensually evokes the physicality of what it's representing – language that is itself inspired by the environment.[124] Some indigenous peoples attribute the origination of the sounds and structure of their language to the land they inhabit. Observers have noticed an affinity between the rhythms and sounds of an area's natural soundscape and the rhythms and sounds of the native people's speech and music.[125] The Amahuaca of the Amazon rainforest are explicitly able to mimic the cries of local birds and mammals and use these to communicate during hunting excursions.[126]

When a storyteller uses the local names of individual species and land features, they convey something of the soundscape from which the story originates and help to teach the lexicon that codes knowledge of the corresponding ecosystem.[127] For these reasons, I don't think storytellers should shy away from including such unfamiliar terms and spelling out their meaning as necessary, even in stories from very distant lands, so long as they don't ascribe to themselves an authoritative knowledge they don't possess.

Comprehending the stories of the non-human

Stories extend your imagination to see the world from perspectives other than your own. When you hear someone's own story, your empathy is engaged and you recognize that other person as a conscious being capable of suffering and joy. When this takes place in a public setting, it may nurture trust between groups and stimulate conversations that could lead to useful action.[128] That's another reason it's been important to human rights movements to give a platform to individuals from oppressed demographic groups to tell their own stories. How might this input of storytelling into the nurturing of empathy and ethics encompass the stories of non-human creatures? Since they can't speak human languages to tell us stories, let's consider the potential of human advocates to convey the experiences and perspectives of non-human creatures on their behalf.

Since the Enlightenment the Cartesian dualism embedded in Western thought has regarded animals and plants as objects, without souls or sentience, that we can treat in any way we please. This perception has sanctioned the massacring of wild animals for profit or sport, and cruelties such as factory farming, not to mention the wholesale destruction of habitats. The prevailing monetary value system can only justify the existence of wildlife and wilderness in terms of their providing some (ultimately economic) benefit to humans, such as opportunities for tourism or the discovery of new pharmaceuticals. Given that frame of values, it's troubling that computer-generated imagery, as in simulated nature documentaries like *Monsters We Met* and *Extinct*, about species that humans have driven into extinction, now enables people to consume the sights of nature without the real thing even needing to exist.

But contemporary zoology is revealing that the more intelligent animals experience an existence whose sensory and behavioural complexity may be compared to that of humans.[129] Neuroscientists suspect that most mammals have dreams and a conscious awareness of the present moment.[130] Every species inhabits an 'umwelt' – a world as that particular species perceives it – which may include sensory and semiotic experiences beyond the range of human experience, such as the low-frequency utterances of elephants and whales which facilitate social interaction across large distances. So complex are the umwelten of animals like elephants, whales, wolves, bears and apes that it may be supposed they also possess an 'innenwelt' – an inner world of sentience and feelings comparable to yet fascinatingly different from our own.[131]

Meanwhile ecology is revealing the immense complexity of nature as a whole, its physical complexity being compounded by the sum of the umwelten of each separate species, each with 'a story of some unique way of living in this world'.[132] As industrial civilization expands its domain, this complexity is progressively diminished by human modification of the environment. Yet it embodies stories that humans have yet to fully learn, such as the process by which the complex dynamic equilibrium of a climax community like primary rainforest comes into being, as well as stories that shed revealing light on human behaviour, such as the heroic endeavours of pioneer species.[133] The fluid complexity of wilderness – in Gary Snyder's words 'a limitless fabric of possibilities, elegant variations a millionfold on the same themes, yet each point unique'[134] – seems to me analogous to the organic, unpredictable, unrepeatable essence of storytelling. The novelist Joyce Carol Oates claims that nature 'inspires a painfully limited set of responses … reverence, awe, piety, mystical oneness'.[135] Her tone betrays an obliviousness to the richness of mystical experience, but her comment is yet a challenge – to the storyteller as well as the nature writers she's critiquing – to consider what diversity of responses could be inspired by a repertoire that includes not only traditional, personal, historical and fictional stories about human protagonists but also stories drawn from the range of experience of other species.

Just as storytellers who tell stories from cultures other than their own should be informed and respectful, so those who tell stories about other species ought to be informed about their lives and depict them with respect. As Nabhan writes:

> Once we have begun to express in our own ways the stories inspired by those other lives, we need to keep seeking out those lives in order to compare constantly the images we have conjured up with the beings themselves … It is time to hear the seabirds singing at the edge of the world and to bring them back, freshly, into our cultural stories, into our dreams.[136]

Traditional stories, especially fables, often represent animals in a highly anthropomorphic way. This invites a degree of empathy, or antipathy, towards animals, but the focus of interest remains human, unengaged with the animals' otherness.[137] Different from anthropomorphism is the implication of a mythopoeic kinship between humans and other creatures, as in Ovid's emphasis of the trope of metamorphosis in Greek myths such as the death of Actaeon:[138] 'while Actaeon is literally de-anthropomorphized, the stag that he turns into becomes humanized', explains Robert Pogue Harrison. 'Now that Actaeon has become a stag we are able to suffer its fate as if it were a human being.'[139] Shifts back and forth between human and animal forms occur in, for example, Scottish tales of selkies and Native American ones about bison people.[140] In Native American traditions, animals are spoken of as 'people', with their own ways different from human people's, and stories mediate what the animals have to teach us.[141] In some indigenous stories, we find, not shapeshifting transitions, but an ambiguity of form and being in which characters like Mantis in San mythology and Flying Fox Woman in New Caledonia are simultaneously human and animal and a sense of the animals' otherness is preserved.[142]

An understanding of universal kinship is normative in many indigenous cultures that attribute spirit not only to animals and plants but also to landforms, water bodies and meteorology. Everything in nature is respected as alive in its own way, able to act upon its own initiative and to speak to people who listen in the right way.[143] In Indo-European traditions such nature spirits have become anthropomorphized as fairies and the like. MacLellan understands the fairies in folktales not simply as a supernatural race but as an expression of nature, in which different kinds of fairies are associated with different habitats. Solitary fairies tend to be more obviously tied to the landscape, featuring in stories about a particular tree, pool or rock.[144]

In his Manx shearwater story, Green is conscious of projecting human feelings on to the bird. He admits that this distorts reality but regards this distortion as no greater than that imposed by the purely scientific account that denies the bird anything like feelings. His telling implicitly universalizes the story, so the shearwater may be interpreted as representing more than just a shearwater *as well as* representing the real shearwater known to natural history: the story thus becomes, as in the Native American model, a means by which nature may teach us.[145] At the still-point of a full-length performance, *Shearwater*, Green and his collaborator Tim Dalling evoke the mystery of the bird's otherness when Green questions the shearwater about its experiences and motivations, and the bird (voiced by Dalling) will reply only, 'I know the way,' and then with silence.

In another show, *Gone Cuckoo*, Green goes a step further by speaking in first person as the cuckoo. This produces a deeper intimacy with the bird, demanding 'more exactitude' of truth, since he's telling the story of a real individual cuckoo, whom he witnessed being tagged in Britain and whose exact route and timing of migration to Central Africa he was thus able to track. He narrates what the cuckoo can see, but doesn't depict its emotions. The transition from 'I, Malcolm' at the start into 'I, Cuckoo' is accomplished through telling a Siberian folktale in which a woman turns into a cuckoo because some children have refused to help her – at which point Green dons a cuckoo mask. He subsequently speaks without the mask, but the mask is worn by his collaborator Joshua Green to perform a cuckoo dance and an incantation based on folk beliefs about what the cuckoo's saying when it's calling.[146]

To enter the viewpoint not merely of another person but of another species, with its own umwelt, may seem an impossible feat, likely always to involve some degree of anthropomorphic projection. Contemplation of that gap of understanding creates a tension, a kind of desire, that can motivate the exercising of the imagination to reach across the gap and at the same time accepts as part of the richness of the universe the mystery of that which is beyond one's comprehension and control.[147]

To cross this gap between minds is exactly what indigenous shamans seek to do, as Abram experienced when he received training from a Nepali jhankri. What it demanded was spending time in the presence of the chosen creature – in his case the raven – and giving it a meditative quality of attention that eventually dissolved the separation of his consciousness from the raven's.[148] In indigenous cultures detailed tacit knowledge of local fauna, totemic relationships with particular species, and altered states of perception all help to facilitate powerful experiences of identification with other creatures.[149] Firebrace explains that when an Aboriginal hunter is stalking a kangaroo, not only his bodily movement but his mind too becomes that of the kangaroo. The same mimetic skill is employed back in camp when the hunter tells the story of his hunt.[150] Indigenous storytellers' superb simulation of animals is widely noted.[151] When I watched Firebrace demonstrate a kangaroo's movement while narrating the process of hunting during a storytelling performance, the dogs in the audience responded with uncanny sensitivity to the realism of his mime. 'They know!' he remarked in response to the barking.

From extended observation you can become familiar with the ways an animal moves, its facial and bodily expressions, its vocalizations – and learn to imitate them. At Brookfield Zoo, Chicago, MacLellan prepared children for storywork by having them watch animals – and be watched by them – and experience different perspectives by looking through a periscope ('like a giraffe') or lying on the ground ('like a rat'). He gets people to try telling a story about an animal while pretending they're that kind of animal.[152] Strauss, drawn to stories about the coyote and the wolf, has spent many hours watching these animals. She feels that she *becomes* Coyote, the Native American trickster, as she delivers his speech and gestures in a story.[153]

The inspiration and enchantment of landscape

Nature's interests include not only the well-being of individual creatures but the ecological health of the landscapes in which they live. The relationship between storytelling and land conservation is an area in which indigenous traditions elsewhere have provided especially strong inspiration to storytelling in Britain.

Landscapes everywhere carry a web of connection with stories native to them,[154] perhaps most elaborately in the Aboriginal 'songlines' of Australia: geographical pathways defined by the wandering of mythic beings in their Dreaming of the landscape and its fauna and flora. The narrative songs associated with the songlines are still chanted by Aborigines as they navigate these routes and enact rituals in which the Dreaming is experienced as an ongoing eternity of creation. They believe the songs need to be sung for the land to continue to exist. Conversely, when landscape features on the songlines are destroyed by modern development the corresponding elements of the Dreaming cease to be. At a practical level the respect for places and creatures (including food sources) mediated by these songs helps to conserve the ecosystem, and the songlines' codification of landscape knowledge facilitates navigation across the land.[155]

Maddern, born in Australia of British ancestry, worked among Aboriginal communities in his youth and was deeply inspired by the concept of the Dreaming. Aware the stories of Australia's Dreaming were not his own, he travelled to the land of his ancestors with a mission to explore the Dreaming of Britain. An invitation from English Heritage to pioneer storytelling on their properties gave him an opportunity to apply the inspiration of the Dreaming to storytelling in historic sites around Britain.[156]

The Aboriginal concept of songlines informs the mythic-visionary experience of walking the South Downs Way related in Philip Carr-Gomm's *The Druid Way*. Lupton and Maddern have both applied the concept to construct 'songlines', composed of sequences of stories, that can be walked across the landscapes of, respectively, Norfolk and Snowdonia.[157] Green has led a project called 'Dreaming the Land', which brought together folklore and archaeology of the far north of England to inspire the creation, with schoolchildren, of new stories that imagined what might have happened long ago in a series of ancient sacred sites and then were performed to local communities during an epic walk from the Holy Island of Lindisfarne to Long Meg, a stone circle in Cumbria. The team of adults doing the walk also shared personal stories round the campfire each night as they reflected upon the inner journey that accompanied the experience of travelling in community across a wild yet storied landscape.[158] These initiatives also bear some resemblance to traditions of travelling the pilgrimage routes to sacred places associated with stories of holy teachers.[159] Kevan Manwaring has charted a King Arthur Way from Tintagel, where Arthur was conceived, to Glastonbury, his resting place, as a pilgrimage route 'enabling walkers to experience the Arthurian legend in an embodied way'.[160]

In every country, notable landscape features, often viewed as sacred, are associated with local myth and legend. The crux of a Pueblo story typically pivots on such a feature.[161] Scotland's isle of Iona is peppered with topographic and archaeological features connected to the life of St Columba and other lore;[162] a map published by the Iona Community pinpoints their locations. The locating of British legends on regional maps in ambitious compilations of these stories conveys how they permeate both landscape and townscape.[163] Pedro Olalla has done the same for the Greek myths.[164] Such efforts give an inkling of how, for indigenous peoples, associations between topography and story constitute a vibrant mythscape that coexists with and informs perception of the physical landscape (see Chapter 4).

In the analogue continuity of indigenous oral tradition, the genres of myth, legend, folktale, history and anecdote blend into one another. Memorable anecdotes evolve into legends. Firebrace's discourse will shift, without pause for breath, between personal experience, an Aboriginal take on British colonial history, and full-blown creation myth. All these different kinds of stories are held by the land. The visual form of the landscape structures the memory of stories, and conversely the stories encode knowledge of the land. This works both for features – such as a fallen tree – associated with recent events and for ancient landforms associated with creation myths.[165]

The 'synaesthetic association of visible topology with auditory recall' in indigenous cultures[166] recurs in modern storytellers' practice of structuring a story as a sequence of 'bones' and then visualizing the scene for each bone. By this means you can fashion a simulation of memory so that you can tell a story that's not your own personal story with such commitment as if it were and your words will spark images in your listeners' minds. Where a story's action weaves through geographical space, the bones can be sequenced on a map of the territory, whether drawn or imagined. When you incorporate in this imaginative work your own memories of relevant places and experiences, the distinction between personal and traditional stories begins to blur; the story becomes your own.[167]

If you visit the *actual* locations that feature in a story, you can infuse in your imagining of the story's scenes real memories of these places.[168] As Goethe put it:

> Now that my mind is stored with images of all these coasts and promontories, gulfs and bays, islands and headlands, rocky cliffs, fields, flower gardens, tended trees, festooned vines, mountains wreathed in clouds, eternally serene plains, and the all-encircling sea with its every-changing colours and moods, for the first time the *Odyssey* has become a living truth to me.[169]

The step beyond this is to tell the story in those very locations – as Maddern and Lupton facilitate in their annual workshop centred on Welsh mythology, which always includes at least one day visiting sites linked to the stories.[170] The inner world of the imagination 'locks in' with the outer world observed by the senses, explains Lupton, producing a state of consciousness in which 'the teller becomes a medium through which the landscape can speak'.[171]

In Apache tradition, relates Keith H. Basso, it's not done to imagine events that are not located in a real place: 'identifying the event's location is essential to properly depicting – and effectively picturing – the event's occurrence'.[172] Abram likens the situation of characters in a story and its landscape to a real person's situation in the narrative of life and the real landscape around us.[173] If the imagined and real landscapes are perceived as one and the same, then the distinction between imaginative and personal stories, again, breaks down and – as Maddern explains – the barrier between the material world and the mythic otherworld dissolves:

> When you bring a story to a place and you tell the story in the place where there is some kind of connection between them, both place and story are lifted beyond what they would otherwise be and you can get a sense of magic and you can go through the gateway into the otherworld.[174]

The spiritual perspectives and practices of indigenous peoples have been a source of inspiration – alongside archaeology's sparse findings about Britain's pre-Christian spirituality, and the stories of Celtic mythology – to the modern communities of Pagans (Druids, Wiccans and others) in Britain who are nurturing new forms of spirituality centred upon respect for land and nature. Their sacred sites are woodland groves and prehistoric monuments believed to be associated with an ancient earth-centred spirituality. Their bards tell stories adapted from native myth and folktale and also personal stories based on their own spiritual experiences, which include encounters with supernatural beings and sometimes are facilitated by hallucinogens.[175] In the 'Ecopagan' road protest subculture of the 1990s, Andy Letcher explains, these contemporary fairy stories were mixed with straightforward anecdotes about the struggle against the road builders, in which protestors identified themselves with fairies in the sense of being guardians of nature. He sees in this a living folk tradition that mediated a sense of connection to the English landscape and contributed to a partially successful defence of that landscape from damaging development.[176]

Modern Pagans affirm the ancient identification of earth with goddess and sometimes compare the land to a woman's body,[177] having common cause with ecofeminists who link the abuse of the earth to the abuse of women by patriarchal social structures.[178] This idea is crystallized in an Arthurian story – part of *The Elucidation*, a medieval French prequel to the Grail quest – in which the maidens who tended the land's sacred wells, and served water to passers-by, were raped by King Amangons and his men, with the consequence the wells dried up and the land became a wasteland.[179] Some Pagans advocate the sharing of goddess myths to extend the tenderness one might feel towards one's lover or mother to a cherishing of the earth as sacred.[180] The coming of the wasteland, meanwhile, chimes with indigenous cultures' respect for nature as powerful[181] and able to exercise that power when humankind abuses the ecosystem, as in the trope of the 'fairies' revenge' (see Chapter 2).

Thus the enchantment of the land through stories helps nurture a conception of the earth as sacred and potent – and of certain places as especially so.[182] Just as landscape and stories serve as mnemonics for each other, so there is a synergy between the protection of landscape features and the transmission of stories. The ban in Aboriginal tradition upon taking weapons to sacred sites associated with one's totem animal creates 'de facto wildlife refuges, where totem animals can regenerate' their numbers.[183] In Ireland a respect for enchanted places has lingered into modern times: efforts may be made to avoid disturbing a tree or rath (ringfort) associated with the fairies.[184] Ian Darwin Edwards of the Royal Botanic Garden Edinburgh envisions the telling of stories in restored and protected woods in order to nurture a sense of these areas as new 'sacred groves'.[185] The National Trust aims to use live interpretation, including storytelling, to evoke in visitors to its properties the 'spirit of the place', acknowledged to be subjectively experienced and different for each visitor. This 'spirit of the place' includes archaeology, history, folklore and natural history. Implicit in this approach are messages about the fragility of the landscape and the importance of conserving for the future each locality's special qualities.[186]

The danger, in a country so heavily populated as Britain and so committed to economic growth based on material consumption, is that we preserve a sprinkling of little heritage reserves – where wildlife may survive till climate change terminates the viability of their mini ecosystems – while all the land between them, except in remote upland areas, is consumed by monoculture and urban development. A bigger vision would aim to use stories to mediate a sense of all land as sacred and thereby to validate a sustainable balance between nature and civilization throughout the land (see Chapter 4). Darwin Edwards wants to see the land 'restored' as an integral part of reforesting Scotland.[187] Such projects of ecological restoration require those involved to listen to the story of the land

– by observing its geology and ecology, listening to its soundscape and learning its history and folklore – so the work may proceed in sensitive partnership with nature.[188]

The environmental condition of an area depends greatly on the attitude of the people who live there, who have a vested interest in its well-being – if their eyes be open to see this. MacLellan's community arts projects forge connections between a community and the local environment through working with people to make a story about their locality.[189] Oral history projects similarly bring community and place together through story. A project at Cowpen Bewley Woodland Park, Stockton-on-Tees, explored the site's folklore, history and natural history, especially the economic relationship between people and the environment – the human ecology. The research culminated in a community storytelling festival and was then applied in practical ways to the interpretation and management of the park.[190]

The mobility of people in modern society works against commitment to the local community and concern for the local environment. But it also creates the possibility of broadening outwards the inward focus of deeply rooted communities in order to make connections between diverse cultures and places. Jared Diamond claims that accelerating cultural homogenization is the main source of hope for peace in the world: 'Loss of cultural diversity may be the price that we have to pay for survival.'[191] This is the voice of cultural imperialism in the guise of scientific reason. It ignores the loss of ecological knowledge that accompanies the extinction of local culture. It abandons the creative pathways that open from respectful encounters between different perspectives.[192] In focusing attention on the particularity of *these people* in *this place*, but being able to bring to this jetztzeit stories from across time and geography, storytelling can help to forge both a sense of connectedness to a locality and the intercultural connectedness necessitated by global ecological crisis.

But all such efforts fly against the powerful forces of global capitalism and are easily marginalized within the domain of recreation or special interest. For modern Western publics, the sense of connection with nature rarely has the life-and-death significance that it does for indigenous hunter-gatherers or subsistence cultivators. Perhaps it never will until the effects of ecological crisis impinge to such a degree that people's relationship with nature becomes tangibly a life-and-death issue. Although the Covid-19 pandemic is such an effect, at the time I'm writing this it's not generally framed in public conversation as ecological. However, there are many people who do already perceive ecology as important enough that they're willing for it to constrain and inspire the way they live. Some perceive it at the all-encompassing level of the sacred. James Cowan says it is the '*collusion* between man and nature' that evokes reverence:[193] a collusion that's achieved through respectful modification of nature (sacred art and architecture) and through embodied stories, music and movement. All these elements come together in ritual at sacred sites in the landscape.

Storytelling as transforming ritual

In many storytelling situations any suggestion of a sacred or spiritual dimension may raise barriers to people's receptivity. Storytellers such as Maddern and MacLellan, who take seriously the spiritual dimension but are accustomed to working with the general public, avoid assuming an openness to spirituality and work with people as they find them – towards encouraging them to respect nature in their actions and to value the place where they live.[194] Firebrace doesn't expect modern Western audiences to believe in the spirit animals of the Dreaming; he's content to use stories from the Dreaming to encourage a secular respect for living creatures.[195]

But, according to Goodison's definition of 'spirituality' as 'the faculty which allows us to feel our connection with other humans, the natural environment and a wider sense of the universe',[196] storytelling is intrinsically spiritual – and so is knowledge of ecology. You don't have to believe in supernatural spirits in order to experience that amplification of your sense of connection to that which is beyond yourself which occurs when storytelling verges into ritual.

In African ritual drama, there's no fourth wall between performers and audience: everyone takes part; everyone enters the liminal space – in which the performance experience is considered real and potent, not merely a fiction – and therefore everyone encounters the possibility of transformation.[197] Storytelling shares something of this. There's generally no fourth wall: storyteller and listeners share the same space.[198] To fully take in a story, the listener must actively contribute to imagining it. Through this participation, and the memory of the experience they take away with them, some part of their being may be changed, connected in new ways with things beyond themselves. Please perceives a ritual quality – 'like the Stations of the Cross' – in the rhythm of a story walk: the group alternately comes together to look at something and hear a relevant story and then breaks up into a band of individuals with space to assimilate the story and observe the surroundings for themselves until the next stop.[199]

In ritual, people are invited to take part physically as well as imaginatively: in *doing* the story rather than simply listening, they cease to be audience and become participants, more susceptible to transformation.[200] Ritual augments storytelling with other art forms: music, dance, poetry, theatre, visuals. At an event at the Ancient Technology Centre, in Dorset, Lupton and Ben Haggarty performed an extract from their Mesolithic creation epic *I Become Part of It*, whose most powerful moment depicted the 'conversation of death' – Lopez's term[201] – between a human hunter and a deer. The alternation of partially repeating verses between hunter and prey evoked a ritual mood at the same time that the incremental transformation of these verses through to a dramatic resolution conveyed the moral acceptability of killing animals in a hunting society. This episode implicitly challenged the disconnect in modern society between the slaughtering of animals and the eating of meat. Immediately after the performance, dinner was served: non-vegetarians like me had to queue up to watch our slice of pork hacked off a spitted pig and slapped on our plate. A connection was thus made, without explanation, between the 'imaginary' of the story and the 'actual' of butchery and eating. The effect of ritual was engineered without crossing into explicit ritual.

What's possible is limited by what the group you're working with are open to. Ana Adnan, having reached the limits of what seemed possible in ordinary storytelling contexts, began to run workshops on her own property in Wales whose primary focus was to create rituals inspired by story and landscape. She advertised only through one of the Druid orders to ensure that all who attended would have previous experience of ritual. Within the parameters she defines of time, place and stories, she cultivates in the group an openness to creative inspiration and going with the flow. This gives space to nature to contribute to the experience, which it does most dramatically through weather. Adnan's property and the surrounding land contain many features that can be linked into stories. One weekend, based around the Greek story of Theseus and Ariadne, culminated in a 'retelling' in which each subgroup presented an episode of the story, incorporating whatever participatory elements they chose. In one episode a woman dressed as the Cretan Snake Goddess led each participant into a dark, dirty shed, where they sat alone for a time in the presence of a Minotaur silhouette, and then took them to walk an outdoor flare-lit labyrinth, which many chose to do naked.[202]

Adnan finds that this kind of work cultivates great sensitivity to one's surroundings. I can appreciate that from my own experience of attending outdoor rites conducted by Druids. In a Lammas rite, for example, the ballad story of 'John Barleycorn' was enacted in a ritual form that was analogous to the Eucharist's enactment of Christ's Passion but gave me a moving sense of connection with the summer landscape which cannot be experienced inside a church building.

The augmentation of storytelling with other art forms helps to meet the challenge of engaging a large congregation. Storytelling to large audiences – especially outdoors and to audiences not self-selected as storytelling enthusiasts – may incline towards a theatrical spectacle that offers more sensory stimulation than can a solitary speaker.[203] At the Eden Project two yurts were available for more intimate storytelling, but the performers also worked in large outdoor spaces and the two giant greenhouse 'biomes'.[204] They used street theatre skills to gather an audience from the visitors drifting by and a high-energy theatrical style to hold them. The Bronx Zoo has used storytelling theatre on an even grander scale, reaching an estimated audience of one million people over twelve months.[205] When storytelling moves towards theatrical spectacle, it becomes more susceptible to Zipes's critique of the disempowering effect of 'spectacle';[206] but fluid and lively outdoor conditions, with large numbers of people roaming around, are unconducive to the level of attention demanded by conventional storytelling.

MacLellan's community arts projects often culminate in a big theatrical 'celebration' of the local environment. He uses traditional stories to spark a creative process involving diverse artistic and investigative activities; later the group may create their own new story. The final event is too ludic to feel threatening to anyone, but, like more overt forms of ritual, it uses a mix of art forms to engage people at different levels and make everyone a participant. Always, amidst the comedy, there will come a still-point – an unplanned moment of connection with something larger than oneself – which brings an intensified awareness of the specialness of the surroundings. This invitation to stillness is not so potent in an indoor venue, MacLellan notes; you can only point towards connection with the environment rather than make the connection for real.[207]

Such a point of stillness occurs within many storytelling occasions, and within individual stories. It marks a liminal space, in which everyday experience is suspended, oppositions are reconciled, and one escapes from the ubiquitous measurement of time according to its economic value[208] – especially so when stories are shared in a liminal place and time, such as around a fire on Halloween. In mythic terms it's a doorway, as Ari Berk puts it, to 'other times and realms where Gods reside and knowledge may be gained'.[209]

In Peter Searles's comic personal narrative *Through Peru* the still-point comes when he compares the squalor of a shanty town with the luxury of the rich: a centre of gravitas nested within the comedy and earned by satisfying the audience's wish to be entertained. In a companion piece, *A Chile Christmas*, comedy gives way to graphic portrayal of Pinochet's brutal treatment of his country's people and ecology, which Searles, drawn into the underground opposition, witnessed first-hand. The show uses personal story to engage the audience with the political reality of recent history. I saw it at a storytelling festival, a context that may have affected some people's expectations. Some couldn't stomach the brutality and left at the interval. Others I spoke to were distracted from the story – and the issues it addressed – by questions about whether Searles had truly experienced everything he was relating and what effect he intended to achieve. He's a professional actor and, from the perspective of seasoned storylisteners, his perfectly choreographed performance perhaps presented a barrier to the relationship of trust that such powerful material demanded.

We come back to the relational nature of storytelling. People can't take too much bad news, Green warns, too much that is serious or shocking, without withdrawing their attention.[210] The storyteller must be sensitive to the audience's response and judge the limits of what they can take. My research suggests that most ecological storytelling emphasizes the positive: eliciting interest, empathy, delight and wonder in response to nature and landscape. But the history of ecological destruction also needs to be known, so that people can learn from the past and see what needs to change in order for the earth to flourish. There are times when the storyteller is called to tell their audience, 'at the risk of their own distress, the secrets of their own heart'.[211] Like Percival seeking the Grail, people must learn to ask, 'What ails thee?' – to confront the real problem, in ourselves and in the world – before the wasteland can be healed.[212] Let us now evaluate the vocation of storytelling, in the fray of public life, to make a difference to the world and its ecological problems.

The vocation of storytelling

Confrontation of listeners with politics or spirituality is likely to meet resistance unless the storyteller has earned their trust to take such a risk. Rob Parkinson warns against 'the "more-esoteric-than-thou" stance ... the "away-with-the-fairies" factor ... the "I'm-doing-something-very-serious-so-just-shut-up-and-listen" posture'.[213] Yet storytelling does need to engage at deeper levels if it's to do more than merely entertain. Part of the challenge is to choose the right time and place for departures from more straightforward storytelling. For storytelling that veers towards ritual, a forest glade at night is a more promising venue, allowing more open-ended expectations, than a marquee at a folk festival. The ritual qualities of *I Become Part of It* – not least the practicalities of lighting a real fire – made that production difficult to perform in theatres and more successful outdoors.[214]

It is possible to shift the mood from bantering light-heartedness to something deeper, but it takes skill, humility and sometimes the cooperation of a compère. Resistance to ethical challenge or the invocation of a ritual mood may arise from a storyteller's insensitivity to the audience's reactions and a failure to embody the wisdom they aspire to share. The storytellers most able to lead us into new places in the heart, to transcend the zeitgeist of irony without coming across too earnest, are those we trust as mature in spirit. Ruth Sawyer noticed

> that the best of the traditional storytellers whom I have heard have been those who live close to the heart of things – to the earth, the sea, wind and weather. They have been those who knew solitude, silence. They have been given unbroken time in which to feel deeply, to reach constantly for understanding.[215]

So the storyteller who wants to make a difference faces the calling to make their own journey of transformation. Through travelling the otherworld of stories, experiencing other cultures, places, creatures, and seeking sources of wisdom beyond their own ego, they may serve, in some ways like a shaman, as a bridge for their audiences between the familiar world and other worlds.[216] To tell nature's stories with authority requires the tacit knowledge that comes only from direct experience of withdrawing from everyday modern life to immerse your senses in nature and find the solitude and stillness in which to deepen your own connection with the living world.

Modern Pagan bards, perceiving nature as spirit-filled, cultivate openness to 'awen' – an energy of creative inspiration they believe to flow everywhere, but especially strongly in sacred or numinous places.[217] Manwaring ventures into wild places to seek inspiration and to prepare himself for storytelling and poetry performances. His perception of exchanging 'energy' with his audiences, his peers and the environment is part of his sense of ecological connectedness.[218] For some years he maintained a special relationship with a small privately run woodland: in return for its nourishment of his spirit, he organized bardic events there and helped to plant trees. He's now cultivating such a relationship with his new environs of Wiltshire downland dotted with prehistoric monuments.[219]

Through the web of ecology and our bodies' physiology, human beings are part of the earth: what we feel and speak is an expression of the environments we frequent.[220] If storytellers spend time in the presence of nature and if they recognize the landscapes of their real-life experience as also the enchanted landscapes of folklore, then in telling personal, traditional, historical and scientific stories associated with these landscapes they give voice to the environment. They may claim, in this sense, to speak for nature.

But does it really make any difference? In a few contexts such as restoration projects and the road protest movement, storytelling has contributed instrumentally to environmental action. Elsewhere storytelling does not in itself produce direct tangible change in the service of ecology. The hope is that people will be moved by stories they've heard to modify their lifestyles, to contribute time or money to ecological work, to support political initiatives that benefit the environment. But neither words nor feelings automatically produce action, especially if it involves a sacrifice of wealth or convenience. You can tell ecological stories, or listen sympathetically to them, or attend a workshop, and imagine you've done your bit for the environment, whereas in fact you've simply done something enjoyable and the environment has yet to reap the benefit.

Much environmental education is geared to children. The resourcing of such work, alongside the lack of will to address the ecological crisis at the level of political economy, suggests a recurring impulse to pass the buck to the next generation to undertake the necessary changes. MacLellan finds that, though adults are willing to challenge themselves intellectually, they often believe they themselves cannot change. They will attend workshops to acquire skills they can use, but often have a resistance to activities that exercise the soul.[221]

Gersie tackles this resistance to change using a therapeutic approach she calls 'storymaking', in which people work with stories to explore challenges that ecological crisis presents to their lives and thereby discover their own responsibility and capacity for change.[222] Mike Wilson raises the question of whether Gersie's emphasis on enabling individuals to cope with difficult circumstances risks leaving unjust social conditions unchallenged.[223] The 'resilience' she seeks to nurture is part of the lexicon of neoliberalism, which expects people to endure the reality of the world rather than change it.[224] However, in Gersiean groupwork the development of individuals coinheres with the development of the group; it's a microcosm of community. Informed by Paolo Freire's pedagogy aiming to empower 'the oppressed', this work bespeaks an 'enlightened self-interest' in which individual self-interest is discovered to be inseparable from concern for others.[225]

Marxist criticism insists on processes that demand change rather than affirm the status quo. That means stories that challenge people's assumptions and promote 'cognition'.[226] How, though, should the burden of change be distributed between individual and collectivity? Myshele Goldberg's model of 'social conscience' comprises three intersecting elements: consciousness, structure and agency. *Structure* means the social structures that constrain people's opportunities to flourish and take action. *Agency* bespeaks individuals' personal power and responsibility. *Consciousness* links the two: enables people to discern the structural problems that need addressing and also their individual capacities to act. Goldberg understands 'consciousness' in terms of people's 'knowledge and awareness of the gap between their ideal world and the real world',[227] but it can also be understood as meta-awareness, or alertness in the moment to one's own perception and cognition.[228] Applying these ideas to storytelling: story content can purvey understanding of social and environmental structures; the empowerment of individuals' voices can boost their agency; and conscious storytelling can promote consciousness (see Chapters 5 and 6).

The temptation abhorred by Marxists is to postpone the earth's restoration to an imagined future that lies beyond the reach of our actions. Islam and Christianity teach that paradise awaits us the other side of death.[229] In the religion of capitalism, advertising images of unpolluted beaches and perfect houses and gardens entice us to indenture our days to soul-deadening jobs.[230] The futurist dreamer pictures a utopia in a future as inaccessible as the mythic golden age of the past, perhaps on another planet.[231] Ursula Le Guin, however, calls for a 'utopian imagination' that recognizes the here and now as the Dreaming[232] – a challenge that brings together storytelling's enchantment of what's around us and the question of transmuting words into action, and puts the emphasis upon process in the present rather than pursuing a vision of the future.

The ecological crisis is unlikely to be effectively addressed until there's a democratic will to do so in the world's more powerful nations. Though a growing number of people in many countries have green sympathies, it may seem to require an unrealistic view of human nature to hope that in the foreseeable future a *majority* of people may be coaxed into prioritizing ecology above short-term economic self-interest.[233] The scale of the crisis is so overwhelming, driven by such huge, largely impersonal forces, that individual people can feel powerless to make a difference[234] and may respond to ecological warnings with nothing more constructive than fear, guilt or denial.[235]

A traditional way to handle crises was for people to come together and share relevant stories. In the stillness granted by storytelling and ritual, people may rise above the immediate situation, find clarity of vision and the inspiration and courage to begin, in the tangible context of community, the transformation of themselves and their society in response to the crisis.[236] But, in Britain at least, many elements of community have decayed in the wake of rapid technological change in conjunction with neoliberal doctrine that valorizes the self-serving individual and corporation above society. The recent turn towards right-wing populism has been spurred by ordinary people's exclusion from meaningful participation in decision-making that has affected their lives. Political leadership appears divorced from the wisdom of the ages, which is sidelined in the academy, or the wisdom of the land, which is largely forgotten. In contemporary 'fast capitalism', change happens so fast and behind such a smokescreen of image and slogan that it can bypass meaningful public debate about the directions in which change should occur.[237]

Paul Wapner suggests that, as environmental concerns become increasingly salient, they may provide the basis for a new kind of civil society.[238] Perhaps the Covid-19 pandemic will help that to happen. In response to a perceived need for new forms of civil society in which more people are included in conversations about public life, Chris Sunderland has promoted new forums for public conversation, in which he's encouraged the telling of stories about personal experiences and past events. He believes that it's the quality of relationships in public conversation that can optimize the way things work out.[239]

Through sharing stories a community formulates a collective memory of what's most worth remembering and negotiates its collective will, including decisions about managing its environment.[240] The indirectness of storytelling facilitates the sharing of competing views without making inflammatory accusations. In welcoming perspectives from different groups in order to negotiate cooperative responses to public issues like the environment, a storytelling-based forum can transcend the exclusive in-group commitment of traditional communities.[241] That can even extend to animals. WWF-Pakistan relate how an upland community shared stories in the course of determining the fate of a snow leopard they'd captured after it had killed someone's goat: in the end, contrary to custom, they consulted WWF via a family connection and arranged for the snow leopard's release.[242]

In traditional autocratic societies the function of the bard was to validate the monarch's regime by narrating the genealogies and victories that justified the monarch's rule.[243] In a democracy the people are supposed to rule themselves. We may envision a role for the expert storyteller as facilitator of people's contribution of their own stories to various forums of democratic deliberation. The storyteller could do so through:

- offering training and personal development enabling people to give voice to their stories;
- providing opportunities for people to explore the significance of selected stories for their lives;
- skilful service as master of ceremonies to ensure everyone gets their opportunity to speak;
- supplementing the people's stories with skilfully presented stories from the longer memory of history, myth and science.

Dream paths towards change

There may seem a vast gulf between scientific interpretation and sacred ritual, but some of the same storytellers work in both these contexts. The ecological crisis demands a creative reconciliation of things that have become disconnected and positioned in opposition to each other: between humankind and nature; between the inner world of myth, spirituality and imagination and the outer world of science, politics and embodiment.[244] The potential of ecological storytelling to bridge the divide between science and the imagination is reflected in the careers of its practitioners. Some, such as Green and MacLellan, were originally educated in the sciences and later became performers. Others, such as Salisbury and the Eden Project team, began as performing artists and boned up on natural history as they moved into ecological work.

Ecologically engaged storytellers and interpreters are recovering some of the skills and outlook of indigenous tradition bearers who mediated a sustainable relationship between their societies and nature; they're thereby helping to cultivate such a relationship in the modern context. In focusing attention on the actuality of the here and now, storytelling helps instil a sensual connection with the environment and provides a channel by which nature can speak to modern society. It builds bridges between people's imagination and the perspectives of other times, other cultures and other beings. It nurtures a perception of landscape as enchanted, even sacred, and of other creatures as conscious and worthy of our compassion. Its dependence on trust and respect for the other subverts the neoliberal-materialist paradigm of quantification, control and the primacy of self-interest. Its relational dynamics demand of listeners an active response. In dissolving the distinction between performer and audience, it can help to build community and facilitate both psycho-spiritual transformation and cooperative decision-making.

The myths of traditional cultures, in mediating the relationship between society and nature, tend to promote the conservation of a status quo and to look to the past.[245] If contemporary storytelling were to be too focused on nostalgic appreciation of tradition, it could well remain marginalized as a folksy entertainment and have little capacity to provoke change.[246] For countries as heavily populated as Britain, there's no practical possibility of reverting to a hunting-gathering or subsistence-cultivating economy. Nor should we want to return to the hardships and fears that such ways of life entailed or to surrender the genuine benefits of scientific knowledge. The modern world, meanwhile, has no stable status quo. The most entrenched contemporary 'pieties' must be jettisoned, says Philip Goodchild, if we're to find our way to a sustainable and tolerable future.[247]

When seeking inspiration for an important decision, the elders of the Dunne-za hunter-gatherers of Canada explore a vast matrix of oral knowledge about their people's territory and history by means of 'dream paths' by which they navigate in dreams through space and time.[248] The challenge of finding the way forward – to a world in which human beings may enjoy the possibility of happiness in coexistence with the rest of nature – requires us to extend our imagination both backwards and forwards through time's patterns of causality: to listen to the stories not only of tradition but also of history, nature and personal experience; and to make new stories that, looking to the future, speak to contemporary society about how to inhabit the earth's ecosystems without destroying them.

Storytelling will not single-handedly save the world from ecocatastrophe or bring into being an ecotopia. Government, science, business, religion and public campaigns and movements will be the major players in determining the earth's ecological fate. But a world in which people live in harmonious relationship with each other and with nature – recognizing themselves as part of the ecosystem – will, I think, be one in which storytelling has a place. Future ecotopias envisioned by Le Guin and Ernest Callenbach – in *Always Coming Home* and 'Chocco' – depict storytellers playing an important civic role, not least in remembering the errors of the past. In both these fictions the ecotopian society has arisen following the catastrophic collapse of our present civilization.[249] Can we find a dream path that will guide us another way there?

2

Storytelling as a means of conversation about ecology and sustainability

When a story is told, there's an interplay between three components:

- the story – a particular sequence of events;
- the storyteller's communicative tools of words, voice, movement and body language;
- the dynamics between teller, listeners and physical environment.

In Charles Sanders Peirce's semiotics, the story corresponds to the *object*, the storyteller's activity to the *representamen*, and the listener's response to the *interpretant*. In Peirce's theory the interpretant produces meaning and can itself become a new representamen; hence the possibility of an unfolding chain of meaning-making, or dialogue.[1] Because, in storytelling, the listeners are physically present, every twitch, murmur, yawn or blink may function as a representamen, prompting an interpretant response in the teller and hence some nuance of metamorphosis of the story. Moreover, the presence of multiple listeners produces, not simply a binary dynamic, but a network of responsiveness through listeners' sublingual awareness of each other's reactions. It's to be receptive to such cues that storytellers keep on the house lights in theatres. The immediate physical environment is likely to condition this dialogic process. Animals, certainly, can contribute their own interpretants to the unfolding story.[2] I know a dog so accustomed to attending monthly storytelling sessions that she'll identify the moment when a story has ended and lead the applause with barking.

Thus storytelling can be construed as a kind of conversation. Although one person is doing most of the talking at any given time, a dialogue of non-verbal communication continues throughout and the situation may provide listeners the opportunity to speak, or to tell stories themselves, while the storyteller may in turn become a listener.³ Such fluidity of who's speaking and who's listening, expressive of a sense of community, is evident in indigenous storytelling sessions.⁴ The meaning of a tale, says Peter Brooks, is 'interlocutionary' – emergent from spaces within the story and its telling, 'born of the relationship between tellers and listeners'.⁵ Good storytelling provides *space* for listeners to be part of the conversation, to exercise agency in responding to the story.

By examining a number of oral stories, we shall in this chapter consider a range of ways in which such space may be provided, and qualities of *intention* that storytellers may bring to doing this. Most of the stories discussed here are examples of my own experimentation, as a reflective practitioner, with different story genres that can facilitate different kinds of response. Since we'll be exploring both the stories themselves and the dynamics of telling them, I shall sometimes allude to particular experiences of telling a story and of listeners responding; these experiences thereby become narratives themselves, equally subject to interpretation. The examples include both stories that point up ecological problems and stories suggesting positive ways forward.

The fairies' revenge: 'The Green Ladies of One-Tree Hill'

The Green Ladies of this English folktale are three beech trees that stood atop a hill where it was said that on moonlit nights you might hear strange eerie music and see three tall green women dancing. After the death of the farmer who owned the land including this hill, the farm was divided among his three sons. The youngest brother received only the smallest portion, but he faithfully followed his father's advice to honour the trees with posies of flowers every Midsummer Eve, and his plot, though small, produced a good yield. The eldest and middle brothers ignored their father's advice and their portions of land did not prosper.

Jealous of the youngest brother, the eldest decided to fell the trees, 'to make a fence around the hill to keep out trespassers like you'. He was killed by the first felled tree as it crashed to the ground. The middle brother, inheriting the eldest's land, was determined to fell the remaining trees. But when he cut down the second tree he was killed by a branch falling from the third. The brothers' hired men, too fearful of the hill to participate in the felling, said the ladies of the trees had taken their revenge. After that, few people ever went up that hill. They said it was cursed. Thus the youngest brother came into possession of the whole of his father's land, which flourished under his care. That hill is still there, they say, and upon it a beech tree still stands. That's why the hill is known today as One-Tree Hill. On moonlit nights, they say, the music can still be heard, very faint, and a single Green Lady can be glimpsed dancing all alone.[6]

If storytelling is dialogic, the telling of a traditional tale like this one can be a springboard for listeners to explore the applicability of the story's patterns to the world around them and to their own lives. What exactly are those patterns? Arran Stibbe's method of ecolinguistic analysis identifies within a text the 'stories' the text mediates. By 'stories' he means not stories in the narrative sense I use that word, but rather 'mental models', which I shall refer to as 'beliefs'. These matter because they 'shape how we perceive reality' and therefore condition our behaviour – in ways that may or may not be ecologically beneficial.[7]

What beliefs does 'The Green Ladies of One Tree Hill' convey? Taking the story literally, we might infer:

- Trees (or some of them) are conscious, feminine beings.
- Farms will only prosper if you give offerings to certain special trees.
- You will die if you cut down these special trees.
- Everything will be fine if you faithfully follow your father's teaching.

Traditional cultures worldwide have held beliefs of this kind. The fourth one sounds like a general principle of conservatism. The preceding three are likely to be dismissed by the norms of contemporary thought as beyond credibility. But from a comparative mythological perspective the tale is one example of a recurring trope in world myth and folklore: the 'fairies' revenge'. If you disrespect the gods, the fairies, the spirits of nature, if you take too much, then you'll suffer for it and they may kill you. In Greece there was Erysichthon, King of Thessaly, who in felling the oak sacred to Demeter, goddess of the fertile earth, was cursed by the tree's dryad and punished with an unquenchable hunger that caused him to consume everything in his kingdom, including in the end himself.[8] In the Forest of Dean, in England, a knight was granted on a fairy hill a marvellous drink from a jewelled horn; when he then tried to steal the horn, he forfeited his life.[9] Pueblo mythology tells of the Corn Maidens who brought the people the gift of maize but then departed when the people started wasting the harvest; starvation followed, and then desperate efforts to seek the Corn Maidens and beg them to come back.[10]

We may, then, seek another level of meaning via metaphor. If the Green Ladies are a metaphor of ecological forces and the offerings of flowers a metaphor of respect for nature, we may infer from their tale:

- People and agriculture are interconnected with wild organisms within an ecosystem.
- Agriculture will flourish if we treat the ecosystem with care and respect.
- Disrespectful treatment of the ecosystem will have tragic, unforeseen consequences.

So the fairies' revenge is a metaphor of the rebounding consequences of human abuse of nature: cancers caused by chemical pollution of the environment;[11] pandemics caused by increasingly invasive penetration and exploitation of wild ecosystems;[12] or a tormented bull leaping from a Spanish bullring to attack spectators on the terraces. I encourage such an interpretation of 'The Green Ladies' by mentioning explicit ecological details – the hill has never been ploughed; the middle brother's aggressive use of fertilizer and pesticide and intention of ploughing over the hill – and by emphasizing the idea of *caring for the land* in the father's advice and the youngest brother's practice.

The decoding of metaphor takes us so far, but there's a deeper – mythopoeic – level of interpretation, in which metaphors open into a network of multivalent symbols. 'Symbols do not establish facts; they release experiences,' observes Jürgen Moltmann; 'they "give us something to think about", and invite us to new discoveries'.[13] C. S. Lewis contends that stories vary in the extent to which they possess 'mythic' depth susceptible to such interpretation.[14] Here 'myth' is a quality that exists below the level of language, even below the level of narrative structure, though it finds expression in both of these. Laurence Coupe describes myth as 'that narrative mode of understanding which involves a continuing dialectic of same and other, of memory and desire, of ideology and utopia, of hierarchy and horizon, and of sacred and profane'.[15] Lewis adds that perception of this quality may vary from person to person.[16] This brings us back to the listener's participation in producing the story's meaning – through discerning and interpreting these networks of symbols.

The meanings I discover in 'The Green Ladies' develop from the interpretations listed above:

- If we take too much from nature, and treat nature with disrespect, we shall suffer the consequences, but if we treat nature respectfully, then we'll receive the things we need.

The 'if-then' logic of this pair of complementary beliefs implies an expectation that may be true for humankind as a whole but may not necessarily hold true for every individual experience. Here perhaps our interpretation has to let go of the paradigm of *belief* in favour of *imperative*: Don't take too much from nature! Treat nature with respect! Such imperatives are open-ended; they take us into a realm of ethics where what matters are our intentions and we surrender the consequences to trust.

- The wisdom of our forbears can help us treat nature with respect.

Uncritical compliance with conservative norms can certainly sustain the injustices of the status quo – patriarchy; class privilege; violence towards animals, children and outgroups – and traditional stories that perpetuate such norms need to be challenged. But tradition also contains valuable knowledge and wisdom, born of experience, that are worth carrying forward. Thus traditional stories can contribute to a model of culture as 'evolving tradition' in contrast to the paradigm of always favouring innovation. Hence a rationale for, selectively, reincorporating insights from folk traditions into contemporary culture that has forgotten such lessons or never yet learnt them.

- Organisms such as trees possess a quality of being that entitles them to flourish irrespective of their utility to humankind.

This is a precept of deep ecology. I've phrased it to encompass a range of possibilities, from the more narrowly aesthetic or ecological, to theological notions of trees as precious parts of creation, to more animistic ideas that trees have some kind of consciousness. In mystical traditions the tree is a recurring symbol of the awakening of consciousness from roots in matter to branches in heaven.[17] Recent biology demonstrates that trees communicate and learn from each other through fungal networks connecting their roots.[18] Mythopoeic storytelling allows such varied ideas to coexist without the need to pin down a single interpretation. When I tell this tale, all the possibilities I've listed coexist in my mind, alongside imagery blending my memories of the shapes, texture and movement of beech trees with those of dancing women. Simultaneously, each listener will form their own permutation of interpretations, according to their own way of seeing the world. This multivalency of mythic symbolism is one way the listener gains space to form their own response to the story.

This folktale is conservative inasmuch as it locates wisdom in the ways of the past, yet its plot challenges the hierarchy of power relations on the farm. Its mythopoetics enlarges the listener's agency in interpretation. Myth need not 'be explained away as reactionary', writes Coupe, describing Ernst Bloch's Marxist criticism of fairy tales, but should rather 'be celebrated for its utopian potential', its power to suggest that things could be different.[19]

A biodiverse story ecosystem

In oral cultures the transmission of stories depends on memory. Many stories may be told, but only those which are truly memorable get passed down the generations. This causes folktales to have well-defined structure that's easy to remember and readily satisfies an audience, and which folklorists have characterized via various analyses and rules, such as the 'rule of three' that occurs in 'The Green Ladies'.[20] This structural effectiveness makes folktales appealing to storytellers. They're the easiest stories to tell, because much of the work of shaping them has already been done by generations of folk transmission. However, just as different guilds of organisms – carnivores, herbivores, parasites, saprophytes – serve different functions in the ecosystem, so different genres of stories, including non-traditional ones, provide scope for different possibilities of response.

One form of resistance to story diversity comes from attempts to straitjacket stories into standardized templates. Folkloristic analyses sometimes adopt the scientific paradigm of seeking mastery of understanding through reducing the phenomena of study to their simplest components; the mastery of understanding can then potentially translate into authoritative power of application.

Lord Raglan constructed a twenty-two-point template of the idealized 'hero's' biography and then scored the heroes of myth and legend to evaluate how well they fit the template. He used this analysis, interpreted in terms of ritual drama, to debunk claims that the stories of oral cultures could convey factual knowledge of the past.[21] Joseph Campbell's 'monomyth' is a more sophisticated version of Raglan's template: the young (usually male) hero is called upon a quest, navigates a 'road of trials' and wins 'the ultimate boon' that brings transformation.[22] The Jungian underpinning of this 'hero's journey' lends it to psychotherapeutic application.[23] Its use in the movie *Star Wars* also catalysed its exploitation in commercially successful screenwriting and novel-writing.[24]

There's a comparable relationship between reductionism and commercial success in Christopher Booker's 'seven basic plots', all but two of which – comedy and tragedy – comply with Campbell's model of the proactive hero with a mission.[25] The novels and films with which Booker illustrates his scheme were all very commercially successful; his examples of traditional tales are well-known fairy tales from Charles Perrault, Hans Christian Anderson and the Brothers Grimm. With circular reasoning he dismisses as 'unsuccessful' those stories which don't neatly fit his system.

Kendall Haven makes a case, evidenced with neurological and psychological research, for the efficacy of stories to promote learning, logical thinking, meaning-making, motivation, language skills, memory and a sense of belonging. His findings may hearten those of us wanting to use storytelling to promote ecological thinking and living. However, he makes clear that the only stories worthy of calling 'stories' are the kind that will have the desired impact – circular reasoning again – and defines these stories thus:

> *Story: n.: A detailed, character-based narration of a character's struggles to overcome obstacles and reach an important goal.*[26]

This pattern is closely akin to Campbell's monomyth and also to 'classical design' in screenwriting, or 'archplot' as Robert McKee also calls it, in which 'an active protagonist struggles against primarily external forces of antagonism to pursue his or her desire ... to a closed ending of absolute, irreversible change';[27] a structure that cinema adheres to in order to satisfy the expectations the audience are conditioned to expect and thereby to deliver the required return on investment.

How well does this normative concept of a 'good story' fit the 'The Green Ladies'? The youngest brother is presumably the hero, and his actions do lead to him receiving the fortune and well-being he evidently deserves. But he's not really proactive. He shows little sign of desire or struggle. He undergoes no climactic transformation. He simply works hard and follows his father's advice. In fact it's the elder brothers, the 'antagonists', who drive the story, generating the karma that produces their own downfall. The story doesn't really fit the models of Campbell, McKee and Haven. It centres less on a desiring protagonist than on the Green Ladies' otherness and their mysterious power to bless and to punish while yet being tragically vulnerable. The values in play are different and these entail a different kind of plot.

I'm not denying the existence of such widespread narrative patterns, or their anthropological or psychological interest. However, insistence on replicating them to serve an instrumentalist purpose, commercial or otherwise, reduces the diversity of stories that will be experienced, paralleling the way that single-minded exploitation of useful natural resources reduces the ecological diversity of organisms and habitats. When stories are reduced to entertainment, information or persuasion, says Lopez, they lose the cultic power – 'the elevating and healing event, the exchange of emotions ... [t]he life-sustaining magic, the reincorporation of ourselves into the river of life' – that's needed to help us endure times of crisis.[28] In valorizing the striving individual, the story models discussed above comply with the doctrine of neoliberal political economy, whose hallowing of the egoic instincts of self-interest has erected so great a barrier to ecological sustainability.

Another story is needed. Lots of them. We need an 'ecosystem' of stories, vast and diverse as the planetary ecosystem. In ecology, diversity signifies ecosystemic health; it's also what *produces* ecosystemic health. If you elevate one story above all others – whether it be the neoliberal story of the individual struggling to achieve a goal, or the Christian story of Fall, redemption and resurrection, or the Marxist story of revolution that will overthrow capitalism – then you invite conflict with those who follow other stories. If Haven is right that story is fundamental to the working of our minds,[29] then to impose *one* story, your story, upon other people, is to do violence to who they are.

In his Moroccan memoir *In Arabian Nights*, Tahir Shah is prompted to seek out his own story, meaning not the story of his life, but a traditional story that speaks to the needs of his soul; he navigates the great universe of tales of the Muslim world, in which the several hundred tales of *The Thousand and One Nights* are but one stratum. *The Kathā Sarit Sāgara*, a comparably vast collection, is but one part of the legendarium of India. The index of folktale 'types' developed by Antti Aarne and Stith Thompson, and expanded by Hans-Jörg Uther, contains thousands of different tale types recorded in Europe and West Asia.[30] Each of these is a generalized plot embracing many individual stories from different countries. Thousands more tale types come into play if the field is extended to other regions – or beyond 'folktales' in the narrow sense of *folk fiction*, to include *folk legends*,[31] a genre that has yet to be fully classified.[32] Then there are all the stories of everything that's happened, all the remembered experiences of everyone who's lived, all the stories of other creatures' experiences that we've found out about, all the stories that have been written and could yet be told aloud, and all the things that *might* have happened, all the things that *may* happen in the future, and all the things that could never happen but which someone can imagine.

Let us not constrain possibility with seven plots or one monomyth. Stories are as countless as the earth's creatures. One thing we can be sure about is that the world will keep changing. Just as we cannot know what vital importance each obscure species of plant or animal may play in human existence, we cannot know which stories a particular individual or community may sometime need to hear, to take into their heart, to inspire their actions.

Personal stories: 'The Gloucestershire Flood'

The summer of 2007 was exceptionally wet, especially in my home county of Gloucestershire. The wettest day was Friday 20 July. When my wife, Kirsty, got away from work in Swindon that day, the rain had stopped the trains running. She managed to get a bus, but it broke down just outside Swindon and they had to wait for a replacement. The driver boldly forded the flooded roads, so deep that water was soon swilling back and forth *inside* the bus. She refused to continue beyond Cirencester, half the way home to Stroud. So I had to rescue Kirsty from there by car. It was high ground most of the way and we soon made it safely back.

But just downhill from our house the stream burst its banks and the pharmacy and minimarket were completely filled with water. The main road to Gloucester was washed away. Tewkesbury became an island. In parts of Stroud there was no mains water. We filled buckets, bowls and bath with water. Bottled water was being rationed in the supermarket. The floodwater even threatened an electricity substation. The army were there, defending it with sandbags. You could see it on TV – the water lapping centimetres away from spilling over to knock out the power supply of the whole area. For a few days, it seemed, civilization as we knew it in Gloucestershire teetered on the brink.

But the rain stopped, the floods receded and the repair work began. Some friends' insurance firm demanded they move their electric sockets higher on the wall in case there was another flood. Was there going to be another flood? How likely was that? And why had the flooding been so bad anyway? Freak weather? Climate change? Or had it anything to do with the fact the flood plains had been built on, the wetlands destroyed, the hill slopes ploughed for arable crops, and so much land had been covered with concrete and tarmac that when it rained heavily the water had nowhere to go except into the roads? Looking to buy a house that summer, I noticed that many front gardens were paved over for extra cars. At the property we bought I pulled up the flagstones from the garden so the rain could sink into the soil and the weeds and wild flowers could spring forth.[33]

More powerful personal stories might be related by people who've experienced bushfires in Australia, desertification in East Africa, sea-level rise on Pacific atolls or hurricanes in Louisiana. Someone relating a personal experience has tremendous authority within the sphere of what they've directly experienced in their own body in a physical place. It's a different kind of authority from the abstract authority of scientific data and models. It depends in part on how trustworthy the speaker is perceived to be. In some times and places the spoken testimony of respected individuals has carried more authority than written records even when the latter were available.[34]

'The Gloucestershire Flood' contains some direct testimony of my own and also draws on my wife's narration of her experiences, which I trust as reliably true. Yet, however, significant such experiences were to us, their horizon was limited to what our senses could perceive; they might be dismissed as mere anecdote from having wider significance. Moreover, the accuracy or honesty of memory may be doubted. In my story, therefore, I supplement our personal experiences with allusions to the bigger picture gleaned from press, television and other people. I also use tentative language, including rhetorical questions, to speculate about connections to climate change and land development; thereby I frame myself as not an expert. This is both to remain honest, since I don't have a thorough scientific understanding of the event, and also to invite listeners' responsiveness. Rather than make a firm claim that they would then be positioned to either accept or reject, I give them space, through my own uncertainty, to consider what they think about the matter.

When I tell this story anywhere near Gloucestershire, it provokes a shower of stories from listeners' memories of the same event. The result is a mosaic of perspectives more persuasive and complex than the account of a single individual. In fact Friday 20 July 2007 has become legendary in British storytelling, since a big storytelling festival was supposed to begin that day, so droves of storytellers can tell of their adventures trying to get there. Such collectivity of anecdotal experience adds up to an authoritative claim that these floods were a truly significant event, however the metrics of science might evaluate them.

Allowing everyone's voice to be heard

Storytelling is itself an embodied social experience in a physical place. When someone tells of a lived experience, they enact it within a new lived experience for everyone present, which may in turn be re-enacted in subsequent retelling.[35] By analogy with Roland Barthes' 'déjà-lu' – prior experience of other writings that intertextually inform one's experience of the text in hand[36] – there's a 'déjà-entendu', of narratives previously heard and memories that are themselves latent narratives, that interweaves with our telling or hearing a story.

This cascading of influence, through story and memory, has consequence for what communities of people believe and feel about the world. Thus Wilson emphasizes the political importance of the interchangeability of storytelling and listening, as opposed to the privileging of the expert storyteller's voice.[37] Here the practicalities of context come into play. When I told 'The Gloucestershire Flood' as part of a strictly timed set on stage at a festival, listeners could only share their own stories in private conversation afterwards. In other settings, I can engineer space for a public exchange in which others can speak.

Sometimes the exchange arises spontaneously. In African traditions a discussion is the conventional sequel to a story;[38] I once I told an English folktale after dinner at a scientific field station in the Gabonese rainforest and, as soon as I finished, my audience of Gabonese biologists launched into a spirited discussion of the story's message and alternative ways the protagonist could have acted. In Britain a presentation of local ghost legends usually precipitates, like 'The Gloucestershire Flood', the sharing of personal experiences. In response to prompts after a story, pre-adolescent children will readily offer comments, ask questions, suggest improvements or share their own stories. Some may also wish to speak *during* the story, requiring the storyteller to discriminate between useful collaboration and compulsive attention-seeking. Zipes emphasizes the importance of empowering children by giving them opportunity to voice their thoughts and feelings in response to a story.[39]

To elicit public conversation among adult listeners in Britain generally requires some management of expectations.[40] People who've come to what's been advertised as a performance won't normally be expecting to speak themselves. With the event organizer's agreement, and if time allows, you can create space for discussion after a story or set of stories. It's good to signal this before you start, so the listeners will be anticipating it, and to give them freedom to opt out. It's also helpful to pre-empt the convention at public talks of merely asking questions of the speaker, and explicitly invite the sharing of thoughts or memories prompted by the stories. The physical configuration of space is important: storytelling can segue into discussion more easily if everyone's sitting in a circle than if you're standing on a stage before rows of seats. Out of the silence with which a discussion time sometimes begins, the inhibition of being the first to speak, can emerge the things most pressing to be shared. The storyteller, now facilitator, needs to bring a clear intention to hold the silence, patiently waiting, so that it's a space of invitation rather than awkward and embarrassing. Sometimes an encouraging word will help someone cross the threshold to speaking.

Other kinds of storytelling events can be advertised as involving discussion. For example, I had a church group that wanted a story session about climate change and were happy to break into small groups to discuss the stories. In more informal situations – participants on a story walk, a small class of students, some elders in a care home – it can be natural to alternate between listening to stories and opening to discussion. This structure gives listeners more space to process what they find in the stories and is less mentally tiring than a continuous sequence of stories. Sessions of these kinds are an intermediate step towards the more structured conversations and activities of a 'workshop'.

Another model of session, typified by storytelling clubs, offers anyone present the opportunity to contribute a story.[41] Regular attenders at clubs commonly prepare a story they want to tell. Impromptu contributions from people who are not experienced storytellers are often personal stories. Such stories already exist in your memory; all you have to do is find the courage and words to share them. In this kind of session, storytellers aren't beholden to a commercial imperative to entertain, so there's freedom to tell stories that engage with issues you care about.

The packaging of beliefs and values within stories facilitates more friendly public exchange than when polarizing views are explicitly articulated. Thus the sharing of stories can be usefully applied in sensitive contexts such as peacebuilding. Oelrich observes that the very *process* of storytelling conduces a warmth of fellow feeling. The telling of a story enters both the conceptual and physical space between people, offers new possibilities of connection between them. At a conference promoting dialogue and conciliation among different political factions of Iraq, Oelrich was able to soften the delegates' wariness of each other, first by telling them folktales from their own country, then by inviting three delegates each morning to share a personal story and indicate on a wall map of Iraq where the experience had happened. The process brought a quality of listening quite different from that to be expected in the charged negotiation of concerns and needs. This included a tacit understanding that the personal stories on the map were *not* to be discussed; they produced a respectful connectedness that served its purpose through silence.[42]

The opportunity to voice in public something you've experienced may have not only political or ecological significance, but also psychological importance to the speaker: 'when we feel seen and heard', says Oelrich, it can 'bring out hidden talents and richness of being'.[43] The memory of having told, Gersie emphasizes, will have consequences in future situations in the teller's life.[44] People courageous in other areas of life can sometimes have great fear of public speaking. There's a vulnerability in standing before an audience and letting your voice be heard, especially when, as in most storytelling, there's no script to hide behind. The first time I told a story in a public venue – a folk club in a pub – I was shaking with nerves when I began; but halfway through the story I realized, 'I can do this! I know the story! Words are coming out of my mouth! Everyone is listening!' I stopped shaking and began to enjoy the energy sparkling through me. It was an empowering epiphany. It changed me.

I've witnessed many other people tell a story in public for the first time and undergo something similar. Nearly anyone can hold an audience's attention with a five-minute story, whether an anecdote, a joke or a familiar tale. Storytelling is well suited to being a democratic community art, as Wilson advocates, in which everyone can actively participate and there's a fluidity in the attribution of expertise and authority, productive of citizen engagement.[45] However, 'active participation' includes not only having your voice heard, but also learning to listen. Active listening requires and contributes more than being a 'consumer' of narrative, and good storytellers help to cultivate it. Moreover, to tell a thirty-minute story is far more demanding than a five-minute anecdote; it requires skill, experience and preparation. This is one reason why a flourishing storytelling culture will not only provide spaces for everyone's voice to be heard but also value the specialist expertise of those who've cultivated their skills and knowledge as storytellers.

In a contemporary culture that so emphasizes self-expression, in which social media enable you to express yourself irrespective of whether anyone is listening, storytelling confronts you with the necessity to actually communicate. Whereas 'media' involve transmission from a *sender* (e.g. a television presenter) to a *receiver* (the viewer), storytelling is a form of interpersonal communication in which any sender (speaker) must simultaneously be a receiver.[46] Storytelling involves mutual respect between tellers and listeners: the listeners give the teller their attention; the teller shares something worth hearing and is sensitive to the listeners' needs.[47]

However, there's a delicate relationship between the definition of the social situation in which storytelling takes place and the question, delineated by Doug Lipman, of who is the intended 'beneficiary' – the teller or the listeners.[48] In therapeutic contexts a therapist may sometimes share a story they think will help the client, but the cathartic needs of clients or groupwork participants will also be served through *their* telling stories.[49] Storytelling clubs are an intermediate situation; and some community storytelling events, focused on sharing personal stories, give more tacit permission to tellers to be the beneficiary. When a storyteller gives a professional performance, on the other hand, the beneficiary should clearly be the audience. The gold standard, for me, is to bring an intention that the story you're about to share shall be a precious gift to your listeners.[50]

Communicating science: 'Bat Milk'

When it comes to understanding ecology, and knowing what is true, personal stories lack the reliability demanded by scientific conceptions of truth. Memory can be fallible. This limitation leads us to genres of true-life stories that are based on recorded scientific and historical data. Here's a story I heard from knowledge ecologist Ron Donaldson, dating from his days with the government conservation agency English Nature.

A man called James came to work for English Nature to investigate a decline in the internationally important population of greater horseshoe bats (*Rhinolophus ferrumequinum*) in southwest England. It was straightforward to protect the bats' roosts, but what about the areas where they fed at night, navigating along hedgerows and lines of trees? Talking to the farmers, James found out that much of the farming was non-organic; the antibiotics given the cattle caused their dung to be essentially sterile. However, the Weston family had farmed organically for many years. When no antibiotic is used, the dung is rich in bacteria and attracts insects such as dung beetles – so the cowpats are like pizzas covered with all the bats' favourite toppings. James therefore encouraged other farmers to use organic practices and to plant more hedges and trees to provide navigational routes for the bats; he helped them apply for government grants to do so. At the meeting in which he presented the project's results to the farmers, they cheerfully boasted about the numbers of bats crossing their land and were pleased the decline in bat numbers had halted. The Weston family branded their milk cartons with an image of a bat and the words, 'Our land and cows are farmed organically – This provides abundant dung beetles for an internationally important population of greater horseshoe bats which feeds around our farm.' The government subsequently implemented a policy of grants from the Countryside Stewardship Scheme to support bat-friendly farming, and an increase in bat populations was recorded.[51]

This is a story of a scientific experiment; you may discern the structure of methods, results and conclusion. Presenting the experiment in the form of a story is more affectively engaging than scientific exposition.[52] The findings are more likely to be remembered and more likely to inspire and motivate.[53] In situations where more rigorous evidencing is required, it's possible to interlace narrative and exposition and to supplement the story with visual presentation of data on a screen. 'Bat Milk' is suited to a casual anecdotal style and can easily be embedded within other modes of speaking and conversation. You could tell it during a meeting without the likely crunch of incongruity if you suddenly started telling a fairy tale.

One could map the scientific report's 'methods, results, conclusion' on to Aristotle's famous definition of a story as comprising 'beginning, middle and end'.[54] The openness of Aristotle's definition doesn't constrain possibilities like the classic screenwriting model of 'setup, confrontation, resolution', which implies that a story must involve conflict and must resolve,[55] or Campbell's 'separation, initiation, return', which presumes there must be a departure and return.[56] Aristotle's description may seem pretty obvious, but it does capture the essence of a story. If a story is to progress through a middle to an end, there needs to be at least one 'turning point' in which something happens that *turns* the course of events in a new direction. A story can be turned, teaches McKee, by either action or revelation.[57]

From this structural perspective, a key turning point in 'Bat Milk' is when the farmers are 'encouraged' to cooperate. In the story as I received it, this moment isn't dramatized. The elision of the farmers' decisions, crucial to the story's outcome, is a gap, a lacuna of knowledge, which invites questions about the farmers' motivations. Access to government funding was evidently important, but the story also presents the farmers as proud of the conservation benefits of their actions and emphasizes James's willingness to converse with and learn from them. The Westons, meanwhile, capitalized on organic practices they were already doing. How willing might the other farmers have been to go organic if no government money had been forthcoming?

There have been political changes since the time of these events; English Nature no longer exists, nor does the Countryside Stewardship Scheme. The question of how the greater horseshoe bat is faring today requires knowledge beyond the scope of this story as it stands. The scope of true-life stories of the environment also includes 'ecopolitical' stories in which the emphasis is less on the science than on the dynamics of conflict and negotiation between competing ethical positions and the people and organizations representing them.

Talking about politics: 'The Byker Incinerator'

In 1979 a waste incinerator began operation in Byker, an inner-city district of Newcastle upon Tyne. Local people were unhappy that the heating it provided was more expensive than promised, and about the pollution it caused. When, in the late 1990s, the Council planned to replace the incinerator with a new one, residents formed a Campaign Against Incinerating Refuse and demanded a public meeting. The people attending feared that the new incinerator would be worse than the old one. The upshot was a community working group, BAN (Byker and Newcastle) Waste, to explore with the Council the options for waste disposal. The meetings were like battles. Residents were angry that poorer areas took the brunt of polluting industries and that ordinary people had to give unpaid time out of busy lives to dialogue with paid Council representatives who actively resisted their concerns. So BAN Waste set up a Select Committee to investigate alternative ways of dealing with waste. The costs of bringing expert witnesses to its hearings posed difficulty until a charity, Atlantic Philanthropies, came to the rescue. BAN Waste also persuaded the Council to do a *health* as well as environment impact assessment. It transpired the Council had used ash from the old incinerator on footpaths, including in allotments, and this ash was contaminated with toxic dioxins. BAN Waste worked hard to educate the public and keep up the pressure. The Select Committee's conclusions were to oppose the new incinerator in favour of recovering resources from the waste. Finally the Council yielded: the old incinerator closed and the heating it had provided was replaced by natural gas. Members of BAN Waste subsequently helped the Council develop a strategy of resource recovery.

Besides making a point about the ways disadvantaged communities are disproportionately affected by environmental problems, this story offers encouragement to other campaigners in that it ends in success. It's an unusual story in having no individual protagonists, as would be essential in film or prose fiction. In telling it I respect the absence of named individuals in the published sources.[58] By sticking to what's on public record, I wish to signal the story's 'facticity'.[59] In my tone of voice, the deployment of facts and figures, and the sparseness of imaginative detail, I invite trust that I'm representing in good faith the known facts of something that really happened. The absence of characters puts an onus on me to give life to the story by means of my own personality as I narrate it. What motivates me to tell this story is the pathos of the uneven balance of resourcing between ordinary people, giving their time for a cause, and council officials, representing business as usual, who were being paid to resist them. It conveys something of the cost of changing the way things are done.

For listeners outside the Newcastle context, the story may elicit thoughts about *comparable* situations. In my home district in Gloucestershire a similar campaign has failed to prevent the building of a huge waste incinerator, this time in the countryside, surrounded by farmland. Whereas BAN Waste were active during a Labour government, the Gloucestershire campaign had to contend with Conservative legislation that enabled the contractors to appeal to the Secretary of State for Communities and Local Government, who overruled the local authorities' refusal of planning permission.[60]

'The Byker Incinerator' brings concerns of ecology and social justice within the same frame. Conflict is sometimes construed between ecological concerns, especially the biocentric values of deep ecology, and the needs of disadvantaged groups of people, as if a choice must be made between one or the other.[61] Real-world situations do present ecological conflicts that require choices to be made, but if people are part of nature the way forward has to be a synthesis of social *and* deep ecology.[62] Human history is inseparable from ecological history.

Ecological history: 'The Tasmanian Genocide'

When sea level rose at the end of the last ice age, 12,000 years ago, Tasmania became separated from Australia by 200 miles of open sea. The native people were isolated from the rest of humankind until European sailors arrived in the seventeenth century. The 5000 hunter-gatherers the island could support survived through cooperation between tribes so everyone could access vital resources. Early encounters with Europeans were friendly; French naturalist François Péron reported a warm welcome in 1802 from a young woman, Ouray-Ouray, and her community. However, British sealers, based on offshore islands, began to kidnap Tasmanian Aboriginal women. The British also established a brutal penal colony. When convicts were released to settle the land, they ran into conflict with the Aborigines who lived there. When the Aborigines resisted, the British Governor, George Arthur, declared martial law. The Aborigines were shot on sight. Their numbers decreased rapidly, many lives being lost also to European diseases. It's on record that British policy was to facilitate the Aborigines' extinction.

A missionary, George Robinson, won the trust of a young Aboriginal woman, Truganini, possibly Ouray-Ouray's daughter. She persuaded 135 surviving

Aborigines to entrust themselves to Robinson, who settled them on Flinders Island in the Bass Strait. Most soon died because the living conditions were so poor. Truganini returned to the mainland and joined a band of outlaws who robbed and sometimes killed British settlers. When the band were captured, Robinson gave false testimony that the women among them were blameless pawns, and so only the men were hanged. By 1869 Truganini was one of only three surviving full-blooded Tasmanian Aborigines. When the last man, William Lanner, died, physicians competed to secure pieces of his body, believing his race to be a 'missing link' in evolution. Truganini begged to be buried at sea; but after she died in 1876 her skeleton ended up on display at the Tasmanian Museum. With her death the Tasmanian Aborigines were believed to be extinct. However, people with native ancestry lived on, assimilated into settler society. In the 1950s some began to claim their heritage and today thousands of people identify as Tasmanian Aborigines. Only in 1976 were Truganini's bones cremated and the ashes scattered at sea as she'd requested.[63]

As with 'The Byker Incinerator', I convey the facticity of this story by means of dates, names and statistics and a sparseness of imaginative detail. But the story's content is far more harrowing. To hear such a narrative told to you face to face is more shocking than to learn about the events from reading or television. The direct relationship between storyteller and listeners makes the telling of the story feel confrontational and personal, almost demanding a response.

Historical stories are likely to provoke different kinds of conversation than will a traditional tale. Listeners may have questions about the facts of the matter; some may want to voice prior knowledge relating to the story or its context – or seek further information on the spot via their smartphones. People may want to share their feelings and views about what happened. A story like this reveals the close connection between empathy and ethics: the affective responses it elicits give energy to ethical enquiry. Some listeners want to know why I would tell such a story. They may also ask for confirmation that it's true.

Facticity and truth

Because listeners' empathetic and ethical response to a story like 'The Tasmanian Genocide' hinges on its facticity, there's a moral onus on the storyteller to honour the known facts of the matter. However, any presentation of history is an interpretation. Although I'm no expert on Australian history, I've selected for inclusion in the story only a fraction of the information available to me. An informed listener might challenge, for instance, my emphasis on Truganini and point out that she was outlived by Suke, a full-blooded Tasmanian Aboriginal taken by sealers to an offshore island, and that the last speaker of a Tasmanian language, Fanny Cochrane Smith (of mixed heritage), lived until 1905. They might also comment that the British convicts too were victims of history.

A historical story has to be shaped out of the amorphous tangle of real-life events. You have to deal with conflicting information, with tantalizing gaps, with events petering out anticlimactically, with the need to simplify a complex reality. So there's a tension to be held between respect for the facts and constructing a good story.[64] An oral story requires a particular degree of simplification. If you included more thorough contextual information, you'd end up with a narrative too stodgy for storytelling and better suited to prose non-fiction. If you tried to build up the mimetic elements of description, action, dialogue and characters' thoughts, you'd end up with a work of fiction with reduced facticity.

Theorists of narrative spell out that narratives of the past are never strictly 'true'; they're always an abstraction from the lived experience, which can never be fully recovered, even in the memory of people directly involved.[65] Claims to express authoritative truth will tend towards either an unpalatable clutter of carefully hedged facts or the facile rhetoric of propaganda.[66] Should we even attempt to tell truth-claiming historical stories? I believe they do need to be told, to counter the rhetoric that shields powerful vested interests and to provide a provocative ethical gravitas complementary to other genres of stories that are easier to enjoy and easier to ignore; but told with integrity and humility, including honesty where there's uncertainty.

Why and when would you tell such a story?

My main motivation for telling 'The Tasmanian Genocide' is a conviction that such history should be known, so that those who suffered and died may be honoured in memory, and in the hope that the memory may help to prevent such atrocities recurring. The revival of nationalist xenophobia during the 2010s is a reminder of how easily the lessons of history can be forgotten. The pride of the British that they resisted facism in Europe in the 1940s masks Britain's failure to engage soul-searchingly with its imperialist impact on vast territories and populations elsewhere, whose consequences continue to reverberate.[67] Moreover, the small geographical scale of Tasmania's story helps to expose the ecological underpinnings that may be occluded in larger-scale situations. The island ecosystem could support only a small human population living as hunter-gatherers. The conflict between the indigenous Tasmanians and the British settlers was between two populations competing to use the same land resources, and played out in a similar way to conflicts between humans and wildlife: the settlers killed the Aborigines as if they were vermin.

But there needs to be a specific reason to tell a particular story on a particular occasion. Sensitivity is required with a story like this one. This may involve managing expectations, for example through negotiating with an organization the purposes of a storytelling event. I once told 'The Tasmanian Genocide' and a slightly more positive story – about the evolution, near extinction and teeth-of-time preservation of the American bison – in an ecumenical worship service, where there was an accepted agenda of engaging with questions of ecology, peace, justice and interfaith understanding; the minister had planned to lead us in song afterwards to lift the mood, but decided in the end to keep a prayerful silence rather than palliate the feelings the stories evoked. Expectations of a public performance can be managed through advertising its themes. That will likely attract people who are already willing to engage. Preaching to the converted, perhaps, but if change is to happen, it will probably begin with those who are receptive. It may be useful, for example, for people concerned about the environment to know more about the legacy of imperialism.

Another approach is to carefully subvert expectations – for example, to embed the hard-hitting story within a matrix of more palatable material, in the spirit of Idries Shah's explanation, of Sufi teaching tales, that the pleasure of stories makes the ideas they contain 'palatable to the mind' just as the flesh of a peach enables the seed within to be sown.[68] A challenging story can be embedded within a story set, allowing *time before* to build rapport with the listeners and earn the right, through entertaining them, to challenge them, and also *time after* to bring them back to a positive, if questioning, state of mind. Lupton and Nick Hennessey's *The Liberty Tree* embeds within an entertaining main story-plus-songs about Robin Hood three powerful stories from the history of dissent and land rights in England, about John Ball and the Peasants' Revolt, Gerard Winstanley and the Diggers, and the revolutionary Thomas Paine. Although any performance must stand on its own merits, storytellers like Lupton who've built a renown for excellence have an enhanced opportunity to reach broader audiences with challenging material, as Lupton also does in *On Common Ground* (performed with Chris Wood), presenting the peasant-poet John Clare's traumatic experience of the enclosure of the Northamptonshire countryside.[69]

Space, intention and emergent outcomes

When stories involve historical cruelty, injustice or moral blindness, the storyteller has to beware of slipping into a ranting tone that comes across as judging or punishing the listeners. You may want to challenge them with unfamiliar history, but they themselves were not responsible for those events. Moreover, the listener needs space for their own feelings to arise in response to the story. While rehearsing a story, I let myself feel and sometimes voice strongly the emotions of my own response to the events. When it comes to telling the story to others, it's not so much that I suppress my feelings as that I bring an intention of compassion towards my listeners when I'm aware the story may raise uncomfortable feelings. One can speak of this as 'holding the space' in which the story is being shared. The 'space' here is simultaneously the *external* space – the room, say, or the space around a campfire – that contains the storytelling group, and the *internal* space within each listener in which they experience the story, imaginatively, emotionally and cognitively. The intention of compassion helps you stay conscious of feelings that begin to arise, and thereby let them pass without unconsciously amplifying them.[70]

I once listened to David Holt tell a personal story he'd received from one of the last survivors of the *Titanic*. As one of the women in the lifeboats, she had watched the ship go down and then waited while the circle of fully loaded boats kept their distance from the men (including their own husbands) struggling in the frigid water lest the boats get swamped by them. I vicariously shared the horror, guilt and grief of those survivors. Holt then segued into a blues tune on his banjo to hold a wordless space in which we listeners could process our feelings. The knowledge this was an eye-witness story of a real event made it very emotionally powerful. Its unredemptive ending left me with unresolved feelings which implied an unresolved question: How could things have been otherwise? One ecological perspective might evaluate the lifeboat situation in pragmatic terms of the consequences of need exceeding resource, a parable of the implication of right-wing political economy that some people may be considered expendable in times of resource scarcity.[71] A more ethical 'solution' to the tragedy of the *Titanic* can only be found by expanding the frame backwards in time in order to pre-empt aspects of the crisis. The deeper ecological theme is hubris, the delusion of human power over nature, that this ship was unsinkable, hence the errors in preparedness, such as in the provision of lifeboats.

A similar parable of industrial civilization's hubris is the doomed 1840s expedition of Sir John Franklin in search of the Northwest Passage.[72] Whereas

Holt uses music as a coda to an emotionally potent story, David Metcalfe tells the Franklin story as preface to singing the ballad 'Lord Franklin' and invests the weight of emotion in the music. His telling is informally matter-of-fact, but draws attention to certain facets of the story: the mariners' confidence in the British technological supremacy encapsulated on-board their ships; the failure for years afterwards to realize that indigenous Inuit oral tradition might hold answers to the mystery of what became of the expedition after the ships had presumably foundered in the ice; the Inuit account of some hunters encountering a large party of Europeans in the Arctic wastes and abandoning them, knowing that this barren country couldn't support so many men who lacked knowledge how to survive there; the prediction that global warming is melting the Arctic ice so fast that soon the Northwest Passage may be navigable all year round. Metcalfe thereby brings to the story an ecological agenda; he relies chiefly upon irony, and lightness of tone, to give space to listeners' cognition that will then inform their reception of the ballad. Whereas Holt crafts a powerful emotional experience and leaves you to your own devices in responding to what you may conclude was simply a terrible tragedy, Metcalfe provides a structure of commentary that invites but does not impose particular pathways of response.

John Austin's speech act theory distinguishes *locution* – just saying something – from *illocution* – speech functioning as an action, such as a promise, curse or oath – and *perlocution*, where speech attempts to persuade the hearer of something.[73] When something seems important, you may feel strongly motivated to persuade people to believe what you want them to believe, so they will act accordingly. Hence the craft of salesmanship, propaganda, public relations, political rhetoric. Its power is evident in the way the UK's departure from the European Union was accomplished through sustained rhetoric, playing upon latent insecurity and alienation, to build a heartfelt conviction among millions of voters.[74]

The ever-increasing urgency of the ecological crisis may seem to demand a kind of storytelling that will persuade people of that urgency so they will act to preserve habitats and wildlife and to reduce pollution, waste and consumption. Even better, we might think, would be a style of storytelling and a repertoire of stories both tested to reliably produce those results. That would be to adopt the kind of quantifiable outcomes-based approach, now familiar to university educators, that derives from the paradigm of industrial production and the scientific method, demanding replicability and control. In demonstrating experimentally the power of stories to improve learning outcomes, Haven is applying this paradigm of control to bring about desired ends, and to do so he prescriptively defines a (good) 'story' as one in which an individual protagonist overcomes obstacles to reach their goal.[75] Thus both the *use* of story and the story *content* he envisages recapitulate the same structure of satisfying a preconceived goal as does the model of scientific 'proof' on which his analysis is based. Certainly the qualities that he indicates stories can promote are desirable; however, the will to control the outcome of an activity is the will to dominate – which in the case of storytelling means to dominate the listener.

Some degree of perlocutionary intent is inherent to any kind of educational activity, including the aims of this book. There is a place for persuasive rhetoric in a healthy society. I'm trying to persuade you of an argument right now! There's a place too for applied science. The accomplishment of some goal according to a planned design is the essence of 'craft', as R. G. Collingwood distinguishes it from 'art', in which he says there should be no distinction between means and ends.[76] Whether or not storytelling be recognized as art, it involves a relationship of trust between storyteller and listeners. If a storyteller has rapport with their listeners, then maybe there'll be some sharing of values or insight; if the storytelling is truly dialogic, the sharing may flow both ways and any learning may be emergent between them. But if the storyteller seeks to produce a specific predetermined response in their listeners, then they do violence to the trust of that relationship and to the listener's agency and imagination. And if the listener realizes that an attempt is being made to manipulate them, they may resist.

The 'intention of compassion' that I mentioned above is one example of the importance of intention in storytelling. 'Intention' differs from goal-seeking in being open-ended.[77] It brings chosen qualities or attitudes into play on the storyteller's part but allows the agency of the listeners – and the environment – in what comes about. It's the same kind of dynamic that Jim Cheney and Anthony Weston describe as an 'etiquette' of openness with respect to the non-human world: 'the task is to create the space in which a response can emerge or an exchange coevolve'.[78] The relational dynamics of the storytelling situation thus model the relational dynamics to be cultivated in our inhabitation of the earth. Besides openness to others' agency, these dynamics include the capacities to listen and attend, to remember and imagine, to be consciously present, to feel a sense of connectedness with others, to be empathetically responsive, to observe patterns of desire and consequence, to speak and act respectfully, to recognize and tame the demands of ego and to experience stillness. Once you've got to grips with them, all of these capacities become facets of intention.

The storyteller may clarify in their own mind beforehand what intentions they wish to bring. Some intentions may be specific to a story. In the case of 'The Tasmanian Genocide', they might include, besides compassion towards the listeners, intentions of restraint from adopting a condemnatory tone in speaking of the British actions, and of care in lexical choices when speaking of the Aborigines. Other qualities of intention may be brought into mind as part of one's regular practice, such as the openness and presence just referred to, and the intention the story shall be a precious gift. The magic of intention is that such intentions shouldn't need to be forcefully sustained throughout; with practice, it's enough to declare them to yourself before you begin, and then trust them to stay with you.

In Gersie's storymaking, the *listeners'* intentionality is activated by means of 'response tasks'. A response task is an open-ended expressive task that participants do *after* hearing a story. It may involve speaking or another activity such as writing, drawing, painting, movement, sound-making or dramatic impro. Crucially, the task is specified *before* the story is told. It thereby sets up, firstly, an intention of active listening, since the listeners will have to listen attentively enough to be able to respond to the story; and, secondly, a galvanization of their responsiveness to the story in the particular direction suggested by the response task. The reason for a particular response task should not be spelt out, Gersie emphasizes, because to do so would risk closing down intention into goal-seeking, by producing an impetus to perform the task in a way that meets the participant's perception of an outcome desired by the facilitator. The open-endedness of the tasks enables each participant to discover their own response, while their practical specification channels the manifesting of that response in the social context of the group. Gersie has devised many 'structures' for storymaking workshops, employing diverse response tasks. Each structure is designed to take participants through a psychological journey that recapitulates the dynamics of a particular story the facilitator will tell at a certain point in the session, the story being chosen to open a particular area of psychological concern.[79] The response tasks encourage the participants to engage not only with the stories but also with each other as thinking, feeling beings. Gersie's tried-and-tested methodology has been shown to help people gain curiosity, confidence and self-esteem and care more for themselves, others and the environment.[80] The outcomes identified have a more relational cast than the effects of 'story' identified by Haven. Although Gersie's session structures are prescriptive, they provide spaces in which participants' active agency is encouraged and demand responsivity from the facilitator to what's happening.

I've used simple response tasks as a tool to initiate conversation after telling historical stories. At a workshop with university students I specified this task for 'The Tasmanian Genocide':

> After the story, please share with your partner which moment in the story evoked the strongest feeling – and where in your body you felt that feeling.

The task was worded to require them to attend to the *whole* story, since they won't know until the story's end which moment has elicited the strongest feeling. It also requires a double attention, to both the story and their own body. The partner work opened the way to a freer conversation among the whole group, in which a diversity of story moments and areas of the body came to light. 'I felt it *here*,' some students said, making a gesture that indicated a part of the body and suggested an internal movement of the sensation. This conversation in turn led participants to volunteer thoughts and feelings about a number of topics emergent from the story, including racism and sexism, the relationship between cooperation and ecological living, the impact upon human bodies of imperialist barbarity, the religious dimension of European imperialism, the relevance of such historical events today and the import of whether the story was 'true'.

Although my narration of 'The Tasmanian Genocide' was very spare, lacking mimetic detail, it was evident from their comments that some listeners had filled that gap with dynamic imagery, just as their emotional reactions had filled the space left by my emotional restraint. The 'space' within a story can take many forms. It may include, for example, the unspoken significance of what's happened, or questions that the story leaves unresolved. If a story is too complete, too neatly resolved, then it leaves no space for imagination and cognition.[81]

To maximize the size of audiences, and hence profits, the culture industries have, in M. T. Anderson's analysis, simplified the stories they present, minimized their particularity and prioritized spectacular action.[82] Linked to this is the vogue for stories considered 'relatable' because they present types of characters and situations already familiar to the target audience. These commercial pressures tend to close down cognition.[83]

Stimulating questions may, in contrast, be raised by particularities of content that are *unfamiliar*, owing perhaps to geographical remoteness or, in the case of the following story, remoteness in time. The story is adapted from Haggarty's graphic novel *Mezolith*, which developed from his storytelling work in *I Become Part of It*.

Prehistoric fiction: 'The Bull Hunt'

Long ago, in the Stone Age, a boy was lying in the grass dreaming what creatures he could see in the clouds, when a bee alighted on his nose. Pretending to be a hunter, he pursued the bee into a wood, where, losing the bee, he discovered a huge wild bull. He raced home to camp and reported the beast to the men. The Chief thought maybe the bull had come down near the coast looking for a mate because it was spring. That gave them a plan how to hunt him. They were keen to hunt him; they needed his meat for food, his hide to make clothes, his bones to make tools, his fat to light their lamps. The boy, to his displeasure, was told to stay with the women by the wood's edge. 'Everyone has a part to play in this hunt,' said his dad. 'Your part is to stay with the women.'

The men divided into two groups: one, with the Chief, waited down in the marsh; the other, led by the boy's father, crept into the wood with the dogs. The Chief blew on his horn a mooing sound like a cow's to lure the bull from the wood. The men and dogs gave chase. The women screamed and waved to divert the bull towards the marsh. The boy's father threw his spear and missed. The lad, desperate to help, darted out to recover the spear. But the bull suddenly turned, gored him, tossed him – would have killed him had not his mother rushed out, grabbed the spear and thrust it into the bull.

The dogs and men drove the wounded beast down into the marsh, where he couldn't escape the Chief's men who sprang up around him. Before delivering the coup de grâce, the Chief thanked the bull for the gifts of his body. 'Great bull, sing your death song, and the wind will lift your spirit beyond the earth, beyond the sky, to a world of grass, flowers and dew where you will rest and wander and forage until you're called to this earth once again.'

Meanwhile the women dressed the boy's wound. When the materials butchered from the bull had been dealt with, the tribe gathered round the fire while the Storyteller told the story of the hunt. The boy, lying in his tent, wondered if he'd ever become a hunter like his dad, or whether he'd end up a storyteller instead. Later the Chief and Storyteller laid the bull's skull in the sacred glade and sprinkled it with petals. A bee hovered for a moment above the skull and then zipped away.[84]

This story is neither a traditional nor a true-life story, but a work of fiction. Its truth claims differ accordingly, as do the 'beliefs' its subtext carries. It comes across as *realistic*, meaning that everything depicted could plausibly have happened, and implying that the representation of culture and ecology accurately reflects archaeological knowledge of the Mesolithic setting, and yet the mimetic detail of narration signals that the story is to be received as fiction rather than fact. Applying a Stibbean analysis, we might infer from this story the following beliefs:

- A way of life dependent on animal products involves brutal violence.
- A prehistoric society requires animal products in order to satisfy basic needs.
- A hunting people manage their feelings about killing animals by means of spiritual beliefs and practices.
- Those who defy normative social roles place themselves and others at risk.
- When circumstances demand, normative social roles can be transcended.

The realism includes deeper psychology and hence more nuanced interplay between the beliefs than in 'The Green Ladies of One Tree Hill'. The first three beliefs noted above exist in tension with each other, as do the latter two. These tensions invite ethical questions. The fact the story has such a remote setting also begs questions about the relevance of these ethical questions to modern society. We may wonder whether the brutality of the animal-killing may be avoided in modern meat production, but then remember that, before he got hunted, the bull enjoyed a wild and free life that many domestic livestock today are denied. We may ask which commodities that in the Stone Age could only be obtained from animals may today be provided by other means. Or whether the prescribed gender roles were justified by the physicality of hunting in a way that's irrelevant in a more technological culture. Or how accurately this and other speculative elements of the story's imagining of prehistoric culture accord with the reality of that distant past.

The characters' perception of reality as involving spirits and another world does not disrupt the realism, because listeners will accept that prehistoric people would perceive the world differently from the normative perspectives of our own time. Coexisting with the realism, however, is a whiff of mythopoeic symbolism. It's there with the bee at the beginning: the bee is a mythological symbol of divine knowledge[85] and in this story it incites the chain of events, appearing almost to metamorphose into the bull, only to reappear after the bull is dead. Secondly, the boy's story has the mythic structure of Campbell's hero's journey: call to adventure, a series of trials, supreme ordeal, rescue and return, and the possibility of transformation.[86] Campbell's formulation mirrors adolescent rites of passage in traditional societies, in which the youth is taken from his home into the wilderness, where he acquires the knowledge and skills of manhood and undergoes an ordeal such as circumcision; thus transformed into a man, he returns to take his place in the community. The venture towards manhood in 'The Bull Hunt' is premature, because the boy is too young. In place of the Campbellian 'meeting with the goddess' to prepare him for his ordeal, he has to be rescued by his mum. Thirdly, the bull has a potent presence in European mythology. It features in Palaeolithic cave paintings; in evidence of sacred rites in Neolithic Anatolia and Britain and Bronze Age Crete and India; in association with gods such as Zeus, Poseidon, Shiva and Mithra; and in the ancient Irish epic *Táin Bó Cúailnge*. The notion of the bull's spirit departing to another world from which he may later return is also redolent of shamanic cosmologies, and especially the Blackfoot story of the origin of the Buffalo Dance, which enables bison slain by humans to return to life.[87]

Irrespective of how truly these mythopoeic resonances might relate to the beliefs of the long-lost Mesolithic cultures of Northwest Europe, they subtly destabilize the story's realism and thereby add weight to the characters' spiritual worldview, as revealed most explicitly in the Chief's speech to the bull, and invite the inference of other beliefs:

- An invitation from some kind of divine presence may lead to transformative experiences.
- Animals possess eternal spirits that may be reborn in this and other worlds.
- Animals should be honoured as inspired beings even when they're killed to serve human needs.

Questions now arise from the tension between these interpretations and normative contemporary assumptions about the nature of reality. One might point out that the paradise to which the Chief directs the bull's spirit is much like what the beast was previously enjoying. When I invited a group of university students to suggest what 'feelings' might be experienced from perspectives within the story, only one person (the students' tutor) offered the bull's perspective: 'I feel pain.' After I told the story to stimulate primary school children to devise their own Stone Age stories, they came up with lots of violent interaction with wild animals (predators as well as hunting quarry), but a number of children spontaneously recycled in their compositions the image of petals sprinkled on a slain animal's skull. It struck me that they intuitively recognized the importance of offering some recompense for taking an animal's life.

The range of possible interpretations, both ethical and metaphysical, complicates the idea that a text mediates discrete beliefs. The story may instead open a field of possibilities in tension with each other – a latent internal dialogue.

We may think of this as a 'structured space' within which the listener's mind and heart may respond in 'cognition' (Darko Suvin's term encompasses both reasoning and feelings[88]). In the group situation a space for conversation about the story externalizes this space within the story to enable a social exchange in which competing facets of interpretation may be negotiated.

Imagining alternatives: 'Trouble with Turtles'

It's easier to tell stories about problems than about how to solve them. It's easier to tell stories presenting lessons from the past than to devise stories imagining how the problems of the present might transform in a positive direction. It's easier, and more lucrative to the creative industries, to imagine a violent dystopian future than a better world. The ecological crisis is producing challenging new situations that demand new ideas, new stories.

One approach to imagining positive change has been the writing of utopian narratives. Classic utopian stories have suffered from two connected problems: the lack of narrative traction as the workings of the utopia are explained; and the presentation of the utopian society as a fait accompli, a fixed vision, whose implementation may be inferred to involve coercion.[89] As the political experiment of the Soviet Union demonstrates, the imposition of a preconceived social system involves a will to dominate that parallels the will to dominate I critiqued above in the use of stories as tools of persuasion. When ends are used to justify means, then the ends, if accomplished, will be contaminated by the violence inherent to the means and so the cycle of conflict will be renewed.[90]

'Utopia' therefore needs to be reconceptualized as, not a goal, but a *process*: a pathway of intention in which the desired qualities are embodied in every step and it's accepted that a terminal ideal state will never be reached, since the world will keep changing. To look at this ecologically, for communities of living people and the ecosystems they inhabit, every step up the ladder of change ought to be viable and tolerable *at the time*, just as the principle of biological homeostasis requires that every step in the evolution of an organism must remain viably functional. A process unfolds through time; it can be represented as a story. A story of utopian process may inspire and motivate without needing to harden into a programme for action. The complexity of such processes lends them to treatment in prose fiction, as in the oeuvre of Kim Stanley Robinson.[91] Storytelling requires concision. It can convey the simplified gist of some dynamic. It invites you to cut through the detail and dramatize the 'turn' that brings about transformation.

Ecological crisis produces many conflicts between groups of people – or between people and wildlife – who are competing for the same resources or have competing strategies about what should be done. We've seen that engagement between stakeholders in a conflict situation may usefully include the sharing of personal stories. It would be a taller order to try to facilitate their collaborative construction of a narrative of how the conflict might be resolved. That's a job for expert negotiators. A conflict may, however, provide material for storytelling, *outside that situation*, to imagine pathways of transformation. 'Storytelling is a form of pattern-making,' says Lopez, which can illuminate problems without condemning those involved in them.[92] Stories, writes Cupitt, can 'teach us how to dream, fantasize and simulate for ourselves, so that we can also carry out our own imaginative experiments into possible future courses of action.'[93]

I once assisted at a workshop for executives of a large conservation organization, in which groups were asked to produce a performed story from a digest of information about a particular conservation dilemma. The time envelope was very tight. In pursuing this objective the participants had little opportunity to grasp that a story's impact depends upon the significance suggested to the listener's imagination by a particular pattern of events. The resulting 'stories' took the form of talking-heads sketches in which characters explained the problems and suggested possible solutions.

The creative challenge, from the starting point of non-narrative material, is to construct a sequence of events involving particular characters interacting in particular locations. Adequate time is needed in which to break down this creative work into several stages through which teams of participants can be guided. For example:

- to identify points of interest and conflict in the material;
- to create at least two characters with conflicting desires relating to the situation;
- to imagine specific locations in which these characters might interact;
- to devise a small number of causally connected events (turning points) in which the characters' desires interact;
- to prepare the story for telling using some combination of visual, somatic and spoken improvisation.

Important to the application to conflict scenarios is that this schema doesn't focus on a *single* 'hero' as in the story models of Campbell, McKee and Haven. One of the group stories produced in a workshop I facilitated along these lines helped to inspire my composition of the following story. It's a response to Dimitrios Theodossopoulos's anthropological study of the prolonged dispute on the Greek island of Zakynthos between a local community, keen to encourage tourism, and conservationists wanting to protect nesting sites of the loggerhead sea turtle (*Caretta caretta*).[94]

Yiorgos, the owner of a lovely island beach, was struggling to make money from his olive orchards behind the bay. He worried about paying for all his daughter Anna's needs. He decided to emulate his peers and clear some of the orchards to build holiday flats. A conservationist from Athens, Maroula, pointed out that sea turtles nested on the beach. Yiorgos wouldn't listen to what she told him about regulations and compensation. When she took out a court injunction to stop the development, he furiously browbeat the young policemen and carried on building. Meanwhile Maroula befriended Anna, showed her the turtles laying their eggs and taught her how to protect the nests with frames of sticks.

Anna's new concerns about the turtles put her at odds with her father. When tourists started coming to stay in the flats, she got a job in a beach cafe to earn money to go away to university. She became friendly with an Austrian tourist, Hans, who liked to watch the seabirds at the far end of the beach. The beach's increasing busyness caused damage to the turtle nests despite Anna's efforts. When the eggs hatched in August, the babies, programmed to crawl towards the moonlight on the sea, made instead for the lights up the beach and fell victim to foxes and gulls.

As the years went by, Yiorgos built steadily further along the bay. Anna felt sad how the place had changed. Hans visited every year – until the year he got badly stung by jellyfish. Bad publicity about monster shoals of jellyfish contributed to a drop in tourist numbers. Anna heard from Maroula that the jellyfish boom might have resulted from there being fewer turtles to eat them. Yiorgos wouldn't listen to her advocacy of less development. He was losing money from empty flats, so he did a deal to fly in tourists from England on a cheap package. These tourists liked to drink and caused much disturbance, and one night Anna was involved in an incident at the cafe which left her shocked and offended.

Torn in his heart, Yiorgos at last listened when Anna explained her sadness how the beach had changed. He listened, too, to Maroula's proposal of a compromise dividing the beach into three zones: a developed zone, a buffer zone where development would be restricted, and an undeveloped wild zone. Maroula also suggested ways to improve the profitability of his olives. Yiorgos agreed to scale down the tourism facilities and restored some of the olive orchards. Anna helped with marketing to attract nature-loving tourists. Hans reappeared. When the changes had been made, Yiorgos was making less money than before. But there were compensations, such as the night when Anna took him and Hans to watch the baby turtles poke out of the sand and crawl towards the moonlight reflected on the sea.[95]

This story is not intended to help resolve the real conflict on Zakynthos. For one thing, some of the turning points stretch plausibility: although I didn't invent the jellyfish factor, which nicely brings in the concept of food chains, I doubt that in reality it would carry quite such consequence. More fundamentally, even if the story did suggest a plausible roadmap for the Zakynthos situation, any attempt to implement it there would be an imposition upon the stakeholders involved. The story offers instead a simplified narrative of what a process of change might look like, including the interplay of motivations and relationships among the characters. It illustrates the application of narrative imagination to intractable situations.

Studies of narrative point out how narrative tends to foreclose the openness and complexity of reality to the extent the narrator's authoritative voice and the use of mimesis impose a particular view of the world.[96] Wilson argues that storytelling's political edge rests on its capacity to keep listeners alert to the fact the story is just a story, and that some more immersive storytelling risks dispelling their critical awareness.[97] I am cautious here about narrowing the range of acceptable storytelling experiences. We may value styles of storytelling – witty, ironic, subversive – that invite a mode of listening that Lipman calls 'leaning forward', in which the listener's dialogic engagement with the storyteller is very apparent; but there's also much to be valued in storytelling that invites the more inward mode of listening that Lipman calls 'leaning back'.[98] If the storyteller builds space into the story in some of the ways discussed in this chapter, then even in immersive storytelling, where listeners may surrender more deeply to the experience, the storyteller can continue to honour the agency of the listeners' imagination and interpretive and affective capacities. Thus the narrative may sustain a dialogic openness allowing the emergence of new insights and feelings in the listener.

'Trouble with Turtles' is intermediately immersive, in that my narration of action and scenery is quite mimetic, but my tone of voice is conversational. Cognitive space is opened by the different motivations of the characters; this story evinces something of the dialogic 'polyphony' that Mikhail Bakhtin associates particularly with novels.[99] It relates ecologically damaging activities to an individual entrepreneur's perception of necessity rather than projecting them upon a faceless corporate other; and I have to beware the risk of reducing the cognitive space if my telling sustains too little sympathy for Yiorgos. In post-story discussion a group can be asked to consider the perspective of each character upon the events, including that of 'the turtles'; this activity can be intensified by inviting individuals to speak for a chosen character in the first person. The story has a resolving ending intended to inspire hope and creativity – and to challenge the entrenched neoliberal dogma that businesses should always seek to maximize profit. Further cognitive space potentially opens beyond the story's end to contemplate that challenge and to consider which factors in the story nudged the course of events in a positive direction and how other conflict situations might be turned towards compromise solutions.

The composition of a story like 'Trouble with Turtles' involves more work than other genres discussed in this chapter. It requires research into the real-world problem in question, the construction of a storyline from scratch, the working out of a potential way forward for the problem, and the transposition of this into character-based narrative. The hardest thing is how to 'turn' the story away from the trends of human activity that are progressively inflicting more and more ecological damage.

Erotic motivation: 'Sunbath'

Many so-called traditional stories in fact derive from literary sources in antiquity and the Middle Ages. Modern literary stories are a less obvious resource for the storyteller because they're technically more distant from the form and sensibility of the oral tale. They focus more upon interior states of consciousness, depend more strongly on nuances of style and tend to be structurally less linear. But they can touch the heart in subtle ways beyond the scope of traditional tales. If you feel sufficiently touched by a literary story to want to retell it orally, you'll have to work out how to adapt it into a form that will accommodate the circumstances of telling and listening, very different from those of the solitary reader viewing a text. The use of such a story will require permission from the copyright-holder, unless it has timed out of copyright, like this one I adapted from D. H. Lawrence.

Juliet, the wife of a New York businessman, was suffering from depression. On doctor's advice, she went away, with her little son Johnny, to a warm country to get some sun. After an initial reluctance to be outdoors, the sight of the sun rising from the sea spurred her to leave Johnny with Marinina, a local woman, and descend to a secluded little beach where for the first in her life she lay naked in the sun. She felt the sun's heat envelop her and penetrate through her. She felt her body dissolving, her chilled heart beginning to melt. She went there every day. As her skin gained colour she felt an inward change too, a sense of detaching from her anxieties and the budding of something new. To satisfy local curiosity she told Marinina she was following doctor's orders. Marinina said, 'A person has to be beautiful to reveal their body to the sun.'

As Juliet became aware of her own beauty, her son became fearful, so she began to take him to the beach with her. Sometimes they passed a muscular, tanned workman from the neighbouring farm. One time on the beach a snake reared up near Johnny. He looked at Juliet, uncertain whether to feel afraid. Calmly she told him not to touch and held the stillness of the moment till the creature's long brown body eased away.

The sun got ever hotter as the summer wore on. One day, after they'd started walking back, still naked in the heat, Juliet chanced upon the workman. He stared at her as if she were a vision from another world – till Johnny caught up and broke the spell. Later, from her cottage, she watched the man working at the farm. She stayed up late, watching the moon on the sea, feeling the desire for another child.

Next day, Marinina appeared at the beach to tell her that Maurice, Juliet's husband, had arrived. When he got to the beach and saw his wife naked in the sun, he didn't know where to look. When he did look, she didn't really seem naked, because her suntan clothed her. Johnny was nonplussed to see his daddy. Juliet told Maurice she couldn't ever go back to New York. When they had lunch back at the cottage, the workman on the farm looked across at them. He seemed to Juliet to be full of the sun. What a fine father he'd make for a child!

She persuaded Maurice to return with her to the beach and undress. He looked like a long white worm, she like a sinuous brown snake. When he glanced at her, she knew from the way she felt inside that her next child would be his.[100]

To tell this story to a live audience brings what is largely – for both protagonist and reader – an inward private experience, characteristic of modern literary fiction, into a social situation. It's helpful to the adaptation that, although the source text – 'Sun' – takes us quite deeply into Juliet's thoughts, feelings and sensations, it sustains also a narrative voice telling us the story and includes plenty of vivid imagery. Adaptation to oral delivery meant shedding the exquisite layered sophistication of Lawrence's prose in favour of crystallizing a sequence of distinct visual tableaux, which provide a structure of memory for both storyteller and listener. Admirers of Lawrence may wonder what will be left – or gained – from such a procedure. What comes through is the story's erotic charge, delightful to the private reader, but electrifying with a live audience.

The storyteller must hold their nerve, hold the space, to make that experience stimulating rather than excruciating.

You have to choose carefully the moment to tell a story like this. I prepared 'Sunbath' as a commission from a Lawrence-loving friend to tell at her wedding. It was part of the evening entertainment around an open fire outdoors after dark. The heat and light of the fire echoed the heat and light of the sun. Unlike other kinds of 'distraction', the visual animation of a fire allows the listener's gaze to move between attending to the teller and attending to the abstract imagery of the flames, maintaining a sense of connection without the need for continuous eye contact. A particular case of 'leaning back'. In this way the fire helped to contain the erotic tension of 'Sunbath'. True to Lawrence's penchant for sexual symbolism in nature, it began to rain just as the story ended. Telling the story indoors, without this mediating role of a fire, is more intense, involving more sustained eye contact with listeners; here a circular seating arrangement is especially helpful to holding the space.

The erotics of 'Sunbath' hinge more upon sensuous experience of the elements than upon sexual dynamics between people. The story foregrounds something that's rarely talked about directly: that the sensuousness of our experience of nature – important to our connectedness to nature[101] – can involve an erotic desire to feel the sun, the air, the water on our body, even a merging with what's around us that expands our sense of self to encompass an 'ecological self'.[102] The very possibility of such experiences depends on the preservation of physical places in which they can happen; if the entire coastline gets built up, for example, then there'll be no opportunity to experience the wildness, privacy and nudity that Lawrence's story makes so appealing. Erotic urges are one of our most powerful motivations, alongside survival. Hence all the love stories! Notions of 'ecosex' and 'environmental erotogenics' affirm the underappreciated synergies between erotic desire and loving the earth.[103] To tell a story like 'Sunbath' mobilizes this theme in a social context of reciprocal attention that is itself 'erotic' in a broad sense, demanding from the storyteller both a vulnerability intrinsic to the material and a capacity to hold the space for whatever feelings the story may bring up in others.

Evolving tradition: 'The Forest Fire'

A little parrot was flying above the treetops of his beloved forest home, when he saw a plume of smoke. A fire – quickly spreading! The parrot called the alarm, and the creatures of the forest fled to take refuge in the river. But the parrot could hear the terrified cries of other creatures trapped by the flames. And the fire was still spreading. Would it destroy the whole forest? He had to do something to try to stop the fire! But what could he do? He was just a little parrot. Well, he did have a beak. He filled his beak from the river and flapped back and forth spitting beakfuls of water upon the inferno.

The great spirits in the sky looked down watching and laughed. But one felt a spark of pity. This spirit transformed into an eagle and appeared before the parrot and asked him why he was pursuing such a hopeless task. The parrot replied, 'I'm just doing the best I can with what I've got.'

Watching from the river, the cormorant could see that the parrot's efforts were futile, but she thought she ought to do something to help so he didn't feel he was struggling all on his own. She dipped her oilless wings in the river and flew to shake out the water on the flames. When the spirit in the form of an eagle then posed the same question to her, she answered, 'I'm just doing the best I can with what I've got.'

The mangabey monkey didn't really understand what the parrot and cormorant were doing, but it looked kind of fun; it seemed to be the thing to do, the new craze. So he scooped up water in his hands and scampered to throw it at the flames. The spirit asked him the same question, and the monkey replied the same way.

One by one, each for their own reasons, and in their own way, all the other animals joined in. Till only the elephant was left. She thought the fire-fighting was quite pointless, but realized that if she was the only one who didn't do anything, that wouldn't look too good, so she filled her trunk and stomped over to spray water on the fire.

As the great spirit watched the animals all struggling against the fire his heart was moved. He began to weep. He transformed into a cloud. His tears became rain that poured down to quench the fire. When the steam and smoke cleared, instead of lush forest there was charred devastation. But drops of water dripped from the ruined trees and sodden animals. Wherever a drop fell, a green bud or shoot appeared. Slowly but surely the blackened wasteland became green and slowly the forest began to grow back to life.[104]

The origin of this story was a tale from the Jatakas – the past lives of the Buddha – which Charlene Collison told to a Tales to Sustain gathering at Cae Mabon. It was selected for the whole group to work on together: we divided it into sections to be developed by small groups, which were then reassembled in a long episodic presentation, in which storytelling was supplemented by acting, movement, sound-making, comedy, and props improvised from the surrounding woods. I took what I liked from the insights and innovations arising from the group – including the catchphrase 'I'm just doing the best I can with what I've got' – and shaped my own retelling.

One element of my retelling draws upon a memory from my years as a teacher in Kenya, when a grassfire that had caught from an untended cooking fire swept across the school compound. The breeze drove it at terrific speed through the dry grass. The students leapt up the trees to pluck sprays of foliage with which to beat the fire's edge to steer it away from the buildings. My contribution was to grab a bucket of water and run to empty it on the flames. Whenever I tell 'The Forest Fire' I recall the elemental power and danger of the leaping flames as I came within their heat, and the futility of my bucketful of water. In this kind of way, the telling of a fanciful tale may be imbricated with personal experience that helps make the story feel real and become in some sense the teller's own story. In contrast to post-structuralist theorization of narratives as 'texts' inhabiting an intertextual universe disconnected from the real world, it's important to ecocritical engagement with the world's problems that there be an entanglement of consequence between story and life.[105] There's an *input* from my experience in Kenya into my telling of 'The Forest Fire'. The *output* from the story back into life is always the harder question.

I've told 'The Forest Fire' to audiences ranging from little children – who'll gladly act out the animals – to an international group of sustainability-minded excecutives, who were interested in the characters' varied motivations to take action, since the psychology of people's response to ecological crisis was important to their mission to bring about change.

The iteration of animal episodes also serves to build up suspense by delaying the resolution of the crisis. This dramatization of cooperative action was introduced by the Tales to Sustain groupwork. No cormorant, mangabey or elephant appears in the original Jataka tale, which moves directly from the parrot's efforts to the eagle spirit's intervention. However, the story's centre of gravity, for me, remains that original trope: the paradox that the transformation of seemingly impossible situations requires an intervention beyond the scope of one's personal agency, and yet that one's committed intention – and in my version the cooperative intention of community – is a necessary step to inviting this transpersonal power of change.

We may also note that the area of forest depicted is not saved; it is ruined, but its capacity for rebirth endures. There may be some ecological truth in that, but even localized destruction of tropical forest can cause irretrievable damage, including 'centinelan extinctions' of whole communities of species endemic to one modest area.[106] Thus, although the story appears to have upbeat closure – making it a usefully positive item of repertoire – it leaves some unresolved questions and contradictions.

I have to admit that, over the years I've been telling 'The Forest Fire' since that group exercise with Tales to Sustain, it evaporated from my mind that in the original the parrot is an incarnation of the Buddha. Only returning to the Jataka tale do I realize that its emphasis on the parrot's pluck as he fights the fire, when he could have flown away, bespeaks that he's a bodhisattva, an enlightened one who remains in the world of suffering to help others. In telling traditional stories I easily forget which elements of the story are 'original', which are my innovation and which come from other storytellers. They all fuse together in my own conception of the story, which I can start thinking *is* the story – until I next hear someone else tell their version! When a tale is preserved in writing, whether in scripture, romance or folklorists' transcriptions, that particular text can acquire apparent authority as definitive or authentic; it's one more way that written culture claims superiority to oral culture. Though the static purity of an oral tradition, too, may sometimes be asserted by elites whose status depends on knowledge of them, I believe that mutability, evolution, is inherent to oral storytelling traditions.

In the case of 'The Forest Fire', then, there has been one further 'dialogic' process, one operating amidst the ecosystem of stories. The story has moved from one cultural context – Buddhist India two millennia ago – into a quite different one and in the process has changed, to the extent that the protagonist's identity as the Buddha is unacknowledged, though his spirit of compassion is perpetuated. Such recycling of stories between cultures brings some contentious questions.

Telling tales from other cultures

A culture's mythology, says Campbell, 'integrates the individual into his society and the society into the field of nature'.[107] Barre Toelken, writing about Native American stories, argues that traditional tales cannot be told authentically without deep knowledge of their cultural context; the difficulty, for an outsider, of gaining sufficient knowledge weighs against the 'expropriation' of stories from other cultures. Toelken's position valorizes a purity of tradition in which stories are reified as resisting interpretation.[108] Wilson critiques contemporary transformations of traditional material that claim 'authenticity' but actually lack it, but he also critiques as reactionary the sanctifying of tradition as timeless and unchanging.[109] Zipes argues that a story taken out of its original context ceases to be 'authentic' but that it can become authentic again if the storyteller truly believes in its capacity to serve a new community.[110] His argument implies two different kinds of 'authenticity' which need to be distinguished.

If the mutability of tradition is accepted, then *cultural* authenticity loses salience, becomes unattainable, and we can attend instead to *personal* authenticity, by which I mean a consistency between inner states of being and outward expression.[111] Toelken links authenticity to *respect*.[112] Certainly, storytellers should bring an intention of respect. It's respectful, and useful, to learn about the cultural context of stories you're drawn to tell.[113] But personal authenticity is compromised if a storyteller's work pretends a cultural authenticity it doesn't, or cannot, have. On this basis, my telling of 'The Forest Fire' would be inauthentic if I were to frame it as an authentic 'Buddhist story', but I'd resist a judgement that it's inauthentic simply because it deviates so much from the source text. For a story to 'serve a new community', it likely will need to change.

Stories vary in their potential to usefully translocate into a different cultural context. 'The Forest Fire' is an example of a 'wisdom tale': a genre of teaching tales that are found worldwide, but associated especially with certain religious traditions, and are attractive to storytellers with a sense of moral mission because they address universal themes.[114] However, the meaning or interest of some traditional stories may depend so crucially on specific cultural knowledge that they have little to offer outside the community of origin. Some local legends, for example, will mean little for listeners unfamiliar with the local topography they enchant (see Chapter 4). Some myths mean little without the ritual that re-enacts them or the cosmology that informs them. Aspects of meaning may be lost without the language in which a tale was originally told. Key teachings in Hawaiian tales, according to Serge Kahili King, are coded in the names of characters and places and the relationships between them; without knowledge of Hawaiian you'll comprehend only the surface adventure story, not the spiritual journey hidden beneath.[115]

Besides concerns about cultural authenticity, the critique of 'expropriation' or 'cultural appropriation' has other, more political aspects and has gained increasing traction from the intensifying of identity politics defending the interests of demographic groups who have suffered injustice. In Edward Said's postcolonialist analysis, 'Orientalist' representations of other (Eastern) cultures misrepresent the latter in such a way as to serve Western imperialist purposes.[116]

Europeans' retellings of traditional stories from non-European peoples may thus represent such peoples in some way that frames them as subordinate to Europeans. This can happen without the storytellers consciously intending it, owing to their internalization of received ideas about these cultures. Another consequence of European imperialism is that indigenous peoples have been compelled to participate in a globalized capitalist economy based on owning property you can use to make money. In this context, cultural heritage such as traditional stories is not only precious to people's identity but may be conceptualized as cultural capital, to be protected along the lines of intellectual property rights.[117]

All these factors are apposite to arguments, strongly held by some Native American storytellers, that non-Natives should not tell Native stories. European colonization dispossessed Native Americans of most of their lands and much of their culture; it did likewise to Australian Aborigines and other indigenous peoples. The moral implication of the discourse of 'appropriation' is that the telling of indigenous stories by outsiders is akin to theft. The same principle logically extends to any borrowing of stories from cultures other than one's own, with the effect that American storytelling, for instance, favours personal and family-based material, except where a storyteller claims the right of ancestry to tell stories from a particular tradition.[118]

The situation in Britain is different. Central to the British storytelling revival have been both the native legendaria of the British Isles and a world repertoire of traditional tales, the latter catalysed by a perceived need in the 1980s for multicultural education.[119] There has been a consistency of purpose, celebratory of diversity, in storytellers' use of an international repertoire and the platforming of storytellers from diverse cultures around the world. There may perhaps be vestiges here of an imperial culture that eclectically took what it wished from the multifarious peoples under British rule, and multiculturalism has been critiqued as facilitating a globalized elite's detachment from community.[120] However, many people attending storytelling events are neither passive consumers nor among the globalized elite; they will retell stories they've heard and make new friends from other countries. Not only the practice of storytelling but an active folk storytelling tradition have been revived, in a way that embraces cultural diversity rather than affirms an exclusive in-group.

Folk traditions involve a different paradigm from that of ownership and 'appropriation'. Throughout the ages, when people from different places have met, stories have been shared, retold, transposed, recombined, transformed,[121] thereby contributing to the mixing of cultures, which, Said acknowledges, are not 'unitary or monolithic' and 'assume more "foreign" elements, alterities, differences, than they can consciously exclude':[122] consider, for example, the wild mixing of motifs from Amazonian, Andean, European and Asian folklore in the visionary paintings of the mestizo Peruvian artist Pablo Amaringo.[123] In such an organic process the stories are not lost, as when lands or objects are stolen; those who previously told them can always tell them again. The loss of stories happens for other reasons, such as the imposition of education systems and entertainment media. Folklorists have charted the geographical transmission of stories between countries and continents.[124] The taxonomies of tale types and tale 'motifs' (narrative building blocks such as characters, objects and actions) bespeak the transcultural nature of folktales.[125] A taxonomy of 'migratory legends' reflects the fact that even local legends, stories tied to particular localities, are routinely translocated.[126] New ones today get called 'urban myths'. On the Greek island of Patmos, to give one example, a resident Dutchman told me that crazy environmentalists had released venomous snakes in the ruins of the acropolis to discourage visitors; the same story recurs on other Greek islands to which the Ottoman viper (*Montivipera xanthina*) is native.

The flipside of the impetus of the 'cultural appropriation' discourse – largely to dissuade people of European origin from telling stories from other peoples – is the expectation that non-European storytellers will always tell stories from their own ancestral culture. So *their* creative freedom too is implicitly curtailed. Afro-Caribbean storyteller TUUP has expressed his freedom and capacity to tell stories from anywhere that speak to his heart;[127] Temi Odurinde, from Nigeria, tells stories from diverse countries as well as his own Yoruba tradition and would be glad to hear other people tell Yoruba stories.[128] Taken to an extreme, the stricture against 'appropriation' would stop English people telling Scottish stories, or Scots telling English stories; it would stop me telling the folktales of my home county Gloucestershire, since I'm a native of Lancashire. It's a form of puritanism in that it puts people under pressure to uphold it in order to demonstrate their moral rectitude and closes down cultural possibilities by inhibiting processes of cultural recycling fundamental to folk traditions and the arts in general. It's divisive in implying the separation of cultures into discrete units between which there shouldn't be cross-fertilization. In valorizing ancestry as basis for the right to tell stories from a particular tradition, it veers towards a racialist pattern of thinking.

Whether serving the interests of a dominant ethnic group, as in right-wing nationalism, or those of demographic groups at the hard end of injustice and power dynamics, virulent identity politics pit the interests of one identity group against another's. The intensification of identity-based rhetoric during the 2010s has channelled the neoliberal impetus of competition among individuals towards the competition among ethnic groups and nations now starkly visible in the turn to right-wing populism, hence setting up the faultlines for violent conflict over natural resources as ecological crisis deepens.

There's a space here for the environmental humanities to clarify how the interconnectivity inherent to ecology necessitates a cooperative interconnectivity of response to people's needs and suffering. Navigation through ecological crisis requires not separation and conflict but mutual understanding and cooperation. It requires creativity rather than the closing down of possibilities. For storytelling, that means accepting the interconnectivity of stories which has always existed but is today intensified by the internet and the availability of printed collections. By attending to the stories of other peoples, you can learn about them, empathize with them, enquire how their insights and experience speak to the needs and challenges of a changing world. Listening is one thing. But when you retell stories yourself you engage in more active learning: the stories move through your heart, you articulate them in your own words, and you may in some way be changed.

To acknowledge that you may have something to learn from other peoples doesn't mean you have to romanticize them. The ecological credentials of indigenous peoples are not impeccable.[129] However, 'indigenous knowledge of culture–nature interdependence', as Hubert Zapf puts it, 'represents a source of imaginative counterdiscourses' that have much to teach industrial civilization. Their traditional knowledge, 'by the very logic of ecological thought, provides the basis for cross-cultural interpretation and dialogue' while yet resisting 'easy appropriation and generalization'.[130] As the Hassidic tale of 'Eisik Son of Jekel', or its English version 'The Tailor of Swaffham', teaches us, wisdom from afar may be what's needed to discover the treasure buried at home.[131]

Indigenous stories of Oceania and the Americas are chock-full of ecology: natural habitats, wild organisms, weather conditions, seasonal cycles and the human ecology of interactions with these things. In Europe, where the ecological content of native folktales is sparser, the similarities of climate and wildlife to North America's are a reason to draw upon Native American folklore. When I was asked to tell stories about beavers when some beavers from Germany were introduced to Slimbridge, my British material comprised only a history I'd composed of the extinction and reintroduction of beavers in Britain, plus one Welsh folktale, about the Afanc, a mythical water beast that helped shape Snowdon's topography and may possibly be interpreted as a beaver. To fill out my set I turned to Native America: I told the Iroquois tale of 'Turtle's Race with Beaver' and a landscape-building myth from the Pacific Northwest about Coyote's battle with a monstrous beaver, Wishpoosh.[132]

That admission exposes that, as a jobbing storyteller, I have a vested interest in the argument for creative freedom I'm making in this section. As an Englishman, I have also to be humbly aware of history: one line of my ancestors were cotton industrialists complicit in the plantation economy of the American South, with its African slaves and erasure of Native cultures; another line were proletarians subject to the class hierarchy of England's internal imperialism. Facts to keep in mind when I say that it's my heart's wish to make this argument in a way that will feel respectful to indigenous storytellers I know.

I'm not advocating that anyone should feel free to tell any story anytime anywhere. Sensitive discernment is always needed about the appropriateness of a story to an occasion. There may be good reason for traditional constraints upon when and where particular tales should be told. The linkage of many tales to particular seasons of the year is an ecological reason to tell these tales in season. Respect for other cultures entails awareness of the limitations of your own knowledge; it means acknowledging beliefs they may have that stories have metaphysical significance, as with sacred myths that would normally be told only in ritual contexts. Hence questions about not only who may appropriately *tell* certain stories, but also who may appropriately *hear* them.[133] However, I believe that it's in keeping with the capacity of storytelling to forge a sense of connection, culturally and ecologically, that people should, in principle, tell stories from cultures other than their own. When Strauss agonized whether to stop telling her beloved Coyote stories because she wasn't Native, a Native friend reassured her, 'But you're not a coyote either.'[134]

Although the immigrant communities in the Americas and Australasia have developed their own legends of place,[135] the bedrock of storied wisdom about these regions' land and wildlife lies in indigenous traditions. The ecological well-being of these lands, the treasuring of their sacredness, might be well served if *all* human communities inhabiting them took to heart the indigenous stories.[136] Let us imagine a scenario in which the immigrant peoples allowed the indigenous peoples to be their teachers; in which everyone learnt the indigenous stories mediating knowledge and feeling for the land and its creatures; in which indigenous storytellers ran workshops to teach others how to tell indigenous stories; in which ecologically destructive practices of the colonists metamorphosed into sustainable inhabitation of the land; in which the indigenous peoples, instead of being marginalized in their own country, became empowered guides and co-creators of a progressive, cooperative way forward. Some may say this is fanciful; that, the way things are, oppressed minorities must simply fight for their rights. But the way things are is unsustainable. It has to change.

Spaces of possibility

This chapter has illustrated a range of ways in which telling stories can open structures of space inviting the listener's agency of response, especially when the storyteller brings a dialogic intention to the experience, rather than a will to accomplish specific outcomes. This space may be provided within the story, in the form of what Ernest Hemingway calls 'omissions',[137] that is, lacunas of information, explanation, emotion, even action; as well as the interpretive openness of metaphor, symbol, irony, uncertainty, questions, contradictions; tensions between competing characters, desires, options, ethical stances, metaphysical possibilities; implications of how things could be different, including the applicability of the story's dynamics to other situations – all of which have potential to stimulate the listener's imagination, cognition and feelings. Space may also be cultivated within the storytelling experience – in the physical space between people; the gap between their minds; the storyteller's restraint, flexibility and silences – and by the provision of opportunities for listeners to speak, share their feelings, negotiate meaning and tell their own stories.

Although such space does not dictate the listener's response, its particularity of structure invites some pathways of response more than others. That is, the narrative – that which is actually said and the way it's said – sculpts the space within and beyond it to provide different nuances of opportunity to the listener's agency to respond. This conception of a story may be compared to a three-dimensional sculpture, or piece of studio pottery, in which the configuration of the material defines the shape of the space inside and around it.[138]

These facets of space in stories and storytelling invoke spaces of possibility. The forces of determinism, dogma, distrust, vested interest and preconceived goals work to close down possibilities. To optimize the possibility of hope requires a maximally diverse ecosystem of stories – a world of stories in dialogue with each other, facilitating a diversity of conversation in which we may discover more about ourselves, our world and its ecological diversity. Celebration of that diversity is the key to its preservation.

3

Time, desire and consequence in ecological stories

This book introduced a story as 'a sequence of events through time which usually are linked by some pattern of causality'. If we look in ecology for processes that unfold over time, then we find stories, whole genres of them. Every ecosystem, every locality, every species, every individual organism has a story. In each of these stories we may discern patterns of cause and consequence – and arguably some kind of 'desire' that drives them.

Before we examine some of these stories, let's first look at a folktale that contains a little ecology. It's a trickster tale told by multiple Native American nations. Sometimes the trickster is Otter; sometimes it's Fox. In light of Chapter 2's discussion of the recycling of stories, it's worth noting that versions of this story also occur in the medieval French *Roman de Renart*, where the trickster is Renart (Fox) and the victim Ysengrin (Wolf), and elsewhere in European folklore. All are variants of Aarne–Thompson (AT) tale type 2, 'The Tail-Fisher'.[1]

Nature in the folktale: 'How Bear Lost His Tail'

In the version I tell, the trickster is Lynx, who envied Bear's lovely long tail because her own tail was short and stubby. She tricked him into lowering his tail down a hole in a frozen lake to try to catch fish. 'When you hear me shout, "Now!" you must pull out your tail as quick and as hard as you can.' By morning, Bear's tail was frozen solid into the ice. Lynx sneaked up and shouted, 'Now!' and Bear pulled quick and hard – and that's how he got the short stubby tail he has today.[2]

Ecologically, the story introduces these two animal species, the observation they're wary of each other, and knowledge that lakes ice over in winter, you can fish by cutting a hole in the ice, and in winter no fish will be found in the shallower water where Lynx got Bear to make his attempt at tail-fishing. However, this explanation of ursine tail morphology does not of course conform with evolutionary biology. It's a 'pourquoi tale', purporting to explain how some feature of the world came to be, but really more of a fable, a teaching tale, not to be regarded as naive proto-science.

In its anthropomorphic characters we can see pressures of desire as typically structure a story. Bear gullibly desires to emulate Lynx's ability to catch fish from an ice hole with a flick of her tail. But the story's true protagonist, who drives the plot, is Lynx. Her envious desire is to cut Bear's tail down to size. Yet, although she's the protagonist, and exhibits the sin of envy, she doesn't get her comeuppance. She's the trickster who serves as teacher. It's in Bear's conduct that lessons may be sought – about conceitedly flaunting one's beauty, ignorance about fish and ice, trusting the untrustworthy, following instructions too literally.

Brooks says that characters in a story serve as 'desiring machines', which engage with the desires of both storyteller and audience.[3] What commitment of desire might a storyteller bring to 'How Bear Lost His Tail'? For me, the centre of gravity is when the tail snaps off and is left stuck in the ice. It's a definitive moment of loss, which echoes other experiences of loss that one could have prevented if one hadn't been so stupid. I don't want to push this too far, because it's a light-hearted story that gets a laugh and doesn't direct attention to a bigger picture; but let us note that the ecological crisis involves human conduct that's productive of loss and may in hindsight be judged stupid. The trickster there is the forces of nature that have the power to teach us hard lessons.

Kenneth Burke writes of a 'third creative motive', beyond self-expression and communication, that entails an actualization of some potential.[4] Whether the aspiration is practical, aesthetic or spiritual, I would name this motive as 'commitment'. In storytelling, various worthy aspirations may be in play, but what's essential is commitment of the heart. By 'heart' I mean a responsivity of feeling, experienced in one's whole being, as opposed to a calculus of the mind.

The tales that storytellers tell are ideally the ones their heart responds to.[5] Having chosen a story, you may then identify its 'emotional centre of gravity' – the *moment* in the story to which your heart most responds. This is likely to involve noticing connections between things in the story and experiences in your own life. Such engagement between story and life – think of the engagement of gears – opens the way to the storyteller making the story their own. The heart's commitment brings into play the storyteller's own desires when they tell the story. The desire I discern in myself in response to 'How Bear Lost His Tail' is the desire not to lose, throw away, that which is beautiful. Desire is the basis of utopian hope, of what Northrop Frye calls the 'apocalyptic' imagining of abundance and flourishing;[6] it provides the motivation to act to bring into being the kind of world you want. But desire need not close down possibilities as 'goals' tend to do; you can be motivated by desire without seeking a specific outcome.

The premise of this book – and the kinds of storytelling it discusses – is the 'ecological desire' for human beings to live in a healthy, sustainable, joyful relationship with a healthy, flourishing ecosystem. Different nuances of that desire motivate the telling of each pertinent story. What, though, is the consequence of that desire? I've suggested elsewhere that there's a 'gap of desire' between the ecological desire that may motivate the telling of stories and the actualization of change in the world.[7] My use of 'gap' draws upon McKee's explanation of the gap that opens between expectation and result when a story protagonist attempts to pursue their desire.[8] The ecological desire a storyteller brings to telling a story will feed into the pattern of desire within the story, where it will intersect with the desires, existing or awakening, of the listeners. If beliefs condition how we act in the world, desire – and its contrary, fear – provides the motive force.

This chapter invites input *from* ecology *into* storytelling by means of exemplar stories emergent from ecological science, and then explores the question of how the chain of desire and consequence within stories may produce desire and consequence back in the physical world. This enquiry will bring to our attention the importance of empathy in the traction of desire. It also begs philosophical questions about causation and the inevitability of consequence which have implications for the possibility of hope and change. Again the main examples are drawn from my own reflective practice.

Life cycle of an organism: 'The Beech Tree'

A beechmast fell to the floor of the wood, where a squirrel ate one of the two beechnuts but buried the other. The nut was keen to germinate, but for two consecutive springs the ground was too dry. The third spring was wetter. The nut germinated, but the little seedling was at peril from munching cows – till a bramble gave it cover to grow into a sapling. Every autumn, the young beech tree's leaves turned brown and fell to the ground. Every spring, it grew new ones, all fresh and green. It was hard work, growing, because it was dark inside the wood, but the beech kept growing till at last, when fifty years old, it reached the height of the other trees and could enjoy the sun on its leaves and spread its roots wide. Caterpillars nibbled its leaves, but the beech tree had plenty to share.

One spring, the tree had an exciting new feeling. For the first time it grew flowers and catkins. Pollen was carried on the wind, and the flowers swelled and hardened into beechmast. Every year, the tree threw its beechmast on the ground, the birds and rodents feasted and the squirrels buried some in the dead leaves. When it was 100 years old this beech stood taller than the other trees. When it was 200 its trunk became hollow, providing homes for woodpeckers, bats and beetles and keeping it strong against the wind. By the time it was 300 the beech was feeling tired and old. Fungus grew in its wood. One winter, the wind blew very hard – and the great tree crashed down, ripping its roots from the earth, and died. In the gap where it had stood, the sun shone down upon the ground. In the spring, hundreds of little beech seedlings pushed up through the dead leaves and began to grow towards the sky.[9]

It's possible to describe the life cycle of an organism in a way that conveys the facts, even the sequence of events, but doesn't feel much like a story. What commonly makes a story compelling is the forward thrust of events which is produced by the protagonists' desires. The word 'desire' has sexy connotations, and indeed the 'desires' that animate nature largely concern reproduction and the survival that's prerequisite to that. The protagonist of 'The Beech Tree' is the individual tree whose life cycle we witness. Its 'desire' is to grow and reproduce. When the tree dies, its desire both comes to an end and gains fullest expression in the opportunity given to its offspring to flourish. I give structure to this process by means of the seasonal rhythm of shedding and growing leaves, spoken as a refrain, and the seasonal dropping and squirrels' hoarding of beechmast.

One time after I told this story in the presence of a beech tree in a Cotswold wood pasture, a seven-year-old boy complained, 'You're talking about the tree as if it's *alive*!' We talked about the ways that trees differ from ourselves – can't walk or talk – and are similar: can grow and reproduce. It may have been the first time the boy had really grappled with the concept that trees are living things, not merely objects. He may also have been reacting to my anthropomorphizing the tree's purposefulness using active verbs: *wanted, was able, grew, succeeded, enjoyed, spread its roots, shook, threw down, felt tired, died*. Stephan Harding has found it educationally effective to speak about natural entities and processes '*as if* they involved interactions between sentient, feeling *persons*'. Doing so engages the imagination, integrating faculties of 'reasoning, feeling, sensing and intuition'.[10]

A tree really does have a drive to grow and reproduce. This may not be experienced in the way that humans are conscious of their desires, but there's an emerging understanding in biology that some kind of 'intelligence' operates in all living things.[11] This insight is a conceptual staging post towards 'ecological animism' that sees the living world as permeated by an 'awakeness that resides in … multiple and diverse forms of intentionality'.[12]

My conversation with the boy was on a story walk designed to interpret the wood pasture at the behest of the conservation charity that owns it. My intentions as a contractor served my client's desire to sustain the flourishing of this habitat and others like it. This desire included eliciting the public's support of their work and educating the public to appreciate such places, their wildlife and the challenges they face. The site being a wood pasture, a habitat where cattle graze, I emphasized in the story the bramble's role in protecting the seedling. I also included the peril of ring-barking by squirrels, because in this locality the younger beech trees were struggling to pass that threshold of vulnerability and the warden knew that the elderly beeches that still flourished here wouldn't live for ever.

To communicating these life-cycle challenges, I brought my own wish to evoke a sense of the tree as a purposeful being and therefore something to care about. We may thus see in the story's telling a potential convergence of the desires of employer, storyteller, tree-protagonist, listeners and living trees. The boy's questioning reaction – not merely accepting my framing – was evidence of cognitive engagement that encompassed the story, me, his family and the 200-year-old beech we were sitting beside.

Species extinction: 'The Golden Toad'

Let's now scale up from an individual organism to stories about a population of creatures, indeed a whole species. Telling stories about species that have been extinguished can be considered a form of mourning, which, as James William Gibson says in relation to devastated landscapes, 'creates a kind of consecration of what has been lost, and a prayer for its resurrection and return'.[13] The story of the golden toad (*Bufo periglenes*) is also the story of these creatures' habitat and of two scientists who studied them.

In 1963 a herpetologist, Jay Savage, heard about a kind of toad, unknown to science, that lived in the cloud forest near Monteverde in Costa Rica. The native people said it was hard to find, but that if you saw one you'd be astounded by its beauty, feel fear and find happiness. There was a story about a man who caught one of the toads but let it go because he didn't recognize happiness when he had it, and another man who also caught one and let it go because he found happiness too painful to bear.

In April 1965 Savage travelled into the cloud forest and found the toads gathered in pools to breed. The males were a brilliant golden orange; amidst the moist greenery they looked like jewels. He named the species the 'golden toad' and studied their habits. Outside the breeding season they disappeared, presumably into damp places underground. The golden toad inhabited only ten square kilometres of cloud forest, rich in biodiversity, and in 1972 the whole area was protected as the Monteverde Cloud Forest Reserve.

Moving on to April 1987: another herpetologist, Martha Crump, found the cloud forest unusually dry because exaggerated El Niño heating had lifted the cloud base above the treetops. The pools where the golden toads were trying to breed dried out, causing their eggs and tadpoles to die. In April 1988 she found the forest dry again. The golden toads and thirty of the fifty other species of frogs and toads in the reserve had disappeared; but whereas the other species had wider ranges, the golden toad lived nowhere else. Not only had these amphibians failed to breed, but something had happened to the adults. It seems that because there were fewer moist places left underground they had to crowd more closely together and this promoted the transmission of a disease.

At last, on 21 May, Crump spotted a single male golden toad waiting by a pond for a mate; the same day, another nine were spotted at another pool. In April 1989 no golden toads were seen until, on 15 May, Crump saw, in the same spot, what she believed to be the same solitary male, still waiting for a mate. The following year, there were none at all.

Savage came back to help in the search, but in 2004 the golden toad was declared extinct. It was known to science for just twenty-five years. I wonder whether Savage thought about those stories: about the man who found a golden toad and let it go because he didn't recognize happiness when he had it – and the other man, who caught a golden toad and let it go because he found happiness too painful to bear.[14]

At first glance the two herpetologists might appear to be the protagonists of this story. Both were motivated by a desire to learn about the golden toad. But, although the story's told from the point of view of these two human individuals, in story-structural terms the central protagonist is the golden toad species. The 'desire' of the species is to endure via reproduction; the story ends when the species fails in this aim and becomes extinct. I'm using the word 'desire' as a figure of speech to refer to something different from the conscious desires of human beings. It equates to the sum of the instincts of all the individuals of this species to survive and reproduce. In the analysis of neo-Darwinists like Richard Dawkins such instincts boil down entirely to the inherent propensity of genes or assemblies of genes in any organisms's DNA to replicate themselves, thereby compelling competition among the individuals that bear them.[15]

The emotional centre of gravity of 'The Golden Toad' is that solitary male. Here the 'desire' of the species to endure becomes one and the same as the sexual desire of that individual for a mate. There's often a fuzziness about extinction, in that it can be hard to be sure no surviving individuals are hiding somewhere, but the golden toad's story appears to present one of those situations of ultimate pathos where a species is down to its last individual, as with Martha the last passenger pigeon or Lonesome George the last Pinta Island tortoise (*Chelonoidis abingdonii*).

By evoking empathy for that last golden toad, the story invites empathy for the whole species he represents. The narration from the scientists' perspective also invites empathy with *them.* Towards the story's end the desires of the two scientists shift from wanting knowledge about the golden toads to desiring evidence they yet survive. Their desires have converged with the desire of the species itself. Thus the receptive listener may share in the desire of both toads and scientists – for the species to survive, for that solitary male to find a mate.

When I listened to Dalling narrate the history of the great auk (*Pinguinus impennis*) during *Shearwater*, my imagination was caught by the image of flotillas of these large flightless birds swimming their migration route across the Atlantic. Although I knew how the story would end – the last pair were killed by professional collectors on 3 June 1844 – I was left with a longing this species could somehow return from oblivion. Barring any Jurassic Park scenario of reconstituting an extinct species from its DNA, this longing equates to a gap of desire that is never closed and instead yawns infinitely open as the species vanishes into the void.

Such longing is what motivates me to tell stories like 'The Golden Toad'. A storyteller makes a choice to tell a particular story and invests their own desire in the pattern of desire within it. Although different listeners will respond in different ways, the invitation to the listener to engage with that pattern of desire implies a choice of values: for a species to endure (rather than become extinct), for a habitat to be preserved (rather than destroyed) – and hence for the conservation of *other* species and habitats that haven't yet been obliterated.

Thus we see how a story's eliciting of empathy implies ethical questions. How much does it matter that this small, rare creature became extinct? What might have been done to save it? What are the implications for the bigger picture of biodiversity? The mobilizing of empathy and ethics in 'The Golden Toad' hinges upon a high level of facticity – 'Of more than 40,000 eggs, Martha saw only twenty-nine tadpoles that lived for longer than a week' – and its corollary, acknowledgement of uncertainty: 'The zoologist Tim Flannery claims it to be the first documented species extinction caused by modern climate change.'[16] The connections between anthropogenic climate change, El Niño events and the golden toad's extinction are complex. I therefore leave space for implied questions rather than suggest a certainty of causation which I don't think is warranted.

We've seen that the telling of stories from history and science requires a simplification of the facts. To scale up yet further, from a species and its habitat to the entire biosphere, involves a yet greater degree of simplification.

Evolution and destiny in deep time: 'The Rare Event'

Sixty-five million years ago ... the high summer of the age of reptiles. The climate was lovely and warm. Flies and bees and butterflies sipped nectar and pollen from flowers filling the land with colour. There were frogs and fish in the ponds and streams. Furry little mammals hid in their burrows by day and crept out by night to feed. There were reptiles, large and small, in the land, sea and air. There were ferns and bushes and trees, and birds flitting among them. The trees were often spaced out by open country because they were browsed so heavily by dinosaurs. The dinosaurs had been around for 160 million years. They were the most sophisticated they'd ever been, and very diverse. Some of them hunted the mammals when they ventured out of their burrows.

But an asteroid ten miles wide was hurtling through space towards the earth. The creatures saw only a streak of brilliant white light as it scorched through the atmosphere. It punched a hole twenty miles deep into the coast of Mexico. The shock rang through the earth like the ringing of a bell. The dinosaurs were thrown off their feet. Tsunamis roared over the land. The debris thrown into the sky spread round the planet and blocked out the sun. For a while the sky was dark. But as the heavier debris fell back it burst into flame. The heat from the burning sky ignited the vegetation. While the fires ran wild the mammals cowered in their burrows, birds hid in the marshes, frogs and fish lurked underwater. But the dinosaurs had nowhere to flee. The smoke mixed with the dust left in the atmosphere from the impact. When the wildfires burnt out, the sky was dark as a starless night. No light or heat from the sun. In the darkness the dinosaurs stumbled amidst the burnt wreckage of trees, their hide seared by acid rain, struggling to breathe as carbon dioxide filled the air. One by one they succumbed. Birds, frogs, fish, mammals survived in their hiding places. When the mammals dared to creep out they found plenty of fresh meat to nibble.

At last the sky cleared and the sun shone. Because there was so much carbon dioxide from the impact, the wildfires and the rotting dinosaurs, the atmosphere heated like a greenhouse. So hot that the surviving vegetation shrivelled up. The pools and streams ran dry. No cloud in the sky. If any dinosaurs were still alive, these stragglers now died. No land animal weighing over twenty-five kilograms survived. The pterosaurs were gone from the skies, the plesiosaurs and mosasaurs from the seas. It was the small creatures, able to hide, that got through – the mammals, birds, frogs, fish and lizards. In the desert soil, seeds and spores waited. When the heat began to ease, and trickles of water returned, a sea of ferns appeared. Then bushes. And trees. With no large animals to browse them, the trees grew into a dense forest that covered the earth. They trapped moisture and pumped out oxygen. The forest buzzed with billions of insects. With the dinosaurs gone, other animals had the chance to grow in size. In ten million years the mammals grew from little ratty creatures into beasts as big as hippos and rhinos. Thus the age of reptiles ended and the age of mammals began.[17]

This story is based on my interpretation, in my novel *Deep Time*, of a welter of scientific interpretation of the 'K–T event', or Cretaceous mass extinction. I became acquainted with the stories of deep time on field trips as an earth sciences student, when we'd gather round an outcrop and someone would say, 'So what's the story here?' and the tutor with the relevant knowledge would then narrate a sequence of palaeoecological and/or petrological events. It was pure storytelling, conducted in the presence of the physical remains of the prehistoric environment in question, and brought the distant past to life in my imagination.

From an anthropocentric perspective the K–T mass extinction can be interpreted as a good thing because, by triggering the diversification of mammals, it facilitated the evolution of humans. It didn't seem so good to the creatures there at the time. This story shows that rapid climate change truly can happen and illustrates the impact on the biosphere of severe ecological catastrophe. The instigating impact was way more powerful than humankind's combined nuclear arsenals, but palaeoecological perspectives do teach us that the cumulative ecological impact of human activity has become a geological force.[18] Listeners may want to reflect on the similarities and differences between these two stories.

Protagonist and desire are less obvious in 'The Rare Event'. My emphasis on the dinosaurs positions them somewhat as protagonist. The 'desire', of this group as a whole, is to survive. But the entire planetary ecosystem is stressed by the bolide impact, so it's truer to say that the biosphere as a whole is the protagonist (although I've limited the story's coverage to the terrestrial ecosystem). The biosphere's *survival* is not really in question; its 'desire', rather, is to flourish, to produce an abundance of biodiversity and numbers of organisms. Here the metaphor of desire brings us up against evolutionary science's strict prohibition against any 'vitalist' notions that evolution can be driven by some preconceived goal. An organism may have instincts to survive and procreate, but ecological and biological processes of transformation are believed to arise entirely from the cumulative effects of chance and consequence.[19]

By speaking of 'desire', I'm imposing upon ecological processes a concept of narrative structure which derives from stories about humans and animals. Yet the impetus to flourish is built into ecological systems. Vegetation grows ebulliently when it's not checked by heavy grazing. Palaeobiologists expect evolutionary patterns such as 'adaptive radiations' – the emergence of many new taxa from a surviving lineage – when a large number of ecological niches have been vacated, as in the diversification of mammals after the dinosaurs' demise. Darwinian biology attributes this impetus to flourish to genetic structures chemically predisposed to reproduce themselves whenever they can, together with random variation arising from mutation and sex. The interpretation of this science has implications for human behaviour and therefore for stories and people's response to them.

For Dawkins and sociobiologist Edward O. Wilson, the genes act deterministically; there's an inevitability of consequence from the sum of factors in play. Their theories use the same 'models of self-interest [and] optimization strategies' as laissez-faire market economics,[20] implying a view of human nature which goes back to St Augustine and came to underpin capitalist doctrine via Luther and Calvin.[21] Behavioural propensities such as suspicion of outgroups, male aggressiveness, and favouring your own and your kin's interests above others' are hardwired into the human genome because they have conferred a selective advantage.[22] This behavioural determinism nourishes neoliberal discourse that there's 'no alternative' and hence, as Zipes observes, the culture industries' production of stories that socialize people to believe that the world produced by global capitalism is 'the only and best world that people could possibly create' and therefore to compete in it in such a way as perpetuates it.[23] Thus the future is predetermined by the past, ecologically destructive activities continue, and ecological science and dystopian science fiction find consensus in predicting the breakdown of civilization and ecosystemic collapse.[24]

Wilson does not relish such a prospect. He has a lively concern about the ecological disasters resulting from human beings' genetic predispositions.[25] Like Dawkins, he tries to advocate a free will by which we may transcend the dictates of our genes; but, being convinced 'the human mind is constructed in a way that locks it inside [the] fundamental constraint' that no species, including us, can possess 'a purpose beyond the imperatives created by its genetic history', he gets mired in a logical conundrum from which there's no coherent escape.[26]

The implications of this deterministic belief system extend beyond capitalism. A similar view of human nature underpins political philosophies advocating authoritarian social control and also seems evident in the pessimistic expectations of Marxist critics such as Fredric Jameson.[27] However, some more hopeful nuances of interpretation of Darwinian biology appear in the thinking of other evolutionary biologists.

Lynn Margulis emphasizes that *symbiosis* between different species generates the major innovations in evolution and underpins the functioning of ecosystems. This understanding sheds light on humankind's dependency on interspecies relationships, affirms the value of cooperation in conjunction with competition, and offers stories of how symbiotic relationships came about – including the way that sex may have evolved from a failed attempt at cannibalism.[28]

For Stephen Jay Gould, the multiple levels – higher than genes – at which causation may occur allow greater freedom of possibility, such that, if you could reset the clock, evolution would pan out in quite different ways from the same starting point.[29] This less rigidly deterministic view allows greater scope for the *emergence* of unpredictable possibilities out of the interactions of complex systems, including positive social change among humankind.[30]

The palaeontologist Simon Conway Morris argues that natural processes have a 'deep structure' that orientates biological evolution towards increasing complexity and increasing capacity for intentionality, as in stories of *convergence* such as the evolution of large brains and camera eyes in multiple zoological lineages. Although he fully accepts, as do Margulis and Gould, that evolution operates through Darwinian selection, he sees the dice as loaded in such a way as to suggest a sense of purpose built into the fabric of the universe.[31]

If we entertain the ideas that natural processes are animated by something akin to 'purpose' and also involve a degree of 'emergence' that's not predetermined,[32] then the trends in evolution towards increasing diversity, complexity, mutuality and intentionality may be aligned with desire in people – including storytellers – that such things should flourish in the world, but without our seeking to control exactly what comes about.

The gravitational dynamics of the solar system over millions of years constitute a complex system, out of which an asteroid's entry into a collision course with the earth is an emergent, stochastic event.[33] From the perspective of ecological evolution on earth, the K–T event was utterly unpredictable; it turned the story in a new direction. If a big asteroid struck the earth today, catastrophe would be equally unavoidable. But that's an extremely unlikely event. Epidemics, droughts, famines and floods are stochastic events too, but they're not unlikely and wise action can minimize their intensity and impact.[34]

However, the dominance of deterministic beliefs traps society in a destructive behaviour pattern, which can be compared to a cybernetic feedback loop in which cause and effect are indistinguishable.[35] To break out of that loop requires some catalyst external to it to induce pause, a space, in which something new can emerge. The Covid-19 pandemic has done that – has interrupted the story of the global economic system. The direction in which events will turn hangs in the balance as I write. The impulse of conservative politicians is to try to restore business as usual. The same old pattern of desire recurs. So there's a need also for a *mental* catalyst external to that pattern. Wilson's model of reality cannot permit this because it subordinates all fields of understanding to deterministic science.[36] However, Gould's concept of 'non-overlapping magisteria' allows understanding that stands outside the competence of science, as in the realm of purpose, meaning and values that traditionally falls under the purview of 'religion'.[37] Conway Morris goes further, allowing the conception that the universe is pervaded by divine desire.[38]

Karen Armstrong writes that, even today when religion has lost intellectual credibility, there's a need for 'myth' to enable us to see 'the importance of compassion', to see beyond 'solipsistic selfishness' and 'to venerate the earth as sacred'.[39] Some communicators of science, such as Carl Sagan, have sought a language with a mythic tone in which to tell science's story of the universe:

> The surface of the Earth is the shore of the cosmic ocean ... Recently, we have waded a little out to sea, enough to dampen our toes or, at most, wet our ankles. The water seems inviting. The ocean calls. Some part of our being knows this is from where we came. We long to return.[40]

Stories of deep time invite a mythic register, as Maddern employs in telling science's 'creation myth' of the evolution of the solar system and of life on earth.[41] Conceptions of a prehistoric earth unspoilt by humankind are an ecological equivalent of the widespread myths of a past 'golden age', which, though it may never have existed, can be projected on to the future to motivate present efforts to work for a better world,[42] as in visions of 'rewilding'.[43] The language that biologist Carl Safina uses to express his hopes of ecological restoration – 'And may that vision of abundance someday gather power to levitate the dead'[44] – is resonant with Native American Ghost Dance mythology that envisages wild game returning to the plains.

However, there's more to myth than tone. Science seeks a singular grand narrative where mythic storytelling is multivalent. Thus, as we encountered in Chapter 1, meetings between these two paradigms can be edgy but interesting. The enigmatic bits of folklore I mention at the beginning and end of 'The Golden Toad' open a little space for more imaginative responses by teeing up metaphors and experiences that run beyond the story's historical and scientific content. In the following story I attempt a more ambitious synthesis between scientific and mythological interpretations of fossil remains and a degraded ecosystem in Australia.

When science meets myth: 'The Coming of the Kadimakara'

Long ago the land was like a paradise – well wooded, well watered, rich with vegetation and animals. The trees were so tall they linked the earth to the sky. From clouds above the canopy, rain fell to replenish the rivers and sustain the abundance of life. In the sky lived mysterious beings called the Kadimakara. They peered down through the branches and spied all the water and vegetation. So enticing! They swarmed down the trees to the earth. They drank the water and ate the vegetation. They drank and they ate until there was almost nothing left. They even pulled down the trees and ate *them*. When they took down the trees, a great hole opened in the sky. There were no clouds now, no rain, only the scorching sun. Bushfires raged, the wind scoured away the soil, and the land became a desert. Without the trees the Kadimakara were trapped on the earth. Without food they starved and died. In the dried-out lakes where they'd sought refuge, their bodies petrified in the sun's heat.

The people of that time watched with dismay as their paradise became a desert. They had to adapt to the new conditions. It required ingenuity, simplicity and discipline, taking from the land only the bare minimum they needed. The bones of the Kadimakara jutting from the sand were the only thing left that connected the people to the memory of paradise. Those places became sacred places where the people did ceremonies to dream the Dreaming and remind them how to live the right way in the land. Thus, over the millennia, the people became the Aborigines, living in balance with their delicate environment.

After many years, countless as the stars in the sky, new people arrived from across the sea. These people didn't know the ceremonies or how to live the right way in the land. They brought beasts that swarmed like a plague through the fragile vegetation. They took the land from the Aborigines. They even tried to take away the Dreaming, the memory of paradise. But some clever men among them came upon the bones of the Kadimakara and by their scientific powers deduced these were the bones of giant mammals that had lived tens of millennia ago when the land was like a paradise, well wooded, well watered.

If the land was like that then, how had it become a desert? It had become a desert, the men learnt, because the climate had got much drier because the trees had disappeared. The trees had disappeared because there were no large animals to trample their seeds into the earth or to munch up the undergrowth to prevent it fuelling ferocious bush fires. The large animals had disappeared because they were easy to kill and the people killed them all. They killed them without restraint because the people in those days were strangers in the land. They didn't know the ceremonies or how to live the right way in the land. They weren't Aborigines. Not yet. They'd come from somewhere else across the sea.[45]

I end this story by asking, 'Who do you think the Kadimakara really were, the ones who destroyed paradise?' The 'gap' of this unanswered question is loaded but ambiguous. Not every listener will deduce the irony that the Kadimakara simultaneously represent Australia's extinct Pleistocene megafauna (giant wombats, giant kangaroos, diprotodons) *and* the Aborigines' own distant ancestors, whom palaeontology suggests drove the megafauna into extinction.[46] The mixing of mythic and scientific narrative produces, to use Hubert Zapf's words, 'cognitive ambiguities' that 'provoke interpretive engagement'.[47] By not spelling out the answer to my question, I allow listeners more scope of response. Some listeners, not personally engaged with Australia's past, have inclined towards interpreting the story more symbolically than historically – in terms, for example, of human behaviour in general: 'The Kadimakara are *us*,' said one student. 'It's what we're doing to the earth.'

Critics may raise concerns about not only the use of Aboriginal myth but also the premise that the Aborigines' ancestors exterminated the megafauna and, from the opposite perspective, the idealization of the Aborigines' adaptation to their environment. Once again the simplification required by storytelling should be acknowledged. The 'overkill hypothesis' is persuasive because the dating of megafauna extinctions in different 'naive lands' (Australia, the Americas,

Madagascar, New Zealand, New Caledonia), where native fauna did not coevolve with human beings, corresponds neatly to the different dates of human settlement.[48] The alternative hypothesis – that global climatic change at the end of the last ice age caused this spate of extinctions – may also be countered by the absence of equivalent megafauna extinctions at the ends of the preceding ice ages, when *Homo sapiens* wasn't about. However, it's improper to use this prehistory to critique the affirmation of indigenous peoples' traditional ways of life as ecologically sustainable, since to do so equates indigenous peoples of recent times with distant ancestors who were *not* indigenous. It's equally improper to critique the 'ecological native' on the grounds of recent activities of indigenous people ensuing from the corruption of traditional culture by European impact.[49] In both these arguments there's an erasure of time and the stories of change it contains. Indigenous cultures continue to be implicitly framed as 'primitive' by being equated with prehistoric Eurasian cultures of many thousands of years ago. Though they did not take Europe's path of developing ever-more powerful technology by which to dominate nature and other peoples, indigenous societies developed over those millennia in *other* ways, producing sophisticated cosmologies and artistic, spiritual and ecological practices.[50]

Aboriginal tradition reveres the ancestors as autochthonous beings of the Dreaming embodied in the land and interprets its myths as 'embodying "truth", purporting to depict what actually happened'.[51] Thus Aborigines might resist my story's deconstruction of the Ngandangara myth of the Kadimakara. The particular political sensitivity of challenging Aboriginal 'truth' (compared with, say, challenging fundamentalist Christian belief in six-day creation) makes 'The Coming of the Kadimakara' a vehicle to stimulate questions about competing truth claims. Another motive for telling it is to indicate the parallels between the ecological impact of prehistoric human colonists and of more recent European colonists, with implications for the ongoing despoilment of nature all around the world. The story is not intended for an Aboriginal audience and its use of Aboriginal myth makes no claim to cultural authenticity.

However, I have found that telling this mythic story brings through a potent energy quite different from the ethical-emotional impact of a historical story like 'The Tasmanian Genocide'. By 'energy' I mean a charged atmosphere in the space (see Chapter 6). This effect was intensified during a performance in which 'The Coming of the Kadimakara' and another Aboriginal myth were supported by a soundscape of digeridoo and tabla played by musicians Sam Bloomfield and Tom Simenauer. The fact the music was both improvised and powerful required me to surrender, to a greater degree than usual, to allowing the experience of the story to emerge out of the dialogue between spoken word, music and the audience's attention. We had an extremely receptive audience, seated in a large circle, illuminated only by a central red lantern. We'd informed them there'd be an opportunity at the end of the performance to respond. What we had in mind was a conversation, but something rather different emerged from the silence after story and music ended. An infant entered the central space to investigate the lantern and made some cute preverbal sounds, which in the quality of silence left by the performance seemed not amusing but weighted with startling significance. Adult members of the audience then joined in and collectively improvised an eerie soundscape with ever-shifting nuances of feeling. When this finally ended, there was no need for words.

In terms of the fusion of the inward and outward, this event was one of the most authentic experiences of storytelling I've ever had. It had a taste of a quality that Snyder calls 'wildness', by which he means 'the essential nature of nature. As reflected in consciousness, it can be seen as a kind of open awareness – full of imagination but also the source of alert survival intelligence'. To bring this quality to our use of language, he argues, 'can lead us back to unmediated direct experience'. Creativity 'is born of being deeply immersed in what is – and then seeing the overlooked connections, tensions, resonances, shadows, reversals, retellings. What comes forth is "new".'[52] His argument connects the capacity to be conscious in language-mediated experiences and the capacity to function consciously in the physical world.

Storytelling already conflates the use of language with the physicality of being together in a place. If a storyteller desires to facilitate the emergence of something 'new', it follows from Snyder's argument that they should cultivate 'wildness' in their practice. Not only should the story provide space for the listener's response, as we saw in Chapter 2, but the manner of telling should be open to the unexpected and emergent. That's a reason to favour extempore (unscripted) telling, and to resist the impulse to rehearse and choreograph to such a degree as to predetermine a particular quality of performance – such as one demonstrating your professionalism – and hence a particular kind of audience response. Storytellers can also cultivate the flexibility and openness of 'wildness' through willingness to change their plans of which stories they'll tell. The building of a repertoire of stories you can tell without rehearsal gives you freedom to select which story feels most apposite to the moment. Furthermore, you can deliberately give yourself space in your stories to improvise descriptive detail; or to invite listeners to contribute details as you go along;[53] or to add commentary that steps outside the story, as I observed Haggarty do to customize a story to the predilections of listeners at an ecospiritual festival and engage them in dialogue. Such strategies require a spaciousness of time, rather than tight cramming of material inside a strict time envelope. The step beyond all this is to improvise stories from scratch, or from the starting point of audience suggestions. Add to that the use of improvised movement and we move beyond storytelling into pure impro such as 'fooling' or 'clowning'.

This idea of 'wildness', that can catalyse something 'new', speaks to the need, noted above, to break the cycle of destructive behaviour. The Buddhist influence in Snyder's thinking is evident here. According to the principle of karma, each thing that happens is the result of previous actions. But Buddhism also emphasizes intention. Because what happens in the future is the result of present action, new karma can be created. 'We *can* change,' says Sogyal Rinpoche. 'The future is in our hands, and in the hands of our heart.'[54] There are moments – potentially any or every moment – when, if you're sufficiently mindful, you can make a choice that's not predetermined by what has gone before. Our perception of the chain of cause and consequence can be eased, suggests Gersie, by the way that different stories shed different kinds of light on a situation.[55] Stories contain such moments of choice – 'turning points' when a character chooses a particular action, which then turns in a new direction the chain of causation the story presents.[56]

In considering the next story, let's be alert to such moments of choice – and their relationship with the dynamics of desire and empathy operating both within the story and in the storyteller's and listeners' experience of it. The story belongs to a genre of ecological stories which we met snatches of in 'The Golden Toad': biographical stories of individuals' interaction with the natural world in a particular place and time. It's also a story about an individual animal.

When animal becomes person: 'The Currumpaw Wolf'

In the Currumpaw Valley in New Mexico, in the 1890s, there lived a notorious wolf the ranchers called 'Lobo'. He led a pack of five other wolves, including his beautiful mate, Blanca. They preyed upon cattle, since little other game remained, and so the ranchers wanted them killed. Exceptionally intelligent, Lobo would protect his pack by preventing them eating poisoned carcasses. When a Texan ranger called Tannerey sought to win the $1000 on Lobo's head, Lobo and his pack led Tannerey's wolfhounds into gullies where they got scattered and the wolves then turned and killed them one by one.

The famed wolf hunter Ernest Thompson Seton was called in. Seton had no better luck with poison baits. So he started using wolf traps. He tried to catch Lobo by positioning traps in an H-shaped pattern to play on his evident habit of turning immediately to one side when he detected something suspicious ahead. But Lobo carefully reversed out of the pattern of traps and flicked stones to spring them. Then Seton noticed from the tracks that one of the pack sometimes ran ahead of Lobo. 'That's Blanca,' said the cowboy working with Seton. 'Lobo would never tolerate one of the other males taking the lead.' This gave Seton an idea. He set some obvious traps around a heifer carcass, but deposited the heifer's head to one side, surrounded by six well-concealed traps. In his way he caught Blanca. When he cornered her, she let out a howl, and from far away came Lobo's deep bass reply. So as not to damage her lovely white hide with a bullet, they throttled her with two lassos pulled on horseback from opposite sides. The whole way transporting her carcass to the ranch, they heard Lobo's heartbroken wailing.

That night, Lobo killed the watchdog and raced recklessly round the ranch in search of Blanca. The following day, Seton set 130 traps confected with the odour of Blanca's carcass and prints from one of her paws. In the morning they found Lobo, all four legs caught in traps. He roared with rage and struggled to break free, then sank down exhausted. For the first time, as Seton looked into the wolf's fierce yellow eyes, he felt pity. Instead of killing him, he staked him out near the ranch and offered him meat and water. Lobo just stared out to the open plains. At sunset he was still staring like that. In the morning he was dead. Seton was so moved by this experience that he never killed another wolf. He became a seminal figure in the wilderness preservation movement and the Boy Scouts of America.[57]

To affirm the facticity of this story, I mention the date of Lobo's death – 31 January 1894 – and that his pelt may be seen in the Seton Memorial Library at the Philmont Scout Ranch in New Mexico. My telling is adapted, without factual innovation, from Seton's own account, in which he declares there to be 'no deviation from the truth.'[58]

A conventional anthropocentric attitude would sympathize with ranchers who are losing livestock to wild predators. However, the story's emotional impact is quite the reverse. 'I have been bitterly denounced,' writes Seton, 'first, for killing Lobo; second, and chiefly, for telling of it, to the distress of many tender hearts.' To which complaints he responds, 'In what frame of mind are my hearers left with regard to the animal? Are their sympathies quickened toward the man who killed him, or toward the noble creature who … died as he had lived – dignified, fearless, and steadfast?'[59]

If we consider Seton as the protagonist, his motivation is to destroy Lobo and his pack. If we take Lobo to be the protagonist, his desire is to protect his pack, including Blanca, as they seek food in order to live. There's a direct conflict between these two desires. Lobo's desire is terminated by his defeat, but Seton's desire changes in the very moments of its fulfilment – to converge with the wolves' desire to live – so that thereafter he works to preserve wild animals instead of destroying them.

Whereas Seton narrates the story in first person, my retelling in third person, though still following Seton's point of view, has a distancing effect that draws Lobo more deeply into the story's emotional centre. In presenting an individual wolf as a conscious, desiring being, this story brings us full circle to the tales about wolves mentioned in Chapter 1; only now it's a *true* story about a *real* wolf, the pattern of empathy is reversed and the listener will likely grieve not rejoice when the wolf meets his end.

It's important in retelling the story not to demonize Seton. I narrate his persecution of Lobo in a neutral tone that leaves space for him to be respected as someone doing his job expertly in service to the ranchers' needs, and thus for the listener to empathize with his change of heart. That Seton truly underwent a change of heart is clear from his own testimony: 'Ever since Lobo, my sincerest wish has been to impress upon people that each of our native wild creatures is itself a precious heritage that we have no right to destroy or put beyond the reach of our children.'[60] That change of heart, of one man, had very significant consequences in the United States. It's an example of a shift of consciousness, a spontaneous choice, in which the course of events changes direction. Let's investigate now the space in the story in which we witness that shift happen in Seton, and the space for emergent feeling that it offers the listener.

The Russian Formalists use the term 'fabula' to distinguish the events in a story – 'what happens' – from 'sjuzet', the way the story's narrated.[61] In the fabula of 'The Currumpaw Wolf', there's no sign of any space for change opening in Seton until the scene in which he finds Lobo caught in the traps. The combination of helplessness, fierce desire and dignity on Lobo's part elicits empathy from Seton. Having sought Lobo's death, he doesn't kill him; it's as if he now desires Lobo to live. This empathy is further evident when, having staked out Lobo, Seton removes the cords from his muzzle and legs and gives him food and water. At the end of my telling I make explicit the transformational effect of this experience by quoting his own words and summing up his ensuing career.

In the sjuzet (of my retelling) the structure of space is wider-ranging. The listener may intuit a mythopoeic, even psychological, logic that, once the beloved Blanca has been killed, it's inevitable that Lobo too will die; he appears to have been so affected by Blanca's demise that he's thrown his usual caution to the wind. There's a space of uncertainty that maybe, in the end, he died of a broken heart rather than the trauma of getting trapped. His gazing out at the open plains, while staked out, implies his desire to be free; suggests another world in which he and Blanca could run free without persecution. It may invite a longing among us humans that we too could run wild and free instead of being trapped in circumscribed lives. In all of this is an *implication* that Lobo is a fully conscious being and thus his desires are true conscious desires, emotionally felt, like a human's. It's implied too in the intelligence with which he dealt with the baits and traps, especially the time he gathered up a sequence of baits into a pile and defecated on them. Furthermore, a space of moral questioning opens from the tension between the wolves' predation upon livestock and the campaign to exterminate them. The matter-of-fact restraint with which I describe the cruel methodology of trapping and killing offers the listener some space to respond as they will, in both their feelings and their judgements.

The flow of time and desire in stories means that their structuring of space is not static, as with a sculpture, but dynamic. A closer analogy may be made with a group of people free-dancing: the arrangement of their bodies in any one moment defines the shape of the space between them, but this space then opens the possibilities for how the dancers will change the arrangement of their bodies as time unfolds, which in turn changes the space; and desire operates in the dancers' impulses of how to move, including the extent to which they choose to come closer to others or to harmonize with others' movements.[62] In storytelling there's a similar dialogic cycle, but the interplay of *desire* applies not so much in people's conduct in the storytelling situation as in mobilizing thoughts and feelings with potential to affect conduct in other situations.

Paradoxically, while a story presents a chain of cause and effect, propelled by desire, it may contain moments in which the inevitability of consequence is resisted, a choice is made and something new happens. Working with stories, Gersie says, builds people's awareness of both the predictable and the unexpected.[63] Tolkien coined the word 'eucatastrophe' to refer to the unexpected turn of events which brings a joyous end to many fairy tales.[64] Although he had a realistic pessimism about the trajectory of history, as we too may have in the face of ecological crisis, he believed it essential to retain hope, and never to despair, precisely because the future is unknown and not predetermined.[65] Eucatastrophe challenges the inevitability of cause and effect: the miraculous deliverance, deus ex machina, may not realistically follow from the trend of events and yet may ring true mythopoetically and inspire hope in darkest times. In life, things do sometimes happen out of the blue; people experience synchronicity. We may construct stories to share these experiences, to try to make sense of them. Stories, in turn, can make us receptive to such novelties of possibility. Their power to do so lies not in the onward march of the plot, but in the gaps where there's a silence, an image, a feeling. In the 'hushedness' of listening to a story, says Gersie, we collectively 'make space for another life-experience'.[66]

Dystopia or utopia: 'The Migrant Maid'

The omnipresence of dystopian visions of the future in contemporary science fiction represents a closing down of possibility.[67] The genuinely utopian impulse in science fiction is most provocative of cognition when there's a refusal of closure – 'an openness to the unfinished potential of historical becoming', as Phillip E. Wegner puts it.[68] Incomplete closure is implied in everything I've said about allowing space for the listener's agency, but the extent of *resolution* of a story's tensions and questions is especially important. If a story fully resolves, its ending points back within the pattern of the narrative and you're left feeling that the story is over and can now be left behind. If this resolution reaffirms the status quo ante, the story's effect may well be politically conservative, as in many fairy tales about princes and princesses and the gamut of 'successful' stories marshalled by Booker.[69] When a story doesn't fully resolve, the audience are entrusted with the task of 'completing' it – through reflecting upon the possibilities and perhaps taking action in the real world.

The invitation to complete the story can sometimes take the form of an explicit question or challenge. At the end of Fire Springs' epic *Robin of the Wildwood*, in which Robin Hood is interpreted as guardian of the woods, Robin dies and the burden of responsibility is offered to the audience with the question, 'Who will protect the wildwood now?' More elaborately, Maddern's one-man show *What the Bees Know* interweaves stories (and songs) with commentary raising a range of practical questions about specific aspects of ecological crisis, including the decline in pollinating bees.

Stories like 'The Tasmanian Genocide' and 'The Golden Toad' may appear to have definitive closure, since they end with extinction, but emotionally and morally there's a refusal of closure. The empathetic desire that's been elicited – for the people or creatures in question to flourish – can never be fulfilled. Thus the end of such stories implicitly points back into the present world, where the energy of that desire can transfer to comparable situations where action needs to be taken.[70] This kind of effect parallels the rationale for 'critical dystopias' in science fiction, that is, dystopian stories written with a utopian motivation.[71] In Paolo Bacigalupi's fiction, for example, the structures of the dystopian society that prevent characters enacting their impulses to make a better world may prompt us to consider what freedom we yet have in our present society to act for the good.[72]

Bacigalupi depicts futures within which hope is no longer possible.[73] This chapter's final exemplar story explicitly withholds resolution of the plot, allowing but not guaranteeing the possibility of hope *within* a dystopian setting not greatly different from conditions that already exist. Its 'ecological' input comes from the imbrication of ecology and economics. It extrapolates possible consequences of Britain's leaving the European Union to imagine a future in which the urban environment has become more alienating, socioeconomic inequality more exaggerated, and deregulated speculation in derivatives has accelerated the liquidation of natural resources. I've adapted the traditional ballad of 'King Cophetua and the Beggar Maid'[74] to present Cophetua as superwealthy business mogul John W. Trumpet and the beggar maid Zenelophon as an 'illegal immigrant' who's fled from war in the Middle East.

John spotted her begging while he was watching people in the streets through his telescope from the top of Trumpet Tower in the City of London. Taken by her beauty, he took her under his wing. Though she wouldn't sleep with him, he installed her in a penthouse, showered her with luxuries, dined her in exclusive eateries. From his talk about his businesses, she realized how countless people around the world were held in bondage by debt to men like him. For him that was just business. He didn't understand that he too wasn't free. But he did perceive that Zenelophon's beauty, of body and soul, shone like a beacon amidst the leaden opulence of his world – *and yet was not his*. He laid plans to seduce her in a remote cottage of his in Wales and so obtain a return on his investment. Though entranced by the woods around the cottage – like a paradise, it seemed to her – she still wouldn't yield to him; refused even to marry him.

'Still you would have bought me. Still you would not love me.' She wept for the millions in poverty whose lives were as miserable as hers had been. 'How can you love me if you don't love them?'

Back in London, John vented his frustration by showering money upon the homeless. Zenelophon asked him, 'What really changes when you give charity?' She became his business counsellor, questioned the purposes of his transactions, boggled when she understood how his companies' financial products transferred wealth to the rich at the cost of the poor and the earth. When he caught her giving away her clothes to vagrants, she at last made him see them as people, each a precious soul like her. At last he comprehended the impact of the trade in repackaged debt upon the world. Governments were toothless to end that. But what if one big corporate player, him, John W. Trumpet, were to write off all the debt he controlled? What chain reaction might ensue through the world's economy? It would suck him dry. He'd have nothing left except his industries that produced things that people actually needed. Would this woman love him because he'd done that? Or would he do it because he loved her and she'd made him love the world?[75]

'The Migrant Maid' has a didactic intention to inform people about the impact of the trade in derivatives, to raise ethical questions about this and to suggest the scale of change needed.[76] Yet the story retains something of the fairy-tale simplicity of the ballad. It doesn't attempt a realistic narrative of change as in a Robinson novel. It offers, rather, a symbolic intention towards a real-world problem of enormous complexity. The most important space in its structure of space is the open ending constructed by the questions Trumpet asks himself. By refusing closure, leaving it to the audience to imagine what might ensue, the story leaves them with whatever constellation of desire and hope it inspires in them.

The thrust of desire and the womb of wisdom

Central to the pattern of desire in 'The Migrant Maid' is Trumpet's amorous desire for Zenelophon and her ambiguous feelings towards him. More directly than 'Sunbath', this story aligns erotic desire with the desire for a greener world. One reason for using the word 'desire' in my analysis of stories, as opposed to 'want' or 'motive', is that its erotic connotation bespeaks the fundamental importance of sexual energies in driving much of human activity, just as they underpin so much of biology.

With reference to Freud, Brooks eroticizes the 'thrust' of desire in narrative as involving 'arousal' into a 'condition of tumescence', in which the complications of the plot restrain the narrative tension 'on the verge of premature discharge', postponing resolution 'to ensure that the ultimate pleasurable discharge will be more complete'.[77] Cupitt similarly writes of narrative having 'steady rhythm' and 'a climactic discharge'.[78] In this model, which matches the 'archplot' discussed in Chapter 2, the climactic end of the story is the *goal* of desire; it's this that elicits arousal and necessitates an 'arabesque' of twists and turns. The story, like the protagonist, is driven by this goal. In this sense, causation within the story works backwards in time. The story's resolution, the discharge of desire, equates to death, explains Brooks, the point at which the meaning of one's life is determined.[79] This narrative model closes down possibilities; the predefined end determines what precedes it. Similarly, in life, our freedom of action can be trapped between the forward march of physical causation and the backward causation from a virtual future defined by the mind's formulation of goals.[80]

Brooks develops his Freudian interpretation of narrative to suggest that when a story grants space for the discovery of meaning, it can facilitate personal transformation through a process analogous to transference in psychoanalysis. A patient's narration of problematic past experiences in the analyst's attentive presence opens up a psychological space that's accessible to the analyst's interpretation and thereby allows 'a transference of past desire into terms that can be realized and made to render real rewards'. Brooks suggests that a story can provide an analogous space in which there can be dialogic transactions between the 'investments of desire' of narrator and audience.[81] In storytelling, this dynamic may be collective but involves each individual's psyche. If we posit that the 'problematic past' relates to ecology, the emergent 'meaning' and 'rewards' may involve healthier inhabitation of the ecosystem. As Roszak says: 'What the Earth requires will have to make itself felt within us as if it were our own most private desire.'[82]

If, instead of allowing meaning to emerge dialogically, the storyteller seeks to impose their own desire upon the listener, the erotic analogy is to 'seduction', which ultimately, Brooks notes, can amount to 'violation of the listener'.[83] A comparison may be made to Tolkien's distinction between a story with 'applicability', on one hand, and 'allegory', a story whose meaning is fixed: 'the one resides in the freedom of the reader, and the other in the purposed domination of the author'.[84] This perspective should be borne in mind when the urgency of ecological crisis seems to demand storytelling that is forcefully persuasive of change.

The ambition of heroic desire may be considered in terms not only of thrusting phallus but also of the aggrandizing and appropriating impulses of ego.[85] According to Joel Kovel, the hegemony of ecologically destructive consumer capitalism represents the 'enshrinement' of egocentrism.[86] Inflated ego is brazen in photographs of big-game hunters standing arrogantly over the carcasses they've shot. If the hero finds wisdom, however, the ego may be tamed, as in Seton's or Trumpet's epiphany.

How else can a story gain traction without the drive of desire towards goal? Le Guin critiques the thrusting phallic plot as inherently masculine and suggests an alternative conception of narrative 'as carrier bag/belly/box/house/medicine bundle', a totality that 'cannot be characterized either as conflict or as harmony, since its purpose is neither resolution nor stasis but continuing process'.[87] The symbols she lists are all containers, suggestive of a womb containing a space from which something new may emerge. By obviating the need for 'resolution', freeing the story from bondage to the goal – whether protagonist's or storyteller's – this narrative paradigm encourages the emergent responsiveness, from space within and beyond the story, that we've been exploring. In the case of storytelling, a space of tension with the audience can be held through the strength of rapport without the need for relentless forward movement. To play with the Freudian analogies, the pleasure may continue without discharge; perhaps death is not the end: perhaps the end of the story is only the beginning of what we'll get from it.

If I valorize here the womb of wisdom, it's not to disparage the thrust of desire. To emphasize the need to cultivate 'yin', says Le Guin, using the Taoist terms, is not to seek the dominance of yin over yang – yin doesn't seek dominance – but rather to seek balance in a civilization that's 'so intensely yang'.[88] Without desire, stories would soon lose their juiciness. In practice the yin and the yang, the phallus and the womb, work together. You can see it in 'The Beech': the young tree thrusts towards the sky, the story's ending sees it fall, withered and spent, but as the tree gains age its hollowing timber provides spaces in which other creatures can live, and its falling opens a space in the wood in which new seedlings can eagerly grow from the beechnuts buried in the earth.

4

Composting snakes and dragons: Ecological enchantment of local landscapes

Local folktales may be considered part of a place's human ecology inasmuch as they help mediate a 'culture of habitat', an embedded connectivity between a human community and its environment, including local wildlife. Forces of change in the modern world that fragment and destroy local folk traditions are linked to ones that damage local ecology.[1] In much of England the web of local community and ecology has unravelled under the cumulative impact of enclosure, industrial revolution and globalization; and the culturally homogenizing effects of Reformation, formal schooling and mass media have erased local folklife, including knowledge of folktales.[2]

In Gloucestershire this process has involved the decline of long-established wool, dairy, cider and mining industries; the ending of rights to graze livestock on once common land; the expansion of urban areas; the conversion of pasture to industrialized arable cropland; and an influx of wealthy commuters into cottages once inhabited by shepherds, weavers and milkmaids.[3] The ecological consequence is dramatic loss of biodiversity and wildlife habitat.[4] In *Cider with Rosie*, his memoir of growing up near Stroud in the early twentieth century, Laurie Lee witnesses the ending of a local culture whose connectivity with the land had continuity deep into the past. Alan Sutton, meanwhile, testifies to the vanishing of Cotswold dialect that retained archaic features from Saxon times.[5]

With the dialect have gone the stories. In many places around the world, it was the realization that folktales were disappearing from common memory that motivated folklorists to record them before they were lost for ever. In England the early collecting of tales was patchy; more diligently undertaken in some counties than others.[6] English storytellers have readily felt drawn to the cornucopia of imaginative, sometimes very elaborate tales harvested in the neighbouring Celtic countries. In a 2002 lecture, Lupton enjoined that England's 'scattered and fragmented' legendarium of folktales should 'be re-assembled and retold', since 'it is the dreaming of these particular landscapes'.[7] In retrospect, his lecture could be a manifesto for the History Press series of Folk Tales books that developed from David Phelps's 2009 collection of his retellings of Herefordshire folktales.[8] The series now covers most counties in the British Isles and has galvanized English storytellers to tell the local tales of their home area.

Although compilation of Gloucestershire folklore began in the nineteenth century,[9] the job wasn't done systematically until Roy Palmer's *The Folklore of Gloucestershire* (1994), so the body of folktales perpetuated in this county was rather fragmentary; many extant tales were mere sketchy snippets. My commission to retell thirty tales in the Gloucestershire volume of the Folk Tales series therefore presented both a challenge and an opportunity. Follow-up volumes of *Gloucestershire Ghost Tales* and *Gloucestershire Folk Tales for Children* (both with Kirsty Hartsiotis) entailed the resurrection of a further forty local tales.

I wanted the retold stories to be shapely enough to engage listeners when performed extempore, and also to have, where possible, an ecobardic applicability to our time. Given the patchy source material, these aims required a creative approach quite different from a folklorist's presentation of tales as recorded from 'the folk'. I approached the work as a kind of 'folklore restoration', analogous to ecological restoration – and arguably part of ecological restoration if folklore be considered part of local human ecology – but with the aim that 'restoration' should imply not a static condition but a dynamic one in which both ecology and stories will keep changing.[10] When we treat stories as part of an 'evolving tradition', then tradition can become 'emancipatory', as Mike Wilson suggests, true to the subversive potential of folk culture.[11]

My ecobardic intention involved two main strategies. First, I wanted to 'enchant' landscapes and townscapes by emphasizing the tales' rootedness in place. Second, I sought to amplify any emergent green themes.

Deborah Lilley's description of land as a 'palimpsest' of accumulated physical traces of change[12] may be compared to a landscape's accumulation, via the collective memory of its inhabitants, of stories arising at different points in time.[13] The association of a tale with a place can strengthen over time, as people repeatedly tell the story, and so deepen the place's 'aura' of significance. Thus the inscribing, or weaving, of a shared mythscape of stories across the land serves to root the human community in the land.

In previously exploring mythological landscapes in Ireland, Greece and Brittany, I had found, like Lupton, that the meeting of my knowledge of myths and legends with my direct experience of the places where these stories are set produced a heightened – 'enchanted' – perception of both the places and the stories.[14] In retelling Gloucestershire's folktales I therefore wanted to evoke the genius loci of the places where they're set and thereby invite a deepened appreciation of these places. 'To preserve our places and to be at home in them,' says Wendell Berry, 'it is necessary to fill them with imagination. To imagine as well as see what is in them.'[15]

But tales may change as they're passed from person to person and, in literate societies, move back and forth between written and oral traditions.[16] In the course of time new tales emerge, whether from oral or literary origins, and enter tradition. When storytellers are able to travel, meet visitors or read, tales are not inextricably tied to place: both constituent motifs and whole tales may be translocated. The metaphor of 'composting' perhaps fits better than 'palimpsest' the organic reality of such story traditions, which travel and evolve across both time and geography.[17] In the compost pile of tradition, stories may decompose through the erosion of memory or through incomplete transmission; fragments of them may get mixed with motifs from other stories, or other versions of the same story, and then recycled to nourish the emergence of new stories, or new versions of the same story, to speak to new audiences in new ways.

There's a tension here I wanted to hold: between respecting the rootedness of particular tales in particular places, on one hand, and working creatively with the tales to ensure they were engaging and that the values they expressed satisfied an 'ecosophy' desiring the flourishing of nature and people.[18]

When you choose a story to tell, you need to be aware what beliefs it implies. It's quite possible to tell a story that conveys ideas you wouldn't endorse if you stopped and worked out what they were. Today the misogyny in some folktales will readily be noted, but what about the glorification of violence, which remains normative in popular fiction, film and games? If, when you've realized you don't agree with the beliefs a story expresses, you have a choice to make. You can discard the story and choose another. You can tell the story as it comes and then make it an object of critical scrutiny in conversation with your listeners. Or you can change the story.

The 'green themes' I found in the Gloucestershire legendarium included ones of social justice. Tales I selected included, for example, the workhouse misery of a man driven there by the fluctuations of an industrial economy; a lawyer's exploitation of the gullible and evasion of tithes; men's exploitation and mistreatment of women; the plight of the poor and needy when the monasteries were dissolved. Themes in other tales convey how the flourishing of people is inseparable from ecology: the effects of enclosure on the rural poor; the need to care for the poor in times of hardship; the suffering of social outsiders and captive animals. Though the circumstances in each case are historical, all these themes have contemporary resonance. Other tales speak more mythopoetically: iterations of the fairies' revenge upon those who disrespect them; and transformation into an owl, in one tale, and a nightmare of ecological devastation, in another, both resulting from lack of compassion for the needy. There's also an origin myth of how the Avon Gauge was excavated by giants; as well as a collage of reports of mystery beasts in the Forest of Dean, which I built into a cryptozoological story of Britain's lost megafauna.[19]

This chapter presents three case studies of my methods of researching and recrafting Gloucestershire folktales for the purposes of both storytelling and the books. I examine the 'composted' narrative tradition that bears upon the tales in question and explain how that tradition together with historical and field research informed my shaping of the stories. The chapter explores also the salience of enchantment in the dynamics between local tales and landscape. Comparisons are made with indigenous Kanak storytelling in New Caledonia, an archipelago in the South Pacific which I've twice visited, where enchantment yields to a mythic perspective of the landscape as inhabited by spirits.

Dragon-slaying: 'The Deerhurst Dragon'

Deerhurst is a village on the bank of the river Severn near Tewkesbury. The legend of its dragon was recorded in 1712 by Sir Robert Atkyns:

> There goes a story, that a serpent of prodigious bigness was a great grievance to all the country about Deerhurst, by poisoning the inhabitants, and killing their cattle. The inhabitants petitioned the king, and a proclamation was issued out, that whosoever should kill the serpent, should enjoy an estate on Walton hill in the parish, which then belonged to the crown. One John Smith, a labourer, undertook it, and succeeded; for finding the serpent lying in the sun, with his scales ruffled up, he struck between the scales with his axe, and struck off his head.[20]

In 1779 Samuel Rudder added that Smith baited the dragon with milk and that the Smith family remained in possession of the estate – and the axe.[21] In 1890 George Butterworth recorded that people in Deerhurst still spoke 'with bated breath of "the flying addard"'.[22] Palmer was told of a 'Dragon Tump' on land still owned by Smiths, but couldn't locate this hillock on the ground.[23] The tale may have arisen to beef up the Smiths' title to their land by purporting to explain the sculpted 'beast heads' adorning Deerhurst Church: two on the chancel arch, two on the west porch arch and three on the exterior.[24]

As a local variant of AT tale type 300, 'The Dragon Slayer', this legend belongs to a widespread tradition composted over many centuries. The broader field of dragon lore also contains other kinds of stories. As a glorification of the snake, known to renew its skin, the dragon symbolizes the immortal energy of being; and in China dragons are sacred and generally benevolent.[25] In the West, though, heroes are keen to slay them. Many hundreds of versions of AT 300 are known throughout Europe and beyond; more than 600 versions from Ireland alone.[26] Kurt Ranke's reconstruction of its type plot – a full-blown wonder tale independent of any specific locality – contains five motifs that recur in the simple Deerhurst legend: the hero comes from a humble background; the dragon is a menace to the country; the king offers a reward of land to whoever slays it; the hero has some practical means to even the odds; the dragon gets beheaded.[27]

The ancestry of 'The Dragon Slayer' goes back to Babylon's creation epic, *Enuma Elish*, which narrates the slaying of Tiamat, symbol of primeval chaos, by her son Marduk to create the world from her body.[28] In India, Indra slew the dragon Vritra to release the cosmic waters and so fructify the earth.[29] Krishna defeated the serpent king Kaliya, whose venom had made the river water undrinkable and whose fire had incinerated the trees; but Krishna then breaks the pattern by pardoning Kaliya and dispatching him and his wild energy to the ocean.[30] Via the destruction of dragon-like serpents in wild places by the likes of Zeus, Apollo, Perseus and Heracles in Greek mythology, the dragon became identified in Christian mythology with ultimate evil, Satan, the serpent in Eden who catalysed the Fall, whose defeat as a dragon in the Apocalypse will usher in the reign of peace.[31] This symbolism is in play in St George's killing of a dragon to rescue a princess and convert her people to the faith, a story definitively coopted into English tradition in Richard Johnson's *The Seven Champions of Christendom*. Two other major inputs into the composting of dragon-slayer narratives in England are the dragon-slayings in the Icelandic *Saga of the Völsungs* and the Anglo-Saxon epic *Beowulf*, episodes Tolkien has made familiar to modern audiences by recycling them in his fiction.[32] Between them the exploits of St George, Sigurd and Beowulf include many of the Deerhurst motifs: the dragon can fly; is ravaging the land; is poisonous; the hero is motivated by the prospect of material gain; employs a stratagem to strike the dragon where it's vulnerable; and beheads it.

From this story tradition have issued numerous English local legends. Folk legends are stories, usually localized in place, whose claims to facticity occupy a grey area between history and folk fiction.[33] A legend is commonly believed to be factual when first current – including legends about dragons, long believed to be real animals[34] – but may become perceived as fictional with the passing of time and its embellishment by storytellers. Jennifer Westwood and Jacqueline Simpson report that English dragon-slayer legends typically point out the location of the drama, the survival of the hero's weapon, some artwork that memorializes the event – all present in the Deerhurst tale – and the hero's tomb.[35] The dragon-slayer is usually either a member of a local landowning family, whose claim to the land is derived from this heroic feat, or a man of humble background, who's rewarded with money, not land, or else dies (like Beowulf) with the dragon. The Deerhurst legend combines these two scenarios: the working-class hero becomes a landowner. Among the gamut of other English dragon-slayer legends occur also the motifs of the dragon preying on livestock, its den being in or beside a hill, and the use of milk as decoy.[36]

The composting of 'The Deerhurst Dragon' is complicated by a 1904 account of a sea monster that once swam up the Severn and preyed on livestock and youngsters at Coombe Hill, a mile south of Walton Hill, until 'Tom Smith' won its trust with food, killed it with an axe and was rewarded with a limitless supply of beer.[37] This story is so similar to the Deerhurst legend that I suspect it derives from it. William Vizard's verse retelling of the legend (1926) explicitly likens John Smith to St George and Hercules.[38] Dinah Starkey retells the story for children in comedic vein, introducing two unsuccessful candidates and stratagems before 'Charlie Blyth' comes up with the ruse of using milk.[39] Peter Cripps's jocular summary on the Glosfolk website renames the hero 'George Smith', thereby claiming St George for Gloucestershire.[40] And in a 1974 folk song by Gwilym Davies, the heroism of dragon-slaying becomes an object of blatant parody:

There was once a serpent in Gloucestershire did dwell,
Who swallowed up sheep and people as well.
He ate up their cattle, he ate up their goats
And occasionally fed on small weasels and stoats.
Singing fol de rol dair-oh, fol de rol day
Remember the dragon that lived Deerhurst way.[41]

In *Farmer Giles of Ham*, Tolkien parodies the whole dragon-slayer tradition, both epic and folk, to mock the values it has conventionally implied. His story shares with the Deerhurst tale the motif of the king passing the buck to the local community to deal with the dragon, which Tolkien exploits to the revolutionary extent that his rustic protagonist defies the King's authority. Crucially, Tolkien elicits sympathy for the dragon as a conscious being, who doesn't in the end get slain; there's perhaps an echo of the Somerset legend of St Carantoc taming a troublesome dragon.[42] Hartsiotis has reworked the Coombe Hill legend in a similar way: emphasizing this part of Gloucestershire's proclivity to flooding, and identifying the monster as a plesiosaur, she has Tom Smith spare the trusting creature and enjoy instead a wild ride downriver astride her before sending her home to the sea.[43]

Beyond this 'taming' move, the story pattern of AT 300 is left behind: modern fantasy contains many dragon stories in which various forms of positive relationship between humans and dragons are imagined. Stories like these no doubt predispose audiences to view dragons and real dangerous animals more sympathetically. A positive development, certainly, but such sentiments can rapidly evaporate when people are confronted with any prospect of threat from real predators, as recent hysteria in Britain about baby-killing foxes illustrates.[44] Thus AT 300 retains currency. In the films *Anaconda* (1997) and *Anacondas* (2004), characters demonstrate their growth as heroes by destroying the giant snakes. We're not expected to feel sympathy for these thinly demythologized dragons. The invitation is to share, as a spectacle, the exhilaration of slaying them.

Tradition and revision

The power of such a long-running story tradition lies in the attitudinal momentum it carries, causing people to continue to think about certain things in received patterns. Though the stories evolve, there's a converse impulse that preserves the continuity of tradition and mediates that which is of value from the past, including symbols, aesthetics, beliefs and the wisdom learnt from past experience which should not be forgotten if we're not to repeat the mistakes of our forebears. In this way, traditional stories help sustain the integrity of society and its human ecology.[45] But with the passage of time this freight from the past may come into conflict with society's changing needs and ethics. Thus choices have to be made. Whatever's no longer useful can be let go. Useful innovations can be added. Thus, if storytellers are mindful of their stories' content, tradition can evolve. Parody is one response to outdated values in a story, but it's a negative one that may weaken the tradition. More constructive is to rework the stories in ways that recycle the compost of tradition to cultivate new configurations of values. Feminist revision of fairy tales is a familiar example.[46]

From an ecocritical perspective, 'The Deerhurst Dragon' is a story about the extermination of megafauna to allow settlement by humans and their livestock. Like most dragon-slayer tales, it implicitly endorses the virtue of the warrior hero and the killing of predators that threaten the community. In a pioneering society such values may be a necessity of survival. Among Maasai pastoralists they were formalized in the customary expectation that young men kill lions.[47] But when the human population gets so large that it demands the use of all available land, conflict with large predators becomes implacable and sustained application of these ideas will lead to the animals' extinction. As the world continues to fill with people, this logic implies the eventual elimination of large predators everywhere inhabitable by humans or livestock and may frame commitments to social justice as standing in opposition to wildlife conservation.

War against predators involves culture as well as economics; we saw in Chapter 1 that European folktales have been complicit in the extermination of wolves. The dragon is the epitome of what David Quammen calls 'alpha predators' (able to kill and eat humans).[48] Western culture's traditional equation of this fabulous superpredator with evil, to be destroyed by the dragon-slayer, implies that the eradication of large predators is prerequisite to civilization. Deeper beneath this is a mythopoetics of dragon-slaying as symbolizing human mastery of nature's wildness.[49] Only when these assumptions are questioned can alternative possibilities be contemplated.

On the premise that the extinction of large predators means a tragic loss not only to ecosystemic health and the richness of human experience but also of the unique universe of being that each species represents, I decided to retell 'The Deerhurst Dragon' in such a way as to recast the values the tale implies. I wanted to impart something of the poignancy of true-life stories about the last survivor of a species (see Chapter 3). To do this, I had to construct a more elaborate story. To make the most of the cultural weight of the composted tradition, I retained all the motifs of the local legend gathered by Palmer, and recycled into this story selected motifs from the wider AT 300 tradition, in expectation that some resonance with the tale-type tradition will haunt the awareness of both teller and listeners when the local tale is told. I also sought inspiration from local history and visiting the area where the story is set.

Research and recrafting

When I sought out the settings of Gloucestershire tales, I found that some locations were easy to find and their association with the stories was well known.

This was especially true of buildings: Berkeley Castle, where Edward II may or may not have been murdered; Chavenage House, where the headless ghost of Charles I claimed the soul of an MP who voted for his impeachment; the manor house in Bisley where the future Elizabeth I died young and was substituted with a boy. Some landscape features were also easy to find. Legends record the Devil's handiwork in a number of landmarks: the Devil's Quoit near Stroat, the Devil's Pulpit overlooking Tintern Abbey, the Devil's Chimney on Leckhampton Hill, and Cam Peak near Dursley. At the mile-wide part of the Severn known as 'The Noose', legend tells of the destruction of invading Roman troops by the bore wave when native druids called upon the goddess Sabrina.[50]

Locations requiring more effort divided into two groups: those which were identified in the tale and could be found with detailed maps and local people's help, and those where the exact location wasn't specified and I had to scout out a spot that seemed to fit. Sometimes it was easy to imagine the story's action in the setting as it appears today. In others the place is greatly changed. For example, the setting of 'Maude's Elm' – Swindon Village, near Cheltenham – is today overrun by an industrial estate and, though 'Maude's Cottage' remains evident, naught remains of the tree that grew from the stake planted through tragic young Maude's heart except a sign marking the spot with the unexplained words 'Maude's Elm'.[51] In the case of 'The Deerhurst Dragon', the present state of the landscape proved the key to reshaping the tale.

St Mary's Church, Deerhurst, is over 1200 years old. It was the minster of an abbey in the Anglo-Saxon kingdom of the Hwicce. The name 'Deerhurst' suggests 'a wooded hillock, Old English *hyrst*, frequented by wild animals, *dēor*, most probably deer'.[52] The name of the nearby hamlet of Deerhurst Walton, close to the Walton Hill mentioned in the legend, suggests a surviving Welsh community (Old English 'walh') who'd established a village nucleus ('tūn') on the Saxon model. In early Saxon times the land was wilder and marshier than today.[53] Saxon settlement probably entailed an expanding population and the clearing of woodland to establish self-sufficient farming communities with arable fields close to the village centre, and pastures further out.[54] Deerhurst today is a small village surrounded by fields of rape, barley, oats, wheat, maize, hay, and pasture for cattle, sheep and horses. I could imagine the villagers gathering among the antique farm buildings near the church to debate what to do, but there was little trace of likely dragon habitat.

I proceeded to Walton Hill, the land granted to John Smith, two miles southeast. There isn't much of a hill, only large flat fields of maize and of grass cut for hay or silage, fringed to the west by a dual carriageway, beyond which the land drops down a modest scarp. The hedgerows are mainly elm, hawthorn, ash, thistles and bindweed. Walton Hill Farm is occupied by the headquarters of a haulage company. When I walked up the drive, my way was barred by a security guard. I tried the dragon story on him. He'd never heard of it and I couldn't gain access to the pools behind the farm – which I'd thought a promising locale, given dragons' association with water, and a pool Vizard mentions – or to seek the Dragon Tump. When on two later occasions I phoned the company to enquire about the legend, I was immediately disconnected. The environs were dispiriting. Rubbish including a bathtub and car tyres had been dumped by a gateway. It was hard to imagine a dragon there.

I descended the scarp to the outskirts of Deerhurst Walton, where slivers of wild habitat survive in the margins between fields and roads: marsh, pools, and thickets of willow, elm, hawthorn, oak, bramble, burdock, nettles, willowherb, meadowsweet and bulrushes. They give a hint of how this area may once have looked, as do the restored willow carr and water meadows of the Coombe Hill Nature Reserve a mile southwest.

My observations, and emotional reactions, made me realize the story was not only about predatory megafauna but also about the domestication of the land: my retelling should suggest how the present state of this environment came to be. I decided to set it quite early in Saxon times, when the Saxons were clearing wild country to settle, and to make the most of the dragon's connection with Deerhurst Church, one of the best-preserved Saxon buildings in England. I envisaged monks setting up a monastery in a lonely spot and this becoming a nucleus for settlers, who would exploit the land's resources in new ways and thereby disturb any equilibrium between the preceding human population and their environment.

I decided that the Walton Hill estate, which the King offers as reward, would be the last tract of wildland in the area – the very place where the dragon was laired. As the settlers cleared the woods, so the dragon's natural prey of wild game vanished and she had to prey on the livestock that took their place. I offer a biological interpretation of her 'poisoning' of thirsty cowherds: 'She liked to wallow in the pools among the willows ... People those days knew nothing of bacteria.' Thus humans came into increasing conflict with the dragon, as they do with predators whenever wilderness is converted into farmland to feed an expanding population. By establishing this back story, and providing insight into the dragon's perspective, I invite empathy for her, 'one of the very last dragons east of the Severn'. I made her female to give an ecofeminist swing to the masculine hero's assault upon the wild, distantly recalling the cosmic feminine represented by Tiamat. Her taking to the wing 'in hope of luring a mate from Wales' plays on the dragon as symbolic of the Welsh, the native people, vanquished by the Saxon invader, their lingering presence witnessed in the name of Deerhurst Walton.[55]

It's a poor man – the everyman John Smith – a man needing land in order to marry and raise a family, who's willing to tackle the dragon to win that tract of wildland. His wish to marry echoes the common motif, in AT 300, of the dragon-slayer winning a bride. The fact that, as in *Farmer Giles of Ham*, the King throws the problem back on the local people, rather than sending in a troop of housecarls, draws attention to how power hierarchies put the less privileged on the back foot and in the brunt of conflict with wildlife.[56] Recycling from AT 300 tradition the motif of the dragon's severed head as proof of slaughter, I have the Abbot equip Smith with axe and milk on pain of losing his hands as a thief if he returns without the dragon's head. This move invites empathy for the human protagonist too, rather than simply reverse the polarization of good and evil between dragon-slayer and dragon by casting the dragon as victim rather than villain.

I set Smith's encounter with the dragon beside a pool in the area between Deerhurst Walton and Walton Hill, depicted as a jungle of marshy thickets where tension builds because both dragon and hunter may readily be concealed. When the dragon basks in the sun after guzzling the milk, Smith strikes the soft skin exposed between the ruffled scales on her *belly*. This echoes the belly blow struck by St George, Beowulf and Sigurd and enables me to draw out the dragon's death. Wounded, she flees up the scarp, through the thickets, to her lair atop a tump. Here Smith corners her – and her infant.

My innovation of this juvenile dragon arose, unplanned, during improvised rehearsal before I tried out the tale at a storytelling club. The two beast heads on the church's chancel arch were carved, I narrate, to replace two real dragon heads hung there 'as an offering to God in thanks for Deerhurst's deliverance from the Devil's minions'. The ecobardic purpose is to deepen the audience's empathy for the dragon at this climactic moment. Smith 'wasn't a heartless man; it pained him to see how the little one nuzzled the mother's headless carcass. But he knew there's no place for dragons in civilised country … The baby dragon's scales were thin and soft. One blow of the axe did the job.'[57] This is the story's emotional centre of gravity. In live performance it's more highly charged than on the page because of the relational dynamic between storyteller and listeners and so has to be managed with care and restraint. By allowing the audience emotional space to respond, and by letting their sympathies hesitate between beast and man rather than driving home a one-sided message, I hope once again to provoke thought about real conflicts between people and wildlife (see Chapters 2 and 3). There's a local applicability here to ongoing efforts to exterminate badgers from parts of Gloucestershire, these animals being framed as a threat to cattle because they can carry bovine TB.

Smith's subsequent clearance of the wildland to begin farming allows me to conclude by alluding to the locality's condition today: 'Only in a few nooks below the scarp do the marshes and thickets remain.'[58] Again I give space for a range of feelings – regret for the passing of the wild, respect for the need for farming, dislike of wild boggy land, significance beyond what the eye sees – and thereby imply questions about how one might desire a place like this to be. The localization of a tale by incorporating real physical details of place imparts an immediacy, relevance, and suspension of disbelief that can intensify one's engagement with the story's thematic content.[59] In other words, there's a synergy between my two ecobardic aims, the enchantment of place and the mobilization of ecological themes, so that in 'restorying' place, to quote Nabhan, one may 'encode deep-seated values within our culture'.[60]

Enchanted springs and women

Thus far I've used the word 'enchantment' in a general way to refer to perceiving something with a deepened sense of its significance. Tolkien uses 'enchantment' in a more specific sense to refer to the art by which may be wrought 'imagined wonder' that is productive of 'secondary belief' – meaning imaginative experience of a 'secondary world' in which things are different from what is empirically observed in the 'primary world' we inhabit.[61] For Tolkien, as for the modern world generally, all this is the realm of 'fantasy', under which heading may be placed stories that feature the supernatural, which nevertheless includes phenomena that folk believed in times past to be real – and sometimes still do.

Among landscape features, springs are especially prone to enchantment. The two further Gloucestershire tales I shall discuss both involve a spring's enchantment, not only by the association of its story, but also in the Tolkienian sense by supernatural properties the story describes. In both stories the protagonist is a woman.

In traditional societies, springs are ecologically vital as sources of the water on which the lives of people and animals depend. The gushing forth of water from underground can also be perceived symbolically as the flow of inspiration or healing energy from a realm beyond, of the divine or the unconscious. Hence a motivation for people seeking inspiration or healing to visit sacred springs. In

Iamblichus's Neoplatonist understanding, the water of a sacred spring purifies the seeker's ochema pneuma – the 'vehicle of the soul', or energy body – in readiness to receive inspiration.[62] Folklore often associates springs with female spirits, saints, nymphs or fairies, who are to be honoured so that clean water will keep flowing. Sometimes they can be very dangerous to the unwary. There's a symbolic association, also, between a spring's physical form as a life-giving opening in the earth and the life-giving opening of a woman's body – an aspect of the widespread trope, in many mythologies, of the earth as mother goddess.[63]

These are two facets of the long cultural association of the feminine with aspects or the whole of nature. This association is problematic because historically it has contributed to the essentializing of women in a dualist mode of thinking that elevates one thing above another: man superior to woman; human superior to non-human; European superior to non-European; *and also*: reason superior to feeling; autonomy superior to relationship; action superior to reception; mental superior to sensual. The consequence has been patterns of dominance in which men have exploited and mistreated women and non-human nature – and less powerful men – and limited their opportunities to flourish.[64] One response to this history is to reject the association between women and the earth; to presume, as Tzeporah Berman summarizes, that any 'association of women and femininity with Nature in environmental discourse perpetuates patriarchal traditions and domination'.[65] To accept that imperative would mean, for storytellers, abandoning large tranches of the world repertoire of traditional stories and reducing high myth to the level of human drama, shorn of the ecological associations of both male and female spiritual beings.

An alternative response, advanced by ecofeminists, is to reverse the way of looking at the problem: if the problem is a dominance pattern based in valuing one pole of each of a set of dyads as superior to the other, then a cultural effort is required to elevate in value the poles previously regarded as inferior and thereby collapse the hierarchy of dominance, but without either denying difference or seeking a new, inverted hierarchy. The polarity here is better understood in terms not of 'binary opposition' but of 'non-oppositional difference', in which feminine and masculine, like yin and yang, are 'principles' rather than 'definitive gender ascriptions'.[66] When the will to dominate is relinquished, means and ends become united. The devalued attributes of feeling, relationality, receptivity, sensuality, conventionally associated with the 'feminine', or yin, are qualities that desperately need to be promoted in the paradigm shift demanded by ecological crisis. Rather than seeking to empower women to compete with men within the existing ultra-yang framework that's destroying the ecosystem, this paradigm shift entails the empowerment of women as integral to the transformation of the world and its structures of domination. It also entails the transformation of men as they integrate the yin qualities from which they've been alienated, and frees everyone from pressure to comply with prescriptive gender norms.[67]

On this basis, storytellers should feel encouraged to tell traditional stories that present female characters not as the sword-toting warriors in battle bikinis by which Hollywood tries to be politically correct while continuing to glamorize violence, but as expressing qualities the world needs. The Gloucestershire tales depict a number of empowered women, some of whom – not all – have associations with nature. There are, for example, young Polly who overcame a serial wife-killer; the psychic treasure-hunter Molly Dreamer; the faithful fairy bride Tegau Goldenbreast; and the Countess of Hereford who protects the poor folk's rights of common from her husband's austerity policy.[68] However, the two stories of enchanted springs both feature an initially empowered woman who becomes a victim of patriarchal forces. In one case the spring's location was known but neglected; in the other the location was unspecified in the source text. Another reason for comparing these two stories is that the same method of field research gave me contrasting experiences at the two sites.

St Arilda's Well – a holy place

St Arilda is a little-known Gloucestershire saint, who some speculate may have come from Gwent and be identified with St Afrella of the sixth century.[69] The legend is that Arilda was beheaded by a chieftain called Muncius because she refused him sex and that her blood stained red the spring in Kington, near Thornbury, known as St Arilda's Well. The waters of this spring have since accomplished miracles of healing and even today have a reddish hue.[70] The appeal of this sketchy tale was its location in South Gloucestershire, where good stories were sparser than elsewhere in the county, and that it featured a female saint, counterbalancing the major Gloucestershire story of St Kenelm. Exploration of the landscape helped me build up Arilda's legend into a more substantial story.

First I visited Oldbury-on-Severn, where St Arilda's Church, in which Arilda was buried, stands on a hill once sacred to Jupiter. Extensive earthworks in the north of the village suggested there'd been a settlement here since antiquity, as was confirmed to me by a local resident employed in the nearby nuclear power station. Modern sea defences, including a sluice gate, implied a past vulnerability

Composting Snakes and Dragons 133

to flooding. In the church, safe on its hilltop, from which there's a view across the Severn to the hills of Gwent, I discovered a hymn about Arilda which mentions she refused Muncius three times before he killed her.[71] This suggested a narrative structure comprising three dramatic moments I would have to concoct.

In nearby Kington I found my way through the fields to St Arilda's Well. Signs asked walkers to keep to the public right of way. The spring was not on the footpath, farm dogs deterred me from seeking permission from the farmer, and the gate was open, so I discreetly followed the stream to the spring. Today it emerges from a cistern and is encircled by barbed wire, but otherwise the pool, the vegetation, the mud were as you might imagine them long ago. I noted the species of trees and other plants and sat for a time, taking in the ambience of the place, and imagined Arilda drawing water there. I then wrote notes – in short lines like verse.[72] I'm no poet, but I've found that this method of field notation allows a freer engagement of my feelings, as well as my knowledge of the folklore, with my sensory observations. Here's what I wrote at St Arilda's Well:

Glistening trickle
thirsty little sound
so discrete, and discreet
in this hollow of holiness
where sex became death
and all that is good was
turned upside down into bad.
Runnel of movement,
rustiness of either the blood-stained water
or the hue of the mud beneath.
Wads of little heart-shaped leaves
of a water flower I do not know
and that has not yet flowered
at this too early season;
squashy and moist between
the array of stones
like an ancient pavement
before the well, now cistern,
shaded round with hazel, bramble and ash,
silhouette twigs budding against the blue.
Great tit calls the alarm
and chatters his lordship,
faint echo of that Saxon lord

who claimed his droit
and was denied
and suffered no check on
his power of sword.
Yet now the place is peaceful.
Her blood has sanctified time
and place, except the barbed wire
that bars me from stepping to the well.
Peace prevails in the end
this millennium and a half later;
the present landlord has not come,
has not threatened me,
though I feared he might, his might.
Chaste martyrdom,
what meaning does that make
of a meaningless death?
Only this story I will magnify
in my own way
and make holy, holier,
this little pocket of peace and wild
in the memory of man
in the years to come.

The interaction between place, story and writing took me into a space of peace and stillness. Note the shift into a spiritual register towards the end of my notes. As a physical place, this locality was not very special; not the kind of beauty spot whose sheer sensory impact will transport your feelings. It was the story that enchanted the place, made it special to me as images from my imagination were overlaid upon the images from my eyes.

The speculation linking St Arilda to St Afrella suggested to me the historical context debouched from the battle of Dyrham in AD 577, at which the West Saxons defeated the Dobunni (Romano-British) kings of Cirencester, Gloucester and Bath and thereby reached the Severn and severed the Britons of Wales from those of Dumnonia.[73] Arilda's location at Kington would have been in the firing line of the victorious Saxons as they swarmed through this now defenceless region. It made sense to make Muncius a Saxon thane.

I also discovered another local tale – about the problems of building her church in Oldbury, which kept collapsing so long as they tried to build it on the green.[74] The reason given in the tale is fire, but the village's topography suggested that inundation by the Severn might be a compelling reason, since the tale narrates how, following an augury involving two heifers, the church was successfully built on the hilltop site of the old pagan temple.

My retelling of Arilda's story thus begins with Romano-British civilization enduring in the fertile Dobunni lands coveted by the West Saxons; then introduces Arilda as a lady from the court of Gwent who separated from her husband in middle age to devote herself to the religious life in a little monastery at Kington. Then came the British defeat at Dyrham and the arrival of Muncius and his warband. He took a fancy to Arilda and crudely propositioned her. He was too proud to take her by force when she refused him. Instead, having billeted his gang on the monastery, he swaggered into the church when she was praying and propositioned her again. Her flight from him prompted drunken mockery from his men and a tide of anger in him. His third attempt came when she was drawing water at the spring. In this scene I juxtapose imagery of her beauty and the natural setting of the spring and hazel bushes and imply that her spiritual purity is part of what attracted him. In the end it's Arilda's declamation of her trust in Jesus Christ that provokes him to murder her and burn down the monastery.

From there I segue into the tale about building St Arilda's Church, mention the continuity of Christian tradition in the Saxon kingdom of the Hwicce that replaced the Dobunni kingdoms, and conclude with a brief description of the well and the healing properties and reddish stain of its waters.[75]

The Well of the Snake – an unheimlich place

I had a more edgy experience of nature when I sought 'the Well of the Snake'. A verse tale of that title was written by the Victorian antiquarian Adin Williams, who calls it 'a legend of Poulton'. It concerns a woman who was spurned by the man she loved because she seemed uncomely. By bathing, upon the invitation of a snake, in the pool of a secret spring she gained magical beauty – alas, too late to win her beloved, who'd already married another.[76] The story's linkage of enchantment, sensuality and the wild was engaging, but the tale lacked enough substance to seem worth retelling. Then I realized I could construct a composite story by joining it to other witchcraft tales from the Poulton area, which centre on Betty Barstoe, a woman who was hanged as a witch and buried at the crossroads named after her (Betty's Grave).

All I knew from Williams about the Well of the Snake's location was that it was hidden in wild woodland somewhere near the village of Poulton. Precious little woodland survives today in this part of the upper Thames Valley. The first spot I checked out was a pond in a small wood near Priory Farm. The pond turned out to be quite large and neatly banked. It probably had been the fishpond of the priory remembered in the farm's name. Needing someplace wilder, I spotted on the map a tiny square of woodland east of Poulton, with a spring nearby. There was no path. I climbed some fences to reach the wood, which was filled with early summer flowers, and then another fence to reach the dry stream leading to the spring. The vegetation was very wild. In my efforts to reach the spring, I nearly had a nasty accident:

> If it weren't for my glasses I'd have lost an eye.
> I was creeping down the dry brook, seeking the spring,
> the Well of the Snake, whose curse and blessing is beauty.
> The spring was a little way on, I was sure.
> I could see a white plastic container I thought floating in a pool.
> My eyes were on where I was going, not where I actually was.
> The dead stub, sticking out like an erection, worm eaten,
> at right angles from Old Man Willow's trunk,
> came at me from 01:00 – blind spot –
> I didn't see a thing,
> only felt the impact ram against my glasses lens
> and deflect to strike my cheekbone just below
> – no, not my cheekbone, the lower orbit of my eye,
> as close as that. There'll be a bruise there tonight;
> I still feel it stinging.
> On the lens you can see the scratch where the stick hit
> and then a line of dirty marking 1 cm long to the lower rim
> where it slipped off.
> I'd have had a blind spot for good.
> How often must the lesson be taught: of respect for
> nature's unforgivingness, especially when you're trying to
> penetrate a secret, sacred, magical place?
> I had to cross to the other stream bank to get to the water,
> a sequence of pools still soaking up from the earth.
> You can see how much deeper it would be.
> Where the water was, the undergrowth is densest, as if
> all the willows, hawthorns, brambles, briars, nettles are
> sucked there in desperate competition for the life-giving liquid
> or else are doing their work of protecting the pool.
> Such darkness after such an airy lightness in the

remains of the wood through which Betty came in search of her boon.
Oak, hawthorn and furry-leaved hazel, and in the
dappled light beneath a paradise froth of cow parsley
laced with the last remnants of bluebells.
In the paddock next door the new life of lambs
crowded together in this secluded unpublic spot
with their alert mothers.
Corrugated patterns of oak bark
lit by lozenges of light,
all glory and beauty and ephemeral daylight in there;
permanent gloom, almost, in here by the spring
among the dark bitter willows.
The permanent price for me, perhaps, if the scratch is too bad,
to buy a new pair of spectacles
– and do honour to Betty, poor Betty, in my tale.

The wildness of this place, and my feeling of intruding where perhaps I shouldn't, chimed with the wildness of the wood in Williams's verse and the implication his heroine is dabbling in something unheimlich. There's a whiff of enchantment in my experience – such as the allusion to Old Man Willow,[77] imputing personality to the tree that bashed me. But the language is more prosaic than in my notes about St Arilda's Well, and my interpretation of the experience weighs towards acknowledging my carelessness in the face of wild nature that has no interest in my well-being.

In retelling 'Betty's' venture to the spring, I allude to the may blossom and cow parsley I saw in the wood, and depict the pool 'in the shade of a great twisted willow, hedged with brambles and briars'. In the ensuing interchange with the snake I emphasize Betty's wish 'I had the power to win what I desire', before she follows the creature's advice to take off her clothes and bathe with him in the chilly pool beneath the rising moon.[78]

Snakes and witches

This encounter with a snake draws upon a line of symbolism that runs back, like the Satanic dragon, to the serpent in Eden and connotations of temptation, forbidden power and sinful sexuality. Beyond that is a bigger picture of associations of serpent with goddess, in which the snake symbolizes sexual powers of the making, taking and regeneration of life; and wisdom and prophecy, as in the 'mother' of ayahuasca who bestows visions to Amazonian shamans; and the spiralling flow of life energy, as in the Chinese concept of 'dragon veins' running through the land and the Hindu concept of Kundalini that can uncoil up through the human body.[79] Echoing the dragon-goddess Tiamat, supernatural beings in various cultures combine a woman's form with a snake's: Adam's first wife Lilith, Nu Kua in China, the naginis of India, Mami Wata in Africa, Melusine and Elvira in France. Many of these are associated with water. When the Zen priest Shinyu climbed Mount Haku to worship the resident goddess, a dragon emerged from a pool at the top. Resolutely he maintained his devotions until the dragon transformed into Guanyin, goddess of compassion.[80]

Anne Baring and Jules Cashford interpret Marduk's slaying of Tiamat as the beginning of 'the replacing of a mother goddess who generates creation as part of herself by a god who "makes" creation as something separate from himself'.[81] Especially in the West, there's a tradition in which the serpent is pictured as *external* to a powerful goddess it's associated with: Inanna rode a storm dragon; Vritra was born of the goddess Danu; Medea enspelled the dragon guarding the Golden Fleece. In Genesis the goddess is reduced to mortal Eve and the serpent becomes her enemy – as recurs in the dragon-slayings of Perseus and St George, where the 'goddess' is abjectified as a girl chained to a rock. Here, argue Baring and Cashford, phallic symbolism positions the serpent as representing not only wild nature but also the instinctive side of man which his conscious will must master.[82]

The phallic symbolism recurs in stories around the world. In Ashanti mythology a python got the first human couples to face each other in the river and sprayed water on the women's bellies so they'd conceive when they lay with their husbands.[83] In New Caledonia the snake Hulipomé would transform by night into a beautiful man. Each woman who wanted to marry him had to wait inside a hut till he squeezed through the doorway in serpentine form and encoiled her body. Only if she showed no fear would he forgo eating her and shed his snakeskin to sleep with her in human form.[84] In Amazonia, conversely, an anaconda married a king's daughter and when he entered her room she lit a candle and saw he'd transformed into a young man; but while they were making love some candle resin dripped into his eye, which then exploded, causing him to change back into an anaconda and ascend into the sky to become the sun.[85] When, in Australia, the Wauwalak Sisters bathed in a waterhole, vaginal blood awoke the sleeping Rainbow Snake, which rose up spraying water like rain, prompting the sisters to make a shelter. The snake coiled around the shelter, then pushed inside, sprayed saliva over them and consumed them and the child with them. The child survives this ordeal to receive the Rainbow Snake's sacred teaching.[86]

The Amazonian anaconda shapes the world during Kallari Timpu (beginning time-space), as the Rainbow Snakes does in the Dreaming. Despite the phallic imagery, the gender of both these beings is rather fluid.[87] They represent a divine creative agency in the world, ultimately beyond gender, reminiscent also of Shesha, the primal serpent in Indian mythology who carries Vishnu and Lakshmi.

What I've sketched here is no discrete tale-type tradition like AT 300 but rather a web of diverse stories and motifs, in which composted traditions mix with inspiration from local ecosystems. In today's interculturally connected world, influences can run every which way through this web. Awareness of these mythemes evokes for me a charged sense, when I tell Betty's story, of a woman's intimate association with a snake in a spring as signifying an empowerment that transcends – transgresses – the usual expectations of women in a patriarchal society. Thus we come to the figure of the witch, the supernaturally empowered mortal woman.

Tales about witches are numerous in Gloucestershire folklore, as elsewhere. Katharine Briggs's *Dictionary of British Folk-Tales in the English Language* devotes 153 pages to witch legends. The stories usually have a negative charge, expressing time-honoured misogyny. A first reaction might be simply not to tell them. However, misogyny remains current; the expression of hatred towards women, together with the rejection of ecological concerns, is conspicuously aligned with the upsurge of xenophobic right-wing nationalism.[88] A purpose may be served in retelling witch stories in ways that expose misogyny for what it is and attempt to right the wrongs of history.

In Gloucestershire's legend of St Kenelm, the saint's elder sister, Quenthryth, Abbess of Winchcombe, is presented as a witch who, having seduced her brother's tutor, commissioned this man to murder him. The characters in this legend are real historical figures. Local historian John Stevinson believes that if there'd been any suspicion Quenthryth was complicit in Kenelm's murder, their father King Kenulf would never have maintained her as abbess of Winchcombe or placed in her care two further abbeys, as records attest he did.[89] There's a conflict between history and legend. 'Don't let the truth get in the way of a good story,' storytellers sometimes joke. But it's no joke today when people promulgate 'fake news' to serve their own interests at others' expense. It's one thing, says Wilson, to encourage multiple interpretations of 'the truth' which challenge the discourse of the powerful; quite another to propagate lies.[90] My approach to the dynamic between history and legend is to respect the known facts of history so far as possible, especially when something's at stake – such as a real person's reputation – but to allow the inventiveness of both folk and personal imagination in the gaps of knowledge. Stevinson attributes the legend's framing of Quenthryth as fornicator, witch and murderess to a misogynistic zeitgeist later in the Middle Ages when the church had become obsessed with celibacy. He believes that the murder was more likely commissioned by the siblings' ambitious uncle.[91] In my version I therefore turn the story upside down and present Quenthryth as innocently trusting the treacherous tutor and grief-stricken when Kenelm's body is brought home.[92]

Adin Williams's verse tale of 'The Well of the Snake' is not misogynistic. It ends with its newly empowered heroine marrying another suitor who 'loved her as none had before',[93] which in my composite story segues neatly into a charming, witch-positive tale, collected by Alfred Williams from the same area, about a beautiful witch – whom I identify as Betty – who takes her husband on magical adventures at midnight.[94] Most of the folk anecdotes actually about Betty Barstoe are misogynistic, but in 2000 Jacqueline Simpson recorded a more sympathetic tale presenting Betty as an innocent victim.[95] I deploy the death of the beloved husband from Alfred Williams's tale to precipitate Betty's mental breakdown and hence the behaviour – wandering around naked at night and difficulty speaking – that in Simpson's tale turns the villagers against her. Illustrating the long history of attitudes towards mental illness, they blame her as a witch for all their problems, as detailed in the other folklore about Betty. Thus the story runs to its grim climax. However, following Simpson's story again, Betty's power was so great that she rose from the grave after repeated hangings – until the villagers promised to keep her grave adorned with flowers. As recently as the 1970s, when the custom of laying flowers halted, Betty's ghost started reappearing and so the custom was hastily resumed.

The aura of sacred places

The stories of both 'St Arilda's Well' and 'Betty's Grave' centre on a woman who receives blessing from nature: Arilda through living a religious life immersed in nature's rhythms, Betty through receiving from the wild a potent magic. Both women were murdered by men who had power over them and were hostile to their otherness as women who didn't comply with their expectations. They each have a symbolic connection with the earth through their association with a spring and so their killing is symbolically linked to the desecration and destruction of nature.

My experiences of nature at the two springs contain hints of two contrasting perspectives on nature. In the nineteenth century, Gould explains, the naturalist Alexander von Humboldt's perception of nature's harmonious complexity as an expression of divine creativity, inspiring of human harmony and creativity, gave way to Darwin's discovery that nature's complexity is generated by a ruthless struggle for existence, against which humans must impose their own ideas of meaning and morality.[96] Ensuing from this, and the insights of Marx, Freud and Nietzsche and legacy of the Reformation, was the disenchantment of supernatural perceptions of the world which had existed since time immemorial.[97] By 1918, writes Ted Hughes, 'the whole metaphysical universe … had evaporated, with all its meanings'.[98] This shift of perspective allowed a confluence of science, business and greed to rationalize the unfettered destruction of habitats and organisms whose significance had been reduced to their economic value.[99]

Tzvetan Todorov defines as 'fantastic' the genre of stories that sustain ambiguity between an explanation of their events according to the accepted 'laws' of the disenchanted world and an alternative (enchanting) interpretation. The assumption that the latter interpretation refers to something 'that has no reality outside language' implies the delusion of those who experience it as real – that is, 'the drug-user, the psychotic … the infant'.[100] However, local legends have commonly implied such an ambiguity, not so much *within* the stories as in people's interpretation of their facticity. They still do. People may today doubt that bathing in a snake-infested spring will bestow magical beauty or that a saint's martyrdom will permanently stain spring water red, but beliefs in the healing powers of holy wells remain widespread. Hence, for example, the votive decorations I saw on the tree beside the spring where Kenelm was murdered. My own framework of assumptions was challenged by the testimony of owners of ancient manors and inns, evidently sane and by their own admission uninclined to paranormal beliefs, about the ghosts that haunt these buildings and sometimes have to be exorcised. In conversations after performances of local ghost legends, members of the audience often take the opportunity to share a mysterious experience they once had. Less metaphysical, but equally challenging to my prior certainties, were the big cats that many claim to have observed at large in Gloucestershire and elsewhere in the British countryside.[101]

Such reports, like Yeats's accounts of Irish countryfolk's encounters with fairies,[102] are apposite to Tolkien's enigmatic reference to 'Faërian drama', in which 'you yourself are, or think you are, bodily inside its Secondary World'.[103] What Tolkien seems to be coyly hinting at are lived experiences that transgress the consensus (disenchanted) reality of the primary world, that feel real to those who experience them, but which he, as a Christian dualist, cannot accept 'primary belief' in. Note the hesitation – characteristic of Todorov's fantastic – in Tolkien's 'are, or think you are'.

I've come to believe that such uncertainty about what is or is not real remains important today to the enchantment of place. We may hesitate between Humboldt's metaphysical perspective of the world, as I experienced at St Arilda's Well, and Darwin's understanding of nature as ruthlessly impersonal, which smacked me in the face near 'the Well of the Snake'. From the evidence of many conversations, it seems clear to me that, even in twenty-first-century Britain, many people do experience a space of uncertainty where enchanted perceptions feel real and you can't be sure they're not.

Useful here is Benjamin's concept of 'aura': an ineffable quality possessed by living beings, and by unique works of art – but missing from mechanical reproductions of them – and by objects and garments used by a known person, such as we see in museums.[104] Eilean Hooper-Greenhill writes, 'Human experiences can be accumulated in artefacts, and because of this objects can be associated with the deepest psychological needs. Objects can be imbued or charged with meaning as significance and emotion are invested in them.'[105] Such aura may attach to places too, somewhat like the more explicitly spiritual Polynesian concept of 'mana', believed to permeate everything, but more powerfully present in some people and objects and in sacred structures like marae (meeting places) and whare nui (meeting houses).[106] The painter Paul Nash felt that 'There are places, just as there people and objects and works of art, whose relationship of parts creates a mystery, an enchantment, which cannot be analysed.'[107] Places, like Nash's chosen 'places', that have become personally special to an individual are one of four kinds of location that Martin Palmer characterizes as 'sacred'. The others are: places where the numinous breaks through from nature's splendour; places hallowed by a tradition of prayer; and places touched by a story from history or legend.[108] In practice these different qualities of aura may coincide in the same place. Temples originated as man-made amplifications or representations of sacred places in nature (especially mountains).[109] Stories, like sacred buildings, provide a means by which a place's aura may be collectively experienced.

The dragon hill, crossroads and springs in the Gloucestershire tales discussed above are liminal places – thresholds between different spaces. Hills and mountains are liminal between sky and earth. Crossroads are thresholds between alternative routes. Springs are liminal between the realms above and below ground and between water and earth. Other liminal places in traditional tales include the seashore, caves, lakes, islands, forest clearings, ancient trees, rocky outcrops, antiquities and graveyards. Certain *times* may be liminal too, as thresholds between different intervals of time: dusk and dawn, midnight, New Year, the moments of waking or falling asleep, of birth or death. In Irish tradition, in certain places, at certain times – especially midnight at Samhain (Halloween) – the veil is 'thin' between the primary world and the otherworld of the sídhe, facilitating travel between them. For the Kanak peoples of New Caledonia the whole area of bush between the cultivated territories of the tribes is a liminal zone – 'spirit-place' – where the rules circumscribing tribal life are loosened and folktales depict unexpected and uncanny events. Similarly, the whole of the night is a liminal, inverted time, when the spirits of the dead walk and the living sleep.[110]

St Arilda's Well had an aura for me because of the tale of Arilda's martyrdom and because people had claimed to have been healed there. The aura existed in my perception and in the collective imagination of a tradition. The place I identified with the Well of the Snake had to my knowledge no pre-existing associations, only the atmosphere produced by its ecology, but through my recognizing a fit between this place and a story, it started to acquire an aura in my perception.

In many traditional societies the attribution of an aura of sacredness to a place may imply supernatural sanctions – 'taboo' in the Pacific Islands – that define who can go there and what they can do.[111] The enchantment of springs as sacred motivates people to care for them, not pollute them, and thus serves the ecological need to sustain the water supply. Stories perpetuating such an aura may narrate the presence of spirits, like St Arilda's, who both personalize and enforce the place's sacredness.

That which is sacred is excluded from economic exploitation; that's why sacredness is anathema to capitalism.[112] Today the identification of particular sites as storied can help them to be protected as 'heritage' – a modern-day taboo preventing them being used in other ways. That's surely a good thing, but sometimes it risks the impact of large numbers of visitors and the place's commercialization – and/or the restriction of access.[113] Stonehenge is an obvious example.

It's one thing to protect individual localities, but what about the rest of the land? Nature conservation in Britain has been trying to expand from a focus on small reserves to promote 'Living Landscapes' that encompass much larger areas where human land use coexists with wildlife.[114] How can stories' enchantment of landscape be extended beyond a scatter of special places?

A storied journey, like a songline or pilgrimage route, that connects a series of localities may enchant to some degree the whole route across the landscape. Hartsiotis came up with the idea of stringing together some of the Devil's escapades in Gloucestershire to make an episodic story in which the Devil roams the county, vainly trying to counter the proverb 'As sure as God is in Gloucestershire'. The route I scouted for my version of this composite story suggested additional incidents: at Hock Cliff, on the Severn, fossil *Gryphaea*, known as 'Devil's toenails', may be found eroding from the shale, so I have the Devil pause to trim his toenails and discard the parings there. Other stories may enchant a broader geography. My telling of 'Betty's Grave' alludes to the whole landscape around Poulton, including the more extensive woodland there before it was cleared for agriculture; Betty's nocturnal adventures with her husband traverse such large-scale landscape features as Lea Wood, Marston Hill and the rivers Coln and Thames.[115]

To pursue more deeply this question of the enchantment of the larger landscape, much may be learnt from indigenous perspectives. Let us consider now the Kanak mythscape of New Caledonia.

Legends and landscape in New Caledonia

The Kanak comprise twenty-eight distinct ethnolinguistic groups, each with their own language and corpus of stories and comprising a number of 'tribes', a term that refers to both the community and its land. Each clan, or extended family, of these tribes has a 'tertre', a mound or rock from which its founding ancestor is believed to have originated. Stories narrate journeys from this place of origin which namecheck an itinerary of localities and thereby inscribe in the landscape a 'living archive' of the rights and responsibilities of the clan and the lineages comprising it.[116] The Kanak independence leader Jean-Marie Tjibaou spells out that in theory the *entire* landscape is permeated by cultural knowledge in the form of stories, songs and custom speeches that mediate a complex network of relationships between living people, the land and a panoply of ancestral, totemic and other spirits.[117] Like Aboriginal myths, most Kanak tales, tied to the landscape by explicit toponyms, are understood to record events that really happened.[118] In this sense they're akin to local legends; but they contain far more supernatural content than do English legends, since the spirits are so central to Kanak cosmology.

Most of New Caledonia's topography was traditionally entailed in economic uses – horticulture in the tribal communes, hunting in the bush, fishing in sea and streams – and yet was at the same time enchanted by the presence of spirits. A few places – burial grounds, certain areas high on mountains – are intensely taboo; elsewhere nuances of taboo determine who's allowed to use which natural resources, in which locations, at which times, for what purposes.[119] Transgressions of taboo often provide crucial dramatic turns in Kanak tales, often resulting not simply in punishment but in complex consequences that stimulate character development or rearrange the relationships in play. In 'The U of the Air World', for example, the protagonist disobeys his mother's injunction not to leave their home when his aunt lures him away to meet his 'brothers', who then ask him to gather fish, fruit and clams from a series of taboo locations. Each time, he reluctantly complies, but accepts none of the food back from the cousins, instead covertly tossing the choicest items to his aunt. The upshot is the reinstatement of the eldest 'brother' who's been dispossessed by the others, who are duly put to death.[120] The protagonist's mother is an U, a spirit of the crops, making him the ancestor of a clan responsible for honouring the U and resolving conflict in the community.[121]

The varied texture of sacredness across New Caledonia's landscape, and its gigantic lagoon, provides a basis for a sustainable economy: the enchantment of land and sea facilitates the economic exploitation of the ecosystem in such a way that it may continue to flourish and sustain future generations. In conditions of capitalist extraction of resources under French colonial governance, the Kanak's perspective of their environment as permeated by spirits aligns their struggle to maintain their distinctive culture with the conservation of ecology – a struggle complicated, however, by the forcible dispossession of many tribes from their ancestral lands and by the cooption of Kanak in extractive industries.[122]

It's commonly noted that indigenous stories draw so much of their significance from the place where they're set that it's difficult for them to be meaningfully told outside the community to whom that location is physically known. They demand an explicit connection between imagination and physical reality.[123] This is arguably the case for many Kanak tales, but I do find quite a number of the stories interesting and compelling purely *as stories*, and some do recur in different ethnolinguistic areas, especially fables like 'The Octopus and the Rat' which may omit localizing toponyms.[124] The isle of Maré even has a version of 'Jack and the Beanstalk' – 'The Two-Headed Ogre'[125] – which so closely follows the English tale that I suspect it was acquired from English missionaries active there before the French expelled them.[126]

During one research trip to New Caledonia, I intended to seek out the locations of Kanak stories I'd read. Very rarely, I did locate a landmark in a story: one was a waterhole on the isle of Lifou, which the spirits had abandoned – causing the water to dry up – when people began to bathe in it.[127] When I sought the seashore location of 'Keny Wazianu', a story about how the first coconut palm to be planted on Lifou nourished the first sons of the land,[128] I discovered that each tribe on the island locates the story on its own land;[129] but I didn't find out where any of these locations were. I soon realized that it wasn't possible to visit story locations as freely as I'd done in Gloucestershire. Even when I'd obtained permission to be in a tribe by performing a customary exchange with the chief ('faire la coutume'), the most enchanted spots, most likely linked to stories, were taped off as taboo. The purpose of faire la coutume is to place the visitor in right relationship with the spirits of the tribe. The enchantment entailed by this ceremony and by stories and taboos is more than an artistic technique as Tolkien defines 'enchantment'. It's part of Kanak perception of reality; a topic we'll return to in Chapter 6.

My lack of access to the precise locations of the stories, together with my limited understanding of Kanak spirituality and social structures, makes it impossible for me to retell Kanak local legends in the *same way* I tell Gloucestershire ones. I'm more keenly aware of this limitation with Kanak material, which I've studied in some depth, than when I pluck from a book of international folktales a story from a country I've never visited. However, I'm also aware that my amplification of the plots and themes of Gloucestershire legends may make them more engaging to audiences unfamiliar with their locations. Might the plots and themes of Kanak stories offer something of interest beyond the confines of local knowledge? Given the depth of ecological knowledge in traditional Kanak culture,[130] might the stories provide ecological insight that outsiders could learn from?

It must be acknowledged that non-European traditional tales are as likely as European ones to be permeated by conservative (patriarchal and xenophobic) beliefs that invite challenge. Tales about witches are as frequent in New Caledonia as in England and just as misogynistic, particularly stigmatizing older women, who can end up not only dead but cooked and eaten, like the ferocious sexy grandma of 'The Grandmother and the Three Brothers'.[131] When it comes to indigenous cultures, anthropologists and ethnographers are often keen to validate cultural authenticity and to criticize 'imaginative' or 'distorted' retelling of traditional stories.[132] In doing so, they risk reifying such cultures as static. Tjibaou placed at the heart of his campaign for Kanak independence the perpetuation of a distinct Kanak culture that had something valuable to contribute to the world, and yet he argued that it should be not static, or retrogressive, but continually renewed.[133]

My conversations with Kanak storytellers gave me more sense of common ground than much of the anthropological commentary I'd read. When I met a Kanak storyteller and told them a British tale as gesture of thanks for food and conversation, they always told me a story in return, usually choosing one with some thematic connection to the story I'd told. It felt like an empathetic reaching towards the universals that transcend geographical distance and cultural difference: 'Yes, we have something like that too.' However, it can be the *unfamiliar* elements in stories from other cultures that have the most impact.

A tale from mainland New Caledonia tells of 'Tamoangui, the Torso-Man', a monstrous being with no arms or legs, only a torso and enormous testicles. He asks some boys, during their break from work, to scratch him – including under his testicles – and then engulfs them through his anus. The boys' father having failed to protect them, their mother kills Tamoangui and cuts open his belly to release them.[134]

A central principle of Kanak society is exchange, formalized in faire la coutume, and enacted in equitable sharing in everyday life. There are many Kanak tales about someone who abuses hospitality, such as 'The Eagle and the Two Women', in which an 'eagle' repeatedly visits a mother and daughter and consumes all their dinner into his testicles, until on the third occasion the mother tricks him with a 'dinner' of a lethally hot stone.[135] Tamoangui goes further, consuming not merely the product of labour but the young labourers themselves, the hope of the future. That he should do so with his anus suggests a reversal of the natural order of things. As with the eagle, the economic symbolism is harnessed to a disturbing sexual dimension. The massive size of Tamoangui's testicles, the absence of description of other parts of his body, and his 'rolling' method of propulsion hint that he is little more than a gigantic penis with testicles and anus at one end. In both stories connotations of sexual misconduct are conflated with the sexual-reproductive linkage between economics and ecology: the villain symbolically consumes the harvest of labour, even the labour itself, to serve his own uncurbed, economically unproductive urges. In both cases, also, it's the mother who kills the hypermasculine villain: a reversal of gender roles that serves to neutralize the disruptive reversal of moral norms but doesn't exactly fit the ecofeminist vision outlined above.

In the course of learning about New Caledonia, I've tried telling some published Kanak tales in the informal setting of storytelling clubs. I wanted to experience them more deeply than I could by simply reading them; I was also interested in listeners' responses. In telling 'Tamoangui' I omitted the toponyms and parents' names in the source text in order to minimize any illusion of cultural authenticity and to be freer to tell the story my own way and give my listeners freedom to interpret it. The story certainly had an impact. One American listener drew an unflattering comparison to a prominent American politician – an allusion to the simultaneous abuse of power at the personal level and in the dynamics of rapacious capitalism. Someone who heard 'The Eagle and the Two Women' acknowledged its strangeness but then said, 'It's exactly in a nutshell what humans are doing to the planet.' These interpretations stand outside the frames of reference within which these stories were originally told, but nevertheless struck me as interesting and strongly felt.

Drawing upon the methods of the Zen koan and of psychiatrist Milton Erickson, Parkinson advocates the storyteller's deliberate use of the unexpected, even the baffling, to 'momentarily arrest habitual patterns of emotions and thoughts' and thereby open a gap for new insights to break through in the listener's mind.[136] Unfamiliar motifs in stories from other cultures can have that effect; it's one more ingredient of the structure of space that stories present. The weirdness of 'Tamoangui' smacks the Western listener awake more dramatically than would, say, 'The Wolf and the Seven Little Kids', which has a similar plot and themes.

Reweaving the land's enchantment

Twenty-first-century Gloucestershire may seem a long way from Tjibaou's enchanted vision of New Caledonia. But maybe not as far as you might think. Lee recalls of his 1920s Gloucestershire boyhood,

> It was something we just had time to inherit ... the blood and beliefs of generations who had been in this valley since the Stone Age. That continuous contact has at last been broken ... But arriving, as I did, at the end of that age, I caught whiffs of something old as the glaciers. There were ghosts in the stones, in the trees, and the walls, and each field and hill had several ... there were certain

landmarks about the valley – tree-clumps, corners in woods – that bore separate, antique, half-muttered names that were certainly older than Christian.[137]

The loss of this enchanted perspective is intrinsic to the instrumentalist attitude that has driven the demolition of ecosystems: '"disenchanted" people', writes Patrick Curry, 'will fall for the first rationalization for exploiting and destroying, and a disenchanted world doesn't feel worth defending'.[138]

We can't expect to preserve the land in a pristine, unchanging state; the land will keep changing, just as stories will, in the weave of time's unfolding. Neither can we wind the clock back to the perspectives people held before Darwin; to the exact stories that were once told and are now forgotten or fragmented; to the landscape as it was before the wildwood was cleared. We have a long way yet to travel to come to terms with the struggle for existence which Darwin revealed in the natural world. We need more than the inspiration of nature's grandeur and intricacy – to which scientists like Sagan and Edward O. Wilson direct us[139] – to motivate the kinds of change the ecological crisis demands. Something else is needed that speaks within our hearts and in doing so connects us beyond ourselves.

The notion of *dis*enchantment invites the possibility of *re*-enchantment. Gibson's broad usage of 're-enchantment', to include any kind of positive regard for nature,[140] risks eliding a distinct and necessary concept of enchantment as an artful process that cannot be pinned down by science. Enchantment in Tolkien's sense engages 'the primal desire at the heart of Faerie';[141] it bespeaks what Verena Andermatt Conley describes as 'a *mobilization* of the heightened consciousness' that's needed to move from 'ecological awareness' towards a 'praxis' of change.[142] Ronald W. Hepburn argues that the sense of 'wonder' that enchantment evokes 'is notably and essentially other-acknowledging';[143] it conveys that the 'other' – person, animal, plant, place, community – has some level of significance beyond its mere physical existence. Thus can enchantment engender, as Curry says, 'respect, compassion and humility'.[144] If Tolkien's 'enchantment' and the ontological uncertainty of Todorov's 'fantastic' are applied beyond literature to the real landscapes and townscapes of local legends, re-enchantment may be experienced in the space between what we know for sure about the world and what we imagine in stories; a space in which folk tradition, nature's agency, the individual's imagination and – for some – the spirits of the invisible world may all speak.

Tolkien distinguishes between 'enchantment', which has an aesthetic purity of desire – or open-ended intention – and 'magic', whose 'desire is *power* in this world, the domination of things and wills'.[145] 'Magic' in this sense encompasses any technique of power, including scientific technologies, by which to impose your will upon others. Curry defines a super-opposite of enchantment: 'glamour', meaning 'Enchantment in the service of Magic', as deployed notably in advertising and propaganda.[146] Something of this kind is implied in Mike Wilson's critique of 'enchantment' as 'depoliticizing the storytelling act', where 'enchantment' appears to be understood as something like a hypnotic trance that disarms the listener's critical mind and thereby disempowers them; thus 'enchantment' and 'enlightenment' are positioned as mutually exclusive functions of different models of storytelling.[147] However, in Parkinson's account, 'trance' can be understood as a state of consciousness that people routinely slip in and out of, especially when attention is focused, as when reading or listening to a story. It need not involve manipulative disempowerment; on the contrary, the relaxing of critical reason can allow new perceptions to arise from one's unconscious.[148] If Tolkienian enchantment involves an altered state of consciousness akin to trance, and if the storyteller mindfully honours the listeners' agency as they open to this, then enlightenment *can* coincide with enchantment.

Lupton writes, 'The land we inhabit is wounded, it has been desecrated as never before ... and it will not recover until it becomes, in some way, sacred again. Part of the process of re-sacrilisation must involve the telling of the myths of landscape, re-storying and re-dreaming the land.'[149] The more stories of local places are known and retold, the more pervasive will be the land's web of enchantment. The Kanak mythscape offers an inkling of how such an enchanted appreciation of landscape might be integrated with the dynamics of inhabiting and using the land. In Gloucestershire some of the local tales I've reworked are being told by others and have thus renewed their presence in tradition. For example, I learnt from chatting with listeners after one performance that teenagers in Cheltenham had become acquainted with 'Maude's Elm' because a girl who'd read *Gloucestershire Folk Tales* had a friend who lived near the site of the vanished tree. As we'll see in Chapter 5, if reconstructed local folktales can renew their place in local human ecology, they can contribute to more caring and ecologically conscious relations between people and the land they inhabit.

Local folktales are not static cultural fossils that inevitably mediate archaic values. They transmute over time through a kind of cultural composting. A simple tale may imply a whole tradition of related stories, which, though evolving through time, carry a momentum of repeating patterns in which certain values are mediated and may themselves change. What matters is that we treat both stories and land with respect and that the ways we change the stories embody the ethics we need, just as the ways the land is reworked should serve the flourishing of all who dwell there, both human and non-human. I found that latent green themes emerged more readily than I expected from Gloucestershire's folklore and that it is possible to foreground and radicalize these themes while at the same time recycling most of the composted local tradition of each tale, together with aspects of the wider tradition of related stories, and thereby harness to the green themes the aura flowing from the tale's roots in place and tradition. I discovered that open-minded encounter with a place can enable the 'spirit of the place' – its ecology, history, topography, energy – to suggest how the tale may be interpreted in a way that rings true to the place. Field research enables you to embed the retelling in local detail so that, as the tale enchants the place, the place also enchants the tale with 'secondary belief' that enhances its capacity to engage the imagination and elicit an empathetic response.

In all this, an ecobardic intention was essential – in the selection of stories, in reshaping their structure of events and in the process of putting them into words.[150] Without such intentionality, tales may be retold in whatever way seems most entertaining, and pre-existing assumptions may be conveyed by default. Without ecocritical awareness the enchantment of place by local legends is vulnerable to commercialization reducing it to exploitative glamour.[151] Hartsiotis also observes that the recent rise of interest in British local folktales marked by the History Press book series can be seen as part of a cultural turn inwards (including increased interest in domestic nature writing, local tourism and locally produced crafts and food) that is not only ecological, but also pulled from the political right by the nationalism and austerity that produced Brexit and pushed from the left by anxieties about 'cultural appropriation'.[152] The importance of balancing the affirmation of local roots with an intercultural openness is one more illustration of the need for cultural leadership from artists who are politically and ecologically aware and understand that ethical commitment need not diminish but may rather stimulate creativity.

5

The listening place: The space of transformative stillness

On one hand, storytelling is an everyday part of conversation, but, as a more deliberate activity, storytelling – together with music and dance – is a primal element of cultic practices that since prehistory have connected the individual's mind and body to community, environment and cosmos.[1] Art of diverse kinds continues to have such a 'cultic' potential today, by which I mean it can invite *participation*, as opposed to mere consumption of entertainment or transmission of information. In challenging times, says Lopez, such participatory experiences 'gave people the psychic means to endure'.[2]

As we saw in Chapter 1, storytelling has some affinity to ritual, owing to participants' embodied presence and agency. The *structure* of many traditional stories is also akin to that of ritual, as in Campbell's 'separation, initiation, return'; or the 'departure, adventure, integration' shared by Greek wonder tales and folk rituals; or the 'diagnosis, prescription, cure' of spiritual awakening in Buddhist legends of the mahasiddhas.[3] In the middle phase the initiate or protagonist undergoes a liminal experience beyond the scope of everyday life. The final phase integrates that transient experience as change. If someone attending to a story be considered equivalent to the 'initiate or protagonist', they may be seen as experiencing at least the structure of a rite of passage; especially so if they're willing to identify with the story's protagonist. They cross a metaphysical threshold from the everyday world into the imagined world of the story. Having shared vicariously in the characters' experiences, they return to the everyday world as the story ends. They may feel moved or challenged by the story, but how likely are they to undergo change?

Martin Shaw explains that even the powerful rite of passage of a vision quest requires integration work afterwards if lasting change is to ensue.[4] In Chapter 2 we looked at the role of conversation and more elaborate storywork in facilitating the integration of people's response to stories. These kinds of integration processes contain much talking and listening, including further storytelling. We arrive back again at the question of how a consequence of change is carried between the realm of words and the realm of human action in the ecosystem.

As a measure of 'change', the discovery of new *meaning* from a story remains at the level of mentation. The expression and fulfilment of *desire* involve the body; so do healing and well-being. The body is the interface between mind and ecology. It's part of the ecosystem; what happens in the ecosystem will eventually impact upon people's bodies. The body is therefore pivotal to the politics of the environment.[5] Richard Stone's rationale for stories' capacity to facilitate healing is that imagined events are experienced in the body as if they're real.[6] The corollary is that toxic stories will negatively impact on one's body as well as mind.[7] The somatic reception of a story is thus a pathway of effect from stories into the ecological domain. In theory, this applies to stories in any medium. However, storytelling delivers a notable range of biosemiotic effects: the acoustic impact of the spoken word upon the physical space, including the bodies of everyone there, whether human beings or other creatures; the reciprocal visual impact of storyteller's and listeners' gaze, expressions, stance, movement and clothing; the arrangement of the participants' bodies with respect to each other and the physical space, including any furniture or vegetation; the *affective* qualities of the rapport between storyteller, listeners, story and place; and also the *energetic* qualities of connection we'll consider in Chapter 6. In all of this a dialogic responsiveness is in play.

None of these effects in themselves equates to caring for the ecosystem; however, they take the participants further than manufactured texts or images can into the ecological actuality of embodied people interacting in a physical place – and therefore closer to the point of action. The point of action is a point of choice: Do I do *this* or do I do *that*? Chapter 3 argued that in the face of ecological crisis it's important to believe that such choices are not inevitable consequences of past causes; that it may be possible, for some people, some of the time, to experience the moment of choice in full awareness, to act in conscious freedom and thereby turn the course of events in constructive ways.

This chapter will describe storyteller Jane Flood's work in a series of three large-scale community projects in Somerset which aimed to awaken rural communities to their own local landscape through storytelling and other creative activities.[8] Flood is alert to the affinity between storytelling and ritual and to the transformative potential of spaces of inner stillness. Emergent from her work on these projects is the concept of 'the listening place', simultaneously a physical place in the land and a receptive state of being. This concept provides us a springboard to zoom into a more detailed study of the potentially transformative dynamics of listening to stories, listening to the land and listening within.

Freedom from clock time: 'Echoes in the Land'

The first project was in the Mendip Hills, a limestone landscape inhabited since prehistoric times and today possessing some legal protection as an Area of Outstanding National Beauty (AONB). 'Echoes in the Land' took place over a year and involved ten villages and ten different groups of people, of all ages, including schools, youth groups, women's groups and the elderly. The aim was to encourage among this diverse community a more engaged and creative relationship with the landscape they inhabited.

Flood began by listening to the people. In the case of the adults, some of whom had local roots going back generations, she asked open-ended questions about important days, places and characters and listened to the stories, memories, traditions and lore they told her. The knowledge of the oldest people, who could remember the great changes in rural life between the World Wars, included practical wisdom about how to inhabit the land, such as the importance of the seasons and, for instance, how essential it was to ensure you had enough wood to keep the fire going in the winter. People recalled fragments of traditional story, intermediate between memory and legend. In the village of Hutton, for example, someone mentioned 'a crazy lady who used to throw her cups and saucers and plates out of the window at the full moon, and that led on to some story about the hill, something that happened at full moon … up on the hill by the spring … "The old story is that the squire used to take his ladyfriend up there and she went crazy because they were found out."' Such trains of folk memory could lead back in time to 'Something that's really odd and difficult to explain. I get a shiver down my spine when something like that happens.'

The children, meanwhile, Flood took out on to the land and got them to make up stories inspired by what they experienced there. She would make sure beforehand she knew something of the place's geography, natural history, weather patterns, the ways the land had been worked. In the field, she'd begin with some general sharing – 'What does it feel like to be out here?' – being aware that many children today aren't used to being outdoors. Then she would engage them with their senses. 'Let's see. Let's play. Let's listen. Let's be still. Let's run really noisily until we haven't got any breath left and then lie down on our backs.' Through these means she and they listened to the land. Then she'd tell them a story, not necessarily a local one, but a story from her repertoire which she could hook on to something there, maybe a tree, the soil or the wind. And then she'd get them to articulate their own stories in response to the place. These she recorded, so that later they could listen to them together, pick out themes and characters and reshape the stories' structure, sometimes using the template of 'problem, quest and resolution'.

'A really important thing is to forget time,' says Flood. 'In schools you have very precise time intervals before it's break. One of the things about these projects is that we take our lunch, we've always got something to sit on with us and we eat when we feel like it, and the sessions are as long or as short as they need to be. That enables the stillness. It enables that listening consciousness.' This stillness is a pivotal concept I'll return to.

Flood incorporated the stories from both children and adults into a series of storytelling performances. In one locality a sculpture trail was constructed through a wood, in which the paper sculptures referred to stories she'd crafted about the wood. People walked the trail and at each sculpture Flood told the corresponding story. When they walked back in the dark, the paper sculptures had been lit up. The experience evoked a sense of 'pilgrimage … earth magic … and belonging'. Flood still meets people who say, 'I never go to that wood without remembering that night.'

'Echoes in the Land' culminated in an ambitious event inside Cheddar Caves, featuring eight storytellers – some professionals, others from the community – and attended by everyone who'd taken part in the project. 'That night!' people still exclaim. 'It was incredible! I've never forgotten it. I never saw the caves like that. Those stories! And that giant! I didn't know that!' Because these performances incorporated stories built from the community's memories and the children's creative interaction with the landscape, the community felt a sense of ownership of the stories and a deepened sense of connection to the place they inhabited.

Returning local lore into the local community: 'Liberating the Landscape'

Flood subsequently delivered the storytelling component of 'Liberating the Landscape', a year-long project in the Blackdown Hills, another AONB, composed of steep hills and deep-cut valleys, with lots of forest and pasture 'and villages snuggled by the waterways'. The project had a similar aim to deepen local people's relationship with their landscape.[9] To the methodology

Flood had developed on Mendip, she and musician Fiona Barrow added the further ingredient of intensively researching Somerset folktales, folk music and traditions of the land which were largely lost from the community but had been recorded by folklorists. The intention was to find creative ways to embed this lore back in the living community. In archives of Somerset folklore they found lots of promising material, including much Gypsy lore because many Gypsies have lived in the area.

Flood and Barrow wove connections within this material and with their broader knowledge of English folktale and folk song. They also familiarized themselves with the Blackdown landscape: walking the paths; meeting people; going in the churches; visiting veteran trees 'and naming them and thinking about what they had seen'. They mapped the folklore from the archives upon their present-day knowledge of the land to create a performance piece designed to take some of this Somerset lore back to the local community from which it had originally come. For example, in the Wytch Wood, on Blackdown, is a magnificent oak tree. The protagonist of the story that Flood devised, Gracie, is a 'chime child', inspired by folklore recorded by Ruth Tongue.[10] Gracie's favourite place to sit was beneath that tree, a location that recurs three times in the story. The surrounding woods, villages and hills are named locations in the story and inspired Barrow's composition of music. Some of the characters were loosely inspired by local people they met. The story also includes traditional sayings, remedies and beliefs, which, though one may no longer accept them as fact, mark a connection with the past and an acknowledgement, as Flood says, 'that there's more to life than we can pin down, that there are other forces at work that we do not have control over'.

As a chime child, born between midnight and cockcrow on a Friday eve, Gracie had one foot in this world and one foot in the other, and so the 'old folk' (fairies) could communicate with her. She was physically weak but free spirited, would wander the fields, watch the clouds, listen to the birdsong and had a far-away look as if she wasn't quite there. The truth was that she heard everything that was said, and she remembered it. People would ask her about the weather, animals, fields and sweethearts, and she was usually right. On wisht nights and holy days she'd sweetly sing the old songs. No one thought she'd ever marry and she seemed content to dream away her days beneath the ancient oak tree.

On the hilltop in the village of Blackwater lived Granny Criddle, a cunning woman knowledgeable about the fairies, who adopted a chance-come boy named Tom Hoy. She brought him up to observe the old ways. One May Eve, when he was walking home, he heard fairy music and came upon the fairy fayre of Staple

Fitzpaine. He bought Granny Criddle a new jug with one piece of silver and thirteen primroses he'd prudently gathered. In the jug he discovered thirteen autumn beech leaves, which by next morning had become thirteen pieces of gold. Now he could buy a fine horse. One day, riding that horse by the Wytch Wood, he met Gracie and soon they were sweethearts.

Everyone expected them to be married within a year, but on Punkie Night, in October, Gracie was missing from home. Tom rode up to her favourite oak, his horse shied and Tom was thrown. When he came to, he discovered Gracie lying beneath the tree, no sign of injury, but cold and dead. Tom became quiet and joyless after that. When Punkie Night came round again, he rode up to the ancient oak and again his horse threw him. When he got up he heard fairy music and discovered the fairies having a party. There he met Gracie with a child on her shoulder. She told him the fairies had taken her because they needed someone to care for this child. 'You buried sticks and stones that day in the church. Tom, I like it here. There's no sickness, no old age, no grief. The only thing I truly miss is you.' But she couldn't come back to him, and he couldn't stay with *them*. Remembering something Granny Criddle had told him, he turned his coat inside out and threw it over the fairies. At once they vanished and the wood was silent.

When Gracie's coffin was dug up, there was no body, only sticks and stones. Tom never again met the fairies, but he always put out for them spring water and fresh cream, as Granny Criddle had done. On wisht nights and holy days, folk would get him to tell his story about the fairies. It's said they're still there, in the high and hidden places. You can glimpse them in the tree roots, hear their laughter in a gurgling stream, and sometimes you may see them dancing by the light of the full moon.[11]

This story presents within it the kind of 'Faërian drama' discussed in Chapter 4; it is at once a story about storytelling and enchantment *and* a story that enchants the real landscape in which it's set. Its ending draws a partial equation between the otherworld of the fairies and the imaginative world into which stories take us. Gracie's foot in each of the two worlds makes her, like a storyteller, a bridge between worlds.[12] Especially relevant to the focus of this chapter is her 'dreaming' capacity to listen inwardly and outwardly.

Gracie's story, interlaced with music, was performed in local pubs, churches, old people's homes, schools and out on the hills. Because the story features places that people knew and could visit, it had a resonance for them in the landscape. Some have told Flood they've gone looking for Gracie's grave in Staple Fitzpaine. The repeated invocation of the fairies, in both the main plot and the folk customs and beliefs woven into the narrative, conveys a sense of this landscape being permeated by these beings, akin to the 'spirits' of other cultures.

The performance provided the springboard for people in the community to create their own stories. Flood told them, 'This is the place where those stories come from. They're your stories. I've told them to you, but the stories belong to you. What are you going to do with them?' She and her collaborators worked with people from across the age ranges: with schools and parents, with a local history group, with ramblers, equestrians, Gypsies, and 'woodlanders' who live off the grid of modern society.

'Liberating the Landscape' culminated in a local revival of Punkie Night, a Somerset tradition that supposedly began when men would get drunk on cider at an annual fair and the women would make lanterns to guide them home. Behind it sits the older tradition of the fire ceremonies of Halloween.[13] The project team reinvented Punkie Night as a celebration of season and landscape. A candlelit procession was organized to the top of Castle Neroche, the site of an Iron Age hill fort and Norman castle. It's a place where people perceive an odd atmosphere, there's a legend about the Devil, 'and the dogs get spooked and you don't want to be up there on your own after dark'. About 400 people attended Punkie Night. Everyone stood round a tree that an artist had decorated with imagery of the four seasons; the children sang songs, read poems and told stories. The event concluded with a tree blessing, the offering of written 'promises for the land', and a bonfire. Thus public ritual emerged out of storywork to connect, as rites traditionally do, personal renewal with nature's well-being.[14]

Where people, land and story meet: 'The Listening Place'

The Mendip and Blackdown projects needed a legacy strategy. People who'd been involved wanted a place where they could continue something of what they'd experienced. In different ways they decided to take action. In one Mendip village a roundhouse was built where people met once a month to tell stories and play music. Word spread and a sense of community developed from people coming together to listen or perform. A similar event came about in another village. After Punkie Night, and the end of the Blackdown project, a local artist-musician said of Castle Neroche, 'We can make this into a "listening place".' Thus Castle Neroche became the first place to be defined as a 'listening place'. Other listening places then popped up on Blackdown. One of them is the oak in Gracie's story.

The first time Flood and Barron performed the story outdoors, it was in a boggy area with lots of hazel, a place that had a fey atmosphere and was quite an adventure just to get to. Somebody had bent some hazel saplings to make a kind of bower. Words had been carved on a log; things like 'Be still. Just watch.' Telling stories here thus inspired the idea of *constructing* a listening place at a chosen point in the landscape. A seat was erected in a spot elsewhere on Blackdown to be a listening place. 'It's hidden away in the middle of nowhere, yet people are going there. There's a new path towards it.' What matters more than the physical seat, emphasizes Flood, is 'the intention of going to that place with the knowledge that somehow you're giving yourself permission to really *be* ... To be introspective, be aware of what's gone before and also the potential of what could come afterwards.'

When Flood was invited to propose a third storytelling project, in North Somerset, she knew what to call it: 'The Listening Place'. The aim was again to inspire among local people a creative response to the landscape – and in this case coastal seascape – that they inhabit. In the methodology she refined through these projects, the first stage was to listen with the people to what was around and within them; telling them stories was part of this. From the stillness of listening they then created stories, music, poems and art. 'The Listening Place' involved ten schools and some community groups. Flood took groups of children to the same place in each of the four seasons. She got them to be still, to listen, look in each direction, use their peripheral vision. She told them stories *of* the place *in* the place and then elicited from them a creative response to being there.

This time she also worked with a landscape artist to help each school design and build a listening place, a permanent location for quiet contemplation and the sharing of creative work. The plan was to build the listening places in the schools' grounds, but the children didn't want them there; they wanted them to be out where everyone could use them. One school decided to make a labyrinth. One school chose a story tree. One school worked with a church to create a listening place on the top of a hill. One school just had a mark on the ground. There were no fixed expectations what to do in the listening place. The children went to them in the different seasons and took their parents with them. Many were children who'd never spent much time outdoors.

Consequences of the community projects

A strength of these projects was their scale. Because they were long-term projects, involving recurrent sessions with the same people over the course of a year, and because they involved diverse groups within each target area, Flood was able to get to know the community and observe change in ways not possible when a storyteller parachutes in for a one-off session: 'It was truly exciting to see how people's perception of their landscape changed: their sense of belonging, even the way they were walking – there was more attention to what was around them.' Even so, Flood believes that with more time more could be achieved. Ideally, she says, projects like these should run over five years. Though people continued to go up to Castle Neroche to tell stories, their wish to restore Punkie Night as an annual event didn't work out. An event of that scale requires lots of preparation and whipping up of enthusiasm, which in turn build the quality of intention that makes ritual a transformative experience. Paid professionals can do this. It's less sustainable for community volunteers to do all that work unpaid, although they often do work very hard and accomplish much.

At the end of sessions of outdoor storywork, Flood often asked the participants, 'How does that make you feel about this place?' Again and again they said, 'I'm going to come back here' and 'I'll never look at it in the same way again.' Having remained in contact with some of them, she has continued to hear, years after a project ended, about its effects on people's relationship with the land. Many say they see their local landscape in a totally new way, perceive the interconnectivity of all beings and the land, feel part of the land rather than merely using it. They notice the transitions of seasons which they didn't notice before. They will stop at a point on a path where storytelling or storywork happened and listen to its echoes in that place. 'It's made me want to look after the place,' they say. 'I've cleaned it up. I go out more. I care.'

This care involves respect and guardianship. 'Even if this is only a tiny place, I'm going to make sure during my lifetime that it stays how I want it to be.' So they keep the place tidy by picking up litter or clearing paths. One woman now never goes out without her secateurs to trim the brambles. One school on Blackdown was inspired subsequently to do a cross-curricular project on Somerset folklore, 'to make sense of how life was and why people were so superstitious and who were the fairies'. However, 'The stories the participants made blew away with the wind,' observes Flood. 'The stories that I offered are the ones they're retelling.' This observation captures something of the dynamic between the experiential strength of storytelling as inclusive and participatory and the role of the expert storyteller as not only facilitator but also creative artist and tradition bearer.

Through this series of projects, there was a pathway of consequence and learning for Flood too: 'I've changed in myself and I've also changed how I live. When I started I was in an ordinary posh four-bedroom house and now I'm living really close to the land.' She stresses that 'to be sustainable we have to *be*. We can't do what we're doing. It has to stop. It has to change. It has to be reborn and shift and shake and shiver and come out as something new.' But, 'In the hustle and bustle, high-wired, fast-forward life that so many of us live today, it's difficult to find a place and space to stop and take stock in.'

The 'listening place', as it emerged in Flood's projects, is a physical place in the landscape to which you can go, alone or with others, to be and to listen. It's also the state of being you enter when you listen to a story or when you listen to the land with the same attention as when you listen to a story. The act of generous listening can create a sacred space anywhere, a space transcending instrumental purpose.[15] Flood says,

> A good story well told holds the possibility of leading the listener into the place of dreams; into the place where anything is possible, where problems are resolved ... and where we are totally free in our shared imaginations. Something happens as we listen to stories, something akin to alchemy, sorcery or magic. We are transformed. We believe in possibilities beyond the mundane.

While the stories we're hearing feed our imagination, the experience of listening presents a way of being that is still, deep, collective and unselfconscious; 'in that moment your senses become more acute and more attuned' and you can connect with yourself, other people and everything around you. The storyteller 'creates an inner stage', writes Oelrich, 'through living images spoken in words, where the thinking, feeling and willing of the listener is activated'.[16] John S. Dunne infers that there's always more than we can tell, and so listening involves listening 'not only to the things we can tell but also to each other's awareness of things we may not be able to tell'; a way of being that segues into a broader consciousness akin to 'listening to the earth'.[17] Flood believes 'that if we can nurture and develop this way of being ... we will eventually be able to connect not only with each other but with the very life pulse of the planet' and we will know what we need to do.

Storytelling, listening and transformation

The implication here is that the psychological transformation of individuals, in relationship with community and environment, underpins the transformation of behaviour, individual and collective, in such a way as to serve ecological well-being. In the mythopoeic terms of the Grail quest, the healing of the wasteland, the wounded world, coinheres with the healing of the Fisher King, who symbolizes the inner being of each one of us.[18] The argument of this book is that oral storytelling is well suited to sustaining the dialectic between the social negotiation of meaning and ethics, necessary to reforming the structures of society, and the internal process by which the sharing of story can be transformative in its own right. Key to that argument, as we explored in Chapter 2, is the opening of 'space' in which people can respond to story. The gaps in a story, observes Gersie, are equivalent to 'the potential, transitional area in therapeutic practice where insight, discovery and change happen'.[19] Equally key is that storytelling is a profoundly embodied experience.

Activities like reading, watching TV and using computers and phones are embodied in the sense that we're in our bodies as we do these things. However, the effect of these technologies is to distance your conscious experience from what's physically around you. Reading takes you inwards; screen-based media hold your attention on a flat interface with a simulated world that may or may not represent part of the real world. Storytelling does take you inwards, but also, like theatre, directs your attention to live performers in the physical space before you. Ritual drama offers a yet closer analogy with its imaginative evocation of another world coexisting with the physical one. Storytelling, like the chime child, bridges the inner world of the story and the outer world of the telling and is therefore an ideal vehicle of the function of the imagination, as Lindsay Clarke defines it, to bring together the inner and outer worlds of human experience.[20] The story exists invisibly in the mind, the body's senses are attuned to the physical reality around you, and yet both the stimulating of your imagination and the direct sensory impact of the telling can elicit a bodily response through the nervous and endocrine systems;[21] and the body in turn is entangled in ecology. Michael A. Uzendoski and Edith Felicia Calapucha-Tapuy write of Amazonian storytelling,

> the body and its presence have multiple capacities to elicit imaginative and social relations with people as well as with the larger ecological and spiritual world. Stories are social acts that explore the aesthetics of bodily experiences and potentialities, potentialities that are grounded in a rich communicative and sentient landscape of people, plants, rivers, trees, animals, insects, and other socialities.[22]

Story-listeners have an embodied presence in the physical venue where storytelling is taking place. The choosing of a good location for a 'listening place' in Flood's projects brings matters of ergonomics into relation with ecology and atmosphere. Too often, storytelling audiences are expected to sit on uncomfortable seats, or in discomfort on the floor or ground, or outdoors simply to stand, even in the rain! Physical discomfort undermines the capacity to listen with the sustained attention that storytelling requires. Sometimes storytellers need to be assertive with event organizers, and even the listeners themselves, to optimize the seating arrangements. Hence the importance when scouting a story walk of planning how to arrange the audience at each stop. And it's essential in any season that an outdoor event have a fallback venue indoors in case the weather's bad. 'Don't worry, it's June!' an organizer once assured me; both audience and performers looked like drowned rats by the end.

Surface, depth and gaze

Moreover, the storyteller has an embodied presence before the listeners' embodied presence. Storytelling doesn't usually involve *tactile* contact. It can do, as in my first encounter with the legendary Scottish storyteller Duncan Williamson, who sat up close, knee to knee, gripping my knee in his hands as he told me a grim tale of the selkies; there was no way to avoid listening! But the main ways that storytellers physically connect with listeners are through gaze and voice.

The storyteller sees the listener; the listener sees the storyteller. They can generally see the whole of each other's body, so the non-verbal signals of the entire bodies of both parties contribute to their dialogic communication, whether expansive gestures by the storyteller or faint cues of response from the listener.

Vision engages you with the surface of the other, hence its tendency to objectify them, to produce a sense of separation between subject and object.[23] Thus visual communication, including print and screen media, can amplify the experience of the self as separate, and also of the self as a *surface* produced through communicative exchange. On the basis of this understanding of self, Cupitt sees stories primarily as connected sequences of events and information, overlooking the capacity of metaphor, symbol, irony and feeling to give a story *depth* that in turn engages the depth of being of its audience. In his view a continuous stream of narration produces and sustains our sense of 'selfhood', which is 'all on the surface'.[24] This self-narration, however, is really the means by which the *ego* is constructed.[25] There's nowhere for a space – within a story, within the psyche – out of which the new insights and attitudes we need can emerge. All that Cupitt can propose is that we keep coming up with new stories, as if these are an adequate end in themselves; the actuality of change is forever deferred.

In the meeting of gaze between living beings, however, a deeper connection is possible. The reciprocity of seer and seen, the sense of 'I and Thou',[26] allows the distinction between subject and object to begin to dissolve; you become aware of the inner being of yourself and the other.[27] There's a tremendous range of nuance to the quality of eye contact that storytellers can share with their listeners. A softness of gaze can allow your inner self to be seen and at the same time can open your receptivity to the gaze of others. In the holding of one person's gaze for the length of a single clause of speech, before you turn to another listener, there can be a meeting, even a momentary blending, of consciousness.[28]

Voice, rhythm and silence

The feeling of 'transportation' that can be produced by any art form is experienced as sensations in the body.[29] We saw in Chapter 2 how attending to correlations between moments in a story and feelings in different parts of the body can elicit connections between one's embodied existence and facets of ethics, empathy and desire.[30] Important to storytelling's capacity to arouse such feelings in the body are the sonic qualities of the voice.

Sound is a vibration through the air which makes an acoustic impact on the whole of the body, not only the ear. Thus, Ong explains, we experience sound in the depths of our being and simultaneously we're immersed within it. Immersion in the field of sound supports a sense of being central to the cosmos, while sound's penetration of one's body engages a sense of interior consciousness; hence a merging of inside and outside, subject and object, in contrast to the objectifying tendency of sight. Because the storyteller's spoken word is composed of sound, it's experienced in this way, but in addition, Ong writes, 'the spoken word proceeds from the human interior and manifests human beings to one another as conscious interiors'.[31] Such mutual recognition of consciousness is the basis of empathy and community. As stories are shared and memories thereby brought to mind, says Stone, 'those gathered together begin to build a bond of closeness made of common pains, losses, and joys'.[32]

The acoustic impact of the voice upon the listener's body means that storytellers have to attend not only to the words they speak but also to the qualities of voice with which they speak them. If I tell a challenging story in a harsh ranting way, the listener's body may contract defensively and so resist emotional engagement, whereas a sensitive understated tone helps to relax the listener physically and so make them more open to their own feelings. A storywork participant may sometimes serve their own cathartic needs by venting strong feelings vocally, but when the listeners are the beneficiaries the storyeller has to carefully manage the expression of passion. You may sometimes powerfully voice a character's grief or rage, but then drop straight back into a calm narrative voice that lets the audience feel safely held and allows space for their feelings. Not only the words but every sigh, grunt or onomatopoeic noise the teller utters will enter the listener's body, as will noises from other listeners or the surroundings.

Once this principle is grasped, huge scope opens up for storytellers to develop their consciousness of the qualities of their voice and to expand the range of pitch, volume, resonance and intonation available to them.[33] Chloë Goodchild's voicework teaching takes this exploration beneath the level of skilful control, to facilitate the emergence of a maximally authentic 'naked voice' from one's innermost being and to cultivate a consciousness in using the voice which overrides impulsive reaction or habit.[34] The vocalization of the spoken word then ceases to be a dualist exercise of 'impacting' on the listener and becomes rather a shared experience of speaking–listening in which the storyteller is vulnerably open and simultaneously holds the space for the listeners.[35] Goodchild draws upon Indian spiritual traditions in which each syllable is understood to evoke particular nuances of feeling in both speakers and listeners. Different Indian musical modes (ragas) evoke different patterns of feelings (rasas) which express or reflect distinct attitudes to the world.[36] One implication of all this is that the storyteller may formulate an intention of voice (and gesture) evocative of the particular emotional dynamics of the story to be told.[37] Another is to bring to your voice an awareness of the kinds of emotional energy you're putting into the world.

Complementary to the sonic qualities of spoken words is the rhythm of speech – imparting pace, reflecting the rhythm of life and mediating the rhythm of narrative, which pre-exists both story and language, being found in walking, in sport, in sex, in music, in a mother's rocking play with her infant. Speech's rhythm of sound and pause 'entrains' listeners and speaker with each other and is a vital part of the tension that keeps the listeners engaged.[38] The pauses of silence provide spaces in time where something new can come through.

Whereas readers can create space themselves by pausing for thought, in storytelling the teller must provide the space. Maddern, for example, tells with a rhythmic energy that draws listeners in and carries them along; then right at the end, after the last word, he'll sustain a silence by freezing his body and smile, so the listeners can discover their reaction to the completed story, before he lets go and they break the silence with applause. In verbatim 'text-telling', sometimes employed for scriptural or literary stories,[39] the management of pauses between words is critical to inflecting and inviting meaning, since the words are fixed. In extempore storytelling, there's a more dynamic relationship between pauses and words. Because the words are not fixed, they can be seen as *emerging* from silence, even when the rhythm is rapid. The sound of the words arises from the space *between* the words, from *before* and *after* them, from the consciousness *beneath* them; as too does the listener's response to them. Oelrich encourages us 'to become aware of the threshold of our lips … to grasp hold of what we really want to say and to find a space of freedom, if only just for a moment'.[40] In this gap of silence, however brief, you have a choice which words you'll speak, with which tone and gesture, that feel right for this moment. In this same gap of silence the listeners have agency to form an interpretant, hence to influence the storyteller non-verbally at the same time as they discover new insights in themselves. This conception of storytelling is beautifully captured in Lopez's translation of the Inuit term for 'storyteller' ('isumataq') as 'person who creates the atmosphere in which wisdom reveals itself'.[41] For the storyteller to manage this process well requires not only verbal dexterity but a mindful presence to the moment, a capacity to hold the points of stillness when they come.

In a sense, the liminal space alluded to above is available in every pause. But, as we learnt in Chapter 1, a story may contain some particularly charged point of stillness. In William Labov and Joshua Waletsky's analysis, oral stories 'contain a moment of "evaluation," a moment where the speaker calls attention to and reflects on the "point" of his story, and explicitly or implicitly calls the listener to attention, asking him to judge the story as important'.[42] A storyteller may have their own feeling of where a particular story's emotional centre of gravity is located. For me, in 'The Golden Toad', a still-point comes when I say, 'The next year, there were none at all,' because it's these words that signal the extinction of the species.[43] But there may be more than one still-point in a story, different people will perceive still-points in different places, and a quality of stillness may pervade a whole story.

I once told a Women's Institute group the Scottish folktale of 'The Seal Wife', in which a fisherman deceives a selkie woman into becoming his wife, by stealing and hiding her sealskin; when years later she discovered the skin, she abandoned him and their children and returned to the sea, to become a seal once more.[44] In telling the final part of this story, I could feel an intense energy of attention from my listeners, all women over fifty, and was conscious of the varied possibilities of life history, of loss of loved ones, they could have experienced, all unknown to me. I felt a responsibility, as I spoke and paused, to hold the space in which they could each experience the story's resonance with their life and feel whatever came to them. One woman said to me afterwards with feeling, 'I was there!' – which I took to signify an inward participation in what was presented in the story.

Another time, I told this story to a mixed group including some children. I heard the following morning that one young girl had dreamt a continuation of the story in which the selkie's children acquired furry sealskins and swam off in pursuit of their mother. Her dream had evidently filled the gap of closure left by a mother's separation from her children. Storyteller-dramatherapist Hazel Bradley told this same story to the community around a dying woman; she then told it to the woman herself: narrated the selkie's movement down into the sea as the woman breathed out … and up into the air as she breathed in … and down … and up … and down into the freedom of her true home … and when the last word was said the woman breathed out her last breath.[45] Here the space beyond the story's end is the void of death. The rhythm of breath, of all of us, coincides with the rhythm of speech: there's a pause as you breathe in, then words are sounded as you breathe out. Typically, each sentence or clause of a sentence is spoken on a single outbreath. A pregnant gap of silence can be sustained by holding the breathless space before you take the next breath in.

The space of stillness

The rhythm of breath, Flood's concept of the 'listening place', and the dynamics of listening discussed above all converge upon an experience of inner stillness which has some kinship with the experience of meditation. The meditator uses a range of techniques to bring awareness to the coming and going of thoughts and feelings; and out of the space of consciousness between these thoughts and feelings may emerge new perspectives different from the habitual ones that lock us into particular patterns of thought and being. This practice can with time facilitate an inner transformation of being, which is expressed in the transformation of our activity and attitudes in the world, including our capacities to act with empathy, compassion, kindness.[46]

The paradigm that inner healing is requisite to outer healing requires a space of tranquillity which contrasts with the campaigner's urgency for action before it's too late. The dialectic between tranquillity and urgency has to be managed.[47] Stories unfold in time, as change does. They catalyse rather than provide an instant fix. Lyotard, discussing the purpose of literature, speaks of 'listening to and seeking for what is secluded', and in doing so attending to *feeling*.[48] In Tibetan Buddhism each moment of meditative stillness is a miniature 'bardo', a space between, where what was before passes away and something new comes into being.[49]

When storytelling opens up spaces of transformative consciousness, it does so in a social context of a group of people listening together, and the space is structured by the stories' particular patterns of theme and desire. As Peter Malekin says of the effect of art in general, 'the silence is coloured by what has been experienced' – words, voice, images, gesture – 'though that experience has been transcended'.[50] The end of a story, writes John O'Donohue, can bring you 'to a door that you must open yourself' to enter 'a shape of experience which calls you beyond the familiar, the factual and the predictable'.[51]

This process can't be forced. Sometimes the space of stillness opens unexpectedly from a chance nexus of stories and receptivity. However, the storyteller can facilitate the coming of stillness. Intention is important, that the storyteller should actually want their storytelling to have this effect. It can't be presumed that storytelling will do *some* good even when there's no intention it should. A key strength of Gersie's therapeutic storywork is that it begins from the intention of facilitating transformation.[52] However, storytellers' capacity to elicit stillness among others depends on cultivating stillness within themselves. That may mean a meditation practice, preferably conducting some of this in quiet places in the wild, where the stillness of nature can infuse your being and energize your concern for the well-being of wild places and creatures. Stephan Harding advocates choosing a place you can go to regularly and establish a relationship with.[53] Green has maintained such a practice over many years through overnight stays wild camping in the same remote moorland spot;[54] the inner stillness he's gained from this is evident in his storytelling.

Inner stillness brings to one's listeners a presence and openness that encourage *their* openness,[55] and it brings a quality of listening as you speak. So much discourse about creativity emphasizes self-expression, giving voice to *your* ideas, *your* truth, *your* story, *your* being. That's important to personal development. But when storytelling is supposed to be serving others, then self-expression isn't enough. It keeps you in the domain of ego. There can be a complicity between the egoic needs of the performer and a consumerist desire on the part of the audience to simply be entertained in ways that confirm their prior assumptions.

This psychology underpins Zipes's critique that commercialized storytelling whose purpose is merely to entertain is unlikely to transform anything.[56] According to Kovel, it is consumer capitalism's 'enshrinement' of egoic self-interest as the sacred imperative of existence which is driving ecological destruction; it impedes the relationship between inner and outer worlds.[57] The ego is the sense of a separate self; it serves a purpose in our lives, but the 'sense of connection' that's key to the aspirations of ecological storytelling requires a transcending of separation. To listen truly, without wandering thoughts or the rising of antagonistic feelings, is equivalent to meditation, explains the Buddhist teacher Chögyam Trungpa; the speaker's presence and voice are the focus by which you meet their mind.[58] The storyteller must learn to listen – to other people, to the earth and its creatures – as Flood modelled, and galvanized others, in her projects. The storyteller must also listen, inwardly and outwardly, as they tell. Let me offer an illustration of what I mean.

It was a talk by the Buddhist teacher Jayaraja, the title of which alluded to ecological crisis.[59] He began with a very long silence during which he looked around the audience, meeting people's gaze. Although the audience was large, he held my eyes long enough that I felt not only seen by him but that he was 'listening' to me through my gaze and body language, as if forming an impression of what I needed to hear. The ensuing talk was clearly improvised, did eventually reach the topic suggested by the title, and included long pauses in which Jayaraja again appeared to listen to the audience, and closed his eyes to listen inwards, as he sought inspiration for what to say next. Early in the talk he also invited us to look around at our fellow listeners for a time and allow ourselves both to truly see them and to be seen. I felt touched by the whole experience, motivated to build my capacity for kindness in a world subject to frightening ecological impacts.

Jayaraja appeared to treat the giving of the talk as something like a meditation, one in which we listeners were invited to participate and thereby meet his mind. What's to stop storytelling being like that? One thing is the animus against appearing to take yourself too seriously.[60] Ego inflation and pretentiousness are the very opposite of what I'm describing. Jayaraja's style of speaking undercut such hazards through lots of joking and by evincing vulnerability; at one point he even admitted feeling nervous. The ego's fear of vulnerability can induce storytellers to seek to deliver their stories flawlessly, to demonstrate expertise and thereby to erect a barrier to intimacy with their listeners. But if you allow yourself to be vulnerable you can open an authentic space for everyone: space for sensitive mutual responsiveness, for the emergence of the unexpected; perhaps for the thoughts of the listeners' hearts to be expressed, the possibilities of change to be seeded.

I've noticed that, quite often in public storytelling, authenticity is affected by a quality of voice we can label 'generalized emotion'. By this I mean a tone of voice that conveys a heightened sense of significance, flagging that 'I'm telling a story', and is characterized by a repeating rhythm and a singsong variation of pitch. It sounds a little like someone seeking to cast a spell, as if to fulfil the descriptions of storytelling as 'enchanting' or 'spellbinding', and perhaps indicates an unconscious effort to put listeners into a mild hypnotic trance, as storytelling is believed to often do.[61] My concern is not so much about the possibility of trance actually occurring (see Chapter 4), as about the unconsciousness of what's going on. The use of generalized emotion appears to be propagated via unconscious imitation, since individuals telling a story in public for the first time don't usually exhibit it. As a listener I find that this vocal habit obstructs my reception of the story; it clouds the nuance of what's being narrated. More compelling, says Fran Stallings, 'is when the voice supports and amplifies what the words say'.[62] When storytellers avoid generalized emotion, I become more engaged.

I have to acknowledge that *my* storytelling too can sometimes slip into this habit. It's most likely to when I'm least conscious what I'm doing. Part of the remedy is to ensure you know the story thoroughly, because this frees the mind to be more conscious of the present situation. You can also use intention: to bring a specific vocal quality to each story; and, most importantly, to *be* conscious while telling.

Transformative storywork in a busy distracted world

It's a truism that the ever more complexly woven web of cyberspace is 'connecting' people more than ever before. Ong anticipated that electronic media would bring about a transformation of human consciousness equivalent in significance to that wrought by the written and printed word.[63] This consciousness, says J. Baird Callicott, is characterized by 'simultaneity, interconnectedness, and interactivity'.[64] The internet is normalizing a style of communication that prioritizes links between pieces of information: a flow of connectivity that lacks both materiality and depth. This culture of communication thereby exacerbates people's separation from ecology, on one hand, and fosters a cybernetic construction of human beings as information-processing machines, whose most personal thoughts and feelings may be externalized as text on screens and thence harvested by algorithms for economic and political exploitation.[65]

The digital exchanges of social media can facilitate, like conversation, a dialogic narrative and can do so in ways that collapse time and distance and involve multiple interlocutors.[66] However, the contributions to such exchanges are sequential media transmissions between a sender and a receiver; they're not emergent from shared presence in the way the dialogic spoken word can be.

Videotelephony services such as Zoom, when used live, differ in that they *can* mediate the vocal and visual cues of the telling/listening dynamic. Storytelling in the sense discussed in this book *is* possible through this medium, even though there's no physical presence. The limiting factor may appear to be only the quality of sound and imagery the technology can transmit. Storytellers' widespread use of Zoom during the Covid-19 pandemic raises the question, as in other fields, of whether it works well enough to carry on using it after the pandemic, for the sake of cost and convenience – including the opportunity for people all over the world to 'attend' an event without needing to travel to it.

What are the shortfalls of telling stories in this way? The non-verbal 'dialogue' of eye contact doesn't really work through the camera; you're never quite sure whether someone is looking at you or not. There's a need to project your presence through more assertive use of your voice, which coarsens the nuances of rapport. More effort is needed to sustain your smile and attention; to remember that the other people can see you, that it's not just TV. With practice and better tech, these things will no doubt improve. Do any points of difference, however, depend more fundamentally on physical presence? Human eyes and ears work stereoscopically to construct 3D awareness of the space around us; so our interpersonal communication has a 3D spatial nuance that's lost on the screen. Then there's the intangible sense of 'energy' that performers and listeners experience from each other's proximity (see Chapter 6). Thirdly, there's something special about physical presence which comes down to vulnerability and intimacy. The direct impact of voice and gaze upon another's body can be considered a kind of 'touch'; and if you're physically present, there's the possibility, after storytelling, of a handshake or hug.

It's remarkable that, in this information age, the quintessential way of expressing heartfelt public opinion remains the street demonstration. Whether the focus be war, injustice or ecology, the parading of human bodies aptly underscores that the threats in question impact on our physical being; most powerfully so when protesters resort to the vulnerability of the naked body.[67] The viscerality and affect of embodied presence, Costas Douzinas argues, feed the possibility of embodied action; in the mass gatherings during the Greek financial crisis, c. 2011, bodily proximity catalysed 'new types of collective self-awareness'.[68] There's a resonance between the body's vulnerability and the fragility of other living things and environments under the impact of industrial exploitation. Bodies always exist in a physical place, whereas cyber-connectivity is independent of place. Storytelling is not usually done naked – except in Maddern's hot tub at Cae Mabon – but in the storytelling situation the vulnerable materiality of bodily presence and a conscious meeting of minds coincide.

The possibility of this kind of experience is itself endangered in an ever more technologized and commercialized society. Storytelling cannot compete with a mainstream culture industry that provides through handheld devices instant access, anywhere, anytime, to endless choices of entertainment – including big-budget multi-episode drama series that overwhelm the mind with computerized imagery, orchestral music and violent spectacle – and the ceaseless, addictive opportunity to obtain information about anything or to communicate with anyone you know. My observation from storytelling on the front line is that, outside subcultural enclaves, the general public are becoming progressively less familiar with the experience of sustained dialogic listening. If the written word brought about a turning inwards that compromised our connection with what's around us, as Abram argues,[69] the expansion of ICT in our time has fragmented our capacity for attention either inward or outward.[70] This trajectory of culture, paradoxically, accentuates the need for the very thing it squeezes out: focused awareness of the present moment of being. There remains a precious need for activities, like storytelling, that can help us to connect dialogically with each other's conscious embodied selves.

As Flood says, the way we live has to be reborn if the crisis we face is to be mitigated. The world is made up of individuals, and it is to be hoped that inner transformation, changed perception, will translate into action and thus transform the world. But if the burden of change is placed entirely on the individual, there's risk of complicity with self-serving neoliberal individualism: a person may feel motivated to improve their ecological impact by using an electric car, buying organic food and volunteering with a conservation charity, but this may be but a lifestyle choice that can coexist with other choices (even in the same person) such as owning more than one home, making frequent flights and having multiple children. There has also to be collective change.

In storytelling, the space of stillness is shared by everyone present. Gersie emphasizes that a told story's dynamics aren't limited to 'the projections of an individual's imagination', but engage 'both the intrapsychic and the interpersonal world of teller and listener'.[71] There's an accountability to each other; a single individual who's resistant to the experience can disrupt it by starting a separate conversation or getting out their phone. As the space within the story stimulates space to open within the listeners, space also opens *among* the storyteller and listeners. There's a social space of 'conversation', as discussed in Chapter 2. Moreover, the physical space – the listening place – that exists between the bodies of those present becomes charged with a sense of connection, a 'subtle dialogue', from which some shared feeling or insight – an ethical intuition, a point of empathy, a resonance with experience – may emerge.

The value of community projects like Flood's is that they facilitate the possibility of community-level transformation – the vital link between individual enlightenment and environmental well-being. Imagination, effort and open-hearted collaboration are required to create such opportunities for storytelling's special qualities to serve the ecological challenge and people's perceived needs. Since the projects reviewed in this chapter, Flood has delivered two further big landscape projects elsewhere in Somerset. She's also been invited to work with a psychiatric nurse to conduct outdoor storywork as a 'social prescription' for people whose mental health has been impaired by the Covid-19 pandemic.[72]

There's also a need to expand public and professional *expectations* of the experience of storytelling, which requires innovation in the framing and structuring of activities, perhaps sometimes eschewing the term 'storytelling'. By 'framing' I mean constructing and publicizing a context that will both attract people to take part and set up suitable expectations about what they're going to experience. In Britain, I've observed, many people assume by default that storytelling won't interest them, that it's something for either very young children or an eccentric subculture, but that when they actually experience it, sometimes by accident, they do find it enjoyable and accessible.

The actuality of storytelling can be incorporated in a wide range of training, educational, therapeutic, developmental, community, ritual and social contexts, without necessarily being named 'storytelling'. Suitably designed storywork can satisfy many of Karen Blincoe's aims for sustainability education:

- 'intuition, imagining, wisdom, spirituality and holism, as well as basic knowledge of the interdependence and interconnectedness of all things';
- 'skills in how to relate to other people, how to be part of a community, how to go beyond winning or being first';
- 'the attributes of being true, authentic and content with who they are';

- 'to learn to communicate with their natural environment, expand their senses and increase their intuitive powers, and gain storytelling skills to share their experience'.[73]

Economics, however, is critical. Flood's projects could not have succeeded without proper funding to pay the artists and facilitators. Storytellers are vulnerable not only in their personhood as they stand before their listeners, but also – if this is their vocation – economically as they seek to make a living. Very often, expert storytellers are asked to work for inadequate or no payment, all the more so when the cause is worthy. The very fact that storytelling is a folk art in which anyone can participate complicates the problem: professional storytellers can find themselves competing for a job with others who'd be happy to do it for nothing, and clients may have no basis of understanding to do other than accept the cheapest tender. Hence the role of critics to help to build such understanding.[74] It would also be helpful if academic commentators, in affirming the democratic merits of storytelling, avoided tones of critique implying there's something inherently unethical about earning a living from expertise in this art.

If storytelling is to be sustainably applied in ways that serve the aim of ecological sustainability, then the people who commit time, energy and expertise to that work need to be sustained by adequate remuneration. This means *either* presenting the activities in question as something that customers (whether individuals or organizations) will feel motivated to pay for themselves – that is, as addressing their own perceived needs and desires – *or* accessing external sources of funding; either way without creating false expectations or sacrificing one's intentions and values. It would be consistent with the propensity of storytelling to facilitate an emergent response, rather than compel a desired effect, to bring to this 'marketing' of storytelling an intention to allow the emergence of opportunity from one's commitment and openness, instead of hard-selling one's services in accordance with the Darwinian logic of competition. It will also require faith, as part and parcel of the journey of inner change by which storytellers develop the personal capacity to catalyse the possibility of change among others.

6

Supernatural ecology and the transcendence of normative expectation

Fundamental to Kanak identity in New Caledonia is belief in the existence of diverse spirits who inhabit one and the same world as living people and interact with them through altered states of being, such as dreams, visions, illness, synchronicity, ceremonies and storytelling. The invisible world of spirits of the dead, totemic spirits associated with particular creatures, and fairy-like spirits of forest, sea and sky is interwoven with the social and material world of human beings, plants, animals, minerals and elemental forces to form a kind of supernatural ecosystem.[1] Patrice Godin's diagram of how attributes of 'spirit' and 'blood' circulate through this ecosystem reminds me of diagrams depicting the carbon and nitrogen cycles; nothing is exactly the same as or completely separate from anything else.[2] The complexity of all this is magnified by the fact that each of the twenty-eight ethnolinguistic groups has its own nuances of cosmology, lexicon of spiritual concepts and beings and legendarium of place-based stories. The stories themselves are suffused with spirits: non-human spirits who feature as characters; human protagonists who have since become spirits of the dead; animals that have totemic significance; and yet other spirits implicit in landscape and location. This 'mythic' perspective of the world, as Maurice Leenhardt referred to it, has endured under Christianization and French colonization.[3] The spirits are integral to Kanak's bond with the land.[4] Myth therefore matters politically as well as metaphysically. Belief in the reality of the spirits and their powers is an inextricable part of defending Kanak rights and way of life against the impacts of colonialism.[5]

In diverse cultures elsewhere may be found a recurrent perspective that human beings exist in a network of relationships with an ecosystem understood to be permeated by various kinds of spiritual consciousness and energy, which are imputed to physically distinct entities like animals, plants, rocks and streams and also perceived to have a more intangible presence in the wind, the night, the sea and underground. The Australian Aboriginal understanding of 'country' as a living web of conscious entities is just one example.[6] The Napo Quichuas of Amazonia believe that 'Ecological others, perceived as humans in transformed states, come alive through the musicality of the spoken word and the human voice'.[7] The kind of perspective I'm talking about is thus articulated in the stories of these cultures, and indeed in stories routinely presented to Western children till they're deemed old enough to be educated out of it.[8] It's what was conventionally called 'animism'.

This word has associations with the homogenizing interpretation of European imperialists who dismissed such belief systems as primitive superstition to be dispatched by the truths of science and Christianity. Scholars have therefore deployed other terms, such as 'perspectivism'[9] or 'ecological animism',[10] to allude to this concept. The need for some such term implies that 'animism' might be usefully rehabilitated, in full acknowledgement of the diverse and sophisticated thoughtworlds it's taken to encompass.

An animist dimension is evident even within supposedly monotheistic milieux: the jinn in Muslim lands, for example;[11] or the exotika of Greek folklore, including 'nereids' little changed from the nymphs of antiquity.[12] O'Donohue presents rural Ireland as pervaded by an 'invisible world' in which the presence of God is intermixed with fairies, angels and saints.[13] In India there's a continuum between the animism of countless local devatas and the cosmology of major gods. Supernatural beings populate folklore nearly everywhere. In England a wealth of ghost legends continue to inspire credence that more may be going on around us than our senses or science can ascertain. In my Gloucestershire work I've learnt to respect the lived experiences that people have shared with me about ghostly encounters, just as I had to respect the experiences and awareness of spirits which Kanak shared with me in New Caledonia. By 'respect' I mean not a polite pretence of respect, but genuinely taking people's testimony seriously. Good ethnography, say Thom van Dooren and Deborah Bird Rose, enables the 'weaving or braiding of stories ... in a spirit of openness and accountability to otherness', privileging neither your own belief system nor that of the people you're conversing with.[14]

The consensus of respectable 'rational' discourse is that none of these perceptions amounts to anything that actually exists. They may be poetically delightful, but the existence of what's perceived cannot be demonstrated in a convincing scientific way; moreover, the understanding of reality they imply is inconsistent with the materialist model of the universe which is widely assumed to be demonstrated beyond doubt by science. Ecocriticism can be keen to endorse the dominance of scientific materialism as a description of reality, owing to the urgency of asserting the scientific facts of ecology in the face of postmodernist and constructivist resistance to grand narratives, not to mention the alignment of fundamentalist Christianity (especially in the United States) with anti-environmentalist capitalism.[15] However, in claiming a monopoly on truth, scientific materialism reproduces the framing of animistic perspectives as the delusions of people who need to be educated to know better. From an uncompromising materialist standpoint, as articulated by Dawkins, any kind of spiritualist belief system is a false conception of reality.[16] Postmodernist thought, meanwhile, may appear to allow animism to be as valid as any other description of the world, but if indigenous people were to insist on the truth of their perspective they would discover that it's not recognized as true, will be interpreted only as a 'story', subordinate to a paradoxical grand narrative that rejects the truth claims of grand narratives.[17] Here again there's a contradiction of the respect for the 'other' which is foundational to the ethics and politics of difference. How can you claim to respect a people if you take a position that, explicitly or implicitly, denies their most profound perceptions and beliefs?

This chapter will explore some implications of a loosely constructivist way through this conundrum, summed up by Martin Palmer's argument 'that it is the tension between models of reality that offers us the greatest insights and space for manoeuvre rather than deciding that one side or the other has "the truth"'.[18] If different belief systems are allowed to coexist as 'models' rather than 'truth', they can be subject to critique and at the same time affirmed as authentically engaging, in different ways, dimensions of reality that do exist and can be experienced but cannot be objectively pinned down. This point matters to storytelling, because in many cultures both the content of stories and also the activity of storytelling are understood to mediate spirits and spiritual energies entailed in people's relationship with the environment.[19] Even in the disenchanted context of Britain many storytellers and story-listeners known to me harbour some form of spiritualist, even animist, perspective. One difference between analysing literature and analysing storytelling is that literary criticism can focus purely on texts, whereas storytelling involves a holistic experience in which spiritual aspects cannot necessarily be explained away as mere 'discourse'. Critics risk presuming their own status 'as thinking subject' to be superior to that of the people they're studying, and thus devaluing them 'as possessing less agency', if they premise their critique on assumptions that deny the validity of these subjects' beliefs.[20]

The chapter draws together a number of threads emergent from the preceding chapters. In Chapter 1 we encountered the experience of 'connection', the problem of uncertainty in ecological knowledge, the relationship of storytelling to ritual, and the antinomy between science and mythology. Chapter 2 explored the 'mythic' symbolism of traditional stories, and the alternative models of reality it may imply, as well as the storyteller's need to 'hold the space'. Chapter 3 introduced the idea that moments of conscious choice can interrupt the chain of cause and consequence. Chapter 4 explored 'enchantment' in connection with aura, sacred places, and associations between nature and the feminine. Chapter 5 elucidated an affinity between storytelling and meditation, discussed liminal spaces of stillness and coyly alluded to a quality of 'energy' in storytelling. The field of interest that brings all these things together I have labelled 'supernatural ecology'.

It's a field often dismissed from serious consideration by means of pejorative labels such as 'mysticism' or 'New Age' and by a derisory tone that frames the subject as prejudged on the basis of certain stereotypes. This dismissive stance fails to uphold the standards of criticism it claims to represent. It ignores not only the implications of the ethnographic findings sketched above, but also the corpora of scholarship of the major religious traditions; the testimonies of countless individuals who've undergone 'transpersonal' experiences in which their awareness has transcended the 'skin-encapsulated ego'; and the uncertainties of existence that challenge scientific materialism both as a complete description of the world and as capable of facilitating an adequate response to ecological crisis.

I've come to believe, like others, that the global ecological crisis cannot viably be addressed without some shift – among individuals and collectively – in normative understandings of existence.[21] However, it's difficult for new norms to emerge unless they're framed within the terms of existing norms.[22] In the previous chapters my argumentation has not strayed far outside the consensus reality accessible to science. In what follows I'll consider some limitations of this perspective and explore how stories of experiences that it can't accommodate point to a bigger picture of humankind's relationship with ecology. My analysis here draws on a range of spiritual philosophies and has implications for storytelling in general and especially for the telling of mythic stories in which aspects of transpersonal experience are symbolically presented. I use 'mythic stories' as a collective term for myths, wonder tales and legends with supernatural content.

Materialism, uncertainty and the motivation of action

The scientific method seeks empirical knowledge through conducting replicable experiments that have the potential to falsify hypotheses. The power of science lies in translating this quest for objective truth into technological applications that will reliably function. This entails strict control over the materials employed and is complicit in an ideological will to dominate nature. According to Francis Bacon, 'Nature must be "bound into service" and made a "slave," put "in constraint" and "molded" by the mechanical arts.'[23] The effectiveness of this approach is evident in the achievements of engineering and, to some degree, of medicine. The triumph of Newton's mechanistic model of the universe led eventually to the philosophical worldview of scientific materialism, which inherited from Christianity a meta-premise of exclusive possession of the truth, accepting no metaphysical uncertainty about the nature of reality and no epistemological uncertainty about how truth can be known.[24] In this pattern of belief the tenets held to be incontrovertibly true become part of one's ego, one's sense of identity.[25] The rejection of any place for spirit or divinity within the manifest world reduces nature to a mere assemblage of materials to be exploited at will.[26] The presumption that only the material exists produces an expectation that people's non-material desires can be satisfied by material consumption.[27] Armed with powerful technology and compelled by 'the tyranny of the ego', the agents of materialism – capitalist and Marxist – thus ruthlessly exploit both nature and human beings to serve their scientifically calibrated economic goals.[28]

However, the mechanistic model runs into difficulties with more complex systems such as ecology and society. Complex systems are characterized by networks of interaction whose behaviour is emergent rather than reducible to components.[29] The inherent uncertainties of such systems mean there's a problem when certainty is demanded as the basis for action by an industrial society built on the mechanistic paradigm. Climate is a complex system; the evidence for climate change comprises a vast flux of data together with computer models that crunch the data to calculate probabilities of what may happen. This kind of knowledge contains sufficient uncertainty that those who have vested interests or simply don't want to believe in global warming can claim that it's not proven, and hence there will be insufficient consensus to undertake mitigating actions.[30] The prognosis of global warming is a story, a narrative projected into the future; a story whose detail keeps changing in the light of new data, refined models and ongoing human activity.

It's difficult to impose your will on a complex system. The paradigm of domination and control has exacerbated ecological problems, not only through seeking to maximize economic returns from the extraction of resources but also via attempts to prevent disruptive natural processes such as flooding and bush fires.[31] The evidence that this paradigm cannot take us into a viable future comes not from replicable experiments, but from an experiment already done: the human impact upon ecosystems in the four centuries since the scientific revolution. The record of that impact is a complex tapestry of many stories. Just as the stories of the prognosticed future are necessarily uncertain, so we can never be certain how accurately the stories of history reflect the facts of what happened.

Stories by their nature 'convey unstable truths', says Gersie. In inviting a negotiation of 'shared truth', stories are well suited to engaging with a world of complex systems.[32] The relational nature of storytelling reflects the multiplicity of relationships, at different scales, which complex systems comprise – and the need for our engagement with natural processes and other creatures and people to be, like a dance, relational rather than seeking to dominate.[33] It's an idea captured in microcosm by storyteller-psychotherapist Kelvin Hall's approach to horse-riding: he doesn't use a martingale, a device empowering the rider to force the horse to stop: 'If I want my horse to stop, I ask him to. I trust that he will, because I have a relationship with him.'[34] Hall's trust accepts the uncertainty inherent to letting go of the will to control, just as the storyteller should trust story and listener.

Science's discovery of complex systems reveals that uncertainty is an unavoidable quality of the universe, from the subatomic level to the ecological.[35] Uncertainty not only has to be accepted and managed but can also liberate us from submission to what seems inevitable. It allows spaces in which change is possible.[36] 'When you become comfortable with uncertainty, infinite possibilities open up,' as Eckhart Tolle puts it.[37]

A recurring question in this book is how responses emergent from the storytelling experience can contribute to change at the ecological level. This question has to do with the enactment of the mind's desires in the material world. From a materialist perspective the human mind is an epiphenomenon of matter, emergent from the physical evolution of the biosphere. Within this frame of reference we can entertain that the discovery of new perceptions may prompt us, out of a sense of enlightened collective self-interest, to make changes in our behaviour, such as our consumption habits; to commend our voice and our vote to changes in social and economic structures that impact on ecology; and to participate in work that, directly or indirectly, serves ecological well-being.

However, our will to do any of this will be subject to the biological determinism discussed in Chapter 3: we'll need to be convinced that these actions will somehow better serve the interests of ourselves and our immediate relatives than would adherence to the competitive paradigms of neoliberalism, nationalism or tribalism. We'll be working against genetic predispositions determined by game theory's predictions that the best way to serve your self-interest is indeed to pursue your own self-interest.[38]

The ecological crisis, says Palmer, is 'a crisis of the mind. A crisis of the stories we tell ourselves.'[39] It's not enough to just communicate information; what's needed is the transformation of our sense of self.[40]

The application of systems thinking to organisms, considered as 'living systems', has led to the theorization of 'cognition' as the whole process of life, including perception, decision and action. This step dissolves the distinction between body and mind and allows biologists to impute cognition to all living things, even microbes.[41] By sensorily attending to the agency of natural entities – even non-living ones like logs, mountains and the earth's shadow (the night) – Abram infers in them not merely cognition but intimations of some kind of consciousness.[42]

From an *idealist* perspective, consciousness is the primary reality, through which the material world is perceived and from which, in some sense, it comes into being. This way of thinking gives greater agency to mind, hence a stronger basis for believing that not only insight but the will to act can transcend biological determinism; that people's behaviour need not be conditioned by genetic self-interest. In Cecil Collins's view, art that really touches you can amount to 'an interruption of causality by metaphysical forces'.[43] From an experience in the mind, whether arising from a painting, a story or something else, may be supposed a 'downward causation' upon the individual's body and behaviour.[44] An experience in the mind can also transform your perception of the world in ways that then motivate your attitudes and actions.[45]

Alienation from our own conscious experience alienates us from the world, making us prey to our impulsive, destructive reactions. 'The more I misunderstand myself as a mere thing,' says Herbert V. Guenther, 'the more degraded action becomes, for being valueless myself everything else is equally valueless.'[46] The shift from reaction to transformative consciousness mentioned in Chapter 5 is a microcosm of the kind of collective paradigm shift that could enable humankind to sustainably inhabit the earth.[47]

Systems theory takes us beyond the mechanistic model, but it seems to me that its notion of 'cognition' is essentially a cybernetic one that comes down to the processing of information. To transcend our sociobiological instincts, something else is needed. The 'indeterminacy of behaviour in complex open systems, their temporal structure, and the scope of the possibilities open to them', Moltmann says, suggest 'they possess a subjectivity of their own which is not objectifiable by the human subject';[48] that is, something akin to consciousness from which processes unfolding in time can emerge, as do stories and the telling of them.

Consciousness, energy, and stories of transpersonal experiences

Uncertainty inevitably attends stories that testify to facets of existence that cannot be confirmed by science. To take them seriously does not mean rejecting science, nor does it deny the existence or importance of the material world and people's material needs. What it does require is openness to the simultaneous possibility of *other* kinds of perspective; to let go of philosophical attachment to the 'law of the excluded middle', which demands that each belief we hold about the world should be a binary 'true or false'.[49] 'All our most important problems concerning reality and the psyche have been relegated to a kind of limbo,' writes Philip Rawson. 'But psychic truth demands that such aspects of the world be treated as realities *in their own terms*, not merely translated into a system of general notions derived ultimately from Aristotelian taxonomy.'[50] To talk about these other aspects of reality requires one to step outside the propositional language of conventional academic discourse and use other kinds of language such as metaphor and narrative.

The experiences that Stanislav Grof calls 'transpersonal' may arise spontaneously, or through spiritual practices, or in therapeutic, psychedelic or near-death situations.[51] They occur on 'the same experiential continuum' as everyday experiences,[52] but they collapse the distinction between subject and object upon which the classical scientific method depends. Aspects of such transpersonal experiences which can be accommodated within normative notions of 'objective reality' are often 'intimately interwoven' with other elements that cannot.[53] To the one who undergoes them, says Trungpa, these experiences are 'real beyond question' in a way that 'beggars uncertainty'.[54] The uncertainty comes in one's reception of the story of someone else's experience. If I told you about a transpersonal experience I'd had, you might think I'd only imagined it. I'd also have to utilize metaphor to describe it. The story wouldn't be the same thing as the experience, yet the experience would remain as real to me as other things

I've experienced which would be easier to accept. In both cases my testimony might be more convincing if I shared it with you face to face, so long as my body language supported the authenticity of my words, and/or if you knew me well enough to trust my word.

Transpersonal experiences' dissolution of subject and object has a resonance with storytelling's capacity to bridge between inner and outer worlds and with the cultic potential of art to facilitate what Collins calls 'participation in metaphysical reality',[55] as in the enactment of particular myths in the Greek mystery rites, whose purpose, Aristotle says, was not to 'learn' but to 'experience' and 'be affected'.[56] To be affected is the beginning of change. Kedar Brown tells stories in contexts of ceremony and healing; he says that what matters in listening to 'medicine stories' is not understanding, but to 'notice where you enter the story … where you leave the story … where your attention stops in the story'.[57]

In Napo Quichua culture, storytelling and song are deeply intermeshed with the 'medicine' of healing. To engage on its own terms with this, Uzendoski and (indigenous Quichua) Calapucha-Tapuy deploy William James's notion of 'radical empiricism', in which our experiences, as the basis of our knowing, are inseparable from our sense of significant relations among them. They describe the Quichuas' animistic world as 'not just an "imagined" world' but 'also an experiential world where people and various human and nonhuman others engage in communicative exchanges that involve the whole expressive body'. The enchantment exercised by the power of voice and bodily presence discloses a supersensory 'experience within a living landscape that is rich with the presence of mythological beings and transformations'.[58] Tolkien's 'Faërian dramas' are but discrete tastes of such a vista of transpersonal experience.

Grof acknowledges the cognitive difficulty, in a materialist milieu, of coming to terms with experiences that transcend ordinary experience:

> Transpersonal experiences have many strange characteristics that shatter the most fundamental assumptions of the Newtonian–Cartesian paradigm and of the monistic, materialistic worldview. Researchers who have studied and/or personally experienced these fascinating phenomena realize that the attempts of mainstream science to dismiss them as irrelevant products of human fantasy and imagination or as hallucination … are naive and inadequate.[59]

Any way of talking about such experiences will involve metaphor, but if we accept that the world exists independently of our textual construction of it, then the experiences themselves do not reduce to metaphor. They imply aspects of reality that really do exist but extend beyond human understanding and have been described by different cultures using different metaphors. This is not to say that anything goes. Patterns may be observed; one has to discriminate between delusion, deception and authentic experience; and, despite studying hundreds of people who'd had transpersonal experiences, what truly convinced Grof of their validity was his own 'deep personal experience'.[60] In my case too, it was personal experience that overcame scepticism.

Until the age of fifty, I had a dualist perspective akin to Gould's 'non-overlapping magisteria'. Having grown up a Christian and been educated in the natural sciences, I believed in a spiritual realm quite separate from science's sphere of empirical observation. My dualist convictions continued when, in my late twenties, the certainties of my faith were replaced by a notion of faith that was based in accepting uncertainty. However, the more I engaged with the ecological crisis, the clearer it seemed to me that resources from beyond the material realm were necessary to console, motivate and empower people. I did have occasional experiences that didn't neatly fit into my belief system. For example, I sometimes felt a numinous awareness of the 'aura' inside older cathedrals and in some locations in mythological landscapes I explored. However, it was a lomilomi (Hawaiian massage) treatment that definitively changed my perception of reality.

I had no prior knowledge how lomilomi might differ from other bodywork I'd received. I knew nothing of its spiritual underpinnings. But in ninety minutes my notion of separate material and spiritual realms collapsed in an experience of perceptions in my body and simultaneously in the space *outside* my body which belied scientific explanation. In the few years since, I've had a range of other such transpersonal experiences while receiving various forms of treatment, while meditating, dancing or singing, and spontaneously at other times, especially outdoors in nature.

The lomilomi practitioner attributed what I experienced to the flow of 'mana', the Polynesian conceptualization of the 'energy' that spiritual traditions worldwide perceive to permeate the human body and the world as a whole. Here 'energy' (or 'subtle energy') is itself a metaphor – not to be confused with the calorific energy of physics – for what might more accurately be referred to in English as 'spirit'; I use the term 'energy' in order to distance the concept from the religious connotations of 'spirit'. Sanskrit *prana*, Chinese *qi*, Arabic *baraka*, Greek *pneuma*, Hebrew *ruach*, Iroquois *orenda*, Quichua *samay*, Tibetan *rlung*, Yoruba *ashe* – each culture understands subtle energy in its own way. It's often associated with breath or wind and is generally perceived as flowing, not static. Sometimes it's personified as a divine being, as in Shakti, the Shekinah or the Holy Spirit.[61] Energy in the body is perceived to form an 'energy body' (or 'subtle body'). Energy's presence in nature may be perceived as some form of 'earth spirit', or as multiple spirits or deities, and as flowing with rivers or along 'dragon veins' through the landscape and being concentrated in certain sacred spots.[62] In India these places are called 'tirthas', or 'pithas' if they're sanctified by a goddess. A myth tells how the pithas came into being when, after the death of his beloved Sati, Shiva roamed the world with her body and pieces of it fell to earth in different places.[63]

If subtle energy permeates the earth, then it's both an aspect of the ecosystem and a way of comprehending the land's sacredness. According to practices like dowsing and feng shui, it interweaves even the built environment. Energy can be experienced as a place's aura, most palpably in structures where for centuries many people have prayed or done ritual.[64] Lupton describes 'a state of inner excitement' he experienced in the ruins of Delphi; a 'weight of inner reality ... that's investing this empty place with meaning'.[65] The idea that certain places are hot spots of energy enhances the motivation to make pilgrimages to them and conduct ceremonies there. On tour buses to Stonehenge, I've told parties of visitors the stories from legend and archaeology and then invited them to try a simple meditation when we get there. Inside the stone circle, some, like me, experience various nuances of energy. The experience is nondual: I can't separate out the flow of energy in myself, the monument and the people around me.

The perception of energy is intimately interwoven with conscious awareness. Experienced subjectively in and around your body, it can't be verified objectively in the way that science can measure physical properties. Energetic experiences can't be forced, only allowed; they come in unexpected and varied ways. One might try to explain them scientifically in terms of interoception and trance. Those faculties are certainly in play but they don't begin to provide a complete explanation. Seeking a line of interpretation between 'naive materialism' and 'naive idealism', Geoffrey Samuel suggests that the energy body be considered 'a kind of view of the brain and central nervous system from within'.[66] This idea appears to fall back to the materialist premise that matter is ontologically prior to consciousness. Nor does it account for the ability of sensitive individuals to read the energy of others, which I can testify they can.

The revival of Druidry has foregrounded 'awen' (Welsh 'inspiration') as a culturally specific concept of energy, with an emphasis on the inspiration of bards composing and performing their work.[67] Before a performance, members of Fire Springs habitually invoke awen by toning 'A–WU–EN' three times, analogous to Sanskrit 'A–U–M'. I've taken part in many storytelling events in which we'd reckon 'the awen is flowing', meaning a sense of mutual enlivenment among the participants. But there could be something else too, which I noticed especially when performing: a palpable sense of connection through the space between storyteller and listeners, like invisible lines of force, charged by a feeling tone resonant with the story. I now believe this to be an experience of energy. It's one reason to arrange the seating in a circle, or at least semi-circle, consistent with the Chinese association of circular forms with a yin energy conducive of rapport. Storytellers' experience of 'holding the space' (see Chapter 2) can be understood as a supportive awareness of the flow of energy in the group.

You have to do your best to remain alertly conscious. When the ego cuts in with, 'This feels great, I'm really connecting with the audience,' you lose the connection. As a listener, I've felt most intensely aware of the energized 'space between' when someone has shared something heartfelt and personal, as when a friend dying of cancer told me, 'If someone offends you, forgive them. Just forgive! Otherwise it twists you up inside.' It was a true 'sharing', in that I was so open to her that I received her spontaneous words as a gift that became an intention for my own conduct. Lopez says,

> The fruit of intimacy is hope. We must find ways to break down the barriers between ourselves and a reawakened sense of the power to do good in the world. With the dark horseman on the horizon, we must carefully seek intimacy, closeness, trust, vulnerability in all that we do.[68]

From the dynamic between consciousness (in the realm of mind) and energy (in the realm of embodiment) comes an empowerment of change.[69] The experience of energy extends your consciousness of self beyond your skin to encompass others.[70]

According to Indian spiritual understanding, in the liminal space of consciousness that precedes the emergence of a thought or feeling there's a stirring of energy, a potential, that then resolves into a specific perception. Implicit in this energy is a kind of unvoiced sound – arising from the divine source of the universe – from which the emergence of voiced sound brings aspects of the manifest world into being. Each sound in the Sanskrit alphabet is believed to have an effect on the human body, owing to the sound's relation to a particular part of the energy body. Utterance of mantric sounds such as 'AUM' or 'AH' empties the lungs of breath to create a space of stillness in which energy may spontaneously arise again. Through mantra and devotional songs that move energy through the body, Buddhists and Hindus believe, one participates in the transformation or unfolding of the world. For them, as for shamans and healers in other traditions, the energetic qualities of the voice can bring the inner world into relation with the outer world, mediating healing.[71]

These ideas speak to the nub of storytelling's capacity to facilitate change. One can theorize the extension of them to other art forms, but the spoken and sung word remains the primary embodied mode of the human expression of mind. When 'the awen is flowing' in the storytelling situation, the voice engages between the energy bodies of speaker and listeners. Energetic interactions *can* be experienced across large distances, as in shamanism and prayer, but they're felt most readily between people in physical proximity. I've come to believe that energy is key to the quality of connection experienced when a storyteller is physically and consciously present to their audience. When the awen is flowing, there's a sharing of consciousness as the story takes shape in the energized space between storyteller and listeners. The space is simultaneously physical and imaginative. The experience is transpersonal.

Energy is synonymous with spirit, and we saw in Chapter 4 how the aura of sacred places, such as springs, can be seen as their enchantment by a guardian spirit. The same is true of sacred buildings: the mana of a Maori whare nui is attributed to a spirit.[72] Likewise other artefacts; Tibetan tangkas (mythographic paintings), for example, not only provide a meditative interface with the supernatural characters in their imagery, but are believed to each have a devata of their own.[73] A told story is not a physical artefact, but, emerging from the energized 'space between' and having its own agency, it can be seen as something like a spirit. For the Quichuas, 'To tell a story is to invoke a living presence, a world of complex interrelations.'[74]

A further step is to conceive that each story in a culture's repertoire equates to a distinct spirit. The Ekoi of Nigeria conceptualize each of their stories as a 'story-child', who makes certain demands on those who tell that story.[75] In the Korean tale of 'The Story Bag' a boy who was told many stories by his manservant failed to share them and so they accumulated, disgruntled in a bag, until his wedding day, when they played a series of tricks to punish him. The servant having foiled the tricks, the youth learns the lesson that the stories you hear must be shared with others.[76] If stories possess their own agency, then perhaps they can evade ownership; Oelrich argues that 'stories travel and help wherever they are needed. Who owns such stories? No one and everyone!'[77]

What, though, if both stories and spirits are believed to be attached to particular places or groups of people? Kanak storyteller Sonia Kondolo has been active, with other members of Tragâdé, a storytelling association of New Caledonia's North Province, in encouraging Kanak communities to recover and tell traditional tales. She believes in an evolving tradition and is relaxed about Kanak retelling stories from other Kanak tribes, but doesn't think non-Kanak should tell them. The latter view applies specifically to the *telling* of Kanak tales, rather than their adaptation into new written or dramatic forms. Kondolo's concern is not so much about ownership as about the incapacity of non-Kanak to tell the stories well, because they have no relationship with the spirits entailed in telling them. When I asked what if non-Kanak residents of the country were to develop an awareness of the spirits, she said, 'That wouldn't happen.'[78] In Kanak society your relationship with the spirits of the land, and hence the stories, is determined by the network of kinship relations into which you're born.[79]

Soon after I met Kondolo, another Kanak acquaintance drove me high up a forested valley. Outside the vehicle, I listened to the 3D soundscape of the wind moving in the trees in different places around me. Might these sounds be considered voices of the land's spirits? It was the kind of sensory experience that Abram's neo-animism builds from. A couple of days later, I embarked by mountain bike on a five-day journey through New Caledonia's Chaîne Centrale, staying overnight in different tribes. I took with me an intention of being open and respectful to the spirits of the land. When I reached the highest point of the pass over the mountains, I had an experience. There was the sudden sensory impact of the wind and the view, and at the same time a powerful energetic impact that transported me into an ecstatic state. I experienced an epiphany of conviction that different spiritual perceptions, including the Kanak perception of the spirits of their land, are different ways of understanding and experiencing a shared reality.

I don't want to overstate any claims here; I'm simply sharing a story of something I experienced. The story conveys the interplay between perceptions of spirits and experiences of energy and how these may be entangled with the physical environment. It also helped me to understand that you can acknowledge other people's spiritual experience as real, as pertaining to an actually existing reality, without believing that the metaphors with which they describe it represent the literal truth.

The crucible of love

Transpersonal experiences are inseparable from consciousness, and there are different ways of talking about consciousness too. Rupert Spira defines it as 'awareness of awareness', explaining how anyone can experience this through inward observation without needing to subscribe to any spiritual system.[80] For Snyder, consciousness is fundamentally ecological, 'the source of alert survival intelligence'.[81] The animist, the shaman have a sense of relationship with conscious spirits who permeate the ecosystem. Hindus equate consciousness with the atman, the divine within; in Buddhism it's the Buddha-nature, the luminous ground of being; in Judaeo-Christianity, the presence of God. The physicist David Bohm avoids spiritual language by speaking of an 'implicate order' that exists in relation to the 'explicate order' of the manifest world.[82] Some spiritual writers use the word 'presence' in a way that brackets consciousness and energy and is applicable to both a transpersonal or divine presence that pervades everything and also the personal conscious presence each of us can aspire to bring to our actions and interactions.[83]

Personal transformation through spiritual practice is all very well, but change at the ecological level requires *action*! The pathway to action from the dance of consciousness and energy goes by way of desire, and the transforming of motivations. In storywork, Gersie comments, a group may learn 'to notice the subtle energies that signal movement out of stuckness, or the emergence of a commitment to action over inaction'.[84] Our motivations for action arise through energies we feel in the body. We desire, says Campbell, 'the rapture of being alive' that we enjoy when 'our life experiences on the purely physical plane ... have resonances within our own innermost being and reality'.[85] O'Donohue writes of divine consciousness as 'the primal well of presence from which all longing flows'.[86] When you let go of the will to dominate the other, the energetic exchanges arising in the 'relational space' between you and them have a tone of positive feeling.[87] Something's felt in the heart which empowers you to care and take action. The experience of such compassionate feelings is crucial to the environmentalist cause.[88]

In the evolutionary perspective of human nature, according to Edward O. Wilson, an aggressive instinct towards the stranger, the competitor, is hardwired into our genes.[89] It's becoming ever more obvious that the institutionalization of this instinct in neoliberal economics and nationalist politics is the primary obstacle to a greener world, through driving the destruction of ecology and resisting cooperative approaches to environmental problems. This political-economic milieu entrenches as normative an absence of consideration for the well-being of other people, other nations, other species. What's missing from Wilson's well-meaning cogitation to get round this problem is a source of compassion which is independent of the biological logic that cannot provide it.

Diana Durham distinguishes between an inner self (or consciousness), in which we encounter our connectedness to others in Bohm's 'implicate order', and an outer self (or ego), a constructed sense of identity likely to include affiliations such as nationality, ethnicity, religion and gender.[90] The disenchantment produced by materialism, the relentless technological pressure of modern life to live 'in the territory of externality', as O'Donohue phrases it, can alienate us from this inner self.[91] Without access to its wisdom, our ego-motivated compensatory actions end up compounding our problems. If you believe that your outer self is the entirety of who you are, then perceived threats to aspects of your identity can feel like threats to your very existence.[92] Hence the fierce intensification of identity politics in response to resource scarcity.

When we tune into a shared space of consciousness, Durham explains, we can experience a shared 'coherence' of thought and feeling, which may then find expression in a coherence of actions undertaken. Through cultivating consciousness, says Tolle, we can accomplish our emergent purposes – tasks intended to make a better world – without exercising an egoic will to dominate others. Whereas Tolle emphasizes the consciously empowered individual, Durham is describing a *collective* process, based on Bohm's 'Dialogue' groupwork, that acknowledges the collective nature of the transformation of social structures.[93] Thus the cultivation of consciousness in a collective context expands our sense of self to encompass – as a 'social self' – the community of other people. If the same practice is extended to non-human nature, this expansion will also include – as 'ecological self' – the larger community of the ecosystem with which we're interwoven in an ongoing process, in which our very self can be considered a process, an unfolding story, from 'ego-centric' to 'eco-centric'.[94] As ego diminishes, empathy develops;[95] you perceive the other's experience to such an extent that you experience in your own being their 'intrinsic value and being'.[96] The dissolving of the separation of your consciousness and others', says Spira, is the experience of 'love'.[97]

In Durham's analysis the Grail King of Arthurian romance symbolizes the divine presence – or implicate order – within us, and the Fisher King our woundedness, or alienation. The Grail is the opening through which divine energy enters the world; that is, the opened heart. Percival's question – 'What ails thee?' – arises out of compassion for the Fisher King's illness;[98] out of the open heart that Shakti Caterina Maggi calls 'the sublime door between spiritual and material'.[99] With the healing of the soul comes the healing of the wasteland. Only with empathy and compassion can any worthwhile attempt be made to respond to ecological crisis. Storytelling that genuinely seeks to contribute to that effort will need to be conducted in that spirit.

When someone meets you eye to eye, as when a story's told, you encounter the consciousness of another; you see a reflection of yourself, the surroundings and the story.[100] You share an experience that can be a manifestation of love. You accept the unpredictability, the mystery, says Oelrich, in the ways that stories 'can help us unfold our greater potential'.[101]

Storytelling that aspires to be dialogic and transformative might be compared to Bohm Dialogue. Durham explains that Bohm Dialogue works best when its convener has cultivated their capacity for consciousness and 'acts as the seed crystal to help the group cohere'.[102] Similarly, a storyteller or storywork facilitator who brings an ego-transcending consciousness to the circle of other people can open the space for them to tune in, if they're willing, to what Durham calls the 'group presence':[103] in experiencing in some way the energy connecting them, they may feel a warmth towards each other as simultaneously their minds and hearts open to the content of the stories. Some storytellers do this effortlessly; they draw you in, so you really want to engage, rather than holding you away with a performance of ego.

This ability was demonstrated in a talk I attended by the writer Ben Okri. In the awkward setting of a bookshop mezzanine, his back against a railing, Okri asked the scattered listeners to move closer together in front of him. Into the energy of this sudden shoulder-to-shoulder intimacy, he began to speak in a soft, low voice: 'In this book the story is like a bowl that contains different kinds of love … ' The claim he was making for his novel (*Dangerous Love*) encapsulated the same heart experience he catalysed among us there and then. When he later took questions, he responded evasively to attempts to pin down his spiritual beliefs, leaving us to interpret in our own ways the spiritual dimensions of his stories and use of language.

Can any story worth telling be a crucible of love? *The Kathā Sarit Sāgara* begins with Shiva (symbolizing divine consciousness) and Parvati (an incarnation of Shakti, divine energy) together on the sacred mountain Kailasa, from which 'timeless, world-central scene of bliss', says Heinrich Zimmer, all the polarities of the world come forth.[104] Shiva sits Parvati 'on his lap' and at her invitation begins to tell stories to her.[105] This vast compendium of interwoven tales, cross-section of the world's woes, joys and complexities, thus unfolds from the love play of consciousness and energy. It concludes with Shiva's eternal blessing upon 'whoever listens to it with attention'.[106]

We've seen that each story told has its own structure of space, inviting cognition and awareness, and will suggest a particular pattern of desire, engaging the energy of desire within storyteller and listeners. If the telling of the story touches people's hearts, then this particularity of space and desire will be imbricated with particular nuances of feeling. The story will be its own unique crucible of love, transforming 'passion into compassion' in particular ways.[107]

This dynamic is poised to come into play when a storyteller chooses stories 'their heart responds to' and when in preparing a story they explore how it touches them. When you allow a story to 'move through' your heart,[108] it may begin to have some transformative effect on you; this effect upon you is part of what you share with your listeners as you share the story. Dunne's emphasis on not merely what happens in a story, but the unfolding of characters' *relationship* to what happens,[109] bespeaks also the storyteller's and listeners' unfolding relationship to what happens and, by extension, to facets of their own lives. Some stories have more scope for this than others; whether short or long, they contain more latent depth. The particular themes of chosen stories enable storytelling to channel the general dynamic of consciousness, energy and love towards particular areas of concern, behaviour and action in the world. I hope it is clear how such a process is distinct from propaganda's manipulative will to dominate.

Myths, symbols and imagination

My conversations with regular story-listeners affirm that the impact of stories is generally cumulative. The transformation of culture, likewise, involves the cumulative effect of the stories told within it.[110] Yet sometimes a moment in a story may spark an epiphany. There are moments when something prompts a listener to weep; moments of eucatastrophic joy; moments when you see in someone's eyes the penny drop. In ancient Greece an 'epiphany' was a manifestation of a god, as might happen in a dream or ritual. Some moments that have stayed with me as a listener have been epiphanies in this sense: some divine being was presented in a way that elicited in me a lucid image and a shiver of energy. The moment when John Hartoch narrated St Patrick's arriving at the pearly gates only to find there waiting for him his old Pagan sparring partner, Oisín. Or when Hartsiotis evoked the grief of Demeter, after losing her daughter Persephone, when she condemned the earth to be barren. Or when Haggarty embodied the fay otherness of Midir – like an irruption of colour in a monochrome scene – when he appeared in the mortal world in pursuit of his beloved Étain. Or Dave Robertson's powerful *speaking as* Jesus to deliver the terrifying prophecies of end times in Mark 13. Or when, at the end of Lupton and Daniel Morden's *Iliad*, the gods stand appalled by the savagery of mortal men's destruction of Troy.[111]

Through characters who are deities or spirits, the telling of mythological stories mediates the imagining of aspects of divinity, or the invisible world of spirits, and their entanglement in ecology. Supernatural motifs in mythic stories are representations, *within* stories, of transpersonal experiences in life. Experiences like a vision of Jesus or Mary, for example. Or, more humbly, the tingling in my body during lomilomi, which I found replicated in Kanak tales: a character may experience tingling – either explicitly, or metonymically as an ant on the skin – as a harbinger of healing or divination.[112] What implications might there be for the telling of mythic stories of the supernatural in light of the dynamics of consciousness and energy that can be in play in storytelling?

In his workshops Lupton will tell the tale of 'The Man Who Had No Story' to introduce the idea that the storyteller forms a bridge between two worlds. The man, Jimmy, challenged by an innkeeper because he had no story to contribute to the evening's storytelling, stepped outside into the night and chanced upon a boat on the shore of a lake. Upon sitting in the boat he was propelled to the far side of the lake, where he discovered he'd transformed into a woman. He, or rather 'she', soon met a young man, whom she married, had five children with, a whole life together … until one evening she went for a walk, came upon a boat by the lakeshore, got into it and quickly found herself once more at the other side, a man again.

Back at the inn, Jimmy relates his experiences, only to be told by the innkeeper, 'That's the best story we've heard all night.'

'But it's true!' cries Jimmy. 'It really happened!'

'You've only been gone five minutes, Jimmy. But I tell you this: wherever you end up tomorrow night, if someone asks you to tell a story, you *will* have a story to tell.'[113]

The story is a parable of someone entering the other world of experience that from the perspective of the manifest world we call 'imagined'. Lupton calls this invisible world the 'Dreaming', by analogy with the Aboriginal Dreaming. He sees it as formed by the collective imagination over millennia, taking specific local or national forms but also transcending such identities by revealing themes that unite humankind.[114]

Lupton had Jimmy's story from Betsy Whyte, a tradition bearer of the Scottish Travellers. It echoes a story about the Indian seer Narada, who sought to know the secret of Vishnu's Maya – the creative power by which Vishnu dreams the world. Vishnu bid Narada plunge into a pool, from which he emerged as a girl, who went on to marry a prince, become a queen and have children and grandchildren. After a terrible battle in which all her male relatives were killed, she lit their funeral pyre, then threw herself into the flames, only to find herself back in the pool of water, a man again, and Vishnu guiding him out.

The teaching of the tale, declares Vishnu, is that the secret of Maya is unfathomable. The pool, at Narada's request, was made a sacred place whose waters would wash away sin. There are stories within stories here, and symbols within symbols. In Hinduism, writes Zimmer, water is 'a tangible manifestation of the divine essence'. The water of the pool symbolizes Maya – in another version of this story she's an ocean – and Maya is in some sense interchangeable with Shakti, the personification of cosmic energy. Maya-Shakti is 'the creative joy of life ... the beauty, the marvel, the enticement and seduction of the living world'.[115]

There's a pointer here to an affinity between imagination and energy which reflects the relationship between mythic stories and transpersonal experience. The 'imagined' shouldn't be assumed – as the law of the excluded middle expects – to be 'not real'. 'Imagination' refers to the forming or receiving of images: these *may* be invented, or they may be remembered, or they may arise from a transpersonal reality – as, for example, when certain qualities are pictured as gods or goddesses.[116] Imagination can also involve non-visual sense impressions and certainly plays a part in energetic experiences. 'Tingling' is only a metaphor of what I experienced during lomilomi, not the same as the physical tingling of pins and needles or sunburnt skin.

Turn the dynamic around and a mythic image in a story may inflect the energy in the relational space where 'the story moves in the imagination'[117] – as when Haggarty's presentation of Midir through words, voice and embodiment evoked in me in shivery sense of the fey. In Clarke's view, mythic stories are a means by which to integrate the inner and outer worlds, which he represents geometrically as two overlapping circles whose mandorla-shaped overlap symbolizes the imagination. The bigger this overlap, the greater the synthesis of opposites, of yin and yang, self and other, civilization and wilderness, and the more space opens for the birthing of change.[118] The imagination, says Oelrich, 'engenders generosity in relation to others, the ability to hold several viewpoints at one time and the tangible empathetic presence of the heart'.[119]

Myths are not merely a pre-scientific way of understanding the physical world. They engage with the invisible world of transpersonal experience. They function symbolically; the symbols they carry have multivalent meanings and can touch different levels of your mind at the same time. Art desiring to serve a transformative spiritual purpose requires an inner openness in which symbols can evoke – not define – nuances of the invisible world.[120] When religious mythology is interpreted as the literal truth, when believers interpret their faith's metaphors as facts, the result is irreconcilable conflict with science and also irreconcilable conflict with other religions that have different myths. When it's also linked to demographic identity, serving the egoic needs of the members of a group, that conflict of ideas feeds political conflict and destructive consequences that only seem to vindicate Dawkins's view that religion should be dispensed with completely.[121]

Although science's 'evolutionary epic' can be told in mythic style, as Wilson advocates it should to replace religious mythology,[122] it remains wedded to being understood as the literal truth. Myths, with their images and metaphors, provide a symbolic way of speaking about that which is beyond words.[123] They bring life to the void of meaning and desire which is left when any notion of spirit or divinity is rejected, as by Dawkins, as a 'virus of the mind'.[124]

Unreflective attitudes and behaviour that follow from rigid religious beliefs may well exacerbate ecological crisis – as in the American Christian right's commitment to the narrative that God gave humankind dominion over the earth and will provide a new world when this one is destroyed. Jung's notion that mythic stories express a set of timeless archetypes in the psyche raises questions of how any use of storytelling based on that premise could facilitate social change.[125] This idea of universal archetypes is consistent with sociobiological understanding that the template of human nature has been genetically determined by evolution over many tens of thousands of years and is thereby resistant to the needs of a rapidly changing world.

If there is to be change, then, critical awareness needs to be brought not only to traditional stories, as models of human behaviour, but also to aspects of our own nature which stories mirror back to us. A way out of instinct and habit – emergent change – is conceivable if we distinguish the *mind*, as the sum of mental forms that have developed in each of us through biological processes and the self-narration of our lives, from the field of *consciousness* in which these mental structures are experienced.[126]

The inscrutability of Maya evokes the fluid depths of meaning and mystery mediated by myth. Campbell writes that, 'both true and false', myth inhabits the ocean between 'the field of all joy and pain' and the 'other shore' of 'an absolute that is beyond principles'.[127] Myths engage the great themes of meaning, purpose, origins and destiny, not merely in the abstract way of philosophy, but imaginatively. The traditional purpose of myth, says Armstrong, 'was to make people more fully conscious of the spiritual dimension that surrounded them on all sides'.[128] In India, writes Zimmer,

> The mythical tales are meant to convey the wisdom of the philosophers and to exhibit in a popular, pictorial form the experiences or results of yoga. Appealing directly to intuition and imagination, they are accessible to all as an interpretation of existence. They are not explicitly commented upon and elucidated … The tale goes straight to the listener through an appeal to his intuition, to his creative imagination … [The tales'] details impress themselves on the memory, soak down, and shape the deeper stratifications of the psyche. When brooded upon, their significant episodes are capable of revealing various shades of meaning, according to the experiences and life-needs of the individual.[129]

Individual myths lend themselves to ritual use by their association with liminal times in the seasonal cycle and with human rites of passage. By enchanting aspects of nature as inspirited, myths invite attitudes of respect, even reverence, towards them. Indo-European mythologies tend to represent ecological forces and realms as anthropomorphic deities, mapping symbolic connections between non-human nature and the deities' archetypal significance. Apollo, for example, is a sun god and also stands for clarity of mind; Sarasvati is a river goddess and associated with the flow of speech. In animist mythologies, animal spirits are more prominent. They connect between human needs and ecology in diverse ways, including as totems that bind kinship systems to land and wildlife, and as power animals that shamans call upon to aid them.

It wouldn't be impossible to keep telling stories about spirit animals when the corresponding species have vanished from the ecosystem, but to do so would incur a terrible irony. Corresponding totems or power animals would become empty concepts. How can you expect to sustain a spiritual connection with beings whose earthly representatives and habitats your own kind have destroyed? The idea of a level of consciousness that connects you to others implies the possibility of engaging in some way with the innenwelten and umwelten of other species. We might mourn not only the loss of the creatures for their own sake but also our relationship with them and what their existence can teach us. When a species is lost, says Rick Bass, 'We have lost a part of ourselves, of who we were and who we will be.'[130] To tell stories about particular kinds of animals – and plants – is a way to bring them to awareness, even ones we rarely see, and to honour them as teachers.

An invitation to tell stories about butterflies at a heritage venue that has a butterfly house prompted me to investigate traditional tales about these insects. Butterflies' recurrent associations with soul, dreaming, metamorphosis and mortality have obvious connections with their biology and physical appearance. The international tale 'Butterfly Soul' – I tell an Irish version – presents a butterfly's journey through a mini-landscape as symbolizing the inward journey of a human soul in a dream, but also lets us wonder whether the sleeping soul really can leave the body.[131] In a Pueblo story the arch-trickster Coyote is tricked by the butterflies: while he was napping during a trip to Salt Lake to fetch some salt, they transported him home, so he woke up believing he must have only dreamt he'd made the trip, and had to go again.[132] In an O'odham myth, Elder Brother, feeling sad about the transience of created things, creates the butterflies by mixing together a little of the beauty of everything else. Complaints from the birds caused him to silence the butterflies' songs. Ever after, the sight of their beauty evokes a song in the heart of those who see them.[133] In a Tukuna story from Amazonia a *Morpho* butterfly acts as a guide to Cimidyue, a woman lost in the forest, where creatures keep metamorphosing in her perception; it transforms her into a dragonfly so she can cross the river to get home. My retelling of Cimidyue's story drew upon Aaron Shepard's adaptation, which is more structurally satisfying for a Western audience: the *Morpho* instigates Cimidyue's venture into the forest and transforms her into a butterfly not dragonfly.[134] This story evokes for me a sense of the forest as a supernatural ecosystem containing mystery that will remain unfathomable. All four tales have a lightness of mood, evocative of butterflies, yet are mythic; they narrate transpersonal experiences in ways interconnected with ecology and affirmative of butterflies as spiritual teachers.

Stories metamorphose, as do our beliefs and perceptions, as do caterpillars into butterflies. Collins argues that drawing upon symbols from a 'consecrated spiritual tradition' is a way to avoid the solipsism of the modern artist who's concerned entirely with self-expression, yet he believed strongly that such traditions should evolve.[135] Archetypes can be reconceived as mutable, as in Frye's analyses, and thereby coopted in open-ended dynamics of transformation and possibility.[136] Myth can evolve just like other story traditions. Though he asserted the continuing importance of the hero's journey, Campbell acknowledged the need for new myths that would serve the world as a single community rather than serving individual nations.[137] Myths can be used to empower an authoritarian will to dominate, to sustain conservative norms or to propagate apocalyptic expectations that risk becoming self-fulfilling.[138] That's why it's so important that they do evolve, and also why they need to be told and received in ways that elicit compassion.[139]

Myth-telling, story-dreaming and conscious memory

At this point we should perhaps attend to Zipes's warnings to storytellers who aspire to make a difference to the world or to people's lives: 'it is not the role of the storyteller to be the healer, the shaman, the omniscient guru'; he would prefer 'the storyteller' to concentrate on disclosing social realities, like the child in 'The Emperor's New Clothes' who points out the King's nakedness.[140] Parkinson warns against storytelling being taken 'SERIOUSLY' so that it spawns its own 'high priests' and 'cult followings'.[141] The serious concern in both critiques is that of practitioners' ego inflation and will to dominate and the corresponding disempowerment of those they work with. However, there's an animus also in both critiques towards closing down options.

Some expert storytellers, including Parkinson, are practising therapists; they *are* healers. Shaw's approach to 'myth-telling' in conjunction with wilderness rites of passage seems close to a shaman's work;[142] Brown's use of 'medicine stories' is overtly so. Some storytellers are ordained priests. Others are trained teachers, or nurses, or actors, or clowns, or writers. Each brings a unique mix of skills and experience that conditions what they can aspire to do in their storytelling. Just as Zipes makes clear that political dynamics are always in play, both within stories and in the act of storytelling,[143] so it can be contended that energy dynamics too are always in play.[144] It follows that storytellers would do well to cultivate an awareness of energy as they tell and listen, just as they should seek to be aware of the political dynamics. Through cultivating consciousness, you can contain your ego and hold space for other people's responses. These capacities of consciousness need not be limited to healers or shamans with special expertise in working with energy. They require no adherence to particular spiritual beliefs; only an open mind.

Parkinson evinces a preference for a homespun, witty style. Quite often mythological stories are told in a 'low' register, ironic and everyday, which levels down the activities of gods and heroes to the recognizable antics of mortals. Like much contemporary fantasy fiction, this approach tends to relinquish symbolic depth and thereby disenchant the mythic. Richard Kearney calls for the renewal of sacred stories 'in a new spirit of "ludic imagining"'.[145] Playfulness can be delightful and liberating, but the gravity of our times demands more than that. A renewed sense of sacred depth is needed, moving beyond both the dogmatism and tribalism of past religion; not turning back the clock. It's a need that storytelling is well suited to serving through its power to bring to life in communal settings the sacred stories of myth. The question then is how to tell mythic stories in ways not limited by shallow expectations, that can evoke a sense of the sacred, the extraordinary, the tragic, while sustaining a nimble humour and humility.

The 'ladder to the moon' arranges oral story genres in ascending order from personal anecdote, through family memory, legend and folktale to wonder tale, epic and myth.[146] This loosely maps on to Frye's scheme of 'modes': irony, low mimesis, high mimesis, romance, myth – defined by the relative power of action of the corresponding stories' protagonists.[147] These modes are reflected in literature by different registers of language, from 'low' to 'high'. The disenchantment and democratization of modern British culture have made low mimesis and irony the normative expectations; Tolkien is unusual in using the full scale.[148] For the higher modes to ring true, to feel strongly 'mythic', a higher register is needed. In storytelling, the register involves not only language but all the non-verbal tools of voice and body. Through these means, if the listeners are with you, an imaginative space may open in which the energy of the mythic, the transpersonal, can flow.

Hence the energy, the 'charged atmosphere', I reported in Chapter 3 from telling 'The Coming of the Kadimakara'. In 'The Green Ladies of One Tree Hill' I use a lowish register mainly but shift to a higher one when I speak of the dancing trees and their slaying of the elder brothers. I use a yet higher register in the story of 'Erysichthon', since it involves not only a nameless tree spirit, but also Demeter, a major goddess, symbolic of the earth's fertility. With the energy come tones of feeling that bleed beyond everyday experience. In the case of 'Erysichthon' my own feeling responses include the *sacredness* of the oak; the *erotic frisson* of the dryads dancing round it on warm spring nights; the *taboo* of cutting it down; the *pathos* of the dryad's death; the *enchantment* of the oak, all oaks, by association with dryads; the *wrath* of Demeter; the *horror* of personified Hunger; the *foreboding*, in a dream, of Erysichthon's insatiable appetite; the *abjection* of his greedy destruction of everything good in his kingdom; the *tragedy* and *pathos* of his innocent daughter's fate.

The same cultural trends as occur in contemporary literature predispose some participants in storytelling to favour a low style. But mythic stories are so much part of storytelling's currency that storytellers do venture up the modes. The thing is, a higher register is more difficult to do well. You may encounter cheesy archaism from novices; generalized emotion among the more experienced. So there's work to do – in developing the technical skills, and also in learning to be conscious.

Rather like a form of meditation is the technique of visualizing story scenes – 'dreaming the story', as Lupton has described it.[149] In workshop exercises he encourages participants to describe as much detail as they can in a static image of each scene. When you tell the story, the lucid images in your mind then have the power, *without* the need for such detailed description, to enable the listeners to visualize the scenes themselves. Often they'll say things like 'I was really there' or 'I could really see it'. This effect has always struck me as extraordinary, as jumping the gap between minds. I would now conceptualize it in terms of a meeting of consciousness. It doesn't always happen. I know from my own story-listening that a commitment of attention is required of the listener; the challenge of contending with one's own inner chat room is rather like that encountered in meditation. Storytellers who are fully present to audience and story will be best able to elicit this reciprocal attention.

'Ekphrasis' is the Greek term for the description of statues and paintings in classical literature. Critics have since applied it to the description of dreams and landscapes and to verbal representation of other art forms such as music.[150] In modern Greek literature, Margaret Alexiou explains, ekphrases use a high register of language, facilitating mythic resonances, and may evoke altered states of consciousness. She places the ancestry of ekphrasis in the oral traditions that preceded literature, comparing it to the aisling, or dream-vision, of the Irish bards.[151] It can be used in storytelling, sparingly, though it runs against modern expectations that a story should keep moving. When I observed Maddern ekphrastically describe Culhwch approaching King Arthur's court in the Welsh epic 'Culhwch and Olwen', he paused to explain to his teenage listeners that such elaborate description was the medieval equivalent of TV.

Ekphrasis provides a space in time in which we're offered a synesthetic encounter with an image of something special. For the ancient Greeks the image was likely to represent a deity, to be contemplated as icons continue to be contemplated as a spiritual practice in Greek Orthodoxy. In India, where too art has traditionally served a spiritual purpose, of transforming consciousness, the sculptor or painter opens their mind to the divine in order to channel an image of a deity, which, emergent in the making of the art, will in turn have the potential to open the viewer who contemplates it to that aspect of the divine.[152] If you substitute for 'the divine' whatever language you feel comfortable with – 'consciousness', 'implicate order', 'spirit', 'the transpersonal' – I think this methodology suggests a model for telling mythic stories in a way that does them justice. That doesn't mean the telling has to be heavy and portentous. Depending on the story – maybe not 'Erysichthon'! – it could be full of light and laughter. The affinity of visualization in stories to spiritual practice is evident in the *Spiritual Exercises* of St Ignatius of Loyola, in which one imagines biblical scenes, visually and using other senses, from the point of view of being physically present within the scenes and thereby receives the blessing of the divine presence in the story.[153]

The use of a sequence of visualized images as a mnemonic technique derives from the classical 'art of memory', in which items to be remembered are located in 'topoi' (places) in an imagined 'palace of memory'. Though originally a practical tool, in its elaboration especially by Renaissance Neoplatonists the art of memory became a spiritual practice by which to engage with a metaphysical understanding of the cosmos.[154]

Memory is held in the body as well as the mind. Various kinaesthetic techniques may therefore be used to help commit stories to memory and to explore the interplay of physical and emotional dynamics. You can find body positions that capture the essence of each scene; mime your way through the whole story; experiment with gesture and stance while rehearsing the story, including stances evocative of different characters. You can also construct a spatial sense of each scene in the space around your body. Let me give an example of this that also illustrates how awareness of physical space can open a space for energetic experience.

There's a scene in Fire Springs' epic *Arthur's Dream* in which Gawain and Lancelot arrive at the Grail Chapel. As I narrate Gawain's entering the chapel, I have in my mind's eye that *before* me is the altar where a maiden stands holding the Grail, to my *left* is the well into which a spear drips blood, and *behind* me is the doorway where Lancelot has fainted. My 3D sense of the chapel's interior continues throughout the scene. When we performed this show at the Chalice Well, Glastonbury, the audience included some devotees of a spiritual path based on Arthurian mythology. During the Grail Chapel scene, it was evident from their body language that these listeners were treating the story like a guided meditation (one confirmed afterwards he had done so), and there was a charged stillness in the room. The initiative here came from the listeners, who were far more au fait with meditation than I was. I just had to hold the space and allow my voice and pauses to be responsive to them as I told the story.

In this example the physical setting was significant too: the Chalice Well is where legend says Joseph of Arimathea hid the chalice – the Grail! – from the Last Supper. When you tell a story in the proximity of its location, your spatial sense within the story can be aligned with the physical landscape. Outdoors especially, you can also follow the Kanak storytelling practice of pointing in the direction of more distant places referred to, reinforcing awareness of a larger mythscape.[155]

Whatever techniques are used, memory is central to storytelling. The storyteller has to remember the story. The listener has to remember what they've been hearing in order to comprehend the relationships of events through time within the story; they can't turn back the page or rewind the video. The constellation of memory – the stories you've taken in, the stories you've lived, your reflections and feelings about them – becomes part of who you are, in contrast to mere information you access and then forget. That's why it matters which stories you ingest, especially the ones a storyteller selects to take through their heart into the embedded memory of repertoire.

Memory is a technique of the imagination, says Moltmann, by which the past is brought into the present – just as expectation brings the *future* into the present – and so into the creative being of the psyche.[156] Meditation draws attention to the present moment, the actually existing moment in which every joy is experienced, every choice is made;[157] yet consciousness, says Anagarika Govinda, includes both this awareness of the now and a 'storehouse' of 'the fruits of experience' in memory.[158] The Chinese idea of the Tao involves patterns of connectedness woven through time as well as space.[159] A story may be conceptualized as a way of representing something emergent from a complex system of events and processes connected through time; it's easier to understand a complex system like the changing climate as a narrative, of what has happened or might happen, than as a computer model or a set of scientific statements. The vantage point of the storyteller, who can see the shape of the whole of a story at once, is a microcosm of a divine perspective that – like the theory of relativity – holds past and future coexistent with the present. Myth mediates, writes Coupe, between 'the rhythm of temporal existence (chronology)' and the 'timeless paradigm' of eternity.[160]

Therapeutic perspectives point out how 'stories' embedded in the psyche drive habitual reactions, so that past recursively determines present.[161] The emphasis here is on 'stories' as ossified interpretations of the past. However, memory carried in stories also enables experience to be taken into the furnace of consciousness. I want to suggest that in storytelling you can cultivate a capacity for 'conscious memory', in which you hold in mind a lucid memory – of lived or imagined experience – together with awareness of the dynamics of power and emotions it entails. When this conscious memory is brought into relation with conscious presence in the storytelling situation, it can become part of the eternal moment of becoming, in which the story – the story told, the story believed, the story lived – can change.

Journeys to other worlds and the reconciliation of opposing principles

For some storytellers an attractive model, especially when working with stories that are both mythic and ecological, is the shaman. In Siberian shamanic cultures, three genres of 'shamanic' stories are told:

- legends about individual shamans, akin to stories of saints and siddhas;
- stories used in ritual, as myths are in many cultures;
- reports of journeys out of the body into another world, typically undertaken to investigate a problem in the community, such as illness or food scarcity.[162]

That third type of story is the shamanically distinctive one. It's a kind of personal story, though with potential to evolve into legend or even myth. If comparisons are to be made with storytelling, it's important to distinguish between the story and the transpersonal experience the story reports.

When Lupton suggests a kinship between storytelling and shamanism, he's talking about the storyteller's experience, not the listeners': the 'storyteller's job is to enter the Dreaming' … 'to enter invisible worlds, not accessible to everyone … to report back'.[163] At least three strands of this role can be noted, which are worth spelling out because they help to delineate particular abilities an expert storyteller can bring to the communities they serve. Firstly, storytellers 'enter the Dreaming' by familiarizing themselves with the legendaria of traditional tales and, when possible, visiting the physical landscapes connected to them. Secondly, they engage in 'dreaming the story', the meditation-like process of exploring in the imagination the stories they choose to tell. The third entry into the Dreaming is during the telling, when the storyteller becomes the bridge between worlds; here the 'reporting back' is not retrospective but, in effect, a running commentary while you're actually making the journey.[164]

In Western 'shamanic counselling', the process is reversed: instead of reporting back on a journey, the shamanic practitioner guides others to undergo such a journey themselves, as a master shaman might guide an apprentice.[165] This may appear analogous to a storyteller's guiding their listeners on an imaginative journey, as in a guided meditation. However, the journeyer will normally discover their own journey content while the practitioner holds the space. So the comparison to storytelling only really applies to the space the storyteller allows within the story for the listeners to exercise their imagination. I have taken part in a hybrid 'story journey', a guided visualization structured as a plotless story, beginning in shamanic fashion from the roots of a tree, escorted by a hare. It included a number of clearly defined gaps in which we were invited to receive messages from various aspects of nature. This activity illustrates very explicitly the notion of space within a story. Unfortunately I missed some of the messages because I fell asleep!

Shamans have dealings with the spirits, including the spirits of the dead.[166] Throughout the world, people have looked to religious mythology to help them cope with mortality. Death is a major area of interface between ecology and myth. Ecology requires transience: each of us dies to make space for others. Facts of life not easy to accept. The fact of death impacts on our relationship with the fact of ecological crisis. It imposes a time horizon beyond which we won't participate as living individuals in ongoing ecological processes. Whatever ecological scenario may unfold on earth after our death stands as beyond our present experience as religious visions of heaven or hell. Big capacities of imagination and empathy are required to take seriously such future circumstances for the sake of future generations. Those capacities aren't hardwired by our genes. Moreover, the decline of expectations of life after death has given impetus to making the most of this present life, but the very materialism that presumes that death is truly final also produces the expectation of finding fulfilment through maximally consuming products and services that use up natural resources. Dunne observes that 'Immortality never becomes one of the things of life' and hence death is 'a voyage with the unknown into the unknown', in which the journeyer has 'to be led by his discoveries' instead of by desired outcomes.[167]

How, then, to approach that mandatory voyage? What will the consequences be for ecology? On this subject, mythology comes into its own with stories of journeys into underworlds and heavenly realms, and various kinds of otherworld that stand as proxies for the world of the dead and in some cultures merge with a concept of spirit world that's all around us – the invisible world that's encountered in transpersonal experience and that, transposed into language, is the world of stories, the Dreaming. Traditional stories are full of death in one way or another. Caitlín Matthews argues that some genres of Irish bardic tales – the 'immram' (wonder voyage) and 'echtra' (otherworld adventure) – function as reconnaissance of the pathways to the lands of the dead, to be experienced in this life as preparation for when your time comes.[168] Peter O'Connor psychologizes this interpretation of the 'otherworld voyage', seeing the otherworld as a space, representing the unconscious, from which hidden aspects of one's psyche may emerge.[169] This journey of midlife has a different flavour from the journey of adolescence iterated in the hero's journey – as may be seen by comparing Campbell's 'separation, initiation, return' with Dunne's sequence of three 'meetings' that pattern a person's life:

- when you meet one of the major crises of your life;
- when you go into solitude to meet 'the unknown';
- when you return to meet the unknown among others.[170]

How much can stories tell us about the 'unknown' of death? From extensive study of near-death experiences, Stanislav and Christina Grof conclude that the world's mythologies convey with remarkable accuracy the kinds of experience undergone in the early stages of dying. Data are less forthcoming to confirm mythological accounts of death's deeper reaches.[171] Tibetan Buddhism offers complex narratives of the journey through the bardo from death to rebirth in a new body, and hence the possibility of memories from past lives. It also boasts a genre of stories about the post-mortem experiences of 'déloks', people who've returned to the *same* body about a week after dying.[172]

The 'Hades journey' of antiquity, Clarke reminds us, was a rite of passage by which to undergo spiritual rebirth. He observes that in ecological crisis 'the whole powerful culture of our time seems far advanced on a Hades journey of its own'. His remedy is that each of us, rather than exercising our energies in blaming others, should undergo our own imaginative journey in which we face the darkness within and awaken into consciousness and compassion.[173] Sometimes that's forced upon you. It's natural to want to avoid the darkness, to just have a nice life. The problem is that we're all complicit in the ecological crisis, simply by being alive and part of the ecosystem. We're also all mortal. Two things that Covid-19 has reminded us about. Therapy, ritual and meditation are ways to enter the journey willingly. In the hands of skilled guides, storywork can play a part in that.[174]

Telling stories about death is at least a way to engage socially with mortality, which retains an aura of taboo. What I take from the above commentators is that relevant mythic stories can help to prepare and sustain people to navigate the journey inwards, or beyond, when the occasion comes.

Themes of death and otherworld are potently present in the high myths, which are well suited to storytelling and a high style. Told or chanted is how they were originally delivered, in ritual contexts that might involve music and movement. They can be adapted into prose fiction or film, but both these media are inherently disposed towards realism and hence tend to demythologize myth. Epic poetry was historically a medium of myth; it's no longer an accessible form in Western culture but the essence of it has passed into storytelling, evident in the poetic crafting of some of Lupton's work, especially his 'praise song' *The Horses*, which traces through one woman's long life the disappearance of horses from the landscape. Haggarty is a master of high style in his telling of *Gilgamesh*. In narrating the hero's failed quest for immortality, this Mesopotamian epic confronts you with your mortality, the fact that however you twist and turn you can't evade it.

Flood has developed a repertoire of stories to help people come to terms with death. They include *Inanna*, narrating the Sumerian goddess's descent into the underworld. Clarke argues that the Hades journey 'will involve (for both men and women) a transforming encounter with those life-affirming values of the feminine principle which have been neglected and demeaned'.[175] It's there in Campbell's monomyth: 'the meeting with the goddess'.[176] Inanna is one of the thousand faces of the divine feminine. In India she is Shakti, the energy of the living world. In Amazonia the anacondas Yakumama (Mother of All Rivers) and Sachamama (Mother of the Forests) symbolize 'the ecological relations of entire bioregions and ecosystems'.[177] In Christianity the divine feminine is latent in the Virgin Mary and the Holy Spirit, waiting to be re-embraced. In multifarious ways in different cultures she symbolizes the sacredness of earth, water, wind, body, sex, woman, connectedness – all that which was made profane by the dualism that separates the divine from the material world.[178] Even in India, where the goddess has been so adored, society has remained patriarchal and the space for wild creatures has been squeezed ever smaller by the human population.[179] It doesn't follow that the metaphor of the divine masculine, awareness of the infinite and eternal, should be rejected. What's required is to keep seeking in new ways 'the reconciliation of opposing principles'.[180]

'The secret of Maya is this identity of opposites,' writes Zimmer, 'creation *and* destruction, evolution and dissolution'.[181] For the Kanak there's a polarity between 'kamo' – the living and the light – and 'bao' – the spirits, the dead, the darkness; which two can coexist in the 'half-lit third space' of liminal times and places.[182] Inanna's descent – or 'katabasis' – takes the divine energy of the living world into the realm of death. All sexuality and fertility on the earth cease until she's reborn. In the Babylonian version 'Ishtar' makes the descent to rescue her slain son and lover, Tammuz. In the Sumerian one, Inanna dispatches her consort Dumuzu to the underworld as payment for her rebirth.[183] In these dynamic exchanges the duality of life and death is transcended. In church any Sunday, you can participate in a communion ritual re-enacting a katabasis that traces back to this more ancient story. Christian teaching has sought to guarantee the outcome: re-embodied eternal life on a heavenly new earth. But Dunne's 'unknown' remains. Life after death is the ultimate goal that can't be forced; as when you tell a story, you have to surrender to the uncertainty of how the experience will pan out. The reconciliation of life and death, as with all these dialectics, produces not a static condition of unity, but a ceaseless dance of relationship, as in the dynamic and evolving equilibrium of a healthy ecosystem. The 'myths we live by' need to be 'ecological' in this way.[184] Competing myths and metaphors, like the contrasting katabases of Ishtar and Inanna, can be reconciled in what Palmer calls the 'tension between models of reality'.[185]

The dance of duality is there in microcosm in storytelling, when teller and listener meet in a shared experience, a shared story, a shared imagining of scenes, yet each has their own beliefs, their own interpretation, their own images, between which there's a subtle but ceaseless dialogic exchange. Scale up this dynamic to the group situation in which there are multiple listeners – and possibly multiple storytellers – and it's evident that storytelling also encapsulates the reconciliation between individual and collective which is necessary to a healthy society. One individual's voice is privileged through the duration of a story, and the group commits in common cause to listening to that story.

Ecological well-being requires a reconciliation between the needs of the individual and the ecosystem. Mythology expresses the synergy between inner and outer worlds in paradisal imagery that reflects, say the Grofs, the blossoming of the psyche.[186] For Buddhists both the meditative imagining of paradises and the maintenance of a beautiful physical environment nourish the unfolding of conscious being;[187] an ecological focus would emphasize the reciprocity of this relationship – the co-arising of beautiful consciousness and beautiful environment. Hence a reason, in myth-telling, to include eloquent ekphrases of enchanted forests, sacred mountains, secret valleys, kingdoms underground or undersea, and isles of earthly paradise.

Imagined settings provide a geographical structure of space – either coterminous with the physical environment or extending beyond it into a larger supernatural ecosystem – in which the imagination may engage with dynamics of the invisible world. This is one way that myth brings, as Coupe says, 'a promise of another mode of existence entirely, to be realised just beyond the present time and place'.[188] Paul Ricoeur 'speaks of myth as a "disclosure" of "possible worlds"'.[189] The imagining of *dystopian* possible worlds serves a prophetic purpose, but an excess of it risks making the prophecy self-fulfilling.[190] To allow more positive possibilities, we may tell and retell stories that invite the hope of beauty and well-being, during our life in this world and for whatever will be after our death. Hope, Gersie says, 'travels beyond the visible facts'.[191]

Expertise and mystery

The notion of 'medicine story' could aptly be applied to Gersie's capacity to select, from the repertoire she carries in her memory, a story she intuits will speak to a client's needs.[192] Stories of any kind might be said to create a 'sacred space' when they prompt someone's heart to open. Gersie relates the awakening effect on a troubled boy of a story about a raindrop which she was inspired to concoct on the spot by the rain beating against the window.[193] However, the composted symbolism of mythic stories gives them a particular potential to evoke a collective sacred space. Among my strongest experiences of this, on separate occasions as performer and listener, were the Telling Place's team-tellings of St Mark's Gospel to large audiences composed mainly of Christians.[194] For this community this really was a sacred story. The *telling* of it brought a far more powerful energy than you get from passages being read from the lectern, yet most of us had never seen the real landscapes through which the story moves.

I have suggested that when storytellers bring an intention of consciousness to sharing stories, there can be an experience of 'energy' in the space between, a sense of connection that's productive of the empathy, compassion, love necessary to motivate action; and that the stories told can focalize this dynamic in ways unique to each story and each occasion. One might ask whether this approach works. To attempt to *prove* scientifically that it does would be to attempt to fashion another technology of power, in contradiction of this book's line of argument. The evidence I would point to instead would be the stories of experience – stories of people telling and hearing and being touched by stories. I'd point also to the stories of the lives and deeds of individuals who have, each in their own way, been open to spirit and followed a path of love; stories that have inspired others to live better – the stories of the saints, siddhas and shamans, the teachers, healers, campaigners, artists and peacemakers. The older of these have become legends. Among those who've lived more recently are some whose outlook could be described as ecological: Seton and Amaringo, for example, Tjibaou and Govinda, and Masanobu Fukuoka, Jane Goodall, Joan Halifax, Thich Nhat Hanh, Polly Higgins, Anandamayi Ma, Wangari Maathai, George MacLeod, John Muir, Jay Ramsay, Rabindranath Tagore, Pierre Teilhard de Chardin, Gandhi, the Dalai Lama ... Their stories are worth telling.

Tolle argues that, 'In a world of role-playing personalities, those few people who ... function from a deeper core of their Being, those who do not attempt to appear more than they are but are simply themselves ... are the only ones who truly make a difference in this world.'[195] Attempts to address the challenge of ecological crisis, using storytelling or anything else, may well be futile and demoralizing unless they're rooted in some practice of consciousness or spirituality. There are many different ways of experiencing and talking about this. I've tried to weave between the imaginative language of mythic stories, the spiritual metaphors of religious traditions, and a more neutral lexicon that I hope will be accessible to those for whom notions of 'spirit' seem inseparable from implausible belief systems. An encounter with consciousness is available to anyone in any moment. All you need is a willingness for open-minded enquiry.[196]

It dawned on me early in my career as a storyteller that to commit to this path means attending to the whole of your being, since your storytelling will be inflected by every aspect of your body, mind, voice and heart. This means cultivating practical skills of speech and self-presentation and of preparing and delivering stories. It also means entering the Dreaming, to explore the old stories, to dream new ones into being and to explore your inner being, so that as you bring the stories to your listeners you bring them also the fullness of your presence. It means embarking on a journey whose path will be different for each individual and will lead who knows where.

That journey involves an ecosystem of relationships – with other storytellers and listeners, with everyone who has something to teach you, with nature and with stories and the venues in which they're told. In more participatory settings, like workshops and clubs, where storytellers become facilitators of others' storytelling, there's a responsibility for others' well-being: to hold a space that's safe enough for people to share stories from their heart, to reveal who they really are. Part of that safety comes from the acceptance of a diversity of experiences, understanding and metaphors, especially when something that feels sacred is touched upon. Within a safe space that is a physical space, participants can experience the connectedness that I attribute to the flow of energy. Even better when such a listening place is located outdoors in the midst of nature. When you read this you'll know more than I do right now about the ways that culture will be changed by Covid-19. My hope is that the experience of so much physical separation may stimulate a renewed appreciation of direct presence – gaze, voice, touch, energy – in storytelling as in other kinds of face-to-face interaction.

Complex systems such as ecology are unpredictable. As animists have always known, the ecological is inseparable from the spiritual. To commit to the spiritual journey is to open yourself to the unexpected. 'You cannot reach the unknown by walking along the beaten path of the known,' says Osho. 'It is a jump from the known that takes you into the unknown.'[197] You can't predict the actual outcomes of telling a particular story any more than of implementing an environmental action plan. When a process is understood to be spiritual, the destination cannot be prioritized above the journey, ends cannot be divorced from means. This very unpredictability is subversive of power relations. The world will keep changing. Thus we need a utopian process, a compassionate way of undertaking change, rather than trying to enforce upon the world a rigid vision.

Jameson bleakly articulates how the advance of capitalism tends to close whatever loopholes of utopian possibility remain.[198] New technologies like blockchain and artificial intelligence seem likely to intensify the will to control.[199] Meanwhile the health of the biosphere continues to deteriorate. Yet, says Le Guin, utopia always has to begin here and now.[200] Polders of utopia can be found wherever people come peacefully together in one place for a period of time, perhaps at a festival, on a course, to share food, to tell stories.[201]

Those who feel called to apply storytelling to the hope of a greener world cannot predetermine the outcome of their efforts. What they can do is formulate some intentions. You can expand your knowledge and refine your practical techniques. You can dream deeply into the stories your heart calls you to tell. You can cultivate your openness to opportunity and collaboration and even to getting paid for your work. You can seek to contain your ego, become aware of the energy flowing through you and open your heart to the world. You can cultivate space within your stories and the storytelling situation to allow the emergence of something new from the interplay between story, people and place. You can trust that the agency of what emerges may be helpful to someone or something, in a small way or a big way, maybe a way you'll never know, and that it may help you also to experience joy amidst the tragedies that may continue in this world after you've passed into the mystery beyond.

Notes

Introduction

1. Chomsky, *Media Control*; Stibbe, *Ecolinguistics*.
2. Palmer, *Dancing to Armageddon*.
3. Cupitt, *What Is a Story?*, xii.
4. Le Guin, *The Wave in the Mind*.
5. Labov, *The Language of Life and Death*.
6. For example, Glotfelty and Fromm, *The Ecocriticism Reader*.
7. For example, Opperman and Iovino, *Environmental Humanities*.
8. Rose et al., 'Thinking through the Environment', 3.
9. Gablik, *The Reenchantment of Art*.
10. See Manwaring, *The Bardic Handbook*.
11. Nanson et al., *An Ecobardic Manifesto*.
12. Gersie et al., *Storytelling for a Greener World*, 32.
13. Zipes, *Relentless Progress*; Zipes, 'Foreword'.
14. Sheldrake, *The Science Delusion*, 228.
15. Rueckert, 'Literature and Ecology'.
16. Coupe, *Myth*, 177–8.
17. Wheeler, 'How the Earth Speaks'.
18. Zapf, 'Cultural Ecology'.
19. Bate, *The Song of the Earth*.
20. Ong, *Orality and Literacy*, 67.
21. Blewitt, 'New Media Literacy'.
22. See Quammen, *Spillover*.
23. Soper, *What Is Nature?*
24. See Betti, *Twelve Ways*; Pellowski, *The World of Storytelling*.
25. Murphy, 'Ecofeminist Dialogics', 193.

Chapter 1

1. Attributed to Albert Einstein.
2. Wilson, *Storytelling and Theatre*.
3. Shepard, 'Nature and Madness'.

4   Roszak et al., *Ecopsychology*.
5   For example, Abram, *Spell of the Sensuous*; Brody, *Other Side of Eden*; Cowan, *Letters from a Wild State*; Nabhan, *Cultures of Habitat*.
6   Smith, *Storytelling Scotland*, 169.
7   See Brody, *Other Side of Eden*; Guenthar, 'Old Stories'; Lopez, *Arctic Dreams*; Nabhan, *Cultures of Habitat*.
8   Abram, *Spell of the Sensuous*; Manes, 'Nature and Silence'.
9   Stone, *The Healing Art*.
10 Nabhan, *Cultures of Habitat*, 64–5.
11 Ibid., 80.
12 East, 'Fishing Tales'.
13 For example, Cornell, *Sharing Nature with Children*; Holland, *I Love My World*.
14 Lopez, *About This Life*.
15 Goodchild, *Capitalism and Religion*, 201.
16 Philo, 'Television News'.
17 Zipes, *Relentless Progress*, 127.
18 Lopez, *About This Life*; Nabhan, *Cultures of Habitat*.
19 Phillips, 'Is Nature Necessary?'
20 Goodchild, *Capitalism and Religion*.
21 Diamond, *Rise and Fall*; Diamond, *Collapse*.
22 Greenberg, *A Feathered River across the Sky*.
23 Micklin et al., *The Aral Sea*.
24 Huth, *Awakening*.
25 Axelrod and Suedfeld, 'Technology, Capitalism and Christianity'.
26 Nabhan, *Cultures of Habitat*.
27 Von Sydow, 'Geography and Folk-Tale Oicotypes'.
28 Abram, *Spell of the Sensuous*, 269; Nabhan, *Cultures of Habitat*.
29 Day, *Doomsday Book of Animals*; Diamond, *Rise and Fall*; Flannery, *The Eternal Frontier*; Flannery, *The Future Eaters*; Martin, *Twilight of the Mammoths*; Martin and Klein, *Quaternary Extinctions*; Mitchell, *A Fragile Paradise*; Wilson, *The Future of Life*.
30 See Flannery, *The Eternal Frontier*; Goodchild, *Capitalism and Religion*; Palmer, *The Sacred History of Britain*.
31 For example, Flannery, *The Weather Makers*; Latif, *Climate Change*; Leakey and Lewin, *The Sixth Extinction*; Maclean, *Silent Summer*; Thomas et al., 'Extinction Risk'; Williams, *Deforesting the Earth*; Wilson, *The Future of Life*.
32 Carson, *Silent Spring*; Flannery, *The Weather Makers*; Gibson, *A Reenchanted World*; Godrej, *No-Nonsense Guide to Climate Change*; Mickleburgh, *Beyond the Frozen Sea*.
33 Helm et al., 'How Did Britain?'
34 See Capra, *The Web of Life*; Harvey, *The Killing of the Countryside*.

35 Sunderland, *In a Glass Darkly*.
36 See Goodchild, *Capitalism and Religion*; Nanson, *Words of Re-enchantment*; Zipes, *Relentless Progress*; Zipes, *Revisiting the Storyteller*.
37 See Armiero, 'Environmental History'.
38 See, for example, Gibson, *A Reenchanted World*; Spowers, *Rising Tides*.
39 Nabhan, *Cultures of Habitat*.
40 Gelbspan, *The Heat Is On*.
41 Huggan, *Nature's Saviours*.
42 Rushdie, 'Is Nothing Sacred?'
43 See Zipes, *Relentless Progress*; Zipes, *Revisiting the Storyteller*.
44 Benjamin, 'The Work of Art'.
45 Maddern, 'The Sustaining Story'.
46 Goodison, *Moving Heaven and Earth*; Mack, 'The Politics of Species Arrogance'.
47 Oelrich, *The New Story*, 239.
48 Chris Sunderland, interview, Bristol, 18 December 2001.
49 Strauss, *The Passionate Fact*.
50 Simon West, interview, Lyndhurst, 29 January 2002.
51 Davies, 'Voices from the Earth'; Strauss, *The Passionate Fact*.
52 West, interview.
53 Malcolm Green, interview, St Donat's Castle, 7 July 2002.
54 Adrian Tissier, telephone interview, 12 November 2002.
55 Lopez, *Arctic Dreams*.
56 Le Guin, *The Language of the Night*.
57 Davies, 'Voices from the Earth'.
58 Lopez, *Of Wolves and Men*.
59 Strauss, *The Passionate Fact*; Strauss, 'Reconsidering the Big Bad Wolf'.
60 Lopez, *Of Wolves and Men*; Lopez, *Arctic Dreams*.
61 Helmick-Richardson, 'I've Got an Exoskeleton'.
62 Pellowski, *The World of Storytelling*.
63 Francis Firebrace, interview, Bath, 24 November 2002.
64 Ghislaine Walker, telephone interview, 13 September 2002.
65 Tristan Hankins, interview, Eden Project, St Austell, 8 August 2002.
66 Gordon MacLellan, interview, Bath, 20 November 2002.
67 Green, 'Storying Nature'.
68 Strauss, *The Passionate Fact*.
69 Hankins, interview; Jack Morrison, interview, Eden Project, St Austell, 8 August 2002.
70 Michael Moran, interview, Slimbridge, 18 August 2002.
71 Brody, *Other Side of Eden*. See Lopez, *Arctic Dreams*.
72 Maddern, interview.

73   Jon Cree, telephone interview, 10 September 2002.
74   Nan Kammann-Judd, personal communication, 2002; Linda Yemoto, personal communication, 2002; 2020; Yemoto, 'Storytelling versus Interpretation'; https://storynet.org/groups/environmental-storytelling-discussion-group/
75   See Green, 'Kittiwakes on the Bridge'; Green, 'Storying Nature'.
76   https://www.btcv.org/etn
77   Holland, *I Love My World*; Salisbury, 'Wisdom of the Wildwood'.
78   Hibberd, 'Tales from the Wood'.
79   Allan Davies, telephone interview, 12 November 2002.
80   Strauss, *The Passionate Fact*.
81   Chatwin, *The Songlines*.
82   Brody, *Other Side of Eden*.
83   Maddern, interview.
84   Green, interview.
85   For example, Galbraith and Willis, *Dancing with Trees*; Schneidau, *Botanical Folk Tales*; Schneidau, *Woodland Folk Tales*; Jacksties, *Animal Folk Tales*; Thomas, *The Magpie's Nest*.
86   For example, Caduto, *Earth Tales*; Casey, *Barefoot Book of Earth Tales*; East and Maddern, *Spirit of the Forest*; Gersie, *Earthtales*; Keable, *The Natural Storyteller*; Lupton, *The Songs of Birds*; MacDonald, *Earth Care*; Singh, *A Forest of Stories*; Strauss, *Tales with Tails*.
87   Hankins, interview.
88   Sanders, 'Speaking a Word for Nature', 194.
89   Conn, 'When the Earth Hurts'.
90   Hochman, 'Green Cultural Studies'.
91   Ramsden, 'Jewels on Indra's Net'.
92   Crompton and Kasser, *Meeting Environmental Challenges*.
93   For example, Cornell, *Sharing Nature with Children*; Holland, *I Love My World*; Van Matre, *Earth Education*.
94   Goodison, *Moving Heaven and Earth*, 251–2, quoting Jane Roberts.
95   See Gersie et al., *Storytelling for a Greener World*.
96   Green, interview.
97   Moran, interview.
98   See Bartoloni, 'Memory in Language'.
99   Gersie, *Earthtales*.
100 Green, interview.
101 MacLellan, interview; Medlicott, '"Miss, Is Skomar Oddy Extinct?"'
102 Moran, interview.
103 Peter Please, telephone interview, 1 November 2002;
104 Sewall, 'The Skill of Ecological Perception'.
105 Abram, *Spell of the Sensuous*.

106 Wilson, *Storytelling and Theatre*, 56.
107 Abram, *Spell of the Sensuous*.
108 Lopez, *Of Wolves and Men*.
109 Csikszentmihalyi, *Beyond Boredom and Anxiety*, 36.
110 Maddern, interview.
111 Alan Watts quoted in Grof, *The Holotropic Mind*, 74.
112 Evernden, 'Beyond Ecology'.
113 Kroker and Cook, 'Television and the Triumph of Culture'.
114 Hughes, *Winter Pollen*, 148.
115 Sewall, 'The Skill of Ecological Perception', 214.
116 Chris Salisbury, telephone interview, 11 December 2002.
117 Cree, interview; Ben Haggarty, workshop, Bishops Wood Centre, Stourport-on-Severn, October 2000; Moran, interview; Please, interview; Salisbury, interview; West, interview.
118 Moran, interview.
119 Tissier, interview.
120 Cree and Gersie, 'Storytelling in the Woods'.
121 I'm indebted to Malcolm Green and Chris Holland for introducing me to such activities.
122 Green, interview.
123 Yemoto, 'Nature Stories'.
124 Abram, *Spell of the Sensuous*.
125 Ibid.; Armstrong, 'Keepers of the Earth'; Chatwin, *The Songlines*; McLuhan, *The Way of the Earth*; Nabhan, *Cultures of Habitat*.
126 Abram, *Spell of the Sensuous*.
127 Darwin Edwards, 'Re-storying Scotland'.
128 Sunderland, 'Human Nature'; Oelrich, *The New Story*.
129 Diamond, *Rise and Fall*; Lopez, *Of Wolves and Men*; Sunderland, 'Human Nature'.
130 Lewis-Williams, *The Mind in the Cave*.
131 Lopez, *Arctic Dreams*; Lopez, *Of Wolves and Men*; Zapf, 'Cultural Ecology'.
132 Nabhan, *Cultures of Habitat*, 12.
133 Meeker, 'The Comic Mode'.
134 Snyder, *The Practice of the Wild*, 153.
135 Oates, 'Against Nature'.
136 Nabhan, *Cultures of Habitat*, 15.
137 Strauss, 'Reconsidering the Big Bad Wolf'; Payne, 'Dark Brothers'.
138 Ovid, *Metamorphoses*.
139 Harrison, *Forests*, 26.
140 Williamson, *Land of the Sea People*; Thomson, *The People of the Sea*; Campbell, *Primitive Mythology*; Bierhorst, *The Mythology of North America*.
141 Strauss, *The Passionate Fact*; Thomason Sickles, 'Honoring the Other'.

142 Van der Post, *The Heart of the Hunter*; Göröwirijaa, 'Grand-Waka'.
143 See Abram, *Spell of the Sensuous*; Abram, *Becoming Animal*; Gunn, *Spider Woman's Granddaughter*; Manes, 'Nature and Silence'; Silko, 'Landscape, History, and the Pueblo Imagination'.
144 MacLellan, interview.
145 Green, interview.
146 Malcolm Green, telephone interview, 21 May 2020.
147 Lopez, *Of Wolves and Men*.
148 Abram, *Becoming Animal*.
149 Ibid.; Cowan, *The Aborigine Tradition*; Leenhardt, *Do Kamo*.
150 Firebrace, interview.
151 Chatwin, *The Songlines*; Nabhan, *Cultures of Habitat*; Snyder, *The Practice of the Wild*.
152 MacLellan, interview.
153 Strauss, *The Passionate Fact*.
154 Lupton, 'Deep England'; Lupton, *The Dreaming of Place*.
155 Abram, *Spell of the Sensuous*; Chatwin, *The Songlines*; Cowan, *The Aborigine Tradition*; Cowan, *Letters from a Wild State*; McLuhan, *The Way of the Earth*; Snyder, *The Practice of the Wild*.
156 Maddern, interview.
157 Lupton, *A Norfolk Songline*; Maddern, *Snowdonia Folk Tales*.
158 Green, interview, 21 May 2020; https://www.malcolm-green.co.uk/projects/
159 Barnes and Branfoot, *Pilgrimage*.
160 Manwaring, 'Awakening the King'; https://kingarthurway.wordpress.com
161 Silko, 'Landscape, History, and the Pueblo Imagination'.
162 Sheldrake, *Living between Worlds*.
163 Ash et al., *Folklore, Myths and Legends*; Westwood and Kingshill, *The Lore of Scotland*; Westwood and Simpson, *The Lore of the Land*.
164 Olalla, *Mythological Atlas of Greece*.
165 Abram, *Spell of the Sensuous*; Brody, *Other Side of Eden*; Lopez, *Arctic Dreams*; Nabhan, *Cultures of Habitat*; Smith, *Storytelling Scotland*.
166 Abram, *Spell of the Sensuous*, 176.
167 I'm grateful to Hugh Lupton, Shonaleigh Cumbers, Ben Haggarty and Mary Medlicott for introducing me to the techniques described in this paragraph.
168 Lupton, *The Dreaming of Place*.
169 Quoted in McDowell, 'The Bakhtinian Road', 380.
170 Maddern, interview.
171 Lupton, *The Dreaming of Place*, 22.
172 Basso, '"Speaking with Names"', 110.
173 Abram, *Spell of the Sensuous*.

174 Maddern, interview.
175 Letcher, 'The Role of the Bard'.
176 Letcher, 'The Scouring of the Shire'.
177 Edwards, *The Storytelling Goddess*; Matthews, *Arthur*.
178 Kolodny, 'Unearthing Herstory'; Ruether, 'Ecofeminist Philosophy'.
179 Evans, 'The Elucidation'; Gomes and Kanner, 'The Rape of the Well-Maidens'.
180 Edwards, *The Storytelling Goddess*; Manwaring, *The Bardic Handbook*.
181 Lopez, *Arctic Dreams*; McLuhan, *The Way of the Earth*.
182 See Cowan, *Letters from a Wild State*; McLuhan, *The Way of the Earth*; Sheldrake, *Living between Worlds*; Snyder, *The Practice of the Wild*.
183 Nabhan, *Cultures of Habitat*, 196.
184 Yeats, *Writings on Irish Folklore*; Lenihan, *Meeting the Other Crowd*.
185 Darwin Edwards, 'Re-storying Scotland'.
186 Tissier, interview.
187 Darwin Edwards, 'Re-storying Scotland'.
188 Nabhan, *Cultures of Habitat*; Shapiro, 'Restoring Habitats'.
189 MacLellan, interview.
190 Shipp and Nunn, 'Marsh Men'.
191 Diamond, *Rise and Fall*, 212.
192 Palmer, *Dancing to Armageddon*.
193 Cowan, *Letters from a Wild State*, 38.
194 Maddern, interview; MacLellan, interview.
195 Firebrace, interview.
196 Goodison, *Moving Heaven and Earth*, 3.
197 Soyinka, *Myth, Literature and the African World*; Turnbull, 'Liminality'.
198 Harley, 'Playing with the Wall'.
199 Please, interview.
200 Richards, 'Doing the Story'; Schechner, 'Magnitudes of Performance'.
201 Lopez, *Of Wolves and Men*, 62.
202 Ana Adnan, telephone interview, 26 February 2003.
203 MacLellan, interview.
204 Hankins, interview.
205 Simon Garrett, telephone interview, September 2002.
206 Zipes, *Relentless Progress*.
207 MacLellan, interview.
208 Goodchild, *Capitalism and Religion*; Turnbull, 'Liminality'.
209 Berk, 'The Grail in the Uttermost West', 563.
210 Green, interview, 7 July 2002.
211 R. G. Collingwood quoted in Heinrich, 'The Artist as Bard', 14.
212 Murdock, *The Heroine's Journey*.

213 Parkinson, Letter to the Editor.
214 Ben Haggarty, personal communication, 2003.
215 Sawyer, *The Way of the Storyteller*, 29.
216 Abram, *Spell of the Sensuous*; Lupton, 'Betsy Whyte'.
217 Letcher, 'The Role of the Bard'; Manwaring, *The Bardic Handbook*; Restall-Orr, *Druid Priestess*; Shallcrass, 'Awen'.
218 Manwaring, *The Bardic Handbook*.
219 Kevan Manwaring, personal communication, 2020.
220 Sewall, 'The Skill of Ecological Perception'.
221 MacLellan, interview.
222 Gersie, *Earthtales*; Gersie, 'Wild but with a Purpose'; Gersie and King, *Storymaking in Education and Therapy*; Gersie et al., *Storytelling for a Greener World*.
223 Wilson, *Storytelling and Theatre*.
224 Empson, *Subjective Lives*.
225 Freire, *Pedagogy of the Oppressed*; Gersie, *Reflections on Therapeutic Storytelling*; Gersie et al., *Storytelling for a Greener World*.
226 Suvin, *Metamorphoses of Science Fiction*.
227 Goldberg, 'Social Conscience', 106.
228 Spira, *The Nature of Consciousness*.
229 Palmer, *Dancing to Armageddon*.
230 Marshall, *Nature's Web*.
231 See Zubrin, *The Case for Mars*.
232 Le Guin, *Dancing at the Edge*.
233 Axelrod and Suedfeld, 'Technology, Capitalism and Christianity'.
234 Conn, 'When the Earth Hurts'.
235 Gersie, *Earthtales*; Roszak, 'Where Psyche Meets Gaia'.
236 Gersie, *Earthtales*.
237 Shacklock, 'Fast Capitalist Educational Change'.
238 Wapner, *Environmental Activism*.
239 Sunderland, interview.
240 Lopez, *Arctic Dreams*; Sunderland, *In a Glass Darkly*.
241 Sunderland, interview; Oelrich, *The New Story*.
242 WWF Annual Conference, Bristol, 5–7 November 2002.
243 Pellowski, *The World of Storytelling*.
244 Clarke, *Green Man Dreaming*; Goodison, *Moving Heaven and Earth*.
245 Meletinsky, *The Poetics of Myth*.
246 Wilson, *Storytelling and Theatre*.
247 Goodchild, *Capitalism and Religion*.
248 Brody, *Other Side of Eden*.
249 Le Guin, *Always Coming Home*; Callenbach, 'Chocco'.

Chapter 2

1. Cobley, *Narrative*.
2. Hall, 'The Forgotten Tongue'.
3. Benjamin, 'The Storyteller'; Wilson, *Storytelling and Theatre*.
4. Uzendoski and Calapucha-Tapuy, *Ecology of the Spoken Word*.
5. Brooks, *Reading for the Plot*, 258, 260.
6. Summary of my retelling of traditional tale. Sources: East and Maddern, *Spirit of the Forest*; Kane, *The Wildwood King*; Tongue, *Forgotten Folk-Tales*.
7. Stibbe, *Ecolinguistics*, 21.
8. Ovid, *Metamorphoses*.
9. Hartland, *English Fairy and Other Folk Tales*.
10. Wood, *Spirits, Heroes and Hunters*.
11. Carson, *Silent Spring*.
12. Quammen, *Spillover*.
13. Moltmann, *God in Creation*, 297.
14. Lewis, *An Experiment in Criticism*.
15. Coupe, *Myth*, 197.
16. Lewis, *An Experiment in Criticism*.
17. Cook, *The Tree of Life*.
18. Simard, 'Mycorrhizal Networks'.
19. Coupe, *Myth*, 176.
20. See Olrik, 'Epic Laws of Folk Narrative'.
21. Raglan, *The Hero*.
22. Campbell, *The Hero*.
23. For example, Murdock, *The Heroine's Journey*.
24. Henderson, *Star Wars*; Vogler, *The Writer's Journey*; Brayfield, *Bestseller*.
25. Booker, *The Seven Basic Plots*.
26. Haven, *Story Proof*, 79.
27. McKee, *Story*, 45.
28. Quoted in Tydeman, *Conversations with Barry Lopez*, 129.
29. Haven, *Story Proof*.
30. Aarne and Thompson, *Types of the Folktale*; Uther, *Types of International Folktales*.
31. See Briggs, *Dictionary of British Folk-Tales*.
32. Blécourt and Meder, 'A European Classification'.
33. Summary of oral story composed by author.
34. See Sharpe, 'Introduction'; Shearer, *Buddha*.
35. Benjamin, 'The Storyteller'; Ong, *Orality and Literacy*.
36. Brooks, *Reading for the Plot*, 19.
37. Wilson, *Storytelling and Theatre*.

38 Ward, 'What They Told Buchi Emecheta'.
39 Zipes, *Creative Storytelling*.
40 I thank David Metcalfe for introducing to me the idea of expectations management.
41 Metcalfe, 'Voices in the City'.
42 Oelrich, *The New Story*.
43 Ibid., 91.
44 Gersie, *Reflections on Therapeutic Storytelling*.
45 Wilson, *Storytelling and Theatre*; Fagan, 'Citizen Engagement'.
46 Ong, *Orality and Literacy*, 176.
47 Metcalfe, 'Voices in the City'.
48 Lipman, *Improving Your Storytelling*, 120–2.
49 Gersie, *Reflections on Therapeutic Storytelling*; Parkinson, *Transforming Tales*.
50 I'm grateful to Tim Sheppard for teaching me this principle.
51 Summary of 'Bat Milk' composed by Ron Donaldson. My retelling also draws upon Haysom et al., 'Bats'.
52 Strauss, *The Passionate Fact*.
53 Haven, *Story Proof*; Smith and Pottle, *Science through Stories*.
54 Aristotle, *Poetics*.
55 Field, *Screenplay*.
56 Campbell, *The Hero*.
57 McKee, *Story*.
58 Dodds and Hopwood, 'BAN Waste'; https://tyneside.sdf-eu.org/banwaste/home.htm
59 Stibbe, *Ecolinguistics*.
60 https://www.gloucestershire-against-incinerators.org.uk; https://communityr4c.com/about/the-project
61 Naess, 'The Third World'; Bennett, 'From Wide Open Spaces'.
62 Marshall, *Nature's Web*.
63 Summary of oral story composed by author. Sources: Diamond, *Rise and Fall*; Flannery, *The Future Eaters*; Quammen, *The Song of the Dodo*.
64 Nanson, *Words of Re-enchantment*.
65 Cobley, *Narrative*.
66 Frye, *Anatomy of Criticism*.
67 Dorling, *Rule Britannia*.
68 Shah, *In Arabian Nights*, 24.
69 Nanson, *Words of Re-enchantment*.
70 Nanson, 'Jumping the Gap'.
71 Höhler, '"The Real Problem"'.
72 Williams, *Arctic Labyrinth*.
73 Carlson, *Performance*.
74 Browning, 'Brexit Populism'.

75 Haven, *Story Proof*.
76 Collingwood, *The Principles of Art*.
77 I am indebted to my teacher Maya for helping me to understand this distinction.
78 Cheney and Eston, 'Environmental Ethics', 126.
79 Gersie, *Earthtales*; Gersie, *Storymaking in Bereavement*; Gersie and King, *Storymaking in Education and Therapy*; Gersie, *Reflections on Therapeutic Storytelling*.
80 Gersie, 'Bringing Nature Home'; Gersie, 'Wild but with Purpose'.
81 Zipes, *Relentless Progress*.
82 Ibid.
83 Suvin, *Metamorphoses of Science Fiction*.
84 Summary of my retelling of an episode in Haggarty and Brockbank's *Mezolith*. Some dialogue closely follows Haggarty's wording.
85 Travers, *What the Bee Knows*.
86 Campbell, *The Hero*.
87 Campbell, *Primitive Mythology*.
88 Suvin, *Metamorphoses of Science Fiction*.
89 Nanson, '"The Future Has Gone Bad"'.
90 Tolle, *A New Earth*.
91 For example, Robinson, *Pacific Edge*; Robinson, *Green Mars*; Robinson, *Forty Signs of Rain*.
92 Quoted in Tydeman, *Conversations with Barry Lopez*, 16.
93 Cupitt, *What Is a Story?*, 46–7.
94 Theodossopoulos, *Troubles with Turtles*.
95 Summary of oral story composed by author.
96 Cobley, *Narrative*.
97 Wilson, *Storytelling and Theatre*. I thank Mike Wilson for his further thoughts on this topic.
98 Lipman, *Improving Your Storytelling*, 137–40.
99 Holquist, *Dialogism*.
100 Summary of my oral retelling of the unexpurgated version of Lawrence's 'Sun'.
101 Abram, *Becoming Animal*; Abram, *Spell of the Sensuous*.
102 Spowers, *Rising Tides*, 310.
103 Gaard, 'Where Is Feminism?', 85–6.
104 Summary of my retelling of a traditional tale workshopped by Tales to Sustain. Source: Martin, *The Hungry Tigress*.
105 Campbell, 'Land and Language of Desire'.
106 Wilson, *The Diversity of Life*.
107 Campbell and Moyers, *The Power of Myth*, 55.
108 Toelken, 'The Icebergs of Folktale'.
109 Wilson, *Storytelling and Theatre*.

110 Zipes, *Relentless Progress*, 155–6.
111 See Phillips, 'Emotional Well-Being'.
112 Toelken, 'The Icebergs of Folktale'.
113 Schieffelin, 'Listening to Stories'.
114 For example, Feldman and Kornfield, *Stories of the Spirit*; Silf, *One Hundred Wisdom Tales*.
115 King, *Kahuna Healing*.
116 Said, *Orientalism*.
117 Githaiga, 'Intellectual Property Law'.
118 See Nanson, *Words of Re-enchantment*; Stone, *The Healing Art*; Wilson, *Storytelling and Theatre*.
119 Heywood, *The New Storytelling*; Ben Haggarty, talk, Festival at the Edge, Much Wenlock, c. 1999.
120 Zipes, *Relentless Progress*.
121 Ong, *Orality and Literacy*; Parkinson, *Transforming Tales*.
122 Said, *Culture and Imperialism*, 15.
123 Charing et al., *Ayahuasca Visions*; Luna and Amaringo, *Ayahuasca Visions*.
124 Von Sydow, 'Geography and Folk-Tale Oicotypes'; Ranelagh, *The Past We Share*.
125 Aarne and Thompson, *Types of the Folktale*; Thompson, *Motif-Index*; Uther, *Types of International Folktales*.
126 Christiansen, *Migratory Legends*.
127 TUUP, 'Artist Insights'.
128 Temi Odurinde, personal communication, 2020.
129 Krech, *The Ecological Indian*.
130 Zapf, 'Cultural Ecology', 74.
131 Zimmer, *Myths and Symbols*.
132 Bruchac, *Iroquois Stories*; Clark, *Indian Legends*.
133 See Armstrong, *Short History of Myth*; Godin, 'Croyances'; Toelken, 'The Icebergs of Folktale'.
134 Strauss, *The Passionate Fact*, 106.
135 For example, Beatty, *Australian Folk Tales and Traditions*; Polley, *American Folklore and Legend*.
136 Stewart, 'Born of the Land'.
137 Phillips, *Ernest Hemingway on Writing*.
138 I'm grateful to Maya for pointing me towards this idea.

Chapter 3

1 Walker, '"How the Bear Lost Its Tail"'; Ashliman, 'The Tail-Fisher'.
2 Summary of my retelling based on *Canku Ota*, 'How Bear Lost His Tail'.

3   Brooks, *Reading for the Plot*.
4   Burke, 'Hyper-technologism', 98.
5   I'm grateful to Mary Medlicott for introducing me to this notion.
6   Frye, *Anatomy of Criticism*, 141–6.
7   Nanson, 'Jumping the Gap'.
8   McKee, *Story*.
9   Summary of oral story composed by author.
10 Harding, 'Gaia Awareness', 91, 93.
11 Wheeler, 'How the Earth Speaks'.
12 Van Dooren and Rose, 'Lively Ethography', 258.
13 Gibson, *A Reenchanted World*, 90.
14 Summary of oral story composed by author. Full transcript in Nanson, *Words of Re-enchantment*. Sources: Flannery, *The Weather Makers*; Halliday and Adler, *Reptiles and Amphibians*.
15 Dawkins, *The Selfish Gene*.
16 Nanson, *Words of Re-enchantment*, 142, 143.
17 Summary of oral story composed by author.
18 Behrensmeyer et al., *Terrestrial Ecosystems*.
19 For example, Fortey, *Life*.
20 Segerstråle, *Defenders of the Truth*, 355.
21 See Palmer, *Dancing to Armageddon*; Weber, *The Protestant Ethic*.
22 Wilson, *On Human Nature*.
23 Zipes, *Relentless Progress*, 19.
24 Nanson, '"The Future Has Gone Bad"'.
25 Wilson, *The Diversity of Life*; Wilson, *The Future of Life*.
26 Wilson, *On Human Nature*, 2, 18. See Berry, *Life Is a Miracle*; Segerstråle, *Defenders of the Truth*.
27 Jameson, *Archaeologies of the Future*. See Palmer, *Dancing to Armageddon*.
28 Margulis, *Symbiotic Planet*.
29 Gould, *Wonderful Life*.
30 Segerstråle, *Defenders of the Truth*.
31 Conway Morris, *Life's Solution*.
32 See Sheldrake, *The Science Delusion*.
33 Cohen, *The Planets*.
34 See Rigby, *Dancing with Disaster*.
35 Gersie, *Reflections on Therapeutic Storytelling*.
36 Wilson, *Consilience*.
37 Gould, *Rock of Ages*.
38 Conway Morris, *Life's Solution*.
39 Armstrong, *Short History of Myth*, 137.
40 Sagan, *Cosmos*, 5.

41 Stories published as *Earth Story* and *Life Story*.
42 Ashe, *Camelot*; Heinberg, *Memories and Visions*.
43 Martin, *Twilight of the Mammoths*; Taylor, *Beyond Conservation*.
44 Safina, *Song for the Blue Ocean*, 77.
45 Summary of oral story composed by author. Sources: Cowan, *Letters from a Wild State*; Cowan, *The Aborigine Tradition*; Flannery, *The Future Eaters*.
46 Flannery, *The Future Eaters*; Martin, *Twilight of the Mammoths*; Murray, 'Extinctions Downunder'.
47 Zapf, 'Cultural Ecology', 66.
48 Flannery, *The Eternal Frontier*; Flannery, *The Future Eaters*; Martin, *Twilight of the Mammoths*; Martin and Klein, *Quaternary Extinctions*.
49 As in Krech, *The Ecological Indian*.
50 Berndt and Berndt, *The Barbarians*.
51 Berndt and Berndt, *The Speaking Land*, 4.
52 Snyder, *A Place in Space*, 174–6.
53 Medlicott, '"Miss, Is Skomar Oddy Extinct?"'; Salisbury, 'Feeding the Story'.
54 Sogyal, *The Tibetan Book*, 95.
55 Gersie, *Reflections on Therapeutic Storytelling*.
56 McKee, *Story*.
57 Summary of my oral retelling of Seton's 'Lobo, the King of Currumpaw'.
58 Seton, 'Lobo', 254.
59 Ibid.
60 Quoted in Jones, *Epiphany in the Wilderness*.
61 Brooks, *Reading for the Plot*.
62 On this topic I'm indebted to the teaching of Dawn Morgan.
63 Gersie, *Earthtales*.
64 Tolkien, 'On Fairy Stories', 153.
65 Shippey, *The Road to Middle-Earth*.
66 Gersie, *Earthtales*, 29.
67 Nanson, '"The Future Has Gone Bad"'.
68 Wegner, 'Utopianism', 577.
69 Booker, *The Seven Basic Plots*.
70 Nanson, 'Jumping the Gap'.
71 Baccolini and Moylan, *Dark Horizons*.
72 Otto, '"The Rain Feels New"'.
73 Nanson, '"The Future Has Gone Bad"'.
74 Percy, *Reliques of Ancient English Poetry*.
75 Summary of my oral retelling adapted from my published short story 'The Migrant Maid'.
76 See Cable, *The Storm*; Goodchild, *Capitalism and Religion*.

77 Brooks, *Reading for the Plot*, 101–9.
78 Cupitt, *What Is a Story?*, 28.
79 Brooks, *Reading for the Plot*.
80 Guenther, *The Tantric View*; Sheldrake, *The Science Delusion*.
81 Brooks, *Reading for the Plot*, 228, 234.
82 Roszak, *The Voice of the Earth*, 48.
83 Brooks, *Reading for the Plot*, 236.
84 Tolkien, *The Fellowship of the Ring*, 12.
85 Brooks, *Reading for the Plot*.
86 Kovel, *The Enemy of Nature*.
87 Le Guin, *Dancing at the Edge*, 169.
88 Ibid., 90.

Chapter 4

1 Nabhan, *Cultures of Habitat*; Kennedy, 'Folklore and Human Ecology'; Shepard, *Nature and Madness*.
2 See Palmer, *The Sacred History of Britain*; Hutton, *The Stations of the Sun*.
3 Pilbeam, *The Landscape of Gloucestershire*; Ryder, *Portrait of Gloucestershire*: Sale, *Gloucestershire*; Smith and Ralph, *History of Bristol and Gloucestershire*.
4 Studholme and Moore, *State of the Natural Environment*.
5 Sutton, *Cotswold Tales*; Sutton, *Dialect & Folk Phrases*.
6 Dorson, *The British Folklorists*.
7 Lupton, 'Deep England', 7.
8 Phelps, *Herefordshire Folk Tales*.
9 For example, Hartland, *Gloucestershire*; Williams, *Legends, Tales, and Songs*.
10 Shapiro, 'Restoring Habitats'.
11 Wilson, *Storytelling and Theatre*, 28.
12 Lilley, 'Kathleen Jamie', 24.
13 Lupton, *The Dreaming of Place*.
14 Ibid.; Nanson, *Words of Re-enchantment*.
15 Berry, *Standing by Words*, 90.
16 Thompson, *The Folktale*; Warner, *From the Beast*.
17 See Kvartič, 'The Local Impact'.
18 See Stibbe, *Ecolinguistics*.
19 Nanson, *Gloucestershire Folk Tales*; Nanson and Hartsiotis, *Gloucestershire Ghost Tales*; Nanson and Hartsiotis, *Gloucestershire Folk Tales for Children*.
20 Quoted in Palmer, *Folklore of Gloucestershire*, 91.
21 Quoted in Hartland, *Gloucestershire*, 23.

22 Quoted in Palmer, *Folklore of Gloucestershire*, 91.
23 Roy Palmer, personal communication, 2012.
24 Taylor and Taylor, *Anglo-Saxon Architecture*.
25 Hogarth, *Dragons*; Huxley, *The Dragon*.
26 Ó Duilearga, 'Irish Tales and Story-Tellers'.
27 Thompson, *The Folktale*.
28 Baring and Cashford, *The Myth of the Goddess*.
29 Kinsley, *Hindu Goddesses*; Ions, *Indian Mythology*.
30 Zimmer, *Myths and Symbols*.
31 Hogarth, *Dragons*; Frye, *Anatomy of Criticism*.
32 Tolkien, *The Silmarillion*; Tolkien, *The Hobbit*.
33 Briggs, *Dictionary of British Folk-Tales*.
34 Gould, *Mythical Monsters*; Hogarth, *Dragons*.
35 Westwood and Simpson, *The Lore of the Land*.
36 Ibid.; Briggs, *Dictionary of British Folk-Tales*.
37 Turner, *Mysterious Gloucestershire*.
38 Vizard, *In the Valley of the Gods*.
39 Starkey, *Mermaids, Moonrakers and Hobgoblins*.
40 https://www.glosfolk.btck.co.uk/TheLegendoftheDeerhurstDragon
41 Gwilym Davies, 'The Deerhurst Dragon Song', 1974; my thanks to Peter Cripps.
42 Westwood and Simpson, *The Lore of the Land*.
43 Nanson and Hartsiotis, *Gloucestershire Folk Tales for Children*.
44 Crowden, 'Disease-Ridden Vermin'.
45 Kane, *Wisdom of the Mythtellers*.
46 See Zipes, *Relentless Progress*.
47 Saitoti, *Maasai*.
48 Quammen, *Monster of God*.
49 Baring and Cashford, *The Myth of the Goddess*.
50 Nanson, *Gloucestershire Folk Tales*.
51 Ibid.
52 Hooke, *The Anglo-Saxon Landscape*, 2.
53 Ibid.
54 Heighway, *Anglo-Saxon Gloucestershire*; Pilbeam, *The Landscape of Gloucestershire*; Härke, 'Anglo-Saxon Immigration'.
55 Nanson, *Gloucestershire Folk Tales*, 125, 124.
56 See Monbiot, *No Man's Land*.
57 Nanson, *Gloucestershire Folk Tales*, 129.
58 Ibid.
59 Kvartič, 'The Local Impact'.
60 Nabhan, *Cultures of Habitat*, 319.

61 Tolkien, 'On Fairy Stories'.
62 Clarke, *Green Man Dreaming*; Addey, 'Light of the Sphere'.
63 Getty, *Goddess*; Mann and Lyle, *Sacred Sexuality*; Michell, *The Earth Spirit*.
64 Plumwood, *Feminism*; Ruether, 'Ecofeminist Philosophy'.
65 Berman, 'The Rape of Mother Nature', 267.
66 Johnston, 'Subtle Subjects and Ethics', 245.
67 See Plumwood, *Feminism*; Ruether, 'Ecofeminist Philosophy'; Soper, *What Is Nature?*
68 Nanson, *Gloucestershire Folk Tales*; Nanson and Hartsiotis, *Gloucestershire Ghost Tales*; Nanson and Hartsiotis, *Gloucestershire Folk Tales for Children*.
69 Nash Ford, 'St. Afrella *alias* Arilda'.
70 Palmer, *Folklore of Gloucestershire*.
71 Reproduced in Bradshaw, 'St Arilda of Oldbury on Severn'.
72 I'm grateful to Kevan Manwaring for introducing me to this approach to field notes.
73 Savage, *The Anglo-Saxon Chronicles*.
74 Ryder, *Portrait of Gloucestershire*.
75 Nanson, *Gloucestershire Folk Tales*.
76 Williams, *Lays and Legends*.
77 Tolkien, *The Fellowship of the Ring*.
78 Nanson, *Gloucestershire Folk Tales*, 62–3.
79 See Baring and Cashford, *The Myth of the Goddess*; Getty, *Goddess*; Huxley, *The Dragon*; Luna and Amaringo, *Ayahuasca Visions*; Mann and Lyle, *Sacred Sexuality*.
80 Huxley, *The Dragon*.
81 Baring and Cashford, *The Myth of the Goddess*, 273.
82 Ibid.
83 Parrinder, *African Mythology*.
84 Bourret et al., *Littérature orale*.
85 Uzendoski and Calapucha-Tapuy, *Ecology of the Spoken Word*.
86 Cowan, *Myths of the Dreaming*.
87 Ibid.; Luna and Amaringo, *Ayahuasca Visions*; Uzendoski and Calapucha-Tapuy, *Ecology of the Spoken Word*.
88 Gelin, 'The Misogyny of Climate Deniers'.
89 John Stevinson, personal communication, 2011.
90 Wilson, 'Honest Liars'; Wilson, 'Some Thoughts on Storytelling'.
91 Stevinson, *King Kenulf of Mercia*.
92 Nanson, *Gloucestershire Folk Tales*.
93 Williams, *Lays and Legends*, 72.
94 Williams, *Round About the Upper Thames*.
95 Westwood and Simpson, *The Lore of the Land*.
96 Gould, *I Have Landed*.

97   See Weber, *The Protestant Ethic*.
98   Hughes, *Winter Pollen*, 269.
99   Curry, *Defending Middle-Earth*.
100 Todorov, *The Fantastic*, 92, 120.
101 Minter, *Big Cats*.
102 Yeats, *Writings on Irish Folklore*.
103 Tolkien, 'On Fairy Stories', 142.
104 Benjamin, 'The Work of Art'.
105 Hooper-Greenhill, *Museums*, 111.
106 Ibid.; King, *Kahuna Healing*; Howells, *The Heathens*.
107 Nash, *Outline*.
108 Palmer, *The Sacred History of Britain*.
109 Lundquist, *The Temple*.
110 Bensa and Rivierre, *Histoires canaques*; Leenhardt, *Do Kamo*.
111 Howells, *The Heathens*.
112 Goodchild, *Capitalism and Religion*.
113 Howard, *Heritage*.
114 Wildlife Trusts, 'A Living Landscape'.
115 Nanson, *Gloucestershire Folk Tales*.
116 Ramsay, *Nights of Storytelling*, 15.
117 Tjibaou, *Kanaky*; Tjibaou and Missotte, *Kanaké*.
118 Berndt and Berndt, *The Speaking Land*; Leenhardt, *Do Kamo*.
119 Horowitz, '"It's Up to the Clan"'; Tjibaou, *Kanaky*.
120 Göröwirijaa, 'Génie du Milieu des Airs'.
121 Bensa and Rivierre, *Les filles du rocher Até*; Leenhardt, *Notes d'ethnologie*; Salomon, *Savoirs et pouvoirs*.
122 Connell, *New Caledonia or Kanaky?*; Horowitz, '"It's Up to the Clan"'; Horowitz, 'Perceptions of Nature'; Ali, 'Contesting the "Noble Savage"'.
123 Maddern, interview; Abram, *Becoming Animal*; Berndt and Berndt, *The Speaking Land*; Ramsay, *Nights of Storytelling*.
124 Helena, 'Le poulpe et le rat'; Kecine, 'Le pouple et le rat'; Michel, *Légendes et chansons*; Pumwan, 'Pourquoi le poulpe'; Ramsay, *Nights of Storytelling*.
125 Robert, 'L'ogre bicéphale'.
126 See Howe, *The Loyalty Islands*.
127 Hadfield, *Among the Natives of the Loyalty Group*.
128 Bourret et al., *Littérature orale*.
129 Léonard Var, interview, Xepenehe, 1 September 2016.
130 Dahl, 'Traditional Environmental Knowledge'.
131 Goromôtö, 'La grand-mère et les trois frères'.
132 Berndt and Berndt, *The Speaking Land*, 12.
133 Tjibaou, *Kanaky*.

134 Boahnou, 'Tamoangui'.
135 Bami, 'L'aigle et les deux femmes'.
136 Parkinson, *Transforming Tales*, 197.
137 Lee, *Cider with Rosie*, 124–5.
138 Curry, *Defending Middle-Earth*, 59.
139 Sagan, *Cosmos*; Wilson, *The Diversity of Life*.
140 Gibson, *A Reenchanted World*.
141 Tolkien, 'On Fairy Stories', 116.
142 Conley, 'Hélène Cixous', 152.
143 Hepburn, 'Wonder'.
144 Curry, 'Magic vs. Enchantment', 6.
145 Tolkien, 'On Fairy Stories', 143.
146 Curry, 'Magic vs. Enchantment', 403.
147 Wilson, *Storytelling and Theatre*, 75–6.
148 Parkinson, *Transforming Tales*.
149 Lupton, *The Dreaming of Place*, 28.
150 See Nanson et al., *An Ecobardic Manifesto*.
151 Meder, 'The Dutch Law of the Land'.
152 Kirsty Hartsiotis, personal communication, 2019.

Chapter 5

1 Campbell and Moyers, *The Power of Myth*.
2 Quoted in Tydeman, *Conversations with Barry Lopez*, 129.
3 Alexiou, *After Antiquity*; Campbell, *The Hero*; Dowman, *Masters of Enchantment*.
4 Shaw, 'Beyond the Crisis of Return'.
5 Armiero, 'Environmental History'.
6 Stone, *The Healing Art*.
7 Tolle, *A New Earth*.
8 My account of these projects, including the quotations, derives from an interview with Jane Flood in Stroud, 10 December 2010.
9 https://www.neroche.org/art.php
10 Tongue, *The Chime Child*.
11 Summary of oral story devised by Jane Flood.
12 See Lupton, 'Betsy Whyte'.
13 Palmer, *The Folklore of Somerset*.
14 Getty, *Goddess*.
15 Stone, *The Healing Art*.
16 Oelrich, *The New Story*, 274.

17 Dunne, *Time and Myth*, 110.
18 Coupe, *Myth*; Durham, *The Return of King Arthur*.
19 Gersie, *Reflections on Therapeutic Storytelling*, 185.
20 Clarke, *Green Man Dreaming*.
21 Stone, *The Healing Art*; Parkinson, 'Your Body Doesn't Know'.
22 Uzendoski and Calapucha-Tapuy, *Ecology of the Spoken Word*, 5.
23 Ong, *Orality and Literacy*.
24 Cupitt, *What Is a Story?*, 60.
25 Tolle, *A New Earth*.
26 Buber, *I and Thou*.
27 On the topic of this paragraph I'm much indebted to Maya.
28 See Kempton, 'The Magic of Shared Awareness'.
29 O'Sullivan, 'The Aesthetics of Affect'.
30 See Cree and Gersie, 'Storytelling in the Woods'; Freedberg and Gallese, 'Motion, Emotion and Empathy'.
31 Ong, *Orality and Literacy*, 74.
32 Stone, *The Healing Art*, 69.
33 Ramsden and Hollingsworth, *The Storyteller's Way*.
34 Goodchild, *The Naked Voice*.
35 On this point I'm grateful to Chloë Goodchild and participants on 'The Naked Voice' workshop, Hawkwood College, Stroud, 15–19 March 2020.
36 Goodchild, 'The Naked Voice' workshop.
37 Ben Haggarty, workshop, Bishops Wood Centre, Stourport-on-Severn, 2009.
38 Cobley, *Narrative*; Le Guin, *The Wave in the Mind*, 198.
39 Nanson, *Words of Re-enchantment*.
40 Oelrich, *The New Story*, 213.
41 Tydeman, *Conversations with Barry Lopez*, 147.
42 Brooks, *Reading for the Plot*, 236.
43 See Nanson, *Words of Re-enchantment*, 143.
44 Wilson, *Scottish Folk-Tales and Legends*.
45 Hazel Bradley, personal communication, c. 2002; Bradley, 'Therapeutic Storytelling'.
46 My understanding here draws greatly from Maya's teaching. See Osho, *The Perfect Way*; Sogyal, *The Tibetan Book*; Spira, *The Nature of Consciousness*.
47 See Gersie, *Reflections on Therapeutic Storytelling*.
48 Lyotard, 'Discourse of the Secluded', 137.
49 Sogyal, *The Tibetan Book*.
50 Malekin, 'Art and Liberation', 151.
51 O'Donohue, *Eternal Echoes*, 349.
52 Gersie, *Reflections on Therapeutic Storytelling*.
53 Harding, *Animate Earth*.

54 Green and Hennessey, 'By Hidden Paths'.
55 Here again I acknowledge Maya's insight.
56 Zipes, *Relentless Progress*.
57 Kovel, *The Enemy of Nature*.
58 Trungpa, 'Questions and Answers'.
59 Jayaraja, 'Evolution or Extinction'.
60 Parkinson, *Three Angles*; Wilson, *Storytelling and Theatre*.
61 Stallings, 'The Web of Silence'; Sturm, 'The Enchanted Imagination'.
62 Stallings, 'The Web of Silence'.
63 Ong, *Orality and Literacy*.
64 Callicott, 'Worldview Remediation', 152.
65 See Cadwalladr et al., 'America's Most Dangerous Couple?'; Foster, 'Cyberculture'; Nanson, '"The Future Has Gone Bad"'.
66 Wilson, '"Another Fine Mess"'.
67 Carr-Gomm, *Brief History of Nakedness*.
68 Douzinas, *Philosophy and Resistance*, 161.
69 Abram, *Spell of the Sensuous*.
70 Wolf, *Reader, Come Home*.
71 Gersie, *Reflections on Therapeutic Storytelling*, 79–80.
72 Jane Flood, personal communication, 2020.
73 Blincoe, 'Re-educating the Person', 206.
74 Haggarty, *Seek Out the Voice*.

Chapter 6

1 Patrice Godin, interview, Nouméa, 30 September 2016; Godin, 'Croyances'; Illouz, *De chair et de pierre*; Leblic, 'Les Kanak et les rêves'; Leenhardt, *Notes d'ethnologie*; Salomon, *Savoirs et pouvoirs*.
2 Godin, 'Croyances', 331.
3 Leenhardt, *Do Kamo*.
4 Isabelle Leblic, interview, Paris, 29 May 2016.
5 Tjibaou, *Kanaky*.
6 Rigby, *Dancing with Disaster*, 161–2.
7 Uzendoski and Calapucha-Tapuy, *Ecology of the Spoken Word*, 58.
8 Sheldrake, *The Science Delusion*.
9 Uzendoski and Calapucha-Tapuy, *Ecology of the Spoken Word*.
10 Van Dooren and Rose, 'Lively Ethography'.
11 Shah, *In Arabian Nights*.
12 Lawson, *Modern Greek Folklore*; Tomkinson, *Haunted Greece*.

13　O'Donohue, *Eternal Echoes*.
14　Van Dooren and Rose, 'Lively Ethography', 261.
15　See Clarke, 'Science, Theory, and Systems'; Garrard, *Ecocriticism*; Gibson, *A Reenchanted World*; Love, *Practical Ecocriticism*; Segerstråle, *Defenders of the Truth*;.
16　Dawkins, *The God Delusion*.
17　Cupitt, *What Is a Story?*
18　Palmer, *Dancing to Armageddon*, 129.
19　For example, Uzendoski and Calapucha-Tapuy, *Ecology of the Spoken Word*; Ramsay, *Nights of Storytelling*; Cowan, *Letters from a Wild State*; Narayan, *Mondays*.
20　Addey, 'Light of the Sphere', 157.
21　For example, Capra, *The Web of Life*; Clarke, *Green Man Dreaming*; Roszak, *The Voice of the Earth*; Spowers, *Rising Tides*; Tolle, *A New Earth*.
22　Gönenç, 'Litigation Process'.
23　Wirzba, *The Paradise of God*, 81.
24　Sheldrake, *The Science Delusion*; Wilson, *Consilience*.
25　Tolle, *A New Earth*.
26　Sahtouris, 'Mechanistic and Competitive'.
27　Maiteny, 'Finding Meaning without Consuming'.
28　Spowers, *Rising Tides*, 38; Douzinas, *Philosophy and Resistance*; Gaard, 'Where Is Feminism?'; Moltmann, *God in Creation*.
29　Capra, *The Web of Life*.
30　Gibson, *A Reenchanted World*; Flannery, *The Weather Makers*; Godrej, *The No-Nonsense Guide to Climate Change*; Spowers, *Rising Tides*.
31　Meadows, 'Dancing with Systems'; Rigby, *Dancing with Disaster*.
32　Gersie, *Reflections on Therapeutic Storytelling*, 30.
33　Sterling, 'Ecological Intelligence'; Rigby, *Dancing with Disaster*.
34　Kelvin Hall, personal communication, 2019.
35　Capra, *The Web of Life*.
36　Sogyal, *The Tibetan Book*.
37　Tolle, *A New Earth*, 274.
38　Berry, *Life Is a Miracle*; Dawkins, *The Selfish Gene*; Segerstråle, *Defenders of the Truth*; Wilson, *On Human Nature*.
39　Palmer, *Dancing to Armageddon*, 178.
40　Stibbe, *Ecolinguistics*.
41　Capra, *The Web of Life*; Wheeler, 'How the Earth Speaks'.
42　Abram, *Becoming Animal*.
43　Collins, *Vision of the Fool*, 43.
44　Samuel, 'Subtle-Body Processes', 258–60.
45　Spira, *The Nature of Consciousness*.
46　Guenther, *The Tantric View*, 106.
47　See Capra, *The Web of Life*; Tolle, *A New Earth*.

48 Moltmann, *God in Creation*, 50.
49 Dowman, *Masters of Enchantment*; Jeans, *Physics and Philosophy*.
50 Rawson, *The Art of Tantra*, 37.
51 Grof, *The Holotropic Mind*; Grof and Grof, *Beyond Death*.
52 Grof, 'The Akashic Field', 139.
53 Grof, 'The Shamanic Journey', 173. See Samuel and Johnston, *Religion and the Subtle Body*.
54 Trungpa, 'Visualization', 51.
55 Collins, *Vision of the Fool*, 100.
56 Doody, *The True Story of the Novel*.
57 https://kedarbrown.com/listening-to-medicine-stories-the-black-nubian-women/
58 Uzendoski and Calapucha-Tapuy, *Ecology of the Spoken Word*, 170, 78, 157.
59 Grof, 'The Akashic Field', 139.
60 Ibid., 142.
61 Hawken, *Realizations*; Samuel and Johnston, *Religion and the Subtle Body*; Tansley, *Subtle Body*; Uzendoski and Calapucha-Tapuy, *Ecology of the Spoken Word*.
62 Mann, *Sacred Architecture*; Michell, *The Earth Spirit*; Rawson and Legeza, *Tao*.
63 Kinsley, *Hindu Goddesses*.
64 O'Donohue, *Divine Beauty*.
65 Lupton, *The Dreaming of Place*, 8.
66 Samuel, 'Subtle-Body Processes', 252, 254, 262.
67 Letcher, 'The Role of the Bard'; Manwaring, *The Bardic Handbook*; Restall Orr, *Druid Priestess*; Shallcrass, 'Awen'.
68 Quoted in Tydeman, *Conversations with Barry Lopez*, 18–19.
69 Hawken, *Realizations*.
70 Grof, *The Holotropic Mind*; Samuel and Johnston, *Religion and the Subtle Body*.
71 Campbell, *The Roar of Silence*; Goodchild, *The Naked Voice*; Khanna, *Yantra*; Osho, *The Book of Secrets*; Shearer, *The Hindu Vision*; Sogyal, *The Tibetan Book*; Thurman, *The Tibetan Book*; Uzendoski and Calapucha-Tapuy, *Ecology of the Spoken Word*.
72 Hooper-Greenhill, *Museums*.
73 Rawson, *The Art of Tantra*.
74 Uzendoski and Calapucha-Tapuy, *Ecology of the Spoken Word*, 197, 198.
75 Gersie, *Storymaking in Bereavement*.
76 Kim, *The Story Bag*.
77 Oelrich, *The New Story*, 99.
78 Sonia Kondolo, interview, Koné, 9 September 2016.
79 Tjibaou and Missotte, *Kanaké*.
80 Spira, *The Nature of Consciousness*.
81 Snyder, *A Place in Space*, 174.
82 Durham, *Coherent Self*.
83 O'Donohue, *Eternal Echoes*; Tolle, *A New Earth*.

84 Gersie, *Reflections on Therapeutic Storytelling*, 153.
85 Campbell and Moyers, *The Power of Myth*, 5.
86 O'Donohue, *Eternal Echoes*, 379.
87 Betti, *Twelve Ways*, 198; Johnston, 'Subtle Subjects and Ethics'.
88 Nita, '"Inside Story"'.
89 Wilson, *On Human Nature*.
90 Durham, *Coherent Self*.
91 O'Donohue, *Eternal Echoes*, 324.
92 Durham, *Coherent Self*.
93 Ibid.; Tolle, *A New Earth*.
94 Danvers, 'Being-in-the-World'; Naess, 'Self-Realization'; Spowers, *Rising Tides*, 342.
95 Tolle, *A New Earth*.
96 Guenther, *The Tantric View*, 127.
97 Spira, *The Nature of Consciousness*.
98 Durham, *The Return of King Arthur*. See also Campbell and Moyers, *The Power of Myth*.
99 Maggi, 'The Human Journey', 205.
100 Dunne, *Time and Myth*.
101 Oelrich, *The New Story*, 30.
102 Durham, *Coherent Self*, 110.
103 Ibid.
104 Zimmer, *Myths and Symbols*, 199.
105 Somadeva, *Kathā Sarit Sāgara*, vol. 1, 2.
106 Ibid., vol. 2, 625.
107 Campbell and Moyers, *The Power of Myth*, 116.
108 Oelrich, *The New Story*, 98.
109 Dunne, *Time and Myth*.
110 Clarke, *Green Man Dreaming*; Palmer, *Dancing to Armageddon*.
111 See Nanson, *Words of Re-enchantment*.
112 Bourret et al., *Littérature orale*; Göröwirijaa, 'Génie du Milieu des Airs'.
113 Summary of my retelling of Lupton's version of this tale.
114 Lupton, 'Betsy Whyte'.
115 Zimmer, *Myths and Symbols*, 34, 25.
116 Addey, 'Light of the Sphere'; Clarke, *Green Man Dreaming*; Harpur, *The Philosophers' Secret Fire*.
117 Oelrich, *The New Story*, 33.
118 Clarke, *Green Man Dreaming*.
119 Oelrich, *The New Story*, 155.
120 Collins, *Vision of the Fool*; Grof and Grof, *Beyond Death*; Guenther, 'Openness and Compassion'; Maclagan, *Creation Myths*; Malekin, 'Art and Liberation'.
121 Dawkins, *The God Delusion*.

122 Wilson, *On Human Nature*, 201.
123 Campbell and Moyers, *The Power of Myth*; Armstrong, *Short History of Myth*.
124 Dawkins, 'Viruses of the Mind'.
125 Coupe, *Myth*; Wilson, *Storytelling and Theatre*.
126 Spira, *The Nature of Consciousness*.
127 Campbell, *Oriental Mythology*, 336.
128 Armstrong, *Short History of Myth*, 16.
129 Zimmer, *Myths and Symbols*, 39–40.
130 Bass, *The Lost Grizzlies*, 51.
131 Crossley-Holland, *British Folk Tales*.
132 Hayes, *Heart Full of Turquoise*.
133 https://www.firstpeople.us/FP-Html-Legends/HowTheButterfliesCameToBe-Papago.html
134 Kaplan, 'Lowland South America'; Shepard, 'Wings of the Butterfly'.
135 Collins, *Vision of the Fool*, 19.
136 Coupe, *Myth*.
137 Campbell and Moyers, *The Power of Myth*.
138 Campbell, *Primitive Mythology*; Palmer, *Dancing to Armageddon*.
139 Armstrong, *Short History of Myth*.
140 Zipes, *Creative Storytelling*, 224.
141 Parkinson, *Transforming Tales*, 302.
142 Shaw, *Branch from the Lightning Tree*.
143 Zipes, *Creative Storytelling*.
144 See Hamilton, 'Working with Subtle Energy'; Hawken, *Realizations*.
145 Coupe, *Myth*, 196.
146 Hugh Lupton introduced me to this scheme.
147 Frye, *Anatomy of Criticism*.
148 Shippey, *Road to Middle-Earth*.
149 Hugh Lupton, workshop, Festival at the Edge, Telford, July 2000.
150 Alexiou, *After Antiquity*; Doody, *The True Story*.
151 Alexiou, *After Antiquity*.
152 Shearer, *The Hindu Vision*; MaHood, 'Imaginal Yoga'.
153 Ganss, *The Spiritual Exercises*.
154 Yates, *The Art of Memory*.
155 Ramsay, *Nights of Storytelling*.
156 Moltmann, *God in Creation*.
157 Osho, *The Perfect Way*.
158 Govinda, *Way of the White Clouds*, 123.
159 Rawson and Legeza, *Tao*.
160 Coupe, *Myth*, 88.
161 Hawken, *Realizations*; Jeevan, *Embodied Enlightenment*.

162 Van Deusen, 'Storytelling as a Shamanic Art'. See Halifax, *Shamanic Voices*; Kremer, 'Shamanic Tales'.
163 Lupton, *The Dreaming of Place*, 11, 10.
164 Ibid.; Lupton, 'Betsy Whyte'.
165 Harner, 'Shamanic Counseling'. See Abram, *Becoming Animal*.
166 Eliade, *Shamanism*.
167 Dunne, *Time and Myth*, 23, 39, 124.
168 Matthews, 'Quest as Shamanic Journey'.
169 O'Connor, *Beyond the Mist*.
170 Dunne, *Time and Myth*, 86–7.
171 Grof and Grof, *Beyond Death*.
172 Sogyal, *The Tibetan Book*; Thurman, *The Tibetan Book*.
173 Clarke, *Green Man Dreaming*, 246.
174 Gersie, *Storymaking in Bereavement*.
175 Clarke, *Green Man Dreaming*, 247.
176 Campbell, *The Hero*.
177 Galeano, 'On Rivers', 335. See Luna and Amaringo, *Ayahuasca Visions*.
178 Getty, *Goddess*; Campbell and Moyers, *The Power of Myth*.
179 See Thapar, *Land of the Tiger*.
180 Clarke, *Green Man Dreaming*, 10.
181 Zimmer, *Myths and Symbols*, 46.
182 Speedy, 'Introduction', 46. See Leenhardt, *Do Kamo*.
183 Baring and Cashford, *The Myth of the Goddess*.
184 Campbell, *Myths to Live By*.
185 Palmer, *Dancing to Armageddon*, 129.
186 Grof and Grof, *Beyond Death*.
187 Thurman, *The Tibetan Book*.
188 Coupe, *Myth*, 8–9.
189 Ibid., 155.
190 See Nanson, '"The Future Has Gone Bad"'.
191 Gersie, *Reflections on Therapeutic Storytelling*, 168.
192 Ibid.
193 Seymour, 'Interview with Alida Gersie'.
194 See Nanson, *Words of Re-enchantment*.
195 Tolle, *A New Earth*, 107–8.
196 Here again I'm indebted to Maya.
197 Osho, *The Perfect Way*, 39.
198 Jameson, *Archaeologies of the Future*.
199 Tappuni, 'Blockchain Solutions'.
200 Le Guin, *Dancing at the Edge*.
201 Levitas and Sargisson, 'Utopia in Dark Times'.

Bibliography

Aarne, Antti, and Stith Thompson. *The Types of the Folktale: A Classification and Bibliography*. Helsinki: Finnish Academy of Science and Letters, 1961.

Abram, David. *Becoming Animal: An Earthly Cosmology*. New York: Vintage, 2011.

Abram, David. *The Spell of the Sensuous: Perception and Language in a More-than-Human World*. New York: Vintage, 1997.

Addey, Crystal. 'In the Light of the Sphere: The "Vehicle of the Soul" and Subtle-Body Practices in Neoplatonism'. In *Religion and the Subtle Body in Asia and the West*, edited by Geoffrey Samuel and Jay Johnson, 149–67. Abingdon: Routledge, 2013.

Alexiou, Margaret. *After Antiquity: Greek Language, Myth, and Metaphor*. Ithaca, NY: Cornell University Press, 2002.

Ali, Saleem H. 'Contesting the "Noble Savage" on Sustainability: Indigenous Politics, Industry and Biodiversity in New Caledonia'. Paper presented to Annual Meeting of the Society for Applied Anthropology, Tampa, 28–31 March 2007.

Aristotle. *Poetics*, translated by Malcolm Heath. London: Penguin, 1996.

Armiero, Marco. 'Environmental History between Institutionalization and Revolution: A Short Commentary with Two Sites and One Experiment'. In *Environmental Humanities: Voices from the Anthropocene*, edited by Serpil Opperman and Serenella Iovino, 45–59. London: Rowman & Littlefield, 2017.

Armstrong, Jeanette. 'Keepers of the Earth'. In *Ecopsychology: Restoring the Earth, Healing the Mind*, edited by Theodore Roszak, Mary E. Gomes and Allen D. Kanner, 316–24. San Francisco: Sierra Club, 1995.

Armstrong, Karen. *A Short History of Myth*. Edinburgh: Canongate, 2005.

Ash, Russell, et al. *Folklore, Myths and Legends of Britain*. London: Reader's Digest, 1973.

Ashe, Geoffrey. *Camelot and the Vision of Albion*. London: William Heinemann, 1971.

Ashliman, D. L. 'The Tail-Fisher: Folktales of Aarne–Thompson–Uther Type 2'. University of Pittsburgh, 2009–11.

Axelrod, Lawrence J., and Peter Suedfeld. 'Technology, Capitalism and Christianity: Are They Really the Three Horsemen of the Eco-collapse?' *Journal of Environmental Psychology* 15 (1995): 193–5.

Baccolini, Raffaella, and Tom Moylan. *Dark Horizons: Science Fiction and the Dystopian Imagination*. New York: Routledge, 2003.

Bami, Mme. 'L'aigle et les deux femmes de Mwau'. In *Mythes et contes de la Grande-Terre et des Iles Loyauté (Nouvelle-Calédonie)*, edited by Jean-Claude Rivierre, Françoise Ozanne-Rivierre and Claire Moyse-Faurie, 62–73. Paris: Société d'études linguistiques et anthropologiques de France, 1980.

Baring, Anne, and Jules Cashford. *The Myth of the Goddess: Evolution of an Image*. London: Penguin, 1991.

Barnes, Ruth, and Crispin Branfoot. *Pilgrimage: The Sacred Journey*. Oxford: Ashmolean Museum, 2006.

Bartoloni, Paolo. 'Memory in Language: Walter Benjamin and Giuseppe Ungaretli'. *Literature & Aesthetics* 16, no. 2 (2006): 145–56.

Bass, Rick. *The Lost Grizzlies: A Search for Survivors in the Wilderness of Colorado*. Boston: Houghton Mifflin, 1995.

Basso, Keith H. '"Speaking with Names": Language and Landscape among the Western Apache'. *Cultural Anthropology*, May 1988.

Bate, Jonathan. *The Song of the Earth*. London: Macmillan, 2000.

Beatty, Bill. *A Treasury of Australian Folk Tales and Traditions*. Sydney: Ure Smith, 1963.

Behrensmeyer, Anna K., John D. Damuth, William A. DiMichele, Richard Potts, Hans-Dieter Sues and Scott L. Wing. *Terrestrial Ecosystems through Time: Evolutionary Paleoecology of Terrestrial Plants and Animals*. Chicago: University of Chicago Press, 1992.

Benjamin, Walter. 'The Storyteller'. In *Illuminations*, edited by Hannah Arendt, translated by Harry Zorn, 83–107. London: Pimlico, 1999.

Benjamin, Walter. 'The Work of Art in the Age of Mechanical Reproduction'. In *Illuminations*, edited by Hannah Arendt, translated by Harry Zorn, 211–44. London: Pimlico, 1999.

Bennett, Michael. 'From Wide Open Spaces to Metropolitan Places: The Urban Challenge to Ecocriticism'. *Interdisciplinary Studies in Literature and Environment* 8, no. 1 (2001): 31–52.

Bensa, Alban, and Jean-Claude Rivierre (eds). *Les filles du rocher Até: Contes et récits paicî*. Nouméa: Agence de développement de la culture kanak, 1994.

Bensa, Alban, and Jean-Claude Rivierre (eds). *Histoires canaques*. Paris: Conseil international de la langue française, 1983.

Berk, Ari. 'The Grail in the Uttermost West: Vessels of Power, Plenty and Tradition in American Indian Mythology and Literature'. In *Sources of the Grail: An Anthology*, edited by John Matthews, 536–68. Edinburgh: Floris, 1996.

Berman, Tzeporah. 'The Rape of Mother Nature: Women in the Language of Environmental Discourse'. In *The Ecolinguistics Reader: Language, Ecology, and Environment*, edited by Alwin Fill and Peter Mühlhäusler, 258–69. London: Continuum, 2001.

Berndt, Catherine H., and Ronald M. Berndt. *The Barbarians*. Harmondsworth: Penguin, 1973.

Berndt, Ronald M., and Catherine H. Berndt. *The Speaking Land: Myth and Story in Aboriginal Australia*. Rochester, VT: Inner Traditions, 1994.

Berry, Wendell. *Life Is a Miracle: An Essay against Modern Superstition*. Washington: Counterpoint, 2001.

Berry, Wendell. *Standing by Words*. San Francisco: North Point Press, 1983.

Betti, Mario. *Twelve Ways of Seeing the World: Philosophies and Archetypal Worldviews for Understanding Human Consciousness*, translated by Matthew Barton. Stroud: Hawthorn Press, 2019.
Bierhorst, John. *The Mythology of North America*. New York: Oxford University Press, 2002.
Blécourt, Willem de, and Theo Meder. 'A European Classification of Traditional Legends: Towards E-research Using a Digital Harvester of National and Regional Folktale Databases'. *Historical Anthropologist* (2015).
Blewitt, John. 'New Media Literacy: Communication Skills for Sustainability'. In *The Handbook of Sustainability Literacy: Skills for a Changing World*, edited by Arran Stibbe, 111–16. Totnes: Green Books, 2009.
Blincoe, Karen. 'Re-educating the Person'. In *The Handbook of Sustainability Literacy: Skills for a Changing World*, edited by Arran Stibbe, 204–8. Totnes: Green Books, 2009.
Boahnou, Higuè Tein. 'Tamoangui, l'homme-tronc'. In *Contes et légendes de la Grande-Terre*, edited by Jean Guiart, 35–6. Nouméa: Institut français d'Océanie, 1957.
Booker, Christopher. *The Seven Basic Plots*. London: Bloomsbury, 2005.
Bourret, Dominique, Maurice Coyaud, Marie-Joseph Dubois, Loïc Mangematin and Roland Tavernier (eds). *Littérature orale: 60 contes mélanésiens de Nouvelle-Calédonie*. Nouméa: Sociéte d'études historiques de la Nouvelle-Calédonie, 1980.
Bradley, Hazel. 'Therapeutic Storytelling'. *Sahrdaya*, September 2001, 3–9.
Bradshaw, Jane. 'St Arilda of Oldbury on Severn, Gloucestershire'. *Source* 5 (1998).
Brayfield, Celia. *Bestseller: Secrets of Successful Writing*. London: Fourth Estate, 1996.
Briggs, Katharine M. *A Dictionary of British Folk-Tales in the English Language*. 4 vols. London: Routledge, 1970–1.
Brody, Hugh. *The Other Side of Eden: Hunter-Gatherers, Farmers, and the Shaping of the World*. London: Faber & Faber, 2001.
Brooks, Peter. *Reading for the Plot: Design and Intention in Narrative*. Cambridge, MA: Harvard University Press, 1992.
Browning, Christopher S. 'Brexit Populism and Fantasies of Fulfilment'. *Cambridge Review of International Affairs* 32, no. 3 (2019): 222–44.
Bruchac, Joseph. *Iroquois Stories: Heroes and Heroines, Monsters and Magic*. Freedom, CA: Crossing Press, 1985.
Buber, Martin. *I and Thou*. Edinburgh: T. & T. Clark, 1959.
Burke, Kenneth. 'Hyper-technologism, Pollution and Satire'. In *The Green Studies Reader: From Romanticism to Ecocriticism*, edited by Laurence Coupe, 96–103. London: Routledge, 2000.
Cable, Vince. *The Storm: The World Economic Crisis and What It Means*. London: Grove Atlantic, 2009.
Caduto, Michael J. *Earth Tales from Around the World*. Golden, CO: Fulcrum, 1997.
Cadwalladr, Carole, John Naughton, Roger McNamee and Yaël Eisenat. 'America's Most Dangerous Couple?' *The Observer*, 26 July 2020.

Callicott, J. Baird. 'Worldview Remediation in the First Century of the New Millennium'. In *Environmental Humanities: Voices from the Anthropocene*, edited by Serpil Opperman and Serenella Iovino, 133–54. London: Rowman & Littlefield, 2017.

Callenbach, Ernest. 'Chocco'. In *Future Primitive: The New Ecotopias*, edited by Kim Stanley Robinson. New York: Tor, 1994.

Campbell, Don G. *The Roar of Silence: Healing Powers of Breath, Tone & Music*. Wheaton, IL: Quest, 1989.

Campbell, Joseph. *The Hero with a Thousand Faces*. Princeton: Princeton University Press, 1968.

Campbell, Joseph. *The Masks of God: Oriental Mythology*. New York: Viking, 1970.

Campbell, Joseph. *The Masks of God: Primitive Mythology*. Harmondsworth: Penguin, 1976.

Campbell, Joseph. *Myths to Live By*. New York: Bantam, 1973.

Campbell, Joseph, and Bill Moyers. *The Power of Myth*, edited by Betty Sue Flowers. New York: Broadway Books, 2001.

Campbell, Sueellen. 'The Land and Language of Desire: Where Deep Ecology and Post-structuralism Meet'. In *The Ecocriticism Reader: Landmarks in Literary Ecology*, edited by Cheryll Glotfelty and Harold Fromm, 124–36. Athens, GA: University of Georgia Press, 1996.

Canku Ota. 'How Bear Lost His Tail'. 49 (2001).

Capra, Fritjof. *The Web of Life: A New Synthesis of Mind and Matter*. London: HarperCollins, 1996.

Carlson, Marvin. *Performance: A Critical Introduction*. London: Routledge, 1996.

Carr-Gomm, Philip. *A Brief History of Nakedness*. London: Reaktion, 2010.

Carr-Gomm, Philip. *The Druid Way*. Shaftesbury: Element, 1993.

Carson, Rachel. *Silent Spring*. Boston: Houghton Mifflin, 1962.

Carter, Angela. 'The Company of Wolves'. In *Burning Your Boats: Stories*, 212–20. London: Chatto & Windus, 1995.

Casey, Dawn. *The Barefoot Book of Earth Tales*. Bath: Barefoot Books, 2009.

Charing, Howard G., Peter Cloudsley and Pablo Amaringo. *The Ayahuasca Visions of Pablo Amaringo*. Rochester, VT: Inner Traditions, 2011.

Chatwin, Bruce. *The Songlines*. London: Jonathan Cape, 1987.

Cheney, Jim, and Anthony Weston. 'Environmental Ethics as Environmental Etiquette: Toward an Ethics-Based Epistemology'. *Environmental Ethics* 21, no. 2 (1999): 115–34.

Chomsky, Noam. *Media Control: The Spectacular Achievements of Propaganda*. New York: Seven Stories Press, 2011.

Christiansen, Reidar Thorolf. *Migratory Legends: List of Types with a Systematic Catalogue of the Norwegian Variants*. Salem, NH: Ayer, 1977.

Clark, Ella E. *Indian Legends of the Pacific Northwest*. Berkeley: University of California Press, 1953.

Clarke, Bruce. 'Science, Theory, and Systems: A Response to Glen A. Love and Jonathan Levin'. *Interdisciplinary Studies in Literature and Environment* 8, no. 1 (2001): 149–65.

Clarke, Lindsay. *Green Man Dreaming: Reflections on Imagination, Myth and Memory*. Stroud: Awen, 2018.

Cobley, Paul. *Narrative*. Abingdon: Routledge, 2014.

Cohen, Andrew. *The Planets*. London: HarperCollins, 2019.

Collingwood, R. G. *The Principles of Art*. Oxford: Clarendon Press, 1938.

Collins, Cecil. *The Vision of the Fool and Other Writings*, edited by Brian Keeble. Ipswich: Golgonooza Press, 1994.

Conley, Verena Andermatt. 'Hélène Cixous: The Language of Flowers'. In *The Green Studies Reader: From Romanticism to Ecocriticism*, edited by Laurence Coupe, 148–53. London: Routledge, 2000.

Conn, Sarah A. 'When the Earth Hurts, Who Responds?' In *Ecopsychology: Restoring the Earth, Healing the Mind*, edited by Theodore Roszak, Mary E. Gomes and Allen D. Kanner, 156–71. San Francisco: Sierra Club, 1995.

Connell, John. *New Caledonia or Kanaky? The Political History of a French Colony*. Canberra: Australian National University, 1987.

Conway Morris, Simon. *Life's Solution: Inevitable Humans in a Lonely Universe*. Cambridge: Cambridge University Press, 2003.

Cook, Roger. *The Tree of Life: Image for the Cosmos*. London: Thames & Hudson, 1974.

Cornell, Joseph. *Sharing Nature with Children*. Nevada City, CA: DAWN, 1998.

Coupe, Laurence. *Myth*. London: Routledge, 1997.

Cowan, James. *The Elements of the Aborigine Tradition*. Shaftesbury: Element, 1992.

Cowan, James. *Letters from a Wild State: An Aboriginal Perspective*. Shaftesbury: Element, 1991.

Cowan, James. *Myths of the Dreaming: Interpreting Aboriginal Legends*. Bridport: Prism Press, 1994.

Cree, Jon, and Alida Gersie. 'Storytelling in the Woods'. In *Storytelling for a Greener World: Environment, Community, and Story-Based Learning*, edited by Alida Gersie, Anthony Nanson and Edward Schieffelin, 54–73. Stroud: Hawthorn Press, 2014.

Crompton, Tom, and Tim Kasser. *Meeting Environmental Challenges: The Role of Human Identity*. Godalming: WWF-UK, 2009.

Crossley-Holland, Kevin. *British Folk Tales*. London: Orchard, 1987.

Crowden, Peter. 'If These Disease-Ridden Vermin KILL a Child Next Time, Blame the Fools Who Think They're Cuddly'. *Mail Online*, 10 February 2013.

Csikszentmihalyi, Mihaly. *Beyond Boredom and Anxiety: The Experience of Play in Work and Games*. San Francisco: Jossey-Bass, 1977.

Cupitt, Don. *What Is a Story?* London: SCM Press, 1991.

Curry, Patrick. *Defending Middle-Earth: Tolkien, Myth and Modernity*. Boston: Houghton Mifflin, 2004.

Curry, Patrick. 'Magic vs. Enchantment'. *Journal of Contemporary Religion* 14, no. 3 (1999): 401–12.

Dahl, Arthur Lyon. 'Traditional Environmental Knowledge and Resource Management in New Caledonia'. In *Traditional Ecological Knowledge: A Collection of Essays*, edited by R. R. Johannes, 45–53. Gland: International Union for Conservation of Nature, 1989.

Danvers, John. 'Being-in-the-World'. In *The Handbook of Sustainability Literacy: Skills for a Changing World*, edited by Arran Stibbe, 185–90. Totnes: Green Books, 2009.

Darwin Edwards, Ian. 'Re-storying Scotland'. *Facts & Fiction* 40 (2002): 5–7.

Davies, Allan. 'Voices from the Earth: Environmental Storytelling'. Workshop booklet, 1989.

Dawkins, Richard. *The God Delusion*. London: Transworld, 2006.

Dawkins, Richard. *The Selfish Gene*. Oxford: Oxford University Press, 1976.

Dawkins, Richard. 'Viruses of the Mind'. In *Dennett and His Critics: Demystifying Mind*, edited by Bo Dahlbom, 13–27. Oxford: Basil Blackwell, 1993.

Day, David. *The Doomsday Book of Animals: A Unique Natural History of Vanished Species*. London: Ebury Press, 1981.

Diamond, Jared. *Collapse: How Societies Choose to Fail or Survive*. London: Penguin, 2005.

Diamond, Jared. *The Rise and Fall of the Third Chimpanzee*. London: Radius, 1991.

Dodds, L., and B. Hopwood. 'BAN Waste: Environmental Justice and Citizen Participation in Policy Setting'. *Local Environment* 11, no. 3 (2006): 269–86.

Doody, Margaret Anne. *The True Story of the Novel*. London: HarperCollins, 1997.

Dorling, Danny. *Rule Britannia: Brexit and the End of Empire*. London: Biteback, 2019.

Dorson, Richard M. *The British Folklorists: A History*. Chicago: University of Chicago Press, 1968.

Douzinas, Costas. *Philosophy and Resistance in the Crisis: Greece and the Future of Europe*. Cambridge: Polity, 2013.

Dowman, Keith (trans.). *Masters of Enchantment: The Lives and Legends of the Mahasiddhas*. Rochester, VT: Inner Traditions, 1988.

Dunne, John S. *Time and Myth: A Meditation on Storytelling as an Exploration of Life and Death*. London: SCM Press, 1979.

Durham, Diana. *Coherent Self, Coherent World: A New Synthesis of Myth, Metaphysics & Bohm's Implicate Order*. Winchester: O Books, 2019.

Durham, Diana. *The Return of King Arthur: Completing the Quest for Wholeness, Inner Strength, and Self-Knowledge*. New York: Jeremy P. Tarcher, 2005.

East, Helen. 'Fishing Tales and Catching Connections'. In *Storytelling for a Greener World: Environment, Community, and Story-Based Learning*, edited by Alida Gersie, Anthony Nanson and Edward Schieffelin, 180–92. Stroud: Hawthorn Press, 2014.

East, Helen, and Eric Maddern. *Spirit of the Forest: Tree Tales from Around the World*, London: Frances Lincoln, 2002.

Edwards, Carolyn McVickar. *The Storytelling Goddess: Tales of the Goddess and Her Wisdom from Around the World*. New York: HarperCollins, 1991.

Eliade, Mircea. *Shamanism: Archaic Techniques of Ecstasy*. London: Penguin, 1989.

Empson, Rebecca M. *Subjective Lives and Economic Transformation in Mongolia: Life in the Gap*. London: UCL Press, 2020.

Evans, Sebastian (trans.). 'The Elucidation'. In *Sources of the Grail: An Anthology*, edited by John Matthews, 64–8. Edinburgh: Floris, 1996.

Evernden, Neil. 'Beyond Ecology: Self, Place, and the Pathetic Fallacy'. In *The Ecocriticism Reader: Landmarks in Literary Ecology*, edited by Cheryll Glotfelty and Harold Fromm, 92–104. Athens, GA: University of Georgia Press, 1996.

Fagan, Geoff. 'Citizen Engagement'. In *The Handbook of Sustainability Literacy: Skills for a Changing World*, edited by Arran Stibbe, 199–203. Totnes: Green Books, 2009.

Feldman, Christina, and Jack Kornfield (eds). *Stories of the Spirit, Stories of the Heart: Parables of the Spiritual Path from Around the World*. San Francisco: HarperCollins, 1991.

Field, Syd. *Screenplay: The Foundations of Screenwriting*. New York: Bantam Dell, 2005.

Flannery, Tim. *The Eternal Frontier: An Ecological History of North America and Its People*. London: Vintage, 2002.

Flannery, Tim. *The Future Eaters: An Ecological History of the Australasian Lands and People*. New York: Grove Press, 1994.

Flannery, Tim. *The Weather Makers: The History and Future Impact of Climate Change*. London: Penguin, 2005.

Fortey, Richard. *Life: An Unauthorised Biography*. London: HarperCollins, 1997.

Foster, Thomas. 'Cyberculture'. In *The Oxford Handbook of Science Fiction*, edited by Rob Latham, 421–33. New York: Oxford University Press, 2014.

Freedberg, David, and Vittorio Gallese. 'Motion, Emotion and Empathy in Esthetic Experience'. *Trends in Cognitive Sciences* 11, no. 5 (2007): 197–203.

Freire, Paulo. *Pedagogy of the Oppressed*, translated by Myra Bergman Ramos. London: Penguin, 1996.

Frye, Northrop. *Anatomy of Criticism: Four Essays*. Princeton: Princeton University Press, 1957.

Gaard, Greta. 'Where Is Feminism in the Environmental Humanities?' In *Environmental Humanities: Voices from the Anthropocene*, edited by Serpil Opperman and Serenella Iovino, 81–97. London: Rowman & Littlefield, 2017.

Gablik, Suzi. *The Reenchantment of Art*. London: Phoenix, 1991.

Galbraith, Alison, and Alette J. Willis. *Dancing with Trees: Eco-tales from the British Isles*. Stroud: History Press, 2017.

Galeano, Juan Carlos. 'On Rivers'. In *Environmental Humanities: Voices from the Anthropocene*, edited by Serpil Opperman and Serenella Iovino, 331–8. London: Rowman & Littlefield, 2017.

Ganss, George E. (trans.). *The Spiritual Exercises of St Ignatius*. Chicago: Loyola University Press, 1998.

Garrard, Greg. *Ecocriticism*. Abingdon: Routledge, 2004.

Gelbspan, Ross. *The Heat Is On: The High Stakes Battle over Earth's Threatened Climate*. New York: Perseus Books, 1997.

Gelin, Martin. 'The Misogyny of Climate Deniers'. *New Republic*, 28 August 2019.

Gersie, Alida. 'Bringing Nature Home'. In *Storytelling for a Greener World: Environment, Community, and Story-Based Learning*, edited by Alida Gersie, Anthony Nanson and Edward Schieffelin, 194–204. Stroud: Hawthorn Press, 2014.

Gersie, Alida. *Earthtales: Storytelling in Times of Change*. London: Merlin Press, 1992.

Gersie, Alida. *Reflections on Therapeutic Storymaking: The Use of Stories in Groups*. London: Jessica Kingsley, 1997.

Gersie, Alida. *Storymaking in Bereavement: Dragons Fight in the Meadow*. London: Jessica Kingsley, 1991.

Gersie, Alida. 'Wild but with a Purpose: Arts Therapists and the Cry for Social Healing'. In *Cultural Landscapes in the Arts Therapies*, edited by Richard Hougham, Salvo Pitruzella and Sarah Scoble, 19–42. Plymouth: Plymouth University Press, 2017.

Gersie, Alida, and Nancy King. *Storymaking in Education and Therapy*. London: Jessica Kingsley, 1990.

Gersie, Alida, Anthony Nanson and Edward Schieffelin (eds). *Storytelling for a Greener World: Environment, Community, and Story-Based Learning*. Stroud: Hawthorn Press, 2014.

Getty, Adele. *Goddess: Mother of Living Nature*. London: Thames & Hudson, 1990.

Gibson, James William. *A Reenchanted World: The Quest for a New Kinship with Nature*. New York: Henry Holt, 2009.

Githaiga, Joseph. 'Intellectual Property Law and the Protection of Indigenous Folklore and Knowledge'. *Murdoch University Electronic Journal of Law* 5, no. 2 (1998).

Glotfelty, Cheryll, and Harold Fromm (eds). *The Ecocriticism Reader: Landmarks in Literary Ecology*. Athens, GA: University of Georgia Press, 1996.

Godin, Patrice. 'Croyances'. In *Chroniques du pays kanak: Arts et lettres*, edited by Orso Filippi and Frédéric Angleviel. Nouméa: Planète Mémo, 1999.

Godrej, Dinyar. *The No-Nonsense Guide to Climate Change*. London: Verso, 2001.

Goldberg, Myshele. 'Social Conscience'. In *The Handbook of Sustainability Literacy: Skills for a Changing World*, edited by Arran Stibbe, 105–10. Totnes: Green Books, 2009.

Gomes, Mary E., and Allen D. Kanner. 'The Rape of the Well-Maidens: Feminist Psychology and the Environmental Crisis'. In *Ecopsychology: Restoring the Earth, Healing the Mind*, edited by Theodore Roszak, Mary E. Gomes and Allen D. Kanner, 111–21. San Francisco: Sierra Club, 1995.

Gönenç, Defne. 'Litigation Process of Social Movements as a Driver of Norm Transformation?' *Cambridge Review of International Affairs* 32, no. 1 (2019): 43–60.

Goodchild, Chloë. *The Naked Voice: Transform Your Life through the Power of Sound*. Berkeley: North Atlantic, 2015.

Goodchild, Philip. *Capitalism and Religion: The Price of Piety*. London: Routledge, 2002.

Goodison, Lucy. *Moving Heaven and Earth: Sexuality, Spirituality and Social Change*. London: HarperCollins, 1992.

Goromôtö, Clément. 'La grand-mère et les trois frères'. In *Histoires canaques*, edited by Alban Bensa and Jean-Claude Rivierre, 108–29. Paris: Conseil international de la langue française, 1983.

Göröwirijaa, Mme. 'Génie du Milieu des Airs'. In *Les filles du rocher Até: Contes et récits paicî*, edited by Alban Bensa and Jean-Claude Rivierre, 209–29. Nouméa: Agence de développement de la culture kanak, 1994.

Göröwirijaa, Mme. 'Grand-Waka'. In *Histoires canaques*, edited by Alban Bensa and Jean-Claude Rivierre, 89–107. Paris: Conseil international de la langue française, 1983.

Gould, Charles. *Mythical Monsters*. London: Bracken Books, 1989.

Gould, Stephen Jay. *I Have Landed: Splashes and Reflections in Natural History*. London: Jonathan Cape, 2002.

Gould, Stephen Jay. *Rock of Ages: Science and Religion in the Fullness of Life*. New York: Ballantine, 1999.

Gould, Stephen Jay. *Wonderful Life: The Burgess Shale and the Nature of History*. London: Century Hutchinson, 1990.

Govinda, Anagarika. *The Way of the White Clouds*. London: Rider, 1992.

Green, Malcolm. 'Kittiwakes on the Bridge'. In *Storytelling for a Greener World: Environment, Community, and Story-Based Learning*, edited by Alida Gersie, Anthony Nanson and Edward Schieffelin, 206–18. Stroud: Hawthorn Press, 2014.

Green, Malcolm. 'Storying Nature'. *Journal of Interpretation* (1994) [number untraceable].

Green, Malcolm, and Nick Hennessey. 'By Hidden Paths'. In *Storytelling for a Greener World: Environment, Community, and Story-Based Learning*, edited by Alida Gersie, Anthony Nanson and Edward Schieffelin, 74–85. Stroud: Hawthorn Press, 2014.

Greenberg, Joel. *A Feathered River across the Sky: The Passenger Pigeon's Flight to Extinction*. New York: Bloomsbury, 2014.

Grof, Stanislav. 'The Akashic Field and the Dilemmas of Modern Consciousness Research'. In *Science and the Reenchantment of the Cosmos: The Rise of the Integral Vision of Reality*, edited by Ervin Laszlo, 130–43. Rochester, VT: Inner Traditions, 2006.

Grof, Stanislav. *The Holotropic Mind: The Three Levels of Human Consciousness and How They Shape Our Lives*. San Francisco: HarperCollins, 1993.

Grof, Stanislav. 'The Shamanic Journey: Observations from Holotropic Therapy'. In *Shaman's Path: Healing, Personal Growth and Empowerment*, edited by Gary Doore, 161–75. Boston: Shambhala, 1988.

Grof, Stanislav, and Christina Grof. *Beyond Death: The Gates of Consciousness*. London: Thames & Hudson, 1980.

Guenthar, Mathias. 'Old Stories/Life Stories: Memory and Dissolution in Contemporary Bushman Folklore'. In *Who Says? Essays on Pivotal Issues in Contemporary*

Storytelling, edited by Carol L. Birch and Melissa A. Heckler, 177–97. Little Rock: August House, 1996.

Guenther, Herbert V. 'The Indivisibility of Openness and Compassion'. In *The Dawn of Tantra*, edited by Michael Kohn, 26–33. Boulder: Shambhala, 1975.

Guenther, Herbert V. *The Tantric View of Life*. Berkeley: Shambala, 1972.

Gunn, Paula Allen (ed.). *Spider Woman's Granddaughter: Traditional Tales and Contemporary Writing by Native American Women*. London: Women's Press, 1990.

Hadfield, Emma. *Among the Natives of the Loyalty Group*. London: Macmillan, 1920.

Haggarty, Ben. *Seek Out the Voice of the Critic*. Reading: Society for Storytelling, 1996.

Haggarty, Ben, and Adam Brockbank. *Mezolith*, vol. 1. Oxford: David Fickling, 2010.

Halifax, Joan. *Shamanic Voices: A Survey of Visionary Narratives*. Harmondsworth: Penguin, 1980.

Hall, Kelvin. 'The Forgotten Tongue'. In *Storytelling for a Greener World: Environment, Community, and Story-Based Learning*, edited by Alida Gersie, Anthony Nanson and Edward Schieffelin, 294–303. Stroud: Hawthorn Press, 2014.

Halliday, Tim, and Kraig Adler (eds). *The New Encyclopedia of Reptiles and Amphibians*. Oxford: Oxford University Press, 2002.

Hamilton, Diane Musho. 'Working with Subtle Energy in Groups'. *Ten Directions*, 19 August 2015.

Harding, Stephan. *Animate Earth: Science, Intuition and Gaia*. Totnes: Green Books, 2009.

Harding, Stephan. 'Gaia Awareness'. In *The Handbook of Sustainability Literacy: Skills for a Changing World*, edited by Arran Stibbe, 89–93. Totnes: Green Books, 2009.

Härke, Heinrich. 'Anglo-Saxon Immigration and Ethnogenesis', *Medieval Archaeology* 55 (2011): 1–28.

Harley, Bill. 'Playing with the Wall'. In *Who Says? Essays on Pivotal Issues in Contemporary Storytelling*, edited by Carol L. Birch and Melissa A. Heckler, 129–40. Little Rock: August House, 1996.

Harner, Michael. 'Shamanic Counseling'. In *Shaman's Path: Healing, Personal Growth and Empowerment*, edited by Gary Doore, 179–87. Boston: Shambhala, 1988.

Harpur, Patrick. *The Philosophers' Secret Fire: A History of the Imagination*. Glastonbury: Squeeze Press, 2009.

Harrison, Robert Pogue. *Forests: The Shadow of Civilization*. Chicago: University of Chicago Press, 1992.

Hartland, E. S. (ed.). *County Folklore Printed Extracts No. 1: Gloucestershire*. London: Folklore Society, 1895.

Hartland, E. S. (ed.). *English Fairy and Other Folk Tales*. London: Walter Scott, 1890.

Harvey, Graham. *The Killing of the Countryside*. London: Jonathan Cape, 1997.

Haven, Kendall. *Story Proof: The Science behind the Startling Power of Story*. Westport, CT: Greenwood, 2007.

Hawken, John. *Realizations – on the Paths of Transformation*. Strakonice: Paths of Transformation, 2018.

Hayes, Joe. *A Heart Full of Turquoise: Pueblo Indian Tales*. Santa Fe: Mariposa, 1988.

Haysom, Karen A., Gareth Jones, Dan Merrett and Paul A. Racey. 'Bats'. In *Silent Summer: The State of Wildlife in Britain and Ireland*, edited by Norman Maclean, 259–80. Cambridge: Cambridge University Press, 2010.

Heighway, Carolyn. *Anglo-Saxon Gloucestershire*. Gloucester: Alan Sutton, 1987.

Heinberg, Richard. *Memories and Visions of Paradise: Exploring the Universal Myth of a Lost Golden Age*. Los Angeles: Jeremy P. Tarcher, 1989.

Heinrich, Paul. 'The Artist as Bard'. *The Cut*, Winter 1992, 12–15.

Helena, Pa. 'Le pouple et le rat'. In *Toatiti: Textes bilingues nengone–français*, edited by Jacques Haewegene and Raymond Cawa, 41–3. Nouméa: Centre de documentation pédagogique de Nouvelle-Calédonie, 2000.

Helm, Toby, Emma Graham-Harrison and Robin McKie. 'How Did Britain Get Its Coronavirus Response So Wrong?', *The Guardian*, 19 April 2020.

Helmick-Richardson, Gene. 'I've Got an Exoskeleton to Pick with Storytellers'. *Storytelling Magazine* 14, no. 3 (2002): 30–2.

Henderson, Mary. *Star Wars: The Magic of Myth*. New York: Bantam, 1997.

Hepburn, Ronald W. *'Wonder' and Other Essays: Eight Studies in Aesthetics and Neighbouring Fields*. Edinburgh: Edinburgh University Press, 1984.

Heywood, Simon. *The New Storytelling: A History of the Storytelling Movement in England and Wales*. Reading: Society for Storytelling, 1998.

Hibberd, Paul. 'Tales from the Wood'. *Storylines* 4, no. 16 (2001): 3.

Hochman, Jhan. 'Green Cultural Studies'. In *The Green Studies Reader: From Romanticism to Ecocriticism*, edited by Laurence Coupe, 187–92. London: Routledge, 2000.

Hogarth, Peter. *Dragons*. New York: Viking Press, 1979.

Höhler, Sabine. '"The Real Problem of a Spaceship Is Its People": Spaceship Earth as Ecological Science Fiction'. In *Green Planets: Ecology and Science Fiction*, edited by Gerry Canavan and Kim Stanley Robinson, 99–114. Middletown, CT: Wesleyan University Press, 2014.

Holland, Chris. *I Love My World: Mentoring Play in Nature for Our Sustainable Future*. Otterton: Wholeland Press, 2009.

Holquist, Michael. *Dialogism: Bakhtin and His World*. Abingdon: Routledge, 2002.

Hooke, Della. *The Anglo-Saxon Landscape of North Gloucestershire*. Deerhurst: Friends of Deerhurst Church, 1990.

Hooper-Greenhill, Eilean. *Museums and the Interpretation of Visual Culture*. London: Routledge, 2000.

Horowitz, Leah S. '"It's Up to the Clan to Protect": Cultural Heritage and the Micropolitical Ecology of Conservation in New Caledonia'. *Social Science Journal* 45 (2008): 258–78.

Horowitz, Leah S. 'Perceptions of Nature and Responses to Environmental Degradation in New Caledonia'. *Ethnology* 40, no. 3 (2001): 237–50.

Howard, Peter. *Heritage: Management, Interpretation, Theory*. London: Continuum, 2003.

Howe, K. R. *The Loyalty Islands: A History of Culture Contacts, 1840–1900*. Honolulu: University Press of Hawaii, 1977.

Howells, William. *The Heathens: Primitive Man and His Religions*. London: Victor Gollancz, 1949.

Huggan, Graham. *Nature's Saviours: Celebrity Conservationists in the Television Age*. Abingdon: Routledge, 2013.

Hughes, Ted. *Winter Pollen: Occasional Prose*, edited by William Scammell. London: Faber & Faber, 1994.

Huth, Gregory R. *Awakening: In Pursuit of Divine Paradox*. Whitneyville, CT: Ecumenica Press, 2000.

Hutton, Ronald. *The Stations of the Sun: A History of the Ritual Year in Britain*. Oxford: Oxford University Press, 1996.

Huxley, Francis. *The Dragon: Nature of Spirit, Spirit of Nature*. London: Thames & Hudson, 1979.

Illouz, Charles. *De chair et de pierre: Essai de mythologie kanak*. Paris: Maison des sciences de l'homme, 2000.

Ions, Veronica. *Indian Mythology*. London: Paul Hamlyn, 1976.

Jacksties, Sharon. *Animal Folk Tales of Britain and Ireland*. Cheltenham: History Press, 2020.

Jameson, Fredric. *Archaeologies of the Future: The Desire Called Utopia and Other Science Fictions*. London: Verso, 2007.

Jayaraja. 'Evolution or Extinction: A Buddhist's View of Current World Problems'. Talk at Buddhafield Festival, 18 July 2019.

Jeans, James. *Physics and Philosophy*. Cambridge: Cambridge University Press, 1942.

Jeevan, Amoda Maa. *Embodied Enlightenment: Living Your Awakening in Every Moment*. Oakland: New Harbinger, 2017.

Johnston, Jay. 'Subtle Subjects and Ethics: The Subtle Bodies of Post-structuralist and Feminist Philosophy'. In *Religion and the Subtle Body in Asia and the West*, edited by Geoffrey Samuel and Jay Johnston, 239–48. Abingdon: Routledge, 2013.

Jones, Karen R. *Epiphany in the Wilderness: Hunting, Nature, and Performance in the Nineteenth-Century American West*. Boulder: University Press of Colorado, 2015.

Kane, Philip. *The Wildwood King*. Chieveley: Capall Bann, 1997.

Kane, Sean. *Wisdom of the Mythtellers*. Peterborough, ON: Broadview Press, 1998.

Kaplan, Joanna Overing. 'Lowland South America'. In *Legends of the World*, edited by Richard Cavendish, 352–60. London: Orbis, 1982.

Keable, Georgiana. *The Natural Storyteller: Wildlife Tales for Telling*. Stroud: Hawthorn Press, 2017.

Kecine Qatr. 'Le pouple et le rat'. In *Ifejicatre: Textes bilingues drehu–français*, edited by Unë Unë and Drowin Wahetra, 40–3. Nouméa: Centre de documentation pédagogique de Nouvelle-Calédonie, 2002.

Kempton, Sally. 'The Magic of Shared Awareness'. In *On the Mystery of Being: Contemporary Insights on the Convergence of Science and Spirituality*, edited by Zaya and Maurizio Benazzo, 15–18. Oakland: New Harbinger, 2019.

Kennedy, Douglas. 'Folklore and Human Ecology'. *Folklore* 76 (1965): 81–9.

Khanna, Madhu. *Yantra: The Tantric Symbol of Cosmic Unity*. London: Thames & Hudson, 1979.

Kim So-un. *The Story Bag: A Collection of Korean Folktales*, translated by Setsu Higashi. Clarendon, VT: Tuttle, 1960.

King, Serge Kahili. *Kahuna Healing: Holistic Health and Healing Practices of Polynesia*. Wheaton, IL: Quest, 1983.

Kinsley, David. *Hindu Goddesses: Visions of the Divine Feminine in the Hindu Religious Tradition*. Delhi: Motilal Banarsidass, 1987.

Kolodny, Annette. 'Unearthing Herstory: An Introduction'. In *The Ecocriticism Reader: Landmarks in Literary Ecology*, edited by Cheryll Glotfelty and Harold Fromm, 170–81. Athens, GA: University of Georgia Press, 1996.

Kovel, Joel. *The Enemy of Nature: The End of Capitalism or the End of the World?* London: Zed Books, 2007.

Krech, III, Shepard. *The Ecological Indian: Myth and History*. New York: W. W. Norton, 2000.

Kremer, Jürgen W. 'Shamanic Tales as Ways of Personal Empowerment'. In *Shaman's Path: Healing, Personal Growth and Empowerment*, edited by Gary Doore, 189–99. Boston: Shambhala, 1988.

Kroker, Arthur, and David Cook. 'Television and the Triumph of Culture'. In *Storming the Reality Studio: A Casebook of Cyberpunk and Postmodern Science Fiction*, edited by Larry McCaffery. Durham, NC: Duke University Press, 1991.

Kvartič, Ambrož. 'The Local Impact of Migratory Legends: The Process and Function of Localisation'. *Journal of Ethnology and Folkloristics* 6, no. 2 (2012): 87–95.

Labov, William. *The Language of Life and Death: The Transformation of Experience in Oral Narrative*. Cambridge: Cambridge University Press, 2013.

Latif, Mojib. *Climate Change: The Point of No Return*. London: Haus, 2009.

Lawrence, D. H. 'Sun'. In *The Princess and Other Stories*, edited by Keith Sagar, 116–43. Harmondsworth: Penguin, 1971.

Lawson, John Cuthbert. *Modern Greek Folklore: A Study in Survivals*. New York: University Books, 1964.

Leakey, Richard, and Roger Lewin. *The Sixth Extinction: Biodiversity and Its Survival*. London: Weidenfeld & Nicolson, 1996.

Leblic, Isabelle. 'Les Kanak et les rêves ou comment redécouvrir ce que les ancêtres n'ont pas transmis (Nouvelle-Calédonie)'. *Journal de la Société des Océanistes* 130–1 (2010): 105–18.

Lee, Laurie. *Cider with Rosie*. London: Hogarth Press, 1959.

Leenhardt, Maurice. *Do Kamo: Person and Myth in the Melanesian World*, translated by Basia Miller Gulati. Chicago: University of Chicago Press, 1979.

Leenhardt, Maurice. *Notes d'ethnologie néo-calédonienne*. Paris: Institut d'ethnologie, 1930.

Le Guin, Ursula K. *Always Coming Home*. New York: Harper & Row, 1985.

Le Guin, Ursula K. *Dancing at the Edge of the World: Thoughts on Words, Women, Places*. Berkeley: Grove Press, 1997.

Le Guin, Ursula K. *The Language of the Night: Essays on Fantasy and Science Fiction*, edited by Susan Wood. London: Women's Press, 1989.

Le Guin, Ursula K. *The Wave in the Mind: Talks and Essays on the Writer, the Reader, and the Imagination*. Boston: Shambhala, 2004.

Lenihan, Eddie. *Meeting the Other Crowd: The Fairy Stories of Hidden Ireland*. New York: Tarcher, 2004.

Letcher, Andy. 'The Role of the Bard in Contemporary Pagan Movements'. PhD thesis, University of Southampton, 2001.

Letcher, Andy. 'The Scouring of the Shire: Fairies, Trolls and Pixies in Eco-protest Culture'. *Folklore* 112 (2001): 147–61.

Levitas, Ruth, and Lucy Sargisson. 'Utopia in Dark Times: Optimism/Pessimism and Utopia/Dystopia'. In *Dark Horizons: Science Fiction and the Dystopian Imagination*, edited by Raffaella Baccolini and Tom Moylan, 13–27. New York: Routledge, 2003.

Lewis, C. S. *An Experiment in Criticism*. Cambridge: Cambridge University Press, 1961.

Lewis-Williams, David. *The Mind in the Cave: Consciousness and the Origins of Art*. London: Thames & Hudson, 2002.

Lilley, Deborah. 'Kathleen Jamie: Rethinking the Externality and Idealisation of Nature'. *Green Letters* 17, no. 1 (2013): 16–26.

Lipman, Doug. *Improving Your Storytelling: Beyond the Basics for All Who Tell Stories*. Little Rock: August House, 1999.

Lopez, Barry. *About This Life: Journeys on the Threshold of Memory*. London: Harvill Press, 1999.

Lopez, Barry. *Arctic Dreams: Imagination and Desire in a Northern Landscape*. London: Harvill Press, 1999.

Lopez, Barry. *Of Wolves and Men*. New York: Simon & Schuster, 1995.

Love, Glenn A. *Practical Ecocriticism: Literature, Biology, and the Environment*. Charlottesville: University of Virginia Press, 2003.

Luna, Luis Eduardo, and Pablo Amaringo. *Ayahuasca Visions: The Religious Iconography of a Peruvian Shaman*. Berkeley: North Atlantic, 1991.

Lundquist, John M. *The Temple: Meeting Place of Heaven and Earth*. London: Thames & Hudson, 1993.

Lupton, Hugh. 'Betsy White and the Dreaming'. In *Tales, Tellers and Texts*, edited by Gabrielle Hodges, Mary Jane Drummond and Morag Styles, 27–35. London: Cassell, 2000.

Lupton, Hugh. 'Deep England'. Paper presented to Festival at the Edge, Much Wenlock, England, 19–21 July 2002.

Lupton, Hugh. *The Dreaming of Place: Storytelling and Landscape*. Reading: Society for Storytelling, 2001.

Lupton, Hugh. *A Norfolk Songline: Walking the Peddars Way*. Aylsham: Hickathrift Books, 1999.

Lupton, Hugh. *The Songs of Birds: Stories and Poems from Many Cultures*. Bath: Barefoot Books, 1999.

Lyotard, Jean-François. 'Ecology as Discourse of the Secluded'. In *The Green Studies Reader: From Romanticism to Ecocriticism*, edited by Laurence Coupe, 135–8. London: Routledge, 2000.

MacDonald, Margaret Read. *Earth Care: World Folktales to Talk About*. Little Rock: August House, 2005.

Mack, John E. 'The Politics of Species Arrogance'. In *Ecopsychology: Restoring the Earth, Healing the Mind*, edited by Theodore Roszak, Mary E. Gomes and Allen D. Kanner, 279–87. San Francisco: Sierra Club, 1995.

Maclagan, David. *Creation Myths: Man's Introduction to the World*. London: Thames & Hudson, 1977.

Maclean, Norman (ed.). *Silent Summer: The State of Wildlife in Britain and Ireland*. Cambridge: Cambridge University Press, 2010.

Maddern, Eric. *Earth Story*. London: Macdonald, 1988.

Maddern, Eric. *Life Story*. London: Macdonald, 1988.

Maddern, Eric. *Snowdonia Folk Tales*. Stroud: History Press, 2015.

Maddern, Eric. 'The Sustaining Story'. In *Storytelling for a Greener World: Environment, Community, and Story-Based Learning*, edited by Alida Gersie, Anthony Nanson and Edward Schieffelin, 86–96. Stroud: Hawthorn Press, 2014.

Maggi, Shakti Caterina. 'The Human Journey'. In *On the Mystery of Being: Contemporary Insights on the Convergence of Science and Spirituality*, edited by Zaya and Maurizio Benazzo, 204–7. Oakland: New Harbinger, 2019.

MaHood, James. 'Imaginal Yoga in India: A Four Thousand-Year Tradition'. *Temenos* 5 (1984): 193–210.

Maiteny, Paul. 'Finding Meaning without Consuming'. In *The Handbook of Sustainability Literacy: Skills for a Changing World*, edited by Arran Stibbe, 178–84. Totnes: Green Books, 2009.

Malekin, Peter. 'Art and the Liberation of the Mind'. *Temenos* 5 (1984): 139–52.

Manes, Christopher. 'Nature and Silence'. In *The Ecocriticism Reader: Landmarks in Literary Ecology*, edited by Cheryll Glotfelty and Harold Fromm, 15–29. Athens, GA: University of Georgia Press, 1996.

Mann, A. T. *Sacred Architecture*. Shaftesbury: Element, 1993.

Mann, A. T., and Jane Lyle. *Sacred Sexuality*. Shaftesbury: Element, 1995.

Manwaring, Kevan. 'Awakening the King'. *Bardic Academic*, 17 July 2020.

Manwaring, Kevan. *The Bardic Handbook: The Complete Manual for the Twenty-First Century Bard*. Glastonbury: Gothic Image, 2006.

Margulis, Lynn. *Symbiotic Planet: A New Look at Evolution*. London: Weidenfeld & Nicolson, 1998.

Marshall, Peter. *Nature's Web*. London: Simon & Schuster, 1992.

Martin, Paul S. *Twilight of the Mammoths: Ice Age Extinctions and the Rewilding of America*. Berkeley: University of California Press, 2005.

Martin, Paul S., and Richard G. Klein (eds). *Quaternary Extinctions: A Prehistoric Revolution*. Tucson: University of Arizona Press, 1984.

Martin, Rafe. *The Hungry Tigress: Buddhist Myths, Legends, and Jataka Tales*. Somerville, MA: Yellow Moon Press, 2001.

Matthews, Caitlín. *Arthur and the Sovereignty of Britain: King and Goddess in the Mabinogion*. London: Penguin, 1989.

Matthews, Caitlín. 'The Quest as Shamanic Journey in Celtic Tradition'. In *The Encyclopaedia of Celtic Wisdom: Celtic Shaman's Sourcebook*, edited by Caitlín and John Matthews, 350–8. Shaftesbury: Element, 1994.

McDowell, Michael J. 'The Bakhtinian Road to Ecological Insight'. In *The Ecocriticism Reader: Landmarks in Literary Ecology*, edited by Cheryll Glotfelty and Harold Fromm, 371–91. Athens, GA: University of Georgia Press, 1996.

McKee, Robert. *Story: Substance, Structure, Style, and the Principles of Screenwriting*. London: Methuen, 1999.

McLuhan, T. C. *The Way of the Earth: Encounters with Nature in Ancient and Contemporary Thought*. New York: Simon & Schuster, 1994.

Meadows, Donella. 'Dancing with Systems'. *Whole Earth*, Winter 2001.

Meder, Theo. 'In Search of the Dutch Lore of the Land: Old and New Legends throughout the Netherlands'. *Folklore* 122 (2011): 117–34.

Medlicott, Mary. '"Miss, Is Skomar Oddy Extinct?"' In *Storytelling for a Greener World: Environment, Community, and Story-Based Learning*, edited by Alida Gersie, Anthony Nanson and Edward Schieffelin, 268–78. Stroud: Hawthorn Press, 2014.

Meeker, Joseph W. 'The Comic Mode'. In *The Ecocriticism Reader: Landmarks in Literary Ecology*, edited by Cheryll Glotfelty and Harold Fromm, 155–69. Athens, GA: University of Georgia Press, 1996.

Meletinksy, Eleazar M. *The Poetics of Myth*, translated by Guy Lanoue and Alexandre Sadetsky. New York: Routledge, 2000.

Metcalfe, David. 'Voices in the City'. In *Storytelling for a Greener World: Environment, Community, and Story-Based Learning*, edited by A. Gersie, A. Nanson and E. Schieffelin, 220–9. Stroud: Hawthorn Press, 2014.

Michel, Louise. *Légendes et chansons de gestes canaques (1875) suivi de Légendes et chansons de gestes canaques (1885) et de Civilisation*, edited by François Bogliolo. Lyons: Presses universitaires de Lyon, 2006.

Michell, John. *The Earth Spirit: Its Ways, Shrines and Mysteries*. London: Thames & Hudson, 1975.

Mickleburgh, Edwin. *Beyond the Frozen Sea: Visions of Antarctica*. London: Grafton, 1990.

Micklin, Philip, N. V. Aladin and Igor Plotnikov (eds). *The Aral Sea: The Devastation and Partial Rehabilitation of a Great Lake*. Berlin: Springer, 2014.

Minter, Rick. *Big Cats: Facing Britain's Wild Predators*. Dunbeath: Whittles, 2011.

Mitchell, Andrew. *A Fragile Paradise: Nature and Man in the Pacific*. London: William Collins, 1989.

Moltmann, Jürgen. *God in Creation: An Ecological Doctrine of Creation*, translated by Margaret Kohl. London: SCM Press, 1985.

Monbiot, George. *No Man's Land: An Investigative Journey through Kenya and Tanzania*. London: Macmillan, 1994.

Murdock, Maureen. *The Heroine's Journey*. Boston: Shambhala, 1990.

Murphy, Patrick D. 'Ecofeminist Dialogics'. In *The Green Studies Reader: From Romanticism to Ecocriticism*, edited by Laurence Coupe, 193–7. London: Routledge, 2000.

Murray, Peter. 'Extinctions Downunder: A Bestiary of Extinct Australian Late Pleistocene Monotremes and Marsupials'. In *Quaternary Extinctions: A Prehistoric Revolution*, edited by Paul S. Martin and Richard G. Klein, 600–28. Tucson: University of Arizona Press, 1984.

Nabhan, Gary Paul. *Cultures of Habitat: On Nature, Culture, and Story*. Washington: Counterpoint, 1997.

Naess, Aarne. 'Self-Realization: An Ecological Approach to Being in the World'. In *Deep Ecology for the 21st Century: Readings on the Philosophy and Practice of the New Environmentalism*, edited by George Sessions, 225–39. Boston: Shambhala, 1995.

Naess, Aarne. 'The Third World, Wilderness, and Deep Ecology'. In *Deep Ecology for the 21st Century: Readings on the Philosophy and Practice of the New Environmentalism*, edited by George Sessions, 397–407. Boston: Shambhala, 1995.

Nanson, Anthony. *Deep Time*. Stroud: Hawthorn Press, 2015.

Nanson, Anthony. '"The Future Has Gone Bad; We Need a New One": Neoliberal Science Fiction and the Writing of Ecotopian Possibility'. In *Storytelling for Sustainability in Higher Education: An Educator's Handbook*, edited by Petra Molthan-Hill et al., 130–42. Abingdon: Routledge, 2020.

Nanson, Anthony. *Gloucestershire Folk Tales*. Stroud: History Press, 2012.

Nanson, Anthony. 'Jumping the Gap of Desire'. In *Storytelling for a Greener World: Environment, Community, and Story-Based Learning*, edited by A. Gersie, A. Nanson and E. Schieffelin, 140–52. Stroud: Hawthorn Press, 2014.

Nanson, Anthony. 'The Migrant Maid'. In *Ballad Tales: An Anthology of British Ballads Retold*, edited by Kevan Manwaring, 166–74. Stroud: History Press, 2017.

Nanson, Anthony. *Words of Re-enchantment: Writings on Storytelling, Myth, and Ecological Desire*. Stroud: Awen, 2011.

Nanson, Anthony, and Kirsty Hartsiotis. *Gloucestershire Folk Tales for Children*. Cheltenham: History Press, 2020.

Nanson, Anthony, and Kirsty Hartsiotis. *Gloucestershire Ghost Tales*. Stroud: History Press, 2015.

Nanson, Anthony, Kevan Manwaring, David Metcalfe, Kirsty Hartsiotis and Richard Selby [Fire Springs]. *An Ecobardic Manifesto: A Vision for the Arts in a Time of Environmental Crisis*. Bath: Awen, 2008.

Narayan, Kirin. *Mondays on the Dark Night of the Moon: Himalayan Foothill Folktales*. New York: Oxford University Press, 1997.

Nash, Paul. *Outline: An Autobiography*, edited by David Boyd Haycock. London: Lund Humphries, 2016.

Nash Ford, David. 'St. Afrella *alias* Arilda'. *Early British Kingdoms*, 2001.

Nita, Maria. '"Inside Story": Participatory Storytelling and Imagination in Eco-pedagogical Contexts'. In *Storytelling for Sustainability in Higher Education: An Educator's Handbook*, edited by Petra Molthan-Hill et al., 154–67. Abingdon: Routledge, 2020.

Oates, Joyce Carol. 'Against Nature'. In *The Nature Reader*, edited by Daniel Halpern and Dan Frank. Hopewell, NJ: Ecco, 1996.

O'Connor, Peter. *Beyond the Mist: What Irish Mythology Can Teach Us about Ourselves*. London: Victor Gollancz, 2000.

O'Donohue, John. *Divine Beauty: The Invisible Embrace*. London: Bantam, 2003.

O'Donohue, John. *Eternal Echoes: Exploring Our Hunger to Belong*. London: Bantam, 2000.

Ó Duilearga, Séamus. 'Irish Tales and Story-Tellers'. In *International Folkloristics: Classic Contributions by the Founders of Folklore*, edited by Alan Dundes, 153–76. Lanham, MD: Rowman & Littlefield, 1999.

Oelrich, Inger Lise. *The New Story: Storytelling as a Pathway to Peace*. Leicester: Matador, 2015.

Okri, Ben. *Dangerous Love*. London: Phoenix House, 1996.

Olalla, Pedro. *Mythological Atlas of Greece*. Athens: Road Editions, 2002.

Olrik, Axel. 'Epic Laws of Folk Narrative'. In *International Folkloristics: Classic Contributions by the Founders of Folklore*, edited by Alan Dundes, 83–97. Lanham, MD: Rowman & Littlefield, 1999.

Ong, Walter J. *Orality and Literacy: Technologizing the Word*. London: Routledge, 1988.

Osho. *The Book of Secrets: 112 Keys to the Mystery Within*. New York: Osho International, 1974.

Osho. *The Perfect Way*. New York: Osho International, 2017.

O'Sullivan, Simon. 'The Aesthetics of Affect: Thinking Art beyond Representation'. *Angelaki* 6, no. 3 (2001): 125–35.

Otto, Eric C. '"The Rain Feels New": Ecotopian Strategies in the Short Fiction of Paolo Bacigalupi'. In *Green Planets: Ecology and Science Fiction*, edited by Gerry Canavan and Kim Stanley Robinson, 179–91. Middletown, CT: Wesleyan University Press, 2014.

Ovid. *Metamorphoses*, translated by Mary M. Innes. London: Penguin, 1955.

Opperman, Serpil, and Serenella Iovino (eds). *Environmental Humanities: Voices from the Anthropocene*. London: Rowman & Littlefield, 2017.

Palmer, Kingsley. *The Folklore of Somerset*. London: B. T. Batsford, 1976.

Palmer, Martin. *Dancing to Armageddon*. London: HarperCollins, 1992.

Palmer, Martin. *The Sacred History of Britain*. London: Piatkus, 2002.

Palmer, Roy. *The Folklore of Gloucestershire*. Tiverton: Westcountry Books, 1994.

Parkinson, Rob. Letter to the Editor. *Storylines* 4, no. 12 (2000): 6.

Parkinson, Rob. *Three Angles on an Awakening Kiss: Modern Storytelling as if the Moment Mattered*. Reading: Society for Storytelling, 1999.

Parkinson, Rob. *Transforming Tales: How Stories Can Change People*. London: Jessica Kingsley, 2009.

Parkinson, Rob. 'Your Body Doesn't Know It's a Story'. *Storylines* 22 (2003): 6–7.

Parrinder, Patrick. *African Mythology*. New York: Peter Bedrick, 1982.

Payne, Tonia. 'Dark Brothers and Shadow Souls: Ursula Le Guin's Animal "Fables"'. Paper presented at 'Animals in Legend and Story' conference, University of California, Davis, 1–2 August 2001.

Pellowski, Anne. *The World of Storytelling: A Practical Guide to the Origins, Development, and Applications of Storytelling*. New York: H. W. Wilson, 1990.

Percy, Thomas. *Reliques of Ancient English Poetry: Consisting of Old Heroic Ballads, Songs, and Other Pieces of Our Earlier Poets*, edited by J. V. Prichard. 2 vols. London: George Bell, 1876.

Phelps, David. *Herefordshire Folk Tales*. Stroud: History Press, 2009.

Phillips, Dana. 'Is Nature Necessary?' In *The Ecocriticism Reader: Landmarks in Literary Ecology*, edited by Cheryll Glotfelty and Harold Fromm, 204–22. Athens, GA: University of Georgia Press, 1996.

Phillips, Larry W. (ed.). *Ernest Hemingway on Writing*. London: Grafton, 1986.

Phillips, Morgan. 'Emotional Well-Being'. In *The Handbook of Sustainability Literacy: Skills for a Changing World*, edited by Arran Stibbe, 171–7. Totnes: Green Books, 2009.

Philo, Greg. 'Television News and Audience Understanding of War, Conflict and Disaster'. *Journalism Studies* 3, no. 2 (2002): 173–86.

Pilbeam, Alan. *The Landscape of Gloucestershire*. Stroud: Tempus, 2006.

Plumwood, Val. *Feminism and the Mastery of Nature*. London: Routledge, 1993.

Polley, Jane (ed.). *American Folklore and Legend*. Pleasantville, NY: Reader's Digest, 1978.

Pumwan, Leon. 'Pourquoi le poulpe a des taches noires sur la tête'. In *Littérature orale: 60 contes mélanésiens de Nouvelle-Calédonie*, edited by Dominique Bourret, Maurice Coyaud, Marie-Joseph Dubois, Loïc Mangematin and Roland Tavernier, 180–1. Nouméa: Sociéte d'études historiques de la Nouvelle-Calédonie, 1980.

Quammen, David. *Monster of God: The Man-Eating Predator in the Jungles of History and the Mind*. New York: W. W. Norton, 2003.

Quammen, David. *The Song of the Dodo: Island Biogeography in an Age of Extinctions*. London: Pimlico, 1997.

Quammen, David. *Spillover: Animal Infections and the Next Human Pandemic*. New York: W. W. Norton, 2012.

Raglan, Lord. *The Hero: A Study in Tradition, Myth, and Drama*. New York: Vintage, 1956.

Ramsay, Raylene. *Nights of Storytelling: A Cultural History of Kanaky–New Caledonia*. Honolulu: University of Hawai'i Press, 2011.

Ramsden, Ashley. 'Jewels on Indra's Net'. In *Storytelling for a Greener World: Environment, Community, and Story-Based Learning*, edited by Alida Gersie, Anthony Nanson and Edward Schieffelin, 110–23. Stroud: Hawthorn Press, 2014.

Ramsden, Ashley, and Sue Hollingsworth. *The Storyteller's Way: Sourcebook for Inspired Storytelling*. Stroud: Hawthorn Press, 2013.

Rawson, Philip. *The Art of Tantra*. London: Thames & Hudson, 1973.

Rawson, Philip, and Laszlo Legeza. *Tao: The Chinese Philosophy of Time and Change*. London: Thames & Hudson, 1973.

Ranelagh, E. L. *The Past We Share: The Near Eastern Ancestry of Western Folk Literature*. London: Quartet, 1979.

Restall-Orr, Emma. *Druid Priestess: An Intimate Journey through the Pagan Year*. London: Thorsons, 2000.

Richards, Sam. 'Doing the Story: Narrative, Mission and the Eucharist'. In *Mass Culture: Eucharist and Mission in a Post-modern World*, edited by Pete Ward. Oxford: Bible Reading Fellowship, 1999.

Rigby, Kate. *Dancing with Disaster: Environmental Histories, Narratives, and Ethics for Perilous Times*. Charlottesville: University of Virginia Press, 2015.

Robert, Pa. 'L'ogre bicéphale'. In *Toatiti: Textes bilingues nengone–français*, edited by Jacques Haewegene and Raymond Cawa, 37–9. Nouméa: Centre de documentation pédagogique de Nouvelle-Calédonie, 2000.

Robinson, Kim Stanley. *Forty Signs of Rain*. London: HarperCollins, 2004.

Robinson, Kim Stanley. *Green Mars*. London: HarperCollins, 1992.

Robinson, Kim Stanley. *Pacific Edge*. New York: Tor, 1990.

Rose, Deborah Bird, Thom van Dooren, Matthew Chrulew, Stuart Cooke, Matthew Kearnes and Emily O'Gormann. 'Thinking through the Environment, Unsettling the Humanities'. *Environmental Humanities* 1 (2012): 1–5.

Roszak, Theodore. *The Voice of the Earth: An Exploration of Ecopsychology*. Grand Rapids: Phanes Press, 2001.

Roszak, Theodore. 'Where Psyche Meets Gaia'. In *Ecopsychology: Restoring the Earth, Healing the Mind*, edited by Theodore Roszak, Mary E. Gomes and Allen D. Kanner, 1–20. San Francisco: Sierra Club, 1995.

Roszak, Theodore, Mary E. Gomes and Allen D. Kanner (eds). *Ecopsychology: Restoring the Earth, Healing the Mind*. San Francisco: Sierra Club, 1995.

Rueckert, William. 'Literature and Ecology: An Experiment in Ecocriticism'. In *The Ecocriticism Reader: Landmarks in Literary Ecology*, edited by Cheryll Glotfelty and Harold Fromm, 105–23. Athens, GA: University of Georgia Press, 1996.

Ruether, Rosemary Radford. 'Ecofeminist Philosophy, Theology, and Ethics: A Comparative View'. In *Ecospirit: Religions and Philosophies for the Earth*, edited by Laurel Kearns and Catherine Keller, 77–93. New York: Fordham University Press, 2007.

Rushdie, Salman. 'Is Nothing Sacred?' *Granta* 31 (1990): 97–111.

Ryder, T. A. *Portrait of Gloucestershire*. London: Robert Hale, 1972.

Safina, Carl. *Song for the Blue Ocean: Encounters along the World's Coasts and beneath the Seas*. New York: Henry Holt, 1996.

Sagan, Carl. *Cosmos*. London: Macdonald Futura, 1981.

Sahtouris, Elisabet. 'From a Mechanistic and Competitive to a Reenchanted and Co-evolving Cosmos'. In *Science and the Reenchantment of the Cosmos: The Rise of the Integral Vision of Reality*, edited by Ervin Laszlo, 101–8. Rochester, VT: Inner Traditions, 2006.

Said, Edward. *Culture and Imperialism*. London: Vintage, 1994.
Said, Edward. *Orientalism*. New York: Pantheon, 1978.
Saitoti, Tepilit ole. *Maasai*. London: HarperCollins, 1991.
Sale, Richard. *Gloucestershire: People and History*. Marlborough: Crowood Press, 2002.
Salisbury, Chris. 'Feeding the Story'. In *Storytelling for a Greener World: Environment, Community, and Story-Based Learning*, edited by Alida Gersie, Anthony Nanson and Edward Schieffelin, 168–77. Stroud: Hawthorn Press, 2014.
Salisbury, Chris. 'Wisdom of the Wildwood'. *EarthLines* 2 (2012): 47–9.
Salomon, Christine. *Savoirs et pouvoirs thérapeutiques kanaks*. Paris: Presses Universitaires de France, 2000.
Samuel, Geoffrey. 'Subtle-Body Processes: Towards a Non-reductionist Understanding'. In *Religion and the Subtle Body in Asia and the West*, edited by Geoffrey Samuel and Jay Johnson, 249–66. Abingdon: Routledge, 2013.
Samuel, Geoffrey, and Jay Johnston (eds). *Religion and the Subtle Body in Asia and the West*. Abingdon: Routledge, 2013.
Sanders, Scott Russell. 'Speaking a Word for Nature'. In *The Ecocriticism Reader: Landmarks in Literary Ecology*, edited by Cheryll Glotfelty and Harold Fromm, 182–5. Athens, GA: University of Georgia Press, 1996.
Savage, Anne. *The Anglo-Saxon Chronicles*. Godalming: CLB, 1995.
Sawyer, Ruth. *The Way of the Storyteller*. New York: Penguin, 1977.
Schechner, Richard. 'Magnitudes of Performance'. In *By Means of Performance: Intercultural Studies of Theatre and Ritual*, edited by Richard Schechner and Willa Appel, 19–49. Cambridge: Cambridge University Press, 1990.
Schieffelin, Edward. 'Listening to Stories with an Anthropological Ear'. In *Storytelling for a Greener World: Environment, Community, and Story-Based Learning*, edited by A. Gersie, A. Nanson and E. Schieffelin, 154–66. Stroud: Hawthorn Press, 2014.
Schneidau, Lisa. *Botanical Folk Tales of Britain and Ireland*. Stroud: History Press, 2018.
Schneidau, Lisa. *Woodland Folk Tales of Britain and Ireland*. Cheltenham: History Press, 2020.
Segerstråle, Ullica. *Defenders of the Truth: The Sociobiology Debate*. Oxford: Oxford University Press, 2001.
Seton, Ernest Thompson. 'Lobo, the King of Currumpaw'. In *The Best of Ernest Thompson Seton*, edited by W. Kay Robinson, 253–78. London: Hodder & Stoughton, 1949.
Sewall, Laura. 'The Skill of Ecological Perception'. In *Ecopsychology: Restoring the Earth, Healing the Mind*, edited by Theodore Roszak, Mary E. Gomes and Allen D. Kanner, 201–15. San Francisco: Sierra Club, 1995.
Seymour, Anna. 'Interview with Alida Gersie'. *Dramatherapy* 38, nos 2–3 (2017): 124–32.
Shacklock, Geoffrey. 'Fast Capitalist Educational Change: Personally Resisting the Images of School Reform'. *Discourse* 19, no. 1 (1998): 75–88.
Shallcrass, Philip. 'Awen: The Holy Spirit of Druidry'. In *Druidry: Native Spirituality in Britain*, edited by Philip Shallcrass. St Leonards-on-Sea: British Druid Order, 1996.

Shah, Tahir. *In Arabian Nights: In Search of Morocco through Its Stories and Storytellers*. London: Transworld, 2009.

Shapiro, Elan. 'Restoring Habitats, Communities, and Souls'. In *Ecopsychology: Restoring the Earth, Healing the Mind*, edited by T. Roszak, M. E. Gomes and A. D. Kanner, 224–39. San Francisco: Sierra Club Books, 1995.

Sharpe, Richard. 'Introduction'. In *Life of St Columba* by Adomnán of Iona, 1–99. London: Penguin, 1995.

Shaw, Martin. 'Beyond the Crisis of Return'. In *Storytelling for a Greener World: Environment, Community, and Story-Based Learning*, edited by Alida Gersie, Anthony Nanson and Edward Schieffelin, 282–92. Stroud: Hawthorn Press, 2014.

Shaw, Martin. *A Branch from the Lightning Tree: Ecstatic Myth and the Grace in Wildness*. Ashland, OR: White Cloud Press, 2011.

Shearer, Alistair. *Buddha: The Intelligent Heart*. London: Thames & Hudson, 1992

Shearer, Alistair. *The Hindu Vision: Forms of the Formless*. London: Thames & Hudson, 1993.

Sheldrake, Philip. *Living between Worlds: Place and Journey in Celtic Spirituality*. London: Darton, Longman & Todd, 1995.

Sheldrake, Rupert. *The Science Delusion: Freeing the Spirit of Enquiry*. London: Hodder & Stoughton, 2013.

Shepard, Aaron. 'The Wings of the Butterfly'. *Author Online!* (1997).

Shepard, Paul. 'Nature and Madness'. In *Ecopsychology: Restoring the Earth, Healing the Mind*, edited by Theodore Roszak, Mary E. Gomes and Allen D. Kanner, 21–40. San Francisco: Sierra Club, 1995.

Shipp, Fiona, and Martin Nunn. 'Marsh Men and Brick Women'. *Storylines* 4, no. 20 (2002): 8–9.

Shippey, Tom. *The Road to Middle-Earth*. London: George Allen & Unwin, 1982.

Silf, Margaret (ed.). *One Hundred Wisdom Tales from Around the World*. Oxford: Lion, 2003.

Silko, Leslie Marmon. 'Landscape, History, and the Pueblo Imagination'. In *The Ecocriticism Reader: Landmarks in Literary Ecology*, edited by Cheryll Glotfelty and Harold Fromm, 264–75. Athens, GA: University of Georgia Press, 1996.

Simard, S. W. 'Mycorrhizal Networks Facilitate Tree Communication, Learning and Memory'. In *Memory and Learning in Plants*, edited by F. Baluska, M. Gagliano and G. Witzany, 191–213. Berlin: Springer, 2018.

Singh, Rina. *A Forest of Stories: Magical Tree Tales from Around the World*. Bath: Barefoot Books, 2003.

Smith, Brian, and Elizabeth Ralph. *A History of Bristol and Gloucestershire*. Chichester: Phillimore, 1982.

Smith, Chris, and Jules Pottle. *Science through Stories: Teaching Primary Science with Storytelling*. Stroud: Hawthorn Press, 2015.

Smith, Donald. *Storytelling Scotland: A Nation in Narrative*. Edinburgh: Polygon, 2001.

Snyder, Gary. *A Place in Space: Ethics, Aesthetics, and Watersheds*. Berkeley: Counterpoint, 1995.

Snyder, Gary. *The Practice of the Wild*. New York: North Point Press, 1990.
Sogyal Rinpoche. *The Tibetan Book of Living and Dying*, edited by Patrick Gaffney and Andrew Harvey. London: Random House, 1992.
Somadeva. *The Kathā Sarit Sāgara, or Ocean of the Streams of Story*, translated by C. H. Tawney. 2 vols. Calcutta: J. W. Thomas, 1880.
Soper, Kate. *What Is Nature? Culture, Politics and the Non-human*. London: Blackwell, 1995.
Soyinka, Wole. *Myth, Literature and the African World*. Cambridge: Cambridge University Press, 1990.
Speedy, Karin. 'Introduction'. In *Les terres de la demi-lune/Half-Moon Lands*, by Hélène Savoie, 42–63. Paris: L'Harmattan, 2010.
Spira, Rupert. *The Nature of Consciousness: Essays on the Unity of Mind and Matter*. Oxford: Sahaja, 2017.
Spowers, Rory. *Rising Tides: The History and Future of the Environmental Movement*. Edinburgh: Canongate, 2003.
Stallings, Fran. 'The Web of Silence: Storytelling's Power to Hypnotize'. *National Storytelling Journal* 5, no. 2 (1988): 6–19.
Starkey, Dinah. *Mermaids, Moonrakers and Hobgoblins*. London: Kaye & Ward, 1977.
Sterling, Stephen. 'Ecological Intelligence'. In *The Handbook of Sustainability Literacy: Skills for a Changing World*, edited by Arran Stibbe, 77–83. Totnes: Green Books, 2009.
Stevinson, John. *The Lives of King Kenulf of Mercia and His Family and the Legend of His Son St Kenelm*. Winchcombe: n.p., 2005.
Stewart, Anne E. 'Born of the Land', *Facts & Fiction* 41 (2002): 12–14.
Stibbe, Arran. *Ecolinguistics: Language, Ecology and the Stories We Live By*. Abingdon: Routledge, 2021.
Stone, Richard. *The Healing Art of Storytelling: A Sacred Journey of Personal Discovery*. New York: Hyperion, 1996.
Strauss, Kevin. 'Reconsidering the Big Bad Wolf: A Naturalist's Approach to Anthropomorphism in Animal Stories'. *Storytelling Magazine* 14, no. 3 (2002): 23.
Strauss, Kevin. *Tales with Tails: Storytelling the Wonders of the Natural World*. Westport, CT: Libraries Unlimited, 2006.
Strauss, Susan. *The Passionate Fact: Storytelling in Natural History and Cultural Interpretation*. Golden, CO: Fulcrum, 1996.
Studholme, C., and L. Moore. 2011. *State of the Natural Environment Report*. Gloucester: Gloucestershire Environment Partnership.
Sturm, Brian W. 'The Enchanted Imagination: Storytelling's Power to Entrance Listeners'. *School Library Media Research* 2, no. 6 (1999): 1–21.
Sunderland, Chris. 'Human Nature and the Image of God: Social and Biological Factors'. Paper for the 'Churches Together in Britain and Ireland' consultation, 2001.
Sunderland, Chris. *In a Glass Darkly: Seeking Vision for Public Life*. Carlisle: Paternoster, 2001.

Sutton, Alan (ed.). *Cotswold Tales*. Stroud: Alan Sutton, 1991.
Sutton, Alan (ed.). *The Dialect & Folk Phrases of the Cotswolds*. Stroud: Amberley, 2008.
Suvin, Darko. *Metamorphoses of Science Fiction: On the Poetics and History of a Literary Genre*, edited by Gerry Canavan. Bern: Peter Lang, 2016.
Tansley, David V. *Subtle Body: Essence and Shadow*. London: Thames & Hudson, 1977.
Tappuni, Jane. 'Blockchain Solutions for Book Publishing'. *Logos* 30, no. 4 (2020): 7–15.
Taylor, H. M., and Joan Taylor. *Anglo-Saxon Architecture*. 2 vols. Cambridge: Cambridge University Press, 1965.
Taylor, Peter. *Beyond Conservation: A Wildland Strategy*. London: Earthscan, 2005.
Thapar, Valmik. *Land of the Tiger: A Natural History of the Indian Subcontinent*. London: BBC, 1997.
Theodossopoulos, Dimitrios. *Troubles with Turtles: Cultural Understandings of the Environment on a Greek Island*. New York: Berghahn, 2005.
Thomas, Chris, D., et al. 'Extinction Risk from Climate Change', *Nature* 427 (2004): 145–7.
Thomas, Taffy. *The Magpie's Nest: A Treasury of Bird Folk Tales*. Stroud: History Press, 2019.
Thomason Sickles, Dovie. 'Honoring the Other: The Lessons of the Animal People'. *Storytelling Magazine* 14, no. 3 (2002): 24–5.
Thompson, Stith. *The Folktale*. Berkeley: University of California Press, 1946.
Thompson, Stith. *Motif-Index of Folk-Literature: A Classification of Narrative Elements in Folktales, Ballads, Myths, Fables, Medieval Romances, Exempla, Fabliaux, Jest-Books, and Local Legends*. 6 vols. Bloomington: Indiana University Press, 1955–8.
Thomson, David. *The People of the Sea: Celtic Tales of the Seal-Folk*. Edinburgh: Canongate, 1996.
Thurman, Robert A. F. (trans.). *The Tibetan Book of the Dead*. London: HarperCollins, 2011.
Tjibaou, Jean-Marie. *Kanaky*, edited by Alban Bensa and Éric Wittersheim, translated by Helen Fraser and John Trotter. Canberra: Pandanus Books, 2005.
Tjibaou, Jean-Marie, and Philippe Missotte. *Kanaké: The Melanesian Way*, translated by Christopher Plant. Papeete: Éditions du Pacifique, 1978.
Todorov, Tzvetan. *The Fantastic: A Structural Approach to a Literary Genre*, translated by Richard Howard. Ithaca, NY: Cornell University Press, 1975.
Toelken, Barre. 'The Icebergs of Folktale: Misconception, Misuse, Abuse'. In *Who Says? Essays on Pivotal Issues in Contemporary Storytelling*, edited by Carol L. Birch and Melissa A. Heckler, 35–63. Little Rock: August House, 1996.
Tolkien, J. R. R. 'On Fairy Stories'. In *The Monsters and the Critics and Other Essays*, edited by Christopher Tolkien, 109–61. London: George Allen & Unwin, 1983.
Tolkien, J. R. R. *Farmer Giles of Ham*. London: George Allen & Unwin, 1949.
Tolkien, J. R. R. *The Fellowship of the Ring*. London: George Allen & Unwin, 1979.
Tolkien, J. R. R. *The Hobbit*. London: George Allen & Unwin, 1937.
Tolkien, J. R. R. *The Silmarillion*. London: George Allen & Unwin, 1977.
Tolle, Eckhart. *A New Earth: Create a Better Life*. London: Penguin, 2018.

Tomkinson, John L. *Haunted Greece: Nymphs, Vampires, and Other Exotica*. Athens: Anagnosis, 2004.

Tongue, Ruth L. *The Chime Child or Somerset Singers*. London: Routledge & Kegan Paul, 1967.

Tongue, Ruth L. *Forgotten Folk-Tales of the English Counties*. London: Routledge & Kegan Paul, 1970.

Travers, P. L. *What the Bee Knows: Reflections on Myth, Symbol and Story*. London: Penguin, 1993.

Trungpa, Chögyam. 'Questions and Answers'. In *The Dawn of Tantra*, edited by Michael Kohn, 78–92. Boulder: Shambhala, 1975.

Trungpa, Chögyam. 'Visualization'. In *The Dawn of Tantra*, edited by Michael Kohn, 47–52. Boulder: Shambhala, 1975.

Turnbull, Colin. 'Liminality: A Synthesis of Subjective and Objective Experience'. In *By Means of Performance: Intercultural Studies of Theatre and Ritual*, edited by Richard Schechner and Willa Appel, 50–81. Cambridge: Cambridge University Press, 1990.

Turner, Mark. *Mysterious Gloucestershire*. Stroud: History Press, 2011.

TUUP. 'Artist Insights – TUUP'. *YouTube*, 9 March 2019.

Tydeman, William E. *Conversations with Barry Lopez: Walking the Path of Imagination*. Norman: University of Oklahoma Press, 2013.

Uther, Hans-Jörg. *The Types of International Folktales: A Classification and Bibliography*. 3 vols. Helsinki: Finnish Academy of Science and Letters, 2011.

Uzendoski, Michael A., and Edith Felicia Calapucha-Tapuy. *The Ecology of the Spoken Word: Amazonian Storytelling and Shamanism among the Napo Runa*. Urbana: University of Illinois Press, 2012.

Van der Post, Laurens. *The Heart of the Hunter*. London: Hogarth Press, 1961.

Van Deusen, Kira. 'Storytelling as a Shamanic Art: The Udeghe People of the Amur Region'. In *Shamanism and Other Indigenous Beliefs and Practices*, edited by D. A. Funk and V. I. Kharitonova, 96–104. Moscow: Academy of Sciences, 1999.

Van Dooren, Thom Van, and Deborah Rose. 'Lively Ethography: Storying Animist Worlds'. In *Environmental Humanities: Voices from the Anthropocene*, edited by Serpil Opperman and Serenella Iovino, 255–71. London: Rowman & Littlefield, 2017.

Van Matre, Steve. *Earth Education: A New Beginning*. Greenville, WV: Institute for Earth Education, 1990.

Vizard, W. *In the Valley of the Gods: A Nomadic Variorum*. Cheltenham: W. W. Bastin, 1926.

Vogler, Christopher. *The Writer's Journey: Mythic Structure for Writers*. London: Boxtree, 1996.

Von Sydow, Carl Wilhelm. 'Geography and Folk-Tale Oicotypes'. In *International Folkloristics: Classic Contributions by the Founders of Folklore*, edited by Alan Dundes, 137–51. Lanham, MD: Rowman & Littlefield, 1999.

Walker, Micheline. '"How the Bear Lost Its Tail": A Cherokee Fable'. *Micheline's Blog*, 4 August 2013.

Wapner, Paul. *Environmental Activism and World Civic Politics*. Albany: State University of New York Press, 1996.

Ward, Cynthia. 'What They Told Buchi Emecheta: Oral Subjectivity and the Joys of "Otherhood"'. *Proceedings of the Modern Language Association* 105, no. 1 (1990): 85–97.

Warner, Marina. *From the Beast to the Blonde: On Fairytales and Their Tellers*. London: Chatto & Windus, 1994.

Weber, Max. *The Protestant Ethic and the Spirit of Capitalism*, translated by Talcott Parsons. London: George Allen & Unwin, 1930.

Wegner, Phillip E. 'Utopianism'. In *The Oxford Handbook of Science Fiction*, edited by Rob Latham, 573–83. New York: Oxford University Press, 2014.

Westwood, Jennifer, and Sophia Kingshill. *The Lore of Scotland: A Guide to Scottish Legends*. London: Random House, 2009.

Westwood, Jennifer, and Jacqueline Simpson. *The Lore of the Land: A Guide to England's Legends from Spring-Heeled Jack to the Witches of Warboys*. London: Penguin, 2006.

Wheeler, Wendy. 'How the Earth Speaks Now: The Book of Nature and Biosemiotics as Theoretical Resources for the Environmental Humanities in the Twenty-First Century'. In *Environmental Humanities: Voices from the Anthropocene*, edited by Serpil Opperman and Serenella Iovino, 295–311. London: Rowman & Littlefield, 2017.

Wildlife Trusts. 'A Living Landscape: A Call to Restore the UK's Battered Ecosystems, for Wildlife and People'. 2009.

Williams, Adin. *Lays and Legends of Gloucestershire*. London: Kent, 1878.

Williams, Adin. *Legends, Tales, and Songs in the Dialect of the Peasantry of Gloucestershire*. London: Kent, 1876.

Williams, Alfred. *Round About the Upper Thames*. London: Duckworth, 1922.

Williams, Glyn. *Arctic Labyrinth: The Quest for the Northwest Passage*. London: Penguin, 2010.

Williams, Michael. *Deforesting the Earth: From Prehistory to Global Crisis*. Chicago: University of Chicago Press, 2006.

Williamson, Duncan. *Land of the Sea People*, edited by Linda Williamson. Edinburgh: Birlinn, 2010.

Wilson, Barbara Ker. *Scottish Folk-Tales and Legends*. London: Oxford University Press, 1954.

Wilson, Edward O. *Consilience: The Unity of Knowledge*. London: Abacus, 1999.

Wilson, Edward O. *The Diversity of Life*. Cambridge, MA: Harvard University Press, 1992.

Wilson, Edward O. *The Future of Life*. London: Abacus, 2003.

Wilson, Edward O. *On Human Nature*. London: Penguin, 1995.

Wilson, Michael. '"Another Fine Mess": The Condition of Storytelling in the Digital Age'. *Narrative Culture* 1, no. 2 (2014): 125–44.

Wilson, Michael. 'Honest Liars: A Challenge for Our Times'. In *An Introduction to Storytelling*, edited by Christine Willison, 117–20. Stroud: History Press, 2018.

Wilson, Michael. 'Some Thoughts on Storytelling, Science and Dealing with a Post-truth World'. *Storytelling, Self, Society* 13, no. 1 (2017): 120–37.

Wilson, Michael. *Storytelling and Theatre: Contemporary Storytellers and Their Art*. Basingstoke: Palgrave Macmillan, 2006.

Wirzba, Norman. *The Paradise of God: Renewing Religion in an Ecological Age*. New York: Oxford University Press, 2003.

Wolf, Maryanne. *Reader, Come Home: The Reading Brain in a Digital World*. New York: HarperCollins, 2018.

Wood, Marion. *Spirits, Heroes and Hunters from North American Indian Mythology*. Wallingford: Peter Lowe, 1981.

Yates, Frances A. *The Art of Memory*. Harmondsworth: Penguin, 1969.

Yeats, W. B. *Writings on Irish Folklore, Legend and Myth*. London: Penguin, 1993.

Yemoto, Linda. 'Nature Stories – Alfresco'. *Storytelling Magazine* 14, no. 3 (2002): 20–1.

Yemoto, Linda. 'Storytelling versus Interpretation'. *Storytelling Magazine* 15, no. 1 (2003): 14.

Zapf, Hubert. 'Cultural Ecology, the Environmental Humanities, and the Transdisciplinary Knowledge of Literature'. In *Environmental Humanities: Voices from the Anthropocene*, edited by Serpil Opperman and Serenella Iovino, 61–79. London: Rowman & Littlefield, 2017.

Zimmer, Heinrich. *Myths and Symbols in Indian Art and Civilization*, edited by Joseph Campbell. Princeton: Princeton University Press, 1972.

Zipes, Jack. *Creative Storytelling: Building Community, Changing Lives*. New York: Routledge, 1995.

Zipes, Jack. 'Foreword'. In *Storytelling and Theatre: Contemporary Storytellers and Their Art*, by Michael Wilson, xiv–xviii. Basingstoke: Palgrave Macmillan, 2006.

Zipes, Jack. *Relentless Progress: The Reconfiguration of Children's Literature, Fairy Tales, and Storytelling*. New York: Routledge, 2009.

Zipes, Jack. *Revisiting the Storyteller: Reviving the Past to Move Forwards*. Reading: Society for Storytelling, 1996.

Zubrin, Robert. *The Case for Mars: The Plan to Settle the Red Planet and Why We Must*. New York: Touchstone, 1997.

Index

Aarne, Antti 56
Abram, David 25, 29, 32, 36, 173, 183, 190
Aborigines
    Australian 19–20, 22, 33–5, 37, 106–7, 144, 178, 195
    Tasmanian 65–8
Adnan, Ana 40
adolescence 75, 207. *See also* teenagers
Afanc 90
Afrella, St 132, 134
Africa 12–13, 23, 32, 39, 59
air 26
aisling 202
Alexiou, Margaret 202
Amahuaca 29
Amangons 37
Amaringo, Pablo 89
Amazonia 29, 138–9, 163, 178, 208
anaconda 138–9, 208
Anaconda 125
Ancient Technology Centre 40
Anderson, M. T. 73
animal
    commodification 12
    consciousness 30
    as person 109–12
    representation 19, 31–3
    spirit 39, 74–6, 198
animism 97, 178–9, 198
anthropomorphism 31–2, 94, 96, 198
Apache 36
Apollo 198
Aral Sea 13
archaeology 22, 34–6, 74, 187
archetypes 197, 199
archplot 55, 115
Ariadne 40
Arilda, St 132–5, 140, 143
Aristotle 63, 185
Armstrong, Karen 104, 198
Arthur, George 65
Arthur, King 34, 202–3

Ashanti 138
asteroid 100–2, 104
Atkyns, Sir Robert 122
Attenborough, David 17
auk, great 99
aura 120, 142–3, 186–7, 189
Austin, John 70
Australia, 23, 105–7, 138. *See also* Aborigines
authenticity 4–5, 86–7, 107–8, 147–8, 170–1
Avon Gorge 122
awen 43, 187, 189

Babylonia 209
Bacigalupi, Paolo 114
Bacon, Francis 181
badger 130
Bakhtin, Mikhail 80
BAN Waste 64–5
bard 3, 36, 43, 46, 202
bardo 169, 207
Baring, Anne 138
Barrow, Fiona 157, 160
Barstoe, Betty 135, 137, 140
Barthes, Roland 58
Bass, Rick 198
Basso, Keith H. 36
bat, greater horseshoe 62–3
Beowulf 123, 129
bear 93–4
beaver 90–1
bee 74
beech 50–1, 53, 95–7, 117
beliefs 51–3, 74–6, 121, 141, 179, 197
Benjamin, Walter 25, 142
Berk, Ari 41
Berkeley Castle 127
Berman, Tzeporah 131
Berry, Wendell 121
Betty's Grave 135, 140, 144
biosemiotics 5, 154
bird calls 29

Bishops Wood Centre 21
Bisley 127
bison 31, 68
Blackdown Hills 156–61
Blackfoot 76
Blincoe, Karen 174
Bloch, Ernest 54
Bloomfield, Sam 107
bodhisattva 86
Bohm, David 191–3
Booker, Christopher 54, 113
Bradley, Hazel 168
breath 26, 168, 186
Br'er Fox 23
Briggs, Katharine 139
Britain
    Brexit 70, 114, 151
    children in 12
    environmentalism in 14, 37, 143
    history 14, 67
    legends 35
    society 46
    spirituality in 36, 179
    storytelling in 2, 8–9, 21, 33–4, 59, 88, 174
Bronx Zoo 41
Brookfield Zoo 33
Brooks, Peter 50, 94, 115–16
Brown, Kedar 185, 200
Buddha 84, 86
Buddhism 109, 153, 169–70, 188, 191, 207, 209
Buffalo Dance 76
bull 74–6
Burke, Kenneth 94
butterfly 199
Butterworth, George 122
Byker waste incinerator 64–5

Cad Goddeu 26
Cae Mabon 26, 84, 173
Calapucha-Tapuy, Edith Felicia 163, 185
Callenbach, Ernest 48
Callicott, J. Baird 171
Campbell, Joseph 54–5, 63, 75–6, 86, 153, 191, 197, 199, 207–8
campfire 27–8, 34, 83
Canada 22, 48
capitalism 10, 14–15, 45–6, 88, 102–3, 116, 170, 212

Carantoc, St 125
Carr-Gomm, Philip 34
Carter, Angela 19
Castle Neroche 159, 161
cat, big 141
causality 93, 95, 103, 109, 112, 116, 183
Chalice Well 203
change
    ecological 16, 182, 191
    facilitating 3–5, 8, 44–8, 68, 85, 109, 149, 161–3, 173–5, 189, 197
    imagining 77–80, 115
    inner 39, 90, 111, 153–4, 168–9
Charles I 127
Chatwin, Bruce 22
Chavenage House 127
Cheddar Caves 156
Cheltenham 127, 150
Cheney, Jim 71
children's learning 11–12, 33, 44, 59, 76, 155–6, 160, 178
chime child 157, 163
Cashford, Jules 138
Christianity 14, 45, 107, 123, 179, 181, 191, 197, 208–10
church (village) 123, 127–9, 132–5
Cimidyue 199
civil society 46
Clare, John 68
Clarke, Lindsay 163, 196, 207–8
climate change 7, 16, 100–1, 107, 181
coconut palm 146
Collingwood, R. G. 71
Collins, Cecil 183, 185, 199
Collison, Charlene 84
Columba, St 35
community project 38, 41, 154–62, 174
complex system 103–4, 181–4, 204
composted tradition 121–6, 139, 150–1, 210
conflict
    ecopolitical 63–8, 77–81, 90
    of ideas 197
    between stories 22, 56, 139
    in stories 63, 78
    with wildlife 125–30
Conley, Verena Andermatt 149
Conn, Sarah 23
connectedness 6, 23–7, 38, 83, 161–2, 188, 192, 210

consciousness 45, 53, 149, 162, 165, 168–9, 171, 183–4, 187–93, 198, 200, 204
conservativism 48, 53, 104, 113, 146
Conway Morris, Simon 103–4
Coombe Hill 124–5, 128
cormorant 84
Corn Maidens 51
Costa Rica 97
Countryside Stewardship Scheme 62–3
Coupe, Laurence 52, 54, 204, 209
Covid-19 pandemic 6–7, 14–15, 27, 38, 104, 172, 174, 212
Cowan, James 39
Cowpen Bewley Woodland Park 38
Coyote 33, 91, 199
creation story 22, 104, 107
Cree, Jon 21
Cripps, Peter 124
crossroads 135, 142–3
Crump, Martha 98, 100
Csikszentmihalyi, Mihalyi 25
cultural appropriation 86–9, 151
cuckoo 32
Cupitt, Don 1, 78, 115, 164
Currumpaw Valley 109
Curry, Patrick 149–50
customs, folk 157–8
cybernetic 104, 171, 183
cyberspace 6, 171

Dalling, Tim 32, 99
dancing 112
Danu 138
Darwin Edwards, Ian 37
Darwinism 22, 99, 102–3, 141–2, 149
Davies, Allan 22
Davies, Gwilym 124
Dawkins, Richard 99, 102–3, 179, 197
death 40, 74, 116, 168, 206–10
deep time 100–4
'The Deerhurst Dragon' 122–30
délok 207
Delphi 187
Demeter 51, 194, 201
derivatives trade 115
desire 33, 55, 78, 93–9, 101–2, 149, 111–17, 191, 194
determinism 102–4, 183
Devil 127, 144, 159

dialogism 49, 60, 71, 80, 86, 154, 164, 173, 193
Diamond, Jared 38
dinosaur 100–2
disenchantment 141, 149, 192, 200–1
diversity 8, 92
    cultural 38, 88, 178
    of stories 31, 54–7
Dobunni 134–5
dog 33, 49
Donaldson, Ron 62
Douzinas, Costas 172
dragon 122–30, 137–8
dream path 47–8
Dreamer, Molly 132
Dreaming 34, 39, 45, 105–7, 139, 195, 205–6, 211
Druidry 36, 40–1, 187
dualism 30, 131, 142, 186, 208
Dumuzu 209
Dunne, John S. 162, 194, 206–7, 209
Dunne-za 48
Durham, Diana 192–3
Dyrham 134–5
dystopia 77, 102, 113–15, 210

'The Eagle and the Two Women' 147–8
Easter Island 13
ecobardic 3, 120, 129–30, 151
ecocriticism 2–3, 5, 85, 178–9
ecofeminism 37, 128, 131–2
ecological crisis 1–3, 7–9, 12–14, 21, 38, 45, 70, 90, 113, 116, 131, 180, 183, 186, 206–7, 211
ecological history 14, 65–8
ecological restoration 37, 105, 120
ecological self 83, 192
ecology
    cultural 5
    deep 53, 65
    local 11–13, 119
    science of 2, 95
    supernatural 180, 199
ecopoetics 5
ecopsychology 10
ecosophy 121
ecotopia 48
Eden, Garden of 13, 123, 137
Eden Project 20–1, 23, 41, 47
Edward II 127

ego 26, 116, 164, 169–70, 181, 192, 200
'Eisik Son of Jekel' 90
Ekoi 189
ekphrasis 202, 209
Elder Brother 199
elephant 84
Elizabeth I 127
El Niño 98, 100
The Elucidation 37
emotion, generalized 170, 202
emotional centre of gravity 94, 99, 129, 167
empathy 30–1, 66, 99, 109–13, 128–9, 192
'The Emperor's New Clothes' 200
empiricism, radical 185
enchantment 33–9, 47, 120–2, 130, 134, 137, 142–51, 158, 185, 189
energy (subtle) 43, 107, 123, 130–1, 138, 172, 186–93, 196, 200–1, 210
England 14, 50, 90–1, 119–20, 123–3, 146
English Heritage 34
English Nature 62–3
Enuma Elish 123
environmental education 10, 18–19, 44
environmental humanities 2–3, 90
Environmental Trainers Network 21
epic poetry 208
epiphany 194
Erickson, Milton 148
erotic 27, 81–3, 115–17
Erysichthon 51, 201, 203
Étain 195
ethnography 178
eucatastrophe 112
Eucharist 41
Eve 138
evolution 22, 77, 100–5, 197
excluded middle 184, 196
extinction
    centinelan 86
    Cretaceous 100–2
    of experience 11–12
    megafauna 13, 106–7, 126
    species 30, 90, 97–100, 113, 167, 198
eye contact 27, 83, 165, 170, 172, 192

fable 31, 94, 145
fabula 111
facticity 64, 66–7, 100, 141
Faërian drama 141–2, 158, 185
fairies' revenge 37, 50–4, 122
fairy 32, 36, 141, 157–8
fairy tale 54–5, 112–13, 125
fake news 139
farming 62–3, 127, 130
field research 126–8, 132–7, 151
film 16–17, 27, 55, 125, 208
Fire Springs 187
    Arthur's Dream 203
    An Ecobardic Manifesto 3
    Robin of the Wildwood 113
Fisher King 162, 192
Flannery, Tim 100
flood 57–9, 125
Flood, Jane 154–63, 168, 170, 173–4, 208
Flying Fox Woman 32
folklore restoration 120, 157
folk song 124, 157
folktale
    animals in 19, 93–5
    ecological 22–3, 50–3, 90
    local 119–25, 150–1, 157
    recrafting 126–30
    structure 54
    types 56, 89
forest 18, 97–8, 199
'The Forest Fire' 83–7
Forest of Dean 51, 122
Forestry Commission 18, 21
fourth wall 39
fox 93, 125
Franklin, Sir John 69–70
Freire, Paolo 44
Freud, Sigmund 115–17
Frye, Northrop 95, 199, 201

Gablik, Suzi 3
Gabon 59
Gawain 203
gender 131–2, 139, 148
Genesis 22, 138
George, St 123, 129, 138
Gersie, Alida 24, 44, 61, 72, 109, 112, 163, 169, 173, 182, 191, 210
ghost 59, 127, 140–1, 178
Ghost Dance 105
Gibson 97, 149
Gilgamesh 208

Glastonbury 34, 203
Gloucestershire 57–9, 65, 119–44, 146, 148–51, 178
Goethe, Johann Wolfgang von 35
God 129, 178, 191, 197
goddess 36–7, 76, 131, 137–8, 187, 208
Godin, Patrice 177
Goldberg, Myshele 45
golden age 45, 104
Goodchild, Chloë 166
Goodchild, Philip 48
Goodison, Lucy 23, 39
Gould, Stephen Jay 103–4, 141, 186
Govinda, Anagarika 204
Grail 37, 42, 162, 192, 203
'The Grandmother and the Three Brothers' 146
grand narrative 105, 179
Greece 51, 79, 89, 153, 173, 178, 185, 194, 202
Greek mythology 31, 35, 40, 123
Green, Joshua 32
Green, Malcolm 18, 20, 22, 24, 29, 42, 47, 169
  'Dreaming the Land' 34
  Gone Cuckoo 32
  Shearwater 32
'The Green Ladies of One Tree Hill' 50–5, 75, 201
Grof, Christina 207, 209
Grof, Stanislav 184–6, 207, 209
Gryphaea 144
Guanyin 138
Guatemala 16
Guenther, Herbert V. 183
Gwent 132–3, 135
Gypsy 157

Hades journey 207–8
Haggarty, Ben 108–9, 194, 196
  Gilgamesh 208
  I Become Part of It 40, 43, 73
  Mezolith 73
Haku, Mount 138
Hall, Kelvin 182
Halloween 41, 143, 159
Harding, Stephan 96, 169
Harrison, Robert Pogue 31
Hartoch, John 194
Hartsiotis, Kirsty 120, 125, 144, 151, 194
Hassidic 90

Haven, Kendall 55–6, 70–2
Hawaii 87, 186
healing 17, 23, 130, 141, 154, 162, 168, 185, 189, 192
Hebrides 11
Hemingway, Ernest 92
Hennessey, Nick 68
Hepburn, Ronald W. 149
Hereford, Countess of 132
hero 54–5, 75, 78, 116, 123–6, 199, 207
Hinduism 23, 138, 188, 191, 196
Hochman, Jhan 23
Holland, Chris 21
Holt, David 69–70
Holy Spirit 186, 208
Hood, Robin 68, 113
Hooper-Greenhill, Eilean 142
horse 158, 182, 208
Hughes, Ted 27, 141
Hulipomé 138
human nature 45, 102–3, 191, 197
Humboldt, Alexander von 141–2
hunter-gatherers 10, 25, 38, 65
hunting 33, 40, 74–6
Hwicce 127, 135
hyena 23

Iamblichus 131
ICT 6–7, 10–11, 173
idealism 183, 187
identity politics 8, 87–90, 192, 197
Ignatius of Loyola, St 203
illocution 70
imperialism, European 67–8, 73, 87–8, 107, 178
improvisation 107–9, 170
Inanna 138, 208–9
India 56, 123, 139, 166, 178, 187–8, 195, 198, 202, 208
indigenous cultures 8, 13–14, 21–2, 29, 33, 36–7, 107
indigenous stories 19, 23, 32, 35, 88, 90, 145–7
indigenous storytelling 11, 33, 47, 50, 91
Indra 3, 123
innenwelt 30, 198
intention 50, 53, 62, 69–72, 77, 85, 97, 109, 149, 151, 166, 169, 171, 212
interlocution 50
internet 171

intertextuality 59, 85
Inuit 70, 167
Iona 35
Iraq 60
Ireland 37, 123, 141, 143, 178, 199, 202, 206
Ishtar 209
Islam 45, 56, 178

'Jack and the Beanstalk' 145
James, William 185
Jameson, Fredric 103, 212
Jataka 84–5
Jayaraja 170
jellyfish 79
Jesus Christ 135, 195
jetzeit 25, 38
'John Barleycorn' 41
Johnson, Richard 123
Joseph of Arimathea 203
Jung, Carl 197

Kadimakara 105–7, 201
Kailasa 193
Kaliya 123
Kallari Timpu 139
Kanak 143–8, 150, 177–8, 189–90, 195, 204, 208
kangaroo 33
karma 109
katabasis 208–9
Kathā Sarit Sāgara 56, 193
Kearney, Richard 200
Kenelm, St 139–41
Kenulf 139
'Keny Wazianu' 146
Kenya 12, 85
Kew Gardens 20–1
kinaesthetic 203
King, Serge Kahili 88
'King Cophetua and the Beggar Maid' 114
Kington 132–5
koan 148
Kondolo, Sonia 189–90
Korea 189
Kovel, Joel 116, 170
Krishna 123
K–T event 100–2, 104
Kundalini 138

Labov, William 167
ladder to the moon 201
Lakshmi 139
Lammas 40
Lancelot 203
Lanner, William 66
Lawrence, D. H. 81–3
Lee, Laurie 119, 148
Leenhardt, Maurice 177
Le Guin, Ursula 45, 48, 117, 212
legend 35, 56, 87, 89, 91, 122–8, 132, 139–41, 144–6, 151, 205
leopard, snow 46
Letcher, Andy 36
Lewis, C. S. 52
life cycle 18, 22, 95–7
Lifou 146
Lilley, Deborah 120
liminal space 39, 41, 142–3, 153, 167
Lindisfarne 34
linguistics 1, 51
lion 126
listening 61, 113, 155–8, 164, 202
    dialogic 166–70, 173
    exercise 29, 72
    modes of 80
    place 154, 159–60, 162–3, 168, 174, 211
    quality of 18, 27, 60
'Little Red Riding Hood' 19
Lipman, Doug 61, 80
lomilomi 186, 195
London 12, 20, 114
Long Meg 34
Lopez, Barry 25, 40, 56, 78, 153, 188
'Lord Franklin' 70
Lupton, Hugh 26, 36, 119–20, 150, 187, 202, 205
    The Horses 208
    I Become Part of It 40, 43
    Iliad 195
    The Liberty Tree 68
    'The Man Who Had No Story' 195
    On Common Ground 68
lynx 93–4
Lyotard, Jean-François 169

Maasai 126
MacLellan, Gordon 20, 32, 33, 38–9, 41, 44, 47

Maddern Eric 17, 21–2, 26, 34, 36, 39, 104, 166–7, 173
  'Culhwch and Olwen' 202
  What the Bees Know 113
Maggi, Shakti Caterina 192
magisteria, non-overlapping 104, 186
mahasiddha 153
Malekin, Peter 169
mana 142, 186, 189
mangabey 84
Mantis 32
mantra 188
Manwaring, Kevan 34, 43
Maori 189
Marduk 123
Maré 145
Margulis, Lynn 103
Mark's Gospel 195, 210
Marxist criticism 44–5, 54, 103
Mary, Virgin 195, 208
mask 32
materialism 178–82, 185, 187, 192, 206
Matthews, Caitlín 206
'Maude's Elm' 127, 150
Maya 196–7, 208
Mayan Biosphere Reserve 16
May Eve 157
McKee, Robert 55, 63, 95
Medea 138
meditation 168–70, 202–6
memory 24, 35, 54, 58, 61–2, 67, 155, 203–4
Mendip Hills 155, 159
mental health 10, 174
Mesolithic 40, 74–6
metamorphosis 31, 199
metaphor 51–2, 184–6, 190, 197
Metcalfe, David 70
Midir 194, 196
Midsummer Eve 50
Minotaur 40
misogyny 139–40, 146
modes (Frye) 201
Moltmann, Jürgen 52, 184, 204
Monteverde Cloud Forest Reserve 98
moorhen 28–9
Moran, Michael 20, 24, 28–9
Morden, Daniel 195
motifs, tale 89, 121, 123–4, 126
Muncius 132–5

Murphy, Patrick D. 8
music 69–70, 107–8, 157–8, 166
myth 48, 51–4, 75–6, 131, 177, 197–9
  and ritual 87, 91, 185, 198, 205, 208
  religious 123, 197, 206
  telling 200–3, 207–10
  and science 21–2, 104–7
  urban 89
mythic stories 8, 180, 195–208
mythscape 35, 120, 144–6, 150, 204

Nabhan, Gary Paul 11, 31, 130
Narada 195–6
Nash, Paul 142
National Association for Interpretation 21
National Park Study Centre 21
National Storytelling Network 21
National Trust 21, 29, 37
nationalism 5, 67, 89, 139, 151, 191
Native American 19, 31–3, 86, 88, 90–1, 93, 105
nature
  agency and voice 28–9, 40
  conservation 16, 33, 63, 78–9, 99, 143–5
  definition 7
  disconnection from 9–15, 23, 47
  interpretation 18–23
  reserve 16, 37, 98, 128, 144
  speaking for 44
neoliberalism 5, 44, 46, 56, 90, 102, 173, 191
Neoplatonism 131, 203
Nepal 33
New Caledonia 32, 122, 138, 143–8, 177–8, 189–90
New Mexico 109–10
Newton, Isaac 181
Nigeria 89, 189
Norfolk 34
Northwest Passage 69–70

oak 51, 157–9, 201
Oates, Joyce Carol 31
O'Connor, Peter 207
'The Octopus and the Rat' 145
O'Donohue, John 169, 178, 191–2
Odurinde, Temi 89
Odyssey 35

Oelrich, Inger Lise 17, 60, 162, 167, 189, 193, 196
O'odham 12, 199
Oisín 194
Okri, Ben 193
Olalla, Pedro 35
Oldbury-on-Severn 132, 134–5
Ong, Walter J. 6, 165, 171
oral history 38
orientalism 87
Osho 212
otherworld 36, 43, 143, 158, 206–8
Ouray-Ouray 65
Ovid 31
owl 29

Pagan 36–7, 43
Pakistan 46
palaeoecology 100–2
Palmer, Martin 142, 179, 183
Palmer, Roy 120, 126
paradise 45, 76, 105–6, 209
Parkinson, Rob 42, 148, 150, 200
parody 124–5
parrot 83–6
Parvati 193
Patmos 89
Patrick, St 194
peace studies 2
Peirce, Charles Sanders 49
Percival 42, 192
perlocution 70–1
Perseus 138
Péron, François 65
phallic 115–17, 138
Phelps, David 120
pigeon, passenger 13, 99
pilgrimage 34, 144, 156, 187
Pinochet, Augusto 42
Please, Peter 25, 39
Polynesia 142, 186
polyphony 80
postmodernism 179
Poulton 135–6, 144
pourquoi tale 94
predator 110, 125–6, 128
propaganda 3, 67, 70, 150, 194
prose fiction 77, 208
Pueblo 35, 51, 199
Punkie Night 158–9, 161

Pyle, Robert Michael 11
python 138

Quammen, David 126
Quenthryth 139–40
Quichua 178, 185, 189

ragas and rasas 166
Raglan, Lord 54
Rainbow Snake 138–9
Ranke, Kurt 123
raven 33
Rawson, Philip 184
reading 1, 5, 163
realism 74–6, 208
reconciling opposites 8, 23, 41, 47, 65, 196, 208–9
repertoire 28, 31, 88, 108, 156, 204, 210
resilience 44
response task 72–3
restorying 37, 130
rewilding 105
rhetoric 14, 67, 70–1
Ricoeur, Paul 210
rite of passage 75–6, 153, 198, 200, 207
ritual 39–45, 153–4, 159, 161, 163, 185, 209. *See also* myth and ritual
road protest 36, 44
Robertson, Dave 195
Robinson, George 65–6
Robinson, Kim Stanley 77, 115
Roman de Renart 93
Romano-British 134–5
Romans 127
Rose, Deborah Bird 178
Roszak, Theodore 116
Royal Botanic Gardens Edinburgh 21, 37
Rudder, Samuel 122
Rushdie, Salman 17
Russian Formalists 111

Sabrina 127
sacredness of land 37, 47, 91, 145
sacred place 34–7, 39, 43, 74, 105, 130–1, 136, 142–3, 187, 189, 196
sacred space 162, 210–11
Safina, Carl 105
Saga of the Völsungs 123
Sagan, Carl 104, 149
Said, Edward 87–8

Salisbury, Chris 21, 47
Salt Lake 199
Samuel, Geoffrey 187
San 32
Sanders, Scott Russell 23
Sanskrit 188
Santer, Benjamin 16
Sarasvati 198
Satan 123, 137
Sati 187
Savage, Jay 97–8
Sawyer, Ruth 43
Saxons 14, 119, 127–9, 133–5
science
    communication 62–3
    fiction 102, 113–15
    and myth 21–2, 104–7, 197
Scotland 22, 31, 37, 167
Scottish Traveller 11, 164, 195
screen media 6, 26–7, 63, 163, 172–3
screenwriting 54–5, 63
sculpture 92, 156
'The Seal Wife' 167–8
Searles, Peter 41–2
secondary world 130, 142
self, extension of 26–7, 188, 192
selkie 31, 164, 167–8
semiotics 5, 49
Seton, Ernest Thompson 110–12, 116
Severn 122, 127, 134, 144
Sewall, Laura 27
Shah, Idries 68
Shah, Tahir 56
Shakti 186, 193, 196, 208
shaman 33, 43, 138, 191, 198, 200, 205–6
shapeshifting 31–2
Shaw, Martin 153, 200
shearwater, Manx 18, 22, 32
Sheldrake, Rupert 5
Shepard, Aaron 199
Sheshal 139
Shinyu 138
Shiva 187, 193
Siberia 32
sídhe 143
Sigurd 123, 129
Simenauer, Tom 107
Simpson, Jacqueline 124, 140
sjuzet 111

Slimbridge Wildfowl and Wetland Centre 20, 24, 28, 90
Smith, Donald 11
Smith, Fanny Cochrane 67
Smith, John, 122, 124, 127, 129–30
snake 82, 89, 123, 135–9
Snake Goddess 40
Snowdonia 26, 34, 90
Snyder, Gary 31, 108–9, 191
social conscience 45, 121, 126
social justice 65
social media 17, 61, 172
Society for Storytelling 2
Sogyal Rinpoche 109
Somerset 154–61
songline 34, 144
sound 26, 165, 188
soundscape 29, 107–8, 190
South Downs Way 34
Soviet Union 77
Soweto Mountain of Hope 17
space (in storytelling) 1, 50–1, 69–73, 80–1, 108–12, 116–17, 129–30, 163, 173–4, 189
    for discussion 59–60
    holding the 69, 83, 168, 188, 203
    structure of 77, 92, 111, 115, 148, 169, 194, 209
    between words 166–8
spectacle 12, 41
speech 26
    acoustic impact 154, 165–6
    act theory 70
    rhythm 166–8
Spira, Rupert 190, 192
spirit of place 37, 121, 151
spirits 32, 84–5, 131, 143–6, 159, 177–8, 187, 189–90, 195, 206. *See also* animal spirit
spirituality 36, 39, 179, 186, 188, 191, 193, 202–3, 211–12
spring (water) 130–7, 141–3, 146
stag 31
Stallings, Fran 171
Staple Fitzpaine 157–8
St Arilda's Well 132–5, 140–3
Starkey, Dinah 124
Star Wars 54
Stevinson, Jon 139–40
Stibbe, Arran 51, 75

stillness 41, 45, 134, 154, 156, 167–71, 188
Stone, Richard 154, 165
Stonehenge 143, 187
stories. *See also* creation story, indigenous stories, mythic stories
   bardic 206
   biographical 109–12, 210–11
   from ecology 22, 31, 93, 95–105
   fictional 74–81
   historical 65–6
   literary 81–3
   medicine 185, 200, 210
   of the non-human 30–3
   from other cultures 86–92, 190
   personal 16, 34, 36, 42, 57–60, 62, 69, 210
   political 16, 63–5
   prehistoric 22, 74–6, 100–7
   scientific 62–3, 104
   shamanic 205
   utopian 77–81
story
   child 189
   construction 78, 126
   definition 1–2, 55, 63
   ending 55, 69, 81, 115, 158
   locations 126–7, 146, 203–4
   message 1, 19–20, 129
   resolution 63, 113–17
   structure 18, 35, 54, 75, 133, 153, 156
   walk 26, 28, 34, 39, 156, 164
'The Story Bag' 189
storytelling
   as bridge between worlds 43, 47, 158, 163, 184, 205
   clubs 60, 62, 148
   contradicting the consensus 15–17, 142, 180
   as conversation 46, 49–50, 59–60, 73, 77, 141, 147, 174
   definition 1–2
   ecosystem 211
   as embodied practice 6, 27, 58, 153–4, 163–5, 172–3, 212
   marketing 174–5
   marginalization 4, 38, 48
   outdoors 24–5, 28–9, 41, 160, 164, 204
   professional 4, 62, 161, 175
   as relational practice 42, 47, 61, 71–2, 129, 182, 194, 196

   seating arrangement 83, 163–4, 188
   vocation 42–7, 175, 211–12
storywork 4, 33, 44, 72, 84–5, 153–6, 159–61, 169, 171–5, 191
Strauss, Susan, 20, 22, 33, 91
Sumeria 208–9
Sunderland, Chris 18, 46
sustainability 3–5, 85, 145, 174–5
Sutton, Alan 119
Suvin, Darko 77
symbiosis 103
symbolism 52–3, 75, 117, 123, 130–1, 137–8, 141, 196–9, 210

taboo 143, 145–6
tail-fisher 93–4
'The Tailor of Swaffham' 90
Táin Bó Cúailnge 76
Tales to Sustain 3–4, 84–6
'Tamoangui, the Torso-Man' 147–8
Tammuz 209
tangka 189
Tao 204
Tasmanian genocide 65–8, 72–3, 107, 113
teenagers 12, 18, 150
Tegau Goldenbreast 132
television 11–12, 16–17, 27, 61
The Telling Place 210
text-telling 167
theatre 41, 163
Theodossopoulos, Dimitrios 79
Theseus 40
Thompson, Stith 56
The Thousand and One Nights 56
'The Three Little Pigs' 19
Tiamat 123, 128, 138
Tibet 169, 189, 207
Tintagel 34
Tissier, Adrian 29
Titanic, RMS 69
Tjibaou, Jean-Marie 144, 147–8
toad, golden 97–100, 105, 113, 167
Todorov, Tzvetan 141–2, 149
Toelken, Barre 86–7
Tolkien, J. R. R. 112, 116, 123, 141–2, 185, 201
   enchantment 130, 146, 149–50
   Farmer Giles of Ham 124–5, 129
Tolle, Eckhart 182, 192, 211

Tongue, Ruth 157
totem 33, 37, 177, 198
tradition, evolving 23, 53, 83–9, 120–6, 150, 190, 199
Tragâdé 189
trance 150, 171
transpersonal experience 180, 184–6, 189–90, 195–6, 199, 205–6
tree 50–1, 53, 95–7, 100–1, 105–6, 201
Tree of Knowledge 13
trickster 93–4, 199
Troy 195
Truganini 65–7
Trungpa, Chögyam 170, 184
truth, speaking the 14, 17–23, 32, 66–7, 107, 139, 179, 197
Tukuna 199
turning point 63, 78, 109
turtle, loggerhead sea 79–81
'Turtle's Race with Beaver' 91
TUUP 89
'The Two-Headed Ogre' 145
types, tale 56, 89

'The U of the Air World' 145
umwelt 30–2, 198
uncertainty 16, 58, 100, 141–2, 149, 180–4, 209
United States. *See also* Native American
    capitalism and religion in 148, 179, 197
    children in 11
    environmentalism in 68, 110–11
    folktales 23
    history 14, 91
    storytelling in 21, 88
Uther, Hans-Jörg 56
utopia 45, 77, 95, 113–14, 212
Uzendoski, Michael 163, 185

van Dooren, Thom 178
videotelephony 27, 172
viper, Ottoman 89
Vishnu 139, 196
visualization 35, 82, 196, 202–3, 206
vitalism 102
Vizard, William 124, 128

Vritra 123, 138
vulnerability 27, 61, 83, 170, 172–3, 175

Wales 26, 36, 40, 90, 127–9, 202
Waletsky, Joshua 167
Walker, Ghislaine 20
Walton Hill 122, 124, 127–9
Wapner, Paul 46
wasteland 37, 42, 162, 192
Wauwalak Sisters 138
Wegner, Phillip E. 113
West, Simon 18–19
Weston, Anthony 71
Westwood, Jennifer 124
Whyte, Betsy 195
wildness (Snyder) 108–9
Williams, Adin 135, 140
Williams, Alfred 140
Williamson, Duncan 164
Willow, Old Man 136–7
Wilson, Edward O. 102–4, 149, 191, 197
Wilson, Mike 44, 59, 61, 80, 86–7, 120, 139, 150
Winchcombe 139
wisdom tale 87
Wishpoosh 91
witch 135, 139–40, 146
wolf 19, 33, 93, 109–12
'The Wolf and the Seven Little Kids' 19, 148
women
    and nature 37, 131, 140–1
    in traditional stories 132, 139, 146–8, 167–8
Women's Institute 167
wonder tale 123, 153
Wood, Chris 68
WWF 46

Yeats, W. B. 141
Yemoto, Linda 21, 29
yin and yang 117, 131
Yoruba 89

Zakynthos 79–80
Zapf, Hubert 90, 106
Zimmer, Heinrich 193, 196, 198, 208
Zipes, Jack 4–5, 41, 59, 87, 102, 169, 200

Printed in Great Britain
by Amazon